AF412774

Black Man—Red Sand

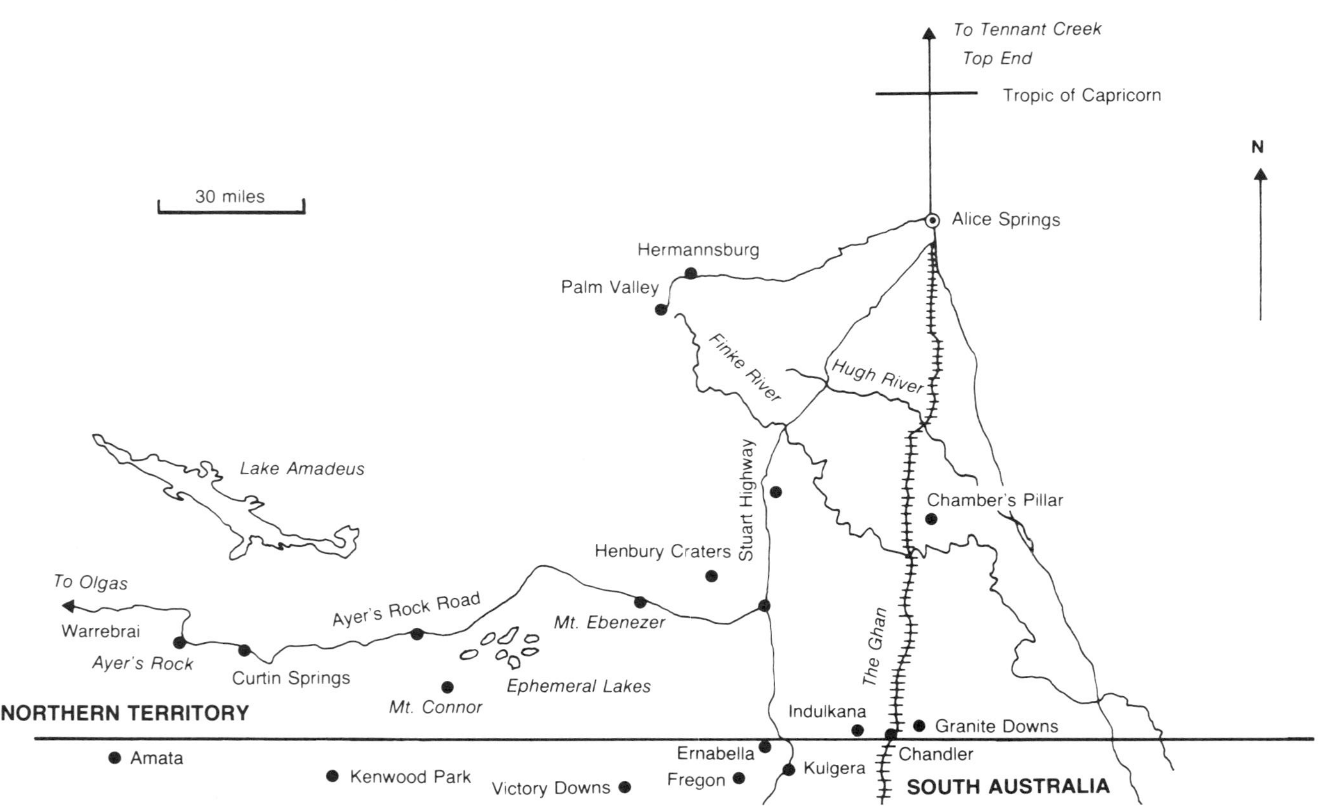

To Tennant Creek
Top End
Tropic of Capricorn
N
30 miles
Alice Springs
Hermannsburg
Palm Valley
Finke River
Hugh River
Stuart Highway
Chamber's Pillar
Lake Amadeus
Henbury Craters
The Ghan
To Olgas
Ayer's Rock Road
Mt. Ebenezer
Warrebrai
Ayer's Rock
Curtin Springs
Ephemeral Lakes
Mt. Connor
Indulkana
Granite Downs
NORTHERN TERRITORY
Ernabella
Chandler
Amata
Kenwood Park
Victory Downs
Fregon
Kulgera
SOUTH AUSTRALIA

BLACK MAN— RED SAND

R. John Rutten, M.D.

VANTAGE PRESS
New York

The places and events recorded in this story are true. Some names have been changed to protect the identities of the characters.

FIRST EDITION

Published by Vantage Press, Inc.
516 West 34th Street, New York, New York 10001

Manufactured in the United States of America
ISBN: 0-533-09199-3

Library of Congress Catalog Card No.: 90-93321

1 2 3 4 5 6 7 8 9 0

To my wife, Laura.
Without her unlimited patience
this book would never have been written.

Black Man—Red Sand

March 1976

"You're out of your mind! Why on earth would you give up a secure practice with a multi-specialty clinic and go back to work for the government?" asked my friend and colleague.

"Because the kids really don't need Laura and me at home now that they've gotten to college age, and we can enjoy a new career, travel, and in eleven years, retire with a government annuity and return to our hilltop home in the Santa Barbara area," I replied.

That was in March of 1976. I had served in the Navy in WWII and the Korean War, and had been invited to return to service with the U.S. Air Force, Europe (USAFE). Stationed in Tehran, Iran, I treated the expatriate community there, and also practiced medicine at the MEDDAC hospital in Tehran. That is, I practiced there when I wasn't working and traveling in Afghanistan, Pakistan, India, Nepal, Bangladesh, and Sri Lanka as a regional medical officer, overlapping with the State Department regional medical officers.

Two and a half years later, I left that area, and served another two-year tour of duty doing the same thing in Central and South America while I was stationed in Panama. Again, it was a fascinating tour of duty, and Laura was able to travel extensively with me in that part of the world.

During my next tour, I had the opportunity to replace an Air Force doctor at the Joint Defense Space Research Facility (JDSRF) in Alice Springs, Australia for my next tour. I would be replacing Doctor Walter Fast, who had himself completed a two-year tour of duty in the very heart of the Australian continent. Laura and I arrived in "the Alice" on 23 September 1980.

The responsibilities of the doctor on this tour included medical care for the American expatriate community as well as monitoring the medical well-being of the Australians who were working at the JDSRF, or "Spyce Byce," as the Aussies called it.

Since the facility was closed to all who did not actually work there, an office had to be provided in the town of Alice Springs for treating dependents of the facility employees. This was a combined medical dental unit in the Community Health Centre located about a mile from the Alice Springs Hospital, a 230-bed acute care hospital that was quite modern. A payment-in-kind arrangement had been made with the Australian government in which the use of the medical office would be equated with the American doctor's services to the Aeromedical Service of the Royal Flying Doctors each Thursday. The duties were to provide medical care for the Pitjantjatjara aboriginals in the medical clinics inside their settlements scattered over an area of about 40,000 square miles in northwestern South Australia and the southwestern part of the Northern Territory.

My first experience with the Royal Flying Doctors' Service was when my predecessor, Walter, introduced me to the staff at the centre next to the hospital in Alice Springs on September 24. It was "sister" Carol's birthday, and they had lots of goodies on the table and invited us to partake. For the next two weeks we were canceled out of our flights for one reason or another, and the first available flight was to Indulkana on October 9. Sister Carol told me that for this first trip out she would have the driver pick me up and take me to the site on the airport that housed the Flying Doctors.

9 October 1980

At 0800 hours they arrived at my house; Carol and Paul. They are late because Carol had made a cake, and it had come alive and toppled into her sink, custard frosting and all; it had taken her some half-hour to put it all back together . . . but not too late to start the trip. Our pilot's name is John. The Royal Flying Doctors are government employees, all of them including the "sisters," Aussie for registered nurse, and not a religious order. I'll mention more about this later. John had already run up the plane, and then shut it down. Pilots do this routinely while waiting for a doctor. Our trip today is down to Indulkana, which is pronounced all in one breath with no accent between the *l* and the *k*. This is about 220 miles from the Alice as the crow flies. The vehicle is a Piper Navajo.

John welcomed us aboard, and we took our seats, with sister Carol back in the passenger area, and me in the right front seat. The plane is equipped to carry two stretchers, and three sitting passengers. The only baggage allowed is the medical equipment and three large boxes of cards that carry abbreviated histories on the patients that we have seen or are about to see. Of course, there's also room for about twenty gallons of drinking water . . . just in case.

Since John has already checked the engines there's no need for preflight check; we touch the master switch, hit the aux fuel pumps, turn on the mags to the port engine, and press the starter. Nothing. Try again. No luck. Three tries. Still nothing. Maybe a cough, but mostly nothing. So, try the starboard. It catches right away. Back to port; like starting a lawnmower. Just enough to keep one trying. Finally, it does catch, holds and then roars into life. Taxi out. Everything looks fine. This plane has double nav-comm (navigation/communication radio), ADF (automatic direction finder), DME (distance measuring equipment), localizer, glide slope, marker beacons, transponder three-axis autopilot, and then a multitude of engine instrument goodies to boot. Oh, yes, there's also an HF (high frequency) radio for real communication, and so we taxi out.

It hasn't rained in this neck of the woods since last November, but there are a few high cumulus clouds that look like they could be wet. We taxi down to runway 30 (there're two of them: 12 and 30—which the tower calls "one-two" and "three-oh"). The tower says, "It's yours, Fox Delta Quebec." We're up to 100 knots indicated when John sneaks it off the runway, turns left, and parallels the Stuart Highway southbound on the east side. Remember, in Australia they drive on the left. We climb to 8,000 feet and trim out. John turns on the autopilot and we sit back and talk. Ahead there are some of those cumuli that look a bit dark. Some of them have gray to black streaks curving out of the bottoms of them.

"Do they go all the way to the ground?" I ask.

"Sometimes," says John. And with that I watch something amazing. The rain is pounding into the desert with such force that the ten months of dust is mushrooming peripherally, like so many bombs are going off. Maybe fifty square miles are involved in this display, and we're quickly through it. The course of the storm is marked by the basins of water left behind in the low spots. From then on there's nothing but desert until we reach the Finke River, about halfway to our destination. The Finke is said by some geologists to be the oldest river in the world.

Now, this desert is different than the desert that Americans are used to seeing. This desert is a red sandstone background, but in lots of places there's water, and the showers like the ones that we just witnessed keep a lot of things alive. There's no real rainy season here in the "centre" like there is up at Darwin, or in Panama. Generally, the summer season between December and January gets about four centimeters of rain, which tapers down from there the rest of the year. But it can rain anytime, or not at all for ten years. The average is about nineteen centimeters a year, though.

"Two years ago they had 114 centimeters in a week," says John. "That's when the Todd River through the Alice flowed for eight months! I've been told also that, geologically, this continent was originally below sea level, then raised to something like 25,000 feet for these mountains. Now, with erosion and subsiding, it has returned to what we see now."

The tops of the mountains look for all the world like the desert that we see in California, because the Alice is almost like Palm Springs or El Centro. It's about the same climate, about 1700 feet above sea level, and the desert will grow just about anything if you put water to it. The water is here, too, like the giant aquifers that feed Las Vegas. They call it "the Artesian Basin," but the big thing is that in the red sandstone that was the original basis of these mountains there have been igneous intrusions of quartz, with cubic zircons, amethysts, rubies, garnets, and of course, opals and gold. GOLD!

"Not much gold around here," John offers, "but there is

south and west, in the area that we're going to on these flights. They say the tourist is only supposed to pick up the baseball size lumps of gold, to guard against hernias, and leave the bigger pieces to the professionals."

This desert is not "un-owned." The "Stations," as the ranches are called, may run to more than a hundred square miles. It takes about ten acres to feed a steer, but like I said, it's a thin forest and not a sandy expanse like the Sahara. The "wattles" grow wherever there's a depression that water can stand in after a rain. They are acacia-like trees, twelve to twenty feet tall, and then, once in a while, there are gum trees (eucalyptus) that stand up to one hundred feet tall. As one flies over the desert, one is amazed at the number of tracks of vehicles that patrol this area. How they ever make those absolutely straight lines in the desert with no sign posts is something else. They go for miles and miles! The cattle trails to the "bores" (wells) are almost straight, too.

An hour and fifteen minutes and John calls the Alice on the radio. We're letting down. Ahead is a range of dry hills, and from twenty-five miles away, one can see the strip that has been cut out of the wattles and the red sand. The village is plastered against the side of the dry, crumbling rocks, and the first of many that I will see of the graveyards for cars; as familiar a sight in the outback here as the water tower is to the towns with railroads in the Dakotas. The approach, the landing, and our local sisters are waiting for us for the monthly clinic.

We transfer the records from the plane to the right-hand drive Bronco. All aboard! We bump our way up to the village and the hospital. It's a trailered-in prefab, with about eight rooms, divided into two- and three-bed rooms, a newborn area, and the delivery room. Then there's the outpatient part that is inhabited by assorted aborigines and dogs. It's not unclean, although there is a layer of dust over everything that seems to be all-pervasive, and about an eighth of an inch thick. There's an isolette without a dust cover, an ancient gas machine for anesthesia, and everything is dirty. Not contaminated, you understand. Just dirty! That's dust and dirt, and it's not stains and grime, and pollution. It's just good, clean dirt. That's for starters.

No, the starters were the dogs. More dogs than people, I think. There are two kinds of dogs; the aboriginal dogs, and the "white" dogs. The dogs are prejudiced; they have definitive racial preferences. The aboriginal dogs look like greyhounds and are uniformly beige or fawn in color. They are not genetically related to the Australian dingo. I've not yet seen a dingo. The aboriginal dog mistrusts the white man and will usually avoid contact. The dogs of the white person are a mixture-type dog, usually spotted and about the same size as an aboriginal dog. They distrust the black man and will generally tolerate their presence or will avoid them all together.

The aboriginals are the real reason for our being here. The resultant concern is akin to the interest that our government shows for our American Indians. Lots of voice, but not much action. What action there is generally tends to downgrade and destroy the aboriginal. There are subsidies for living that are unreal. They give the aboriginal money to spend on liquor and vice, but destroy him and his family. In the States this buys votes for politicians. I can't see a single thing it does for these people except destroy them. Well, maybe that's the point anyway.

Kids under ten years of age are "unisex." No clothes, no restrictions, and the parents dote on them. They rule the primitive world. They really do love their kids, and express this as an intense permissiveness in those children who are less than the age of puberty.

They are black; black as the blackest American Black, but with a different facial appearance. More like Thai, or Vietnamese. Not Chinese or Japanese. The eyes are generally further apart than our North American Black, and the lips are more like Indochinese. The hair is straight and almost blonde, at least at the roots, although at the distal ends it turns dark. It's backwards from the Western peroxide look.

The clinic starts. The sister talks with the "indigenous" sister. These are Caucasian nurses who are hired by the government to live at the settlement for one-year contracts. At the clinics the doctor is going to visit, they line up problems that they're worried about. Here in Indulkana the big thing seems to be kids with infected ears. I look at about a dozen of these, and a couple of pregnant moms, and a couple of "Europeans" who work for the railroad which is only about twenty-five miles away. Talk about a "put-down" class. I'll have more about them later. Big patient of the day is an aboriginal woman whom I'm told has been cough-ing up blood for the past two weeks. Inspection and examination reveals nothing except a moderately plump dark lady who has a Mona Lisa smile on her face.

There is no change in expression on questioning, and finally I ask her, "Okay, cough up some blood."

She coughs twice and fills the palm of her hand with bright red blood! The same look on the face, with no display of emotion. No look of pain. Nothing. We find a place for her on the plane coming back to the Alice.

The children? Every one of them seems to have a white sulfa powder in the external auditory canals. I guess they might as well lose hearing to infection as to hard rock music. No one seems to complain about their kids' ears. It's always something else; a rash, or a non-healing ulcer of an extremity. "Any child can have infected ears, but my child has something unusual," reflects the aboriginal philosophy.

Finally the clinic is over, and we retire for "tea" to the in-digenous sister's house. This is a modified mobile home, but it is homey, and she uses up all her fresh milk from the Alice for those who want cream in their coffee or tea. Then, it's time to depart. We put Eileen with the bloody cough into one of the seats in the Navajo, and crank up. Routine trip home. We wait for the northern tourist plane on the way to Ayer's Rock to depart, and then make a long downwind and final for runway three-oh at Alice. That's all there is to the first trip out to the outback. Next week we're scheduled for Ernabella. What a nice group of people. What an exciting introduction to Central Australian medicine!

16 October 1980

This time it's Peter who is pilot. He arrives a bit early and purloins a bit of petrol from one of the hangers and puts it into the tank of his car, washes down the container and the tarmac, and bids his wife and new baby good-bye. They drive away. We do a preliminary "preflight" on the Navajo and then board it and run it up. Everything seems perfect. The weather is a bit heavier this week than last week, but it seems that our destination is far enough south that it will be clear when we get there. Sister Carol shows up with Paul as her driver, and in no time we're loaded and ready for departure. Same sequence as before, only this time we are taking off on runway three-oh and will make a right turn over Heavitree Gap to pick up our south heading on the east side of Stuart Highway. By the time we've done our "270" (degree turn) we're into some rain squalls, but with the heading and roll locked in on the auto pilot, there's no problem climbing to our cruise altitude of 8,000 feet.

Not much to see on the ground because of the clouds until we approach the Finke River. Then it's all clear on down to the South Australian border. Can't quite see Ayer's Rock to the west, but we do see Mt. Connor to the west. Ernabella is a short way from the airstrip, and the first thing we see from about fifteen miles out is the strip, cut out of the red desert, and then the pile of old cars. We're met at the strip by the local sister, who is happy that we're there. She does have a lot of prenatals lined up for us.

I don't get as much of a tour of this hospital as I did last week in Indulkana. It seems to be less equipped than Indulkana, but has about the same amount of dirt and dust around. The aboriginals are sitting in the dirt under a wattle (acacia tree), and also they sit on the floor of the clinic.

One of our prenatals is thirteen, about twenty-two weeks along and apparently happy. But it's hard to tell with that expressionless look they have. Another is a fifteen-year-old girl who doesn't even have a boyfriend. She's lost three kilos in this past week, and has been going downhill for about the last six months or so. These people don't suffer from anorexia nervosa. The rumor is that someone has "pointed the bone" at her. The "purnu" is a sharp wood rod, two inches to seven feet in length and is made to enter a victim's body by evil magic. A person who is the victim, if he has a sufficiently guilty conscience, will believe that he has been "stung" and will refuse treatment and ultimately die. This little fifteen-year-old had been bitten by a snake about four years ago, and had survived after being treated at the hospital in the Alice. I couldn't find anything physically wrong with her. We decided to bring her back to the Alice in the plane.

Yakiti is an old man who had just returned from the Alice about a month ago after having had the toes of his right foot amputated for gangrene. The story is that he had a stroke a few years ago and is moderately incapacitated by his left-sided paralysis. He is also supposedly diabetic, but like most aboriginals, tends to forget to take medication when it's on a daily basis, particularly if he doesn't feel badly. Now he has ulcerations on the fingers of his right hand, and some black areas on his black skin that look like dry gangrene; this in spite of good radial pulses. The sister says that it looks just like his foot did, and that this thing goes very fast. We decide to take him with us in the plane, too.

Harry is an old man in frank congestive failure. He has been for a long time, but doesn't take his tolbutamide. Poor old chap. He has ascites, too, with a liver margin down on his right hip bone. We decide to take him along. Then a pregnancy that has reached its time. She will come with us, too.

Next there's the little European school marm. "I was coming down the stairs six days ago with the typewriter in my hands, and caught my heel on the next to the last step. I didn't drop the typewriter, but it did land on my left wrist, and it sure hurt," she explains. Exam: She has a fracture, but we don't have room in the plane for her. She'll have to come along in the mail plane on Tuesday. I put her into a "sugar-tong" splint and she has relief from her pain.

Now it's tea time at sister's trailer. We stop and look at the "factory." A European has trained the local women to make Indonesian batiks and other art creations for the market. I understand that she has markets in London, Paris, and New York. The work is beautiful. I understand that it's hard to buy here, though, since everything that really turns out well will be sent to the export markets. Only if you contract for it and pay for it first, are you apt to get one of these art creations for your very own. Well, we'll see next time we're out.

Finally departure time arrives. The plane is really full this time. It takes the whole strip to get us off, and we're winging back to the Alice. The weather is now beautiful. The landing is uneventful, and we're met by the ambulance. Another interesting day in the outback.

Sequels? Sure. The girl with the weight loss never did stay

in the hospital. I was told that she found some relatives down around the Todd River in the Alice, and when last seen was treating herself with Yellow Label sherry, a wine fortified with extra alcohol that is inexpensive and preferred by the aboriginals. We'll probably see her back in Ernabella in a few weeks.

Yakiti? The "gangrene" on his dark-skinned hands was diagnosed as third degree burns. He likes it at the hospital in the Alice, and figured this was a good way to get back. I really thought it was gangrene. Poor old guy. The school marm? I saw her X-rays this last week. She had a fracture of the ulna, about four centimeters above the wrist joint. The radius wasn't fractured. It was in good enough position that nothing else had to be done with it. Harry? I don't know. I guess he just walked out of the hospital. But at 8,000 feet when we we're coming back, he was pretty short of breath. I suppose we'll be seeing him again next time we get to Ernabella. Oh, Eileen who coughed up the blood in Indulkana last week also walked out of the hospital. We'll be seeing her back there, I suppose.

Next week we're off for Amata. We're gradually working our way closer to Ayer's Rock.

23 October 1980

This week it's really heavy weather, and the pilot for the Navajo is Darryl. It's the usual story of the preflight check, and the loading of the boxes of steel files that contain the records of lots of aboriginals. Altogether there seem to always be about three boxes of records for each settlement. Take off is on runway one-two, and before we make our first turn away from the runway, we're in a driving rain. The ground out here is being worked over for some purpose. It almost looks like maybe they're planting tufts of grass, because it looks like rows of holes following the land contours. I didn't have time to ask before we were between cloud layers.

"I doubt we'll get all the way there," Darryl says ruefully. At 8,000 feet we're between layers, but it is smooth. No way to tell when we cross the Finke River this time, except for the DME that says we're ninety-three miles from Alice Springs. Then it begins to loosen up a bit, and here and there you can see the redness of the desert beneath the cloud layer. That's time for sister Carol to serve the coffee and biscuits. There's Mt. Connor just ahead and to the right, and a bit further to the right one can just make out the silhouette of Ayer's Rock. Suddenly all the clouds seem to wash out, and we're in the clear, sunny desert landscape scene again.

The strip at Amata is quite a distance from town, and Darryl is banking for the approach and final before I have a chance to get ready for town, and so the camera wasn't quite ready for anything exciting except the car dump. It's a nice, long strip, again carved out of the red desert, about a hundred yards wide and about a mile long. We're met by the sister of the hospital there who has a full day lined up for us, she says. The four-wheel drive vehicle is piloted by an aboriginal woman who knows two speeds; fast and stop. The road is soft, red dirt, and she makes the van fly, with her elbows held akimbo, face over the wheel, knuckles strained and blanching the skin. A frantic corrective motion to the wheels in the soft sand that makes one wonder when she's going to lose control and the vehicle will roll, and roll, and roll! But she does get us to the hospital, and stops! The metal boxes with the records come shifting forward against the back of the rear seats.

This is the oldest hospital. The sister has just arrived, and will be there for ninety more days waiting for a permanent sister to arrive. Sister Beverly has been a midwife down south in the past; is the mother of grown children, and kind of wonders what she's really doing out here. The hospital has fireplaces in the rooms, but they've been plugged up because the aboriginals tend to take the fire out of the fireplace when it's there, and put it in the center of the room so that they can all gather around. But of course, this does create a fire hazard. So the fireplaces remain blocked up.

It's the usual run of patients: prenatals, and one old gentle-man who has recently returned from Adelaide after having had a cataract removed. He has plastic glasses with his lenses already fitted, although only the left eye has been done and the right eye still has a cataract present as thick as the bottom of a beer bottle. He's delighted with his glasses, and all the others seem a bit envious. I'm told that in about six weeks, the sand and dust will have rendered them opaque, but he'll still look through them blindly. I guess doctors could order more glasses from down in Adelaide, but since they seem to be such a status symbol, it's better not to order them too early, or someone with perfectly normal vision would undoubtedly be wearing them.

Coffee at sister's house after we finish the clinic, and then we're off and away again. This time it's clear all the way home, and we fly just to the east of Mt. Connor. It looks like a chocolate cake rising up from the desert floor. I had been told that it was "unclimbable" by people who had been by it on the way to Ayer's Rock on the road, but that's not so. On the southeastern rim, there's a rock fall that looks wide enough to make a super highway, slanting all the way to the top. It is called the place of the "ice-men" by the Pitjantjatjaras, but looking down on the mesa, it looks just like the rest of the desert floor.

I'm beginning to know my way back and forth now. I can recognize things on the desert floor that tell me where I am without looking at the DME or the map, like Palmer Valley Station. But here and there are large areas, maybe 160 acres or so, that look like they are covered with sand traps for a golf course. I'm told that these are rabbit warrens. Then I was told what the six-foot steel rods that some of the women possess are for. I thought it was strange that they would carry such a heavy thing for a walking stick, but it isn't for that at all.

The women are the rabbit hunters, and when they find a warren like this, they take their steel pikes and plug up the holes of the warren until they only have one left. Then with this one, they thrust and jab into the dirt and follow the burrows until they come to the main cavern. When they strike down with the rod and it comes up tipped with fur and blood, they know they have the game in hand.

They excavate the area around the rod until they open into the cavern, and then reach in their hands and feel for the legs, then the head, and wring each rabbit's neck until there is no more movement. Then they dig them out, and the feast will begin. 'Course, that's not men's work, so you don't see men carrying these rods.

Darryl sets the Navajo down gently, and the trip for this week is over. I'm getting to feel like a pro at this kind of work. It is the high point in the week, really, but I'd better not say too much, or someone will think that this part of the job should be abandoned for some other kind of less interesting work.

30 October 1980

Today, things are different again. This time both of the Royal Flying Doctors' planes are in the shop, and so we go out with a charter flight from the Aero Club, with Roger as pilot. The plane is a nice Piper Aztec, but a lousy plane if you're really planning to med-evac any patients. If we do we'll just have to fly back to the Alice, and have them send out a plane that can accommodate a stretcher. But that's the way the politicians away up in Darwin see it. 'Course, they've never flown out into the outback, so they really haven't seen it, but they're the experts, aren't they? Things out here really do remind me a lot of the way we do things in America.

This is the first day since I've started these trips that the sky is clear. Not a cloud in sight. Off to the east there's smoke rising from a bush fire, but I think it's one of those "on purpose" type that some stations feel are in their best interest. We also have Dr. Hamler with us, a radiologist from Melbourne, who has been touring the country, and obviously knows some folks in high places up in Darwin who have "rung down" to Alice and suggested that it would be nice if he could go with us. Sister Carol shows up with the usual steel cases of files (they're more important than medicine, one would think). But she's distressed, because Paul didn't come by for her, and she just hates to carry these sharp, metal cases in her neat, little sports car. None the less, we're off the runway at 0830 in Aztec VH FTJ.

About an hour and a quarter later, after flying the same old route, except just a tad east, we see the runway at Ernabella. Fregon is about forty miles south of there, and by and by, there's the red, dirt runway, and the pile of old cars. This runway is a bit unique in that there's a hill right in the middle. In short, it's half uphill and half downhill, and when you get low enough on final, it looks like an extremely short runway. No problem. Roger sets it down just fine. Sister Barbara Rexman meets us, and she drives the vehicle back to the hospital. This is probably the smallest hospital in the circuit, but it is reasonably clean and spartan in its accommodations. As usual, the aboriginals are sitting outside under the trees, and are cooking their meal. One is a leg of lamb that seems well charred on the outside. Under a faucet in the courtyard, a naked child sits happily building a dam to hold back the water from the leaky faucet. She's careful not to be too efficient, because then there wouldn't be all this nice, gooey mud to splash all over her dusty, black skin.

The patients are the usual sort. One of the prenatals is about twenty weeks in spite of the fact that she had an IUD placed about two months after her last pregnancy in February. Another is a child with a bad cough, and rales in the right upper lobe. She's had her BCG (Bacillus Calmette-Guerin, an anti-tuberculosis immunization), they claim. Another is Peter, who has diabetes, has had hypertension for years, and even had a nephrectomy about five years ago for recurrent infections that destroyed the kidney. He should be on insulin, but that's impossible. He won't even take his tolbutamide. What's to do?

Then there's Cedric; two years old. He's had recurrent urinary tract infections because of the really tight phimosis of his foreskin. He's already been to the Alice for correction of the problem, but the family left before it was done. These people have a really strong ritual about the pubertal rite in males. The leaders of the rite do an inferior penile slit, actually surgically making a hypospadias with a sharp rock, and so any fooling around with this part of the anatomy could be a disaster for a male child. On the other hand, recurrent urinary tract infections are going to put him into the same boat as Peter, and he's only two. The family does agree that a dorsal slit would be acceptable.

Actually, it isn't the family who agrees; it's the community council of ten aboriginals who say it's okay. So, we plan to take Cedric (and his mom) to the Alice in the Aztec.

Then, there's a European woman who had stepped on a chop bone, and lacerated her foot about six weeks ago. It got quite badly infected, so she had some friends take her to an out-back "doctor," nungkari, who gave her some antibiotics (whatever), and on the way back they were in an auto accident. Now that the infection in her foot has healed (because she's been on erythromycin given by sister Barbara), there seems to be a terrible pain over the medial malleolus of that foot, and I suspect she fractured the bone in the auto accident. But after four weeks, like Dr. Hamler says, "function is the thing," and she seems to be able to walk well in spite of the pain. So, we just leave her alone.

Sister has a nice garden growing outside her trailer with tomatoes, cabbage, broccoli, beets, and other goodies. We have the usual tea, coffee, and biscuits, and she's made a torte that is very good. Back to the plane. Cedric and his mom are waiting. Into the plane, the takeoff. Cedric is very unhappy with the turbulence that bounces the craft around like a cork in a millstream. Back to the Alice, and everyone off to their own thing. Just like it all hadn't happened. But it did happen, and I have the memories and the slides to prove it!

6 November 1980

What a beautiful day for a flight. There's not a cloud in the sky, and the sun is coming up so early now that it's quite a ways above the horizon when I arrive at the airport. It's John, again, as the pilot. Sister Carol hasn't any report yet on Eileen, who coughed up the blood, but she'll ring me as soon as she hears. Eileen did go back to her people, but there just hasn't been a report yet. Fox Delta Quebec is the plane again. Everything works just as smooth as silk. We cruise down at 10,000 feet this time. It doesn't seem to take as long. John is just back from a three-day holiday in Melbourne and feels rested, except for a tad of a headache this morning. He was with friends last night, he says.

Today the "police" plane is also arriving in Indulkana. It seems that there's been a crime wave here in the settlement. Somebody sniffed a little john barleycorn (or maybe it was petrol), and figured every window in town was an enemy. He did a great job in reducing the number of enemies, and then apparently realized what he'd done, and fled. One of the townspeople said, "Well, he didn't hurt anyone, so I don't know why they're looking for him."

But they did look for him, and they found him, and now he's on trial by the Territory ("Territ'ry") Police.

Today the centre looks even dirtier than the last time. We see some of the same people again. No matter what the complaint of the women, they're all pregnant. Did have the European school marm back again. Her arm is better but now she has a lump in her neck. It's her thyroid. I'm going to have Dr. Charley in the Alice see her. She'll go up this week by road. Then there's Andy with the massive furunculosis of the right buttock. He's had it since July. It's never really been treated, because he won't stay on medicine long enough. I take a culture. Tetracycline, 500 mg. q.i.d. (four times a day) for three weeks. He'll never take it that long, I know. The infection actually spreads all the way around the buttock to the groin, and the nodes feel like golf balls. Lymphogranuloma? If so, the culture will grow normal bugs. I didn't ask for them to look for Donovan bodies, a specific finding in lymphogranuloma, but the treatment may be effective.

About fifteen patients, and then tea at sister's. Then we're on the way home again. It's a spectacularly clear day. John and I speculate about the mineral wealth that lies beneath this desert. Probably oil, and natural gas, and innumerable untold goodies that will still be here twenty years from now. We do see a "Ghan" (freight train, so named because in past days the only freight that made it to the Alice from Darwin or Adelaide was carried in camel caravans driven by *Afghan* camel drivers) moving northward slowly on the new tracks. In an hour and five minutes we're on final for one-two. There are four French Mirage jet fighters parked on the tarmac. They almost lost one here yesterday when, the pilot said, his brakes went out. There's a big C–130 on the tarmac, too. I guess it brought spare parts for the landing gear of the Mirage.

"Sometimes when they come down from Darwin, they arrive at the Alice with four minutes of fuel remaining," notes John. "Hardly time for a 'go around' if they mess up the initial approach. They burn 600 gallons an hour," he tells me.

We park the Graham Pitt and casually take our farewells. So much for the fifth trip for me into the Red Centre.

13 November 1980

I mentioned before that Yakiti had been diagnosed at the hospital as having burns on his fingers instead of gangrene. Smart, old guy. He'd figured a way to get around the doc so that he could get a free trip to the Alice and have some wine with his friends under the bridge on the Todd. So did the girl with the curse. Poor old Harry (with the frank congestive heart failure) was back this time, too, looking about twenty pounds lighter, and certainly breathing easier.

We left at the usual time of about 0800 hours. This time it was Glenda and Murray, sister and pilot, respectively. It was a nice day for the flight, again in the Navajo, and the strip looked familiar lying in the valley between the two ranges of dry hills. Sister Judy picked us up, and in no time we were in the hospital and setting up for the patients. Most of them were "ante-natal," but a few were interesting. One who was lying in bed in the hospital has been getting the sisters a bit tired. Her name is Ivy. She kept coming back with high fever and chills and a cough, but they really didn't know what it was. They'd given her a course of Amoxil, and followed that with a course of Vibramycin, but she still stayed sick. I looked at her. She was sure having a shaking chill, and was feverish, but I couldn't see much else. Her chest sounded clear. The sisters are quite insistent, so we agreed to take her back with us in the plane. Glenda doesn't seem to have quite the knack that sister Carol has.

One of the characters we met was Punch Johnston. He's had his picture in the paper and ail. He's one of the higher ups on the aboriginal council and even has his name on the land rights bill. Imagine! I see him for a driver's license exam, and also because he thinks he's having a heart attack because of vague pain in the left lateral chest. I examine him, but when I don't find anything wrong with his heart, I qualify him for the driver's test. (Incidentally, Punch's father's name is "Talk-Talk".)

Then it's time for tea, and I order up two boomerangs from the local artisan. They'll be hand-crafted just for me, and I'll pick them up the next time I'm here. The short, little sister who spells for Judy is named Meg. They kind of look like Mutt and Jeff of the funny papers.

Back to the aircraft. Murray does things just a bit different than the other pilots. Soon we're airborne again, and on our way home. It's difficult to stay awake with the droning of the engines and the warm sun coming through the windscreen. Then Murray is leaning forward and saying, "They're right about here some place. Oh, yes, there they are."

We're making a vertical bank over the Henbury meteorite craters. Geologically, this group of craters was made by a large meteorite some 4,000 years ago, about the same time that Mount Mazama was creating Crater Lake in Oregon. The meteorite exploded after heating in the earth's atmosphere. That's why there are so many craters. It's of recent history sufficient to be included in some of the aboriginal mythology. Murray puts me on the downside of the plane in the bank, and I get some excellent pictures of the craters. Then we're touching down at the airport. Feverish Ivy is taken off the plane by the St. John's ambulance people, and it's the end of another bush trip.

20 November 1980

To everyone's horror, Ivy has been diagnosed as having miliary tuberculosis. It's the most highly contagious form of the disease. So, this day we fly first to Ernabella, because Ivy lived there and sister Pauline Jones is to be dropped off to do Mantouxs (skin tests for tuberculosis) on the folks there that may have had contact with Ivy. Even I'm supposed to have a chest x-ray and then another one in about three months. John is the pilot. It's a lovely day, but a bit hazy. There really isn't all that much to see, so I do my CORE review CME (continuing medical education) on the way.

We don't really see anyone but sister Julie at the strip, and we leave for Amata. It's about fifty miles as the crow flies, and the country is pretty much the same in appearance. Again the hairy ride in the four-wheel drive vehicle with the aboriginal female driver. Wild! One wonders when she's going to roll the vehicle over and over in the bull dust and sand. But we do make it! Again the prenatal exams with the laying on of the hand to feel where the top of the fundus is, and the snuffly children with the runny ears, and the old folks who want their papers filled out so that they can continue to get their "sit down" money. We leave some PPD (purified protein derivative for TB skin tests) here, too, because Ivy had walked between Ernabella and Amata, and had friends in both places. Then lunch at sister's house, and we go back to Ernabella to pick up Pauline. The flight home is uneventful. John has gotten us home safely again.

11 December 1980

We didn't go out on Thanksgiving Day because sister Glenda had mistaken what I had said, and figured that I didn't want to fly on an American holiday. Actually, what I had said was that since I was going to Adelaide on the fourth of December, I really didn't want to miss two trips in a row. But I did miss them, and so, today we're making up for it.

It was Peter this time who was pilot. Sister Glenda accompanied us since it was time to take Ivy home to Ernabella. Take off in the Graham Pitt again, and it is spectacularly clear. A few scattered cumuli nimbus with streaks, but they're away off to the west. Peter is an ex-cop, born and raised in Adelaide; he is also a diver and sailor. He says that Kangaroo Island is an abalone paradise, and also that the crayfish (we call them Australian lobster) are excellent. He's going to build his own boat; going to rig it sloop; and he and his wife and family are going to sail the South Ocean and the reefs. The Graham Pitt lost its hydraulics last week when Peter was at the controls. Seems that they forgot to replace an O-ring when they reinstalled the pump, and so he didn't have too easy a time getting his gear down. Finally all was well, though, and they apparently fixed it (I hope).

Sister Meg is waiting for us when we touch down, and Ivy is welcomed home. Sister Julia is ill with an ear infection and has been having episodes of vertigo. I think we'd better take her back with us. The clinic is the usual. Sister has about thirty patients lined up. One is a forty-ish female who says she's pregnant. Her last papoose was ten years before. I put my hand on her belly. She's about fifteen weeks, I'd guess. It would be sacrilegious in this culture to inspect the female genitalia or do an internal exam, so I'm learning to gauge the length of gestation quite accurately by laying hands on the tummy. She seems to be having no trouble with this pregnancy. I turn to the sink to wash my hands, and discover they have an air conditioner plugged in right next to the sink, so it's difficult to wash and not come in contact with 220 volts. I'm not sure I want to look like a Christmas tree yet. Two European women are pregnant. One has rather nasty varicosities. And there's talk about Bromby Marshal, an aboriginal who is about twenty years old, who has a history of long bouts of drinking, but has been on the wagon for a while. He showed up a few days back looking terrible and died of what they think was lactic acidosis. They think it was petrol sniffing that did him in.

Finally it's lunch time. The sky is really filling up with towering cumulus with glistening snow-white tops and ominous bases that have jagged agonies of brilliance flashing to the ground, but soundlessly, since they're probably fifty miles away yet. We walk from the hospital to the house for lunch. Not a breath of air is stirring, and it's hot. Naked kids, listless men and women, and drowsing dogs bake in the dust under the gum tree, moving only to stay in the shade. No soccer games underway today, for sure. Sister Meg props herself up on three cushions to drive the Toyota four-wheel drive to the strip.

Sister Julie really doesn't feel well at all, but we're off to Fregon for the clinic that was supposed to have been last week. It's only about forty miles south. There's discussion about Ivy's return. She had bought a new dress in the Alice, and there was a lot of conversation about it. It was a red, black and green polyester print, with large flowers, and apparently greatly admired. She was happy to be home, I think. The Graham Pitt takes up the whole strip to get off in the muggy weather. It's bumpy! Sister Julie faints, but there's no vomiting. She just falls over in the seat, restrained by her belt, and then the light comes on showing that the cabin door is unsealed. The noise level climbs to a vacuum cleaner roar, just like the Beechcraft Bonanza I had back in Santa Barbara used to do. No problem. We're at Fregon and landing.

This is the funny strip with the hill in the center so that it looks only half as long as it really is as you come over the approach fence. Sister Barbara meets us. She's still uptight about the radiologist who took all the photos. I have my camera in my hand. It's too hot to leave it in the plane. Some of the aboriginals get upset about having their pictures taken, but I always ask first. Besides, it really isn't any of sister Barbara's business how I handle my own social excursions. I do leave the camera at her house, along with Peter and sister Julie.

We drive back to the hospital with the leaky faucet in the yard. Two little naked kids are playing in the mud this time. The examining room is a grim, dirty ten-by-ten foot enclosure with a Traeger radio plugged into a "No Hassle" twelve-volt battery sitting on the floor. The usual routine of prenatals, and the "sit-down" money people, and finally twenty-five patients have been examined.

We move off to pick up the pilot and patient. Barbara is a lot more relaxed about the camera now, and even seems, in her green, plain dress, almost friendly. While the gear is being loaded on the plane, I take a picture of the settlement with the green trees above a field of white, dead thistles, and the purple-orange-black and white thunderheads above. Then off and away, back past Ernabella, and between the strands of rain beneath the cumulus. Only one of them we catch the edge of; fifteen hundred feet a minute down, and then up so that you feel like your bum is going to go through the seat cushion. Then the top of my hat crushes on the overhead.

This time we have sister Julie on the stretcher. She's lashed in, so I don't know if she just slept or whether she fainted again. Then we're over the Finke, and there's a rainbow to the west; two of them, in fact, with the most brilliant colors I've ever seen. Like a dummy, I admire them and forget what the camera around my neck is for. And then, we're on the ground about 1845 hours and St. John's ambulance is there, ready to help Julie out of the plane. She faints again, poor thing. I hasten along, because there's a staff party for Christmas at the Wilkerson address. I learn later that Julie's thing is probably more of the pain from an *otitis externa* (outer ear infection) than a labrynthitis (inner ear infection). Well, she sure was sick, anyway.

18 December 1980

Today the trip is out to Amata, and Murray is the pilot, and sister Carol is along. Sister Glenda is occupied elsewhere, I guess. The Graham Pitt is run up. The starboard engine smokes a little as it tends to run a bit rich, but Murray says that's okay. Crystal clear day. The tower bids us "g'dye," and it's off on runway one-two, and a right turn out. Set to 240 degrees, and we parallel the new road that we have just come driving up on Tuesday when we returned from a holiday at Ayer's Rock. Past the Henbury meteorite craters, and almost at once on gaining altitude, Mt. Conner comes into view. We aim straight at it. The air is smooth this early in the morning. We cross the Finke, and the Palmer Station, and there's Curtin Springs Station, and Ayer's Rock in the distance with the Olgas just a bit further west.

The road does meander between dry lake beds. That's probably why they can't keep a road in there. When the cloudbursts come they just wash out the road. There are lots of little one-track roads through the bush, too. Amazing how someone on the ground driving a vehicle can make such a straight line through the wattles and rocks.

Mt. Conner, or "Artilla," home of the aboriginal Pitjantjatjara tribe's legendary, fearsome ice-men, sits in a depression; it almost looks like a crater. Again we pass over the southeast corner. It is eroded into about four or five canyons, like fingers from the top, and the erosion debris has formed a sloping surface that could be used to gain access easily (well, not too steep a climb) to the top. Bush and rocks, but nothing that would suggest that a man has ever been on top of it before is all that we see. Then, there's the strip at Amata.

Sister Beverly, the midwife, meets us at the airport with sister Jennie. Beverly is leaving tomorrow for Adelaide to spend Christmas with her family. Her new assignment is going to be at a settlement up the Murray River. She's happy about that. Amata is one of the "newer" settlements. It started about fifteen years ago when the government felt it was best for the nomadic aboriginals to come out of the desert and sit under a gum tree and be fed, housed and clothed by big brother, and, not incidentally—exposed to venereal disease, mumps, chicken pox, measles, etc. which have almost wiped out the race. I'm told that the aboriginals in Amata who are over fifty years of age can tell you about their experience when they first saw the white man: How, at about the turn of the century, there was fear and trepidation when the aboriginal first saw a rabbit! The rabbit soon became a staple in the aboriginal pantry.

I examined one old man, a pensioner from the Social Service who had a 1919 birthdate according to the government, but who according to our records was born in 1926. He seemed to be in robust good health, wiry and lean, except that his teeth were ground down flat, like a horse's, even the cuspids and bicuspids. Ajax was his name.

Amata has to be one of the dirtiest settlements of those I'd seen. A dead dog lies in the road with flies giving it motion. The carrion birds won't come that close to the house. No one thinks of moving the carcass. Junk and brush litter the streets, and people sleep in the dust, under a tree. I see about twenty-five patients, and then it's time to be on the way home.

I do my first aboriginal pelvic, contrary to what my original impression was about the sacrilege of this, on a twenty-five-year-old unmarried girl, who had lost her left eye after surgery for a brain abscess when she was about seven. Now, because of the surgery, no one will even have intercourse with her to give her a baby, let alone marry her. Poor thing! Her mother said that she has a vaginal discharge. After consulting with a woman tribal leader, it is deemed okay for me to do the work. She really doesn't have much of a vaginitis. Everything seems normal. I think it's a socially acceptable reason, though, for her not to have a boyfriend. I recommend a course of Sultrin therapy. Oh, yes. There's nothing unique about the female aboriginal perineum.

The trip home is lovely. We have an aboriginal mother with a ten-month-old baby, and a two-and-a-half-year-old baby. The father is European. The baby has hepatitis, and a urine sugar of 2,000 mg. per deciliter! We'll have him worked up.

I guess I should explain something about race at this point. In the Pitjantjatjara mind, a "European" is a person with white skin. A "white" man is any person who is not an aboriginal. Thus, even an American black man is a "white."

8 January 1981

There have been no trips since the eighteenth, because it was so close to Christmas and New Years. So today is Ernabella, and it gives me a chance to visit with sister Julie, who had returned from her treatment at the Alice hospital for the ear infection. She's doing okay, but still does have some discomfort in that ear. John is the pilot, and again it's the Graham Pitt that we fly in. A rather unsettled morning with several layers of haze that John says we can expect to become cumulus clouds by the afternoon. Yesterday, one of the Northern Territory Airline's Navajos had nose gear trouble, and they had a full-scale exercise with crash wagons and other emergency measures at the airport, but it all came down and locked all right.

We fly right over the Henbury craters again. They really aren't very much to look at. Again, almost over the top of Mt.

Ebenezer, crossing the bitumen road to Ayer's Rock, and then the lakes, and we're letting down. It's hot! We drive into the settlement, and the dogs and kids surround the hospital like they always do. There's one little naked kid, about four years old, in the courtyard with an extra special amount of gunk draining from his nose and down over his upper lip.

"Doesn't it make you want to go, 'sniff,'?" I ask John.

"Not with that much of it," answers John. And, besides, there were half a dozen flies worrying it, and I'll bet you think I'm making this up. I'm not!

It's really a busy day. We have a lot of patients from Ernabella, and then there are a lot who have come up from Fregon, too. The sister from Fregon has brought them up. These are mostly "antenatals," as the Aussies call our prenatals. Incidentally, I'm finding that I'm guessing these gestational dates on their pregnancies as a little further along than they really are by about two weeks. One interesting patient is a man, about forty-five years old, who has, over the last two months, developed an athetotic movement to his right arm. He has left-sided occipito-parietal headaches, and has numbness in his hands on both sides. There's no evidence of muscle wasting, and there are no other localizing symptoms. I think it's a basal ganglion lesion of some sort on the left side of his brain. I'll send him down to Dr. Rick Smith in Adelaide, if the officials concur. Rick is an outstanding neurosurgeon.

Another eleven-year-old boy has a desquamating, vesicular eruption over his face and scalp, and the bathing trunk area that he's had since he was four. The sisters have tried all kinds of topical things on it to no avail. It's getting worse, and it's not only a medical problem, it's a social problem, too. His peers laugh at him, and he's coming up to puberty. He hasn't really been worked up for this, and the last time he was up to the Alice was two years ago. I write a letter to Dr. Barker, the regional supervisor, for permission to send him down to Adelaide; the same as I did for the man with the athetosis. Then it's time for "a drink" at sister's house before we return to the Alice. Here a drink means iced tea or coffee or lemonade, and it's really refreshing.

Sister Meg has bought a large wall hanging ($90) and a small

wall hanging ($20), and a spectacular wrap-around skirt, all of
these local batiks, for $50. They are spectacular examples of the
local art, and would be so much better to bring back with us than
boomerangs and such, although we will have to bring some of
those back, too.

Then we say our good-byes. Sister Julie is leaving. Her tour
of duty is up, and she's returning to Melbourne for a while before
taking her next assignment. The Graham Pitt is waiting for us,
and soon we're in the air. John was right, and the sky is studded
with dumplings; big white cumulus clouds that have lots of
streaks under them, and, where they reach the ground, the ex-
plosions of dust. I sit and study my Core Content Review lesson
(continuing medical education) from last month. The time passes
quickly, and we're home. Sister Glenda says that if Laura would
like to come out with us to Ernabella time after next, I should
talk with sister Kay, who must get permission from the Ernabella
council of aboriginals that it's all right. I don't think there'll be
a problem at all. We'll get the paperwork started.

15 January 1981

Would you believe? It's drizzling out this morning, and sister
Carol Evans calls to say that we're going to be about half an hour
late getting off the ground. So, I drive out at 0815. The mountains
at the gap are partly lost in the mist as I drive. I even have to put
the windscreen wipers on high as I go by the Ross River road to
carry away the mist. The airport is clear, though, and the clouds
are dispersing. Darryl is going to be the pilot this morning, and,
sure enough, at 0845 we're taxiing out to runway one-two. Off
and away in the Graham Pitt. As we turn the right departure,
we're into the clouds. Such spectacular clouds! Rising up like
mountains and canyons, and with rainbows all about in the
morning sun. When you can see ahead, the air is so pure and
washed that you can see detail on the ground for miles and miles.

I uncork the camera to take in some of this for y'all to see. Guess what? I don't have any film left. I've always carried a spare film with the flash unit on the strap of my camera, but the carry case strap had broken at Ayer's Rock (I almost lost the whole thing over the side of the mountain), and I hadn't fixed it yet. So I sit and just daydream as we move between and through these big mounds of white and gray. It's amazing as you watch one of them come up, slowly at first, and then, as you get near, with an amazing rush you're into it. Imagine if it were solid! You wouldn't have a lot of time to pray once you knew that you were going to hit.

Then we come out on top, and cruise at heading 222 degrees over the tops. Curtin Springs Station has an ADF (automatic direction finder) on it, and we head for that. They told us that Amata was in the open, but it sure looks solid as the needle sweeps from "ahead" to "behind" on the ADF. We only have about fifteen minutes more to go. Oh, well, the Navajo has plenty of petrol to get us back if we can't get in. Then, about the time Alice Springs comes back on the air to tell us the latest is that Amata is socked in, the clouds break, and there, just ahead, is the strip with the sun shining on it, the broken clouds making splashes of shade on the desert floor. Ayer's rock and the Olgas off to the right look like purple dinosaurs on the horizon.

The sister here is new. Beverly has gone home for a holiday. Sister Meg has driven all the way over from Ernabella with three patients to be seen, including Ivy, who needs an exam and a letter to sister Pauline Jones of the Health Department. Ivy looks good, and apparently I'm a favorite person for this sixty-five-year-old diabetic aboriginal, who is just recovering from miliary tuberculosis. Well, not everybody out here hates me, as Charlie Brown would say.

There's a young lady here who is going to be leaving for Darwin on the bus tomorrow, but she's come down with every symptom that goes with rheumatic fever. The swelling in her joints has subsided on therapy of penicillin and aspirin, but her sed rate was recorded at 125 mm/hr the week before. I urge her husband to postpone the trip, and for the first time the aboriginals begin to talk with me in English. They have decided that the tjilpi doctor is not a tourist and that they can converse with him in his own language. It's a great feeling!

I forgot to tell you that when we left the Alice, Darryl had left the keys to the lockers on the plane in the pilot's lounge at the airport. So, when we first arrived in Amata, the lockers on the plane were all locked up with our records and equipment in them. Guess what? The key to the Toyota 4-wheel drive fits! We're able to manage. Then, to find the keys after we have finished and are ready to leave, we have to drive all around the settlement to find the Toyota again.

It's a grand tour of the settlement. It's hard to believe the filth and the waste. Houses that have been abandoned for one reason or another with the windows broken out, the solar heaters on the roof blasted with debris, and even holes that have been smashed into the sides of the houses. Filth and dirt, and dogs and debris littering the streets and yards. The natives are lying under the trees in the shade. I hope I can bring home some pictures of this, because you won't believe it unless you can see it. The politicians all crying for someone to do something for the unfortunate black brother. There are some of us sure trying, but the politicians aren't being very helpful with the doles and restrictions on assistance.

Finally coffee at sister's place, and then back to the plane. We have four to go home with us. One young man with his left leg in a cast, to be rechecked at the hospital, and a four-year-old boy with recurrent bladder infections, who has probably also been deaf since birth. With him go Mom, of course, and baby brother who is nine months old. It's a hot day, and Amata is about 2,000 feet above sea level. The Navajo uses up the whole runway, and climbs away at full power at about 200 feet a minute. It's scary when you see the end of the runway five hundred feet ahead, and the airspeed indicates only 80 mph, which is five miles an hour less than one-engine capability. Remember what I said about the clouds coming up fast at the end? The end of the runway does the same thing! But the climb out is neat, and we fly the canyons and through the humps of the mountains all the way home. Then there's the descent, boring holes through the clouds. We're down, and another day is done. More memories to store away for sharing when we get back to America some day.

22 January 1981

It's windy this morning. We're off for Fregon, but there seems to be a feeling among sister Carol and John, the pilot, and me that they really don't need us at Fregon. The sky has clouds, but there seems to be quite a bit of dust in the air. The plane is the Graham Pitt, and the runway is one-two. We're in the air by 0815. It's hazy with the dust and not a good day for sightseeing. I work on my CME lesson from Core Content Review. Carol reads, and John plays with his maps and assists the Alice tower in a radio check. We pass by the Ernabella strip. Fregon is about forty miles further south. John makes a convenience bank for me to take a picture of the settlement, and we land in a strong crosswind. Sister Barbara is there to pick us up, but says that she really has nothing for us to do. So we drive to the makeshift hospital and don't even bother to get the record boxes out of the plane. Sister Barbara invites us for a cup of coffee at her place.

Fregon is the site of the crime wave beginning. It's from this place that the young people first began the petrol-sniffing thing, and then they began to break into houses at their own whim, whether the houses were occupied or not. Since the ringleader of the bunch is the son of one of the council members, there's really not much that can be done about it. I ask Barbara if she is frightened for her personal safety, and she says she really is, because, when they've been on the petrol thing, they really don't use good common sense. The government with the dole is really responsible for the whole problem. Barbara had personally gone to the assistance of one of the other European women on summons of a siren which sounded one night. She says that as she ran across the settlement in her nightie, she suddenly wondered just what she was going to do when she arrived at her friend's house if there happened to be a bunch of young aboriginals there who decided to make use of her. She bravely continued on, and as she approached, the intruders fled in the night. But, what if they hadn't? It seems that the set-up for a massacre of Europeans is really at hand in this situation. I wonder when it will come?

The aboriginals didn't come in for much sympathy today. The girls told the story of the aboriginals who had a problem with the underside of their car. Since they had neither a pit nor hoist available, rather than drive the car up onto a ramp, they simply turned it on its side against a tree and proceeded to fix the problem as best they could standing upright. That's another problem, say the girls. The aboriginal is always happy to fix something whether it needs it or not. Witness, they say, the miles of cassette tape laying around the settlement. Insatiable curiosity to find out where the music is coming from, compels them to break into the cassette and unravel all the tape, and in the end cast it to the wind; still looking for the musicians, I suppose. The families will come back from the city with a player, and the kids will cry and carry on for the "taper," until Mom or Dad hands the thing over to them. They'll push all the buttons on the thing to see what each button does, and then manage to get the cassette out. How? Well, get a stone first and break the little glass door. That's the quickest way.

I was taken into the "store" today. Filthy! There's an "orange drink" on sale, and it's being bought in half liter paper cups like it was going out of style. "Bargains" in the store like canned lamb ham; 630 grams for $7 Australian. That's equivalent to about $5.50 a pound in American currency. The place had been broken into, and all the shoes had been stolen. So, they decided to re-place them— no matter that they really don't need shoes all that much. The craft center has had all its windows broken out since the last time I was here. Additionally, there's a settlement south-west of there that's called Iltur. No one lives there anymore, but one of the men here in Fregon is the council representative to that community. So, he gets paid a rather substantial salary for driving down every couple of months to walk through the dust. It really is pleasant to leave Fregon. Sister Barbara is going to drive her little car the forty miles up to Ernabella to meet us at the clinic up there. On the radio, sister Meg has said that she has five patients she'd like us to stop and see. It isn't going to be a trip for nothing after all.

John takes us into the air, and we fly at a rather low altitude northbound. The rabbit warrens are easily visible from the air, and then we come roaring over the hills and there's Ernabella at treetop level, if there had been any trees. Sister Meg does indeed have a clinic and we see twelve patients. Two are children of

Emily who doesn't seem to want to feed them. So, we bring back both kids with us, naming the diagnosis as "failure to thrive."

I remark to Carol about the rabbit warrens. She says that she's been with the women when they go hunting. She's actually reached into the tunnels and caught the rabbits and wrung their necks. She says that they gut the animals, leave them in the fur, take out just the intestine and leave everything else. Then they singe the fur in a fire, and dig a hole and throw in the fire, rabbits and all, and cover up the hole with dirt. She said they dig the whole thing up after a while (aboriginal luau) and tear the animal to bits. They really don't cook it all that well, so that it's a tad bloody when the feast begins. They'll give the head to one kid, the chest (with heart and lungs intact) to another, etc., still in the fur. I said that I'd like to try it sometime (maybe).

The trip home is interesting. John says he's never seen a day quite like this one. The dust storms across the desert roll up the dirt in a path maybe two miles wide, with the dust reaching our level at 9,000 feet. There are several of these going on at the same time. The wind is from the east. It's not as bumpy as you'd think, but it sure isn't a day for seeing anything. No rain, although by the time we're within two miles of Alice airport, we first see it. The wind is gusting to thirty knots, but it's right down the pike for runway one-two. We turn off at the first taxi-way. Oh, yes. Sister Meg is nailing down the council at Ernabella to accept Laura for the scheduled visit there on the fifth of February.

5 February 1981

There seems to be some confusion this morning, but then there usually is when sister Glenda is in charge of the flight, and, of course, this is the morning that Laura is going to go along. She's been granted permission by the council at Ernabella to come along with her husband, the doctor. Last week there was no flight, although I had gone out to the airport and waited at

0730. No one came along, so I had driven back to the AMS, and was told that the runways were all too wet from all the rain, so they'd canceled. They just hadn't bothered to tell me about it.

Sister Glenda rang me 0800 hours today, and told me that they were going to leave about 0900 or so. We pick up our things, and drive out there. John is the pilot, and the flies are extraordinarily bad this morning. There are thousands of them, and they fly right into your nose or mouth if you keep it open. They're so dumb that you can swat them with your hand. They won't leave you alone and don't even move when you whisk at them.

By and by sister Glenda comes along with three little waifs in tow. They are the two children of Emily that I had brought back two weeks ago for "failure to thrive," and Leo, about nine, who was there for some other reason. John puts in the extra seat just in case, and about 0930 (Greenwich mean time is nine and a half hours behind the time in the Alice) we're taxiing out with Laura in the right hand seat, to runway one-two. And then we're airborne. There seem to be green and water in puddles everywhere, but it's a bit hazy. The little kids drop off to sleep almost at once, except Leo, who is wide-eyed and watching, and Glenda, who is crocheting doilies.

All the salt flats are full of water. We fly down at 6,000 feet, MSL. Laura is all eyes, and it is smooth. John raises her seat up so that she can really see. In about seventy minutes we're making a right-hand bank over Ernabella. There's sure been a lot of rain here, and the creeks are running. Matter of fact, when we came over the Finke, it was running about two hundred yards wide. John makes a nice landing, and we track back to the park. Sister Meg is there to meet us. The road to the settlement is almost washed out in three or four places, and she says that they had fifteen inches of rain in one weekend. That's a whole year's regular fall. She says that the kids were jumping off the bridge, and one of the youngsters got caught in the strength of the water and she did a resuscitation. Successfully, at that. That was why the runway wasn't useable last week. The clouds were too low, and the road was washed out, but the strip held up to its naming, and indeed was "all weather."

The clinic is full. We're late, of course, due to the late start. While I work the clinic, one of the clinic aides takes Laura to the craft store. She buys local art work: a string of beads, note cards, and a "piti" which is a wooden bowl-like object that we'll use for fruit; in the larger size, the aboriginals used to carry their babies in them. We have the usual ante-natals. Payula is pregnant again, less than a year, and so by their law, one of the infants, either the one she's carrying in her womb or the one she's suckling must die. Payula is the aboriginal who did the artwork that Laura bought. She also ordered two skirts, and Meg says that she'll have Munyirijana do the artwork on them. One is $50 and one is $35. I write the check to Meg Carleton for $90. Meg is leaving on the twentieth of this month. She'll let us know where she is, and will pay for the skirts when they are done, and see that they get back to Alice Springs to be delivered to Laura. We'll see. Meg is hoping to return to Israel in the near future. She's Scots, but Jewish.

Finally the clinic ends. We go over to Meg's for tea and lunch, and we talk and discuss so many things. There is a tension in the settlement with the sacking and imminent departure of Brian, who has been there for many years. Seems that the "holy roller" Christians, as Meg calls them, have sacked him for having taken the church Toyota to Adelaide (with the approval of the council). Brian has been the invaluable man who takes care of the running of the bore, the quality of the roads in the settlement, the repair of the tanks, and most of the things that have to be done by someone knowledgeable about such things. They don't even have a substitute for him, but the "Bible Thumpers," as sister Meg calls them, have driven him off. So much the worse for the community in Meg's opinion. And that's the gist of the conversation during lunch. Then we have a tour through the hospital, and then back out to the airstrip. We load in a young man going back for orthopedic follow-up, and two ladies with suckling babies, and we're off. Laura is again in the right front seat. Again, it's smooth at 9,000 feet this time, but still hazy, and Mt. Connor doesn't even show up well.

Then we're home, but it's about 1730 hours, and we make a delayed approach with a 360 over the approach end of runway one-two to let another "bloke" make his landing. The delay does give us some extra time to take pictures of the gap, the Alice, and the base. Then we're down, and instead of a car to take

Glenda and John in, they have to ride the ambulance, at $40 each. A car would have been $10 each. We tease them about being rich.

This's been a fun day. Now Laura has a feeling for the real aboriginal community, although, as I told her, this is the one that comes closest to being truly Europeanized. She'll just have to see Fregon some day to get a truer feeling of how abject it can be. On the other hand, there's now Laura's special recipe for kangaroo. Brian had gotten one (a kangaroo) this morning, and there was to be a luau tonight. The recipe? First get a kangaroo, and kill it, because it won't want to stay on the fire if you don't. Then dig a hole and build a fire, and when the coals are nice and hot, chuck in the kangaroo. That's right! Chuck the whole thing in. If you dress it out, the aboriginals won't eat it. Then when it's all done and the fur has been burned off, and just the skin left, you pull the thing out of the fire and open the belly. Take out the intestines and bury them. They won't smell badly. The heat cooks the contents and they come along as a rubbery mass, and don't contaminate the carcass. Then you start to pull off handfuls of meat. That's the whole recipe. No bay leaves or fancy stuff like that. They say it really is delicious. I suppose I'll have to try that, too, before I come home.

12 February 1981

Sister Carol is the nurse today, and Mark is the new pilot. He's a youngish man who looks about twenty-five or so, and was a pilot with Northern Airlines which is now defunct. He's originally from Adelaide. Peter, it seems, has gone to Port Augusta and bought his boat, and is going to be sailing now. So, Mark is at the controls of Foxtrot Delta Quebec today. It's a nice day, but a bit hazy, and the wind is blowing quite gustily with just a trace of crosswind from the north for runway one-two. The desert looks so green from the air, and all the northwest corners of the rocks and rills have puddles of water where the sun hasn't yet reached to evaporate it.

We fly out on a heading of 230 degrees and this takes us over Hermannsberg Mission. We can see right down into Palm Valley. It almost looks like the Grand Canyon, with steep sides. The tracks of vehicles for the stations are visible here and there across the valley, and interestingly, some of them seem to disappear into mud designs where water has stood in the low places. The ADF, which is maintained by the Department of Transport, points to Curtin Springs, and then in the haze, there's Mt. Connor, and the road to Ayer's Rock. We start to let down for Amata. Mark drops the gear quite a way out, and it's obvious that he's heading across the settlement and will be making a landing towards the south without looking first at the windsock. Well, one chance in four he'll be downwind. Maybe he saw smoke or something on the desert for wind direction that I didn't see. Sure looks like the ground speed is maximum, though. Sure enough, we're committed for a downwind landing, and I'd guess it's gusting to about fifteen knots. But the Navajo has good brakes. No problem!

There's a new sister at the settlement. I don't get her name, and later when I ask sister Carol, she doesn't know either. But Jenny is there; same old radical with the Soweto posters in her quarters, extolling the virtues of that place. I detect a bit of rancor between her and Carol this time. I'm not sure what the problem is.

The first patient is eight-month-old Pita, daughter of sister Chris Halpin, with a bit of "chestiness." Pita also has an awfully big tongue for her mouth, and I'm worried. She really should come into the hospital, but maybe next time. She seems bright and attentive, and a happy baby, but then so does a monkey. I'm worried. Then there's Stanley, and Nancy who is about thirty weeks old; and Ruben with the bad ears; and then Billy, Chris, Nysukulja, Judy, and four-hundred-pound Kitty, and Polly. Iluwanti was hit on the left tibia by her brother last Christmas, and has had recurrent infections over the anterior shin since. Now it's hot and swollen, and I think it might be osteomyelitis. She'll come back with us in the plane.

Then we have Wanyuga, who's about twenty-eight weeks, and Ungakem and Jampawa and Priscilla and Sammy. That about rounds out the sick call. I'd been asked to cancel out this trip in order to be on hand for the departure of the Grace family from the Alice, but that would have really been putting down the sisters. It's not easy to round up a clinic like this. We have tea at Jennie's. Then back to the plane, and off we go, this time into the wind. I get a neat picture of the windmills that pump the bore at the settlement. It's a dozing time all the way back as we watch heavy showers dotting the desert right and left. At 7,000 feet we're flying at the bases of the clouds. It's beautiful! Then we're down, and it's early, only about 1500 hours as I get back into town. Next week I'll be on the Great Barrier Reef. It's supposed to be Fregon, but no matter. When I do Indulkana on the twenty-sixth, I'll catch 'em both.

26 February 1981

Just back from our holiday on the Great Barrier Reef, and there is a big clinic waiting for me at Indulkana. There is a small problem; the rains have washed out the airstrip, so we're going to have to land at Granite Downs and motor over. Just as said, John is the pilot, and sister Glenda is on the line. But we're not flying the Navajo this time. That's on its way down to Adelaide for something. We take the Baron, "Romeo Echo Hotel." We're off the ground by 0800. I take a couple of pictures of the two Royal Australian Air Force Caribous on the ground. The desert is all shades of green and brown and red.

The weather is cloudless, with just a bit of haze. There seems to be water standing all over in puddles. Again, I notice that it seems to cling to the northwest corners of the hills. Almost straight south we fly this time, and in about an hour we're coming low over the station at Granite Downs. Two bores, one north and one south of the place. We spot sister Kay in her Toyota making a cloud of dust towards the airstrip that is about five miles east of the station. There is a strip right at the station, but it's only 2,100 feet long, and 2,000 feet MSL, so on a hot day, it wouldn't be long enough to get the Baron off. (The Baron is about twenty knots faster than the Navajo.)

After unloading, we drive to the station and are greeted by Marg Baxter at the door under the shade of the weeping willows. It's a lovely, old house; stucco with thick walls, and old, old furniture. Solid oak, it is, with the turned feet of a lion at the ends of the legs of the laden dining room table. It's cool inside, and breezy, and just most comfortable. An old piano is sitting against one wall, and Marg has baking powder biscuits, honey, marmalade, cupcakes, and tea and coffee all ready. I examine her for hypertension; then her son, Dougal, for a cold (and eneuresis); and Mitch, the hired hand, for a hiatal hernia. Murray, Marg's husband, is sound. Interesting place in that the hot water is all solar. The electrical system (they even do their own welding on the place) is wind generated. Murray says the station is 75km by 55km. That's just a tad short of a million acres. He flies a Piper Cherokee.

Then it's on to the clinic. Sister Kay has twenty-five for me. It's thirty-four kilometers from the station to the clinic. Most are routine exams. One is Mr. Sydney Ralph with a big liver. He's referred to Adelaide. A cold drink at sister Kay's, and we're on our way back to the plane. We meet a broken down vehicle with South Australian police in it just a few miles east of the railroad community of Chandler. Sister Glenda suggests that we transport them to Granite Downs; we finally convince her that we'd all save time by driving them the few miles to Chandler. Eventually, the men get back to the strip and their plane, and we pick up sausage from Marg (Murray made four hundred pounds of sausage at Christmas), and are airborne at about 1645 hours for home. Too late to get the mail at the APO, but another day of work that's interesting and exciting!

5 March 1981

Glenda forgot to let me know yesterday that we were going at all, but I presumed we were going to Amata, so I drove out to the airport in the early morning. The days are getting a bit shorter, and the sun is just dusting the tops of the buildings at the airport with a rosy glow about the time I get there. It looks peaceful and calm, and like a good time to linger somewhere along the tarmac and watch the birds, and the occasional activity at the airport. Wrong! The flies will fly into your ears and nose, and if you open your mouth to complain, they'll get in there, too. Dr. Stapleton comes along with his accent. He's on his way up north to some place or other that I failed to determine. He's partly Hindu or Malaysian, and partly Aussie. He's a really nice guy, and by and by he leaves in the Baron. About this time our pilot, a new one, Barry, arrives, and then sister Glenda, who still seems kind of at odds. Bob's her stabilizing influence. I don't really know where Bob fits into the scheme of things. Maybe he works for the Aeromedical Service, or maybe it's more than that. It's not important.

The plane this time is a Cessna 310–P called Dog X–ray Dog. It seems much better for short takeoff and landing capabilities than either the Navajo or the Baron. Barry is the first pilot that I've ever been with on AMS flights that smokes. It's kind of disconcerting. The nose of the 310 is built lower, and it gives a much better forward view than either of the other craft. Today is clearer than usual, and there's a good view of Simpson's Gap today, with the early morning sun shadows really identifying the gap. The "spyce byce" with its golf balls is so sharp in the morning sun it almost makes your eyes hurt. Then, there's the dry lakes (some of them not so dry), and Mt. Connor off to the southwest. Behind that it's clear enough to see Ayer's Rock, and even the Olgas as faint purple fly specks on the horizon.

Nice landing at the strip, which is in good condition in spite of all the rain. Sister Julie meets us. She's a little crotchety today; just back from a holiday, and not too happy about it. The other new sister that replaced Meg is Jessie. She's older and taller, but seems competent. The clinic is the usual, but I did see Ivy again;

the recoveree from miliary tuberculosis. Then there's Ronald who is ten years old and really energetic and flying around, but refusing to take his cap off, because the chemotherapy that he received for his acute myelogenous leukemia has removed his hair. They said the therapy didn't help; that there's nothing else to do now, and that it's only a matter of time. He sure looks healthy today. We'll see if he's around the Ernabella clinic next time we come down.

Then it's time for tea at Julie's, and a nice conversation. Now the Fregon contingent arrives. Buxom sister Beth, driving a Toyota with Barry Mackert, the plumber from the settlement, sitting beside her almost looking like he's been scared out of a month's growth—and not from the spider bite on his wrist, either. It's from sister Beth's driving. I guess it was pretty bad. Barry's going to be all right. We see a couple of the people that they brought up with them, and then back into the plane. We have one of the girls who is forty weeks gestation going back with us. We put her in the back behind Glenda, and caution Glenda that if anything starts to happen with the pregnancy, there's no way we can get back there to help her. She'll have to do it all alone, and please don't mess up the plane with placenta and stuff like that. She's not amused.

The ride home is pleasant, with a bit of dozing and reading my CME lesson. Then, we're down, and the day is over. It's 1615 hours.

12 March 1981

It's to be Amata today, and John Everett is there. The Navajo with the brand new engines is just back from Adelaide. Sister Carol arrives about 0805, and we pile in and taxi out to runway one-two. It's a beautiful morning except for the flies which are present in droves as we load up. They seem to be all pervasive, even invading your nose and ears, and landing on your glasses to peer in with their multiwindowed eyes. John gives them a spray in the cabin after we're in. The course is 225 degrees. It's a bit hazier this week than it was last week. We proceed at 8,000 feet MSL. John does a professional job of putting us on the ground, and sister Jennie arrives with the Toyota to take us back to the clinic. Sister Chris Halpin is really in charge of the clinic. There isn't a lot of love lost between sister Jennie and sister Carol. I don't know what the problem is.

First patient is Mich, an older bloke with a dense cataract in his right eye. That's his "shootin' " eye, and he can't do a job on the kangaroo or emu anymore. His friend with bilateral dense cataracts that rendered him totally blind, recently came back from Adelaide after surgery, and "now he can see." It takes me a long time to convince Mich that he has good vision in his left eye, and that's how it's going to remain. We can send him up to the Alice for an examination, but no surgery for right now.

Then there's an aboriginal lady who has lost her "sewing" glasses. I paw through a box of discarded and lost glasses, and finally find a pair with opalescent rims that seem to do the trick. She's delighted. We have a short clinic, and then tea time, and we're back in the plane about 1300 hours.

The take off is a long run since it's hot, and Amata is just about 2,000 feet MSL. No more than climbing out, and John, who has been on the radio telling the Alice we're on the way home says, "Do you mind if we divert to Wandu Hills?"

"Heck, no," I reply. "My day is your day."

"We'll have to go by Ayer's Rock for fuel." We alter course to almost directly north from where we are, and Ayer's Rock is visible in the distance, about forty miles.

Soon we're letting down on the strip that is just on the northeast side of the rock. Good picture of the campground where the Chamberlains' baby of ten months, Azaria, was allegedly taken from her cot by a dingo last fall. Or did the parents sell her? Mr. Chamberlain is a Seventh Day Adventist minister. Anyway, that's for the courts to decide. I get some pictures of the campground and the rock. "Uluru" is the aboriginal name for the largest monolith in the world, standing 348 meters above the plain. The scientists tell us that what we see is only ten percent of the total size of the rock. Just like an iceberg, the ninety percent that we don't see is the major part. It's really the sandstone bed of an ancient lake that has turned up ninety degrees onto its end.

Sister Carol borrows Morris's "utility," and we drive over to see sister Deborrah at the Rock dispensary. Plans are made that in the future, when I'm at either Amata or Fregon, I'll be available for a trip to the Rock dispensary. Sounds like fun to me. Back to the plane, but first, a stop at the store for an ice cream. A bus load of tourists is there. Fat little girls with bikini tops exposing most of the chest. They look photogenic, but I don't take any pictures. I was going to come home and try to tell you that those were all aboriginals. Carol didn't think you'd believe me anyway.

John has the plane all fueled, and we pour it on for takeoff. The end of the strip comes rushing up; airspeed is only about ninety knots when John lifts her off. He has to; there's no place to go but up! The stall warning horn blips on and off, but we're flying. John takes it out over the west parking lots and then cranks it back in so we come back right over the rock cairn on top. Good show! I get pix of Maggie Springs as well. Then off to the west, past the Olgas (Katajuta) and out for the next forty minutes back into South Australia.

Wandu Hills is five miles from the west Australia border. It has a few scars and terraces on the mountains, and John says that it is mining country. He doesn't know what they mine for. The strip is an x-shaped one, but only the east-west is maintained to any degree. We land and meet Mandy, the sister for the settlement. Mandy is dressed in thongs, and one of those Hindu-like skirts that wrap around the bottom like a diaper. Sister Carol is angry. "And she's dirty, too!" she comments to me behind her hand.

"How long have you been out here?" sister Carol snaps.

"Three months and two weeks," replies sister Mandy.

"Well," snaps sister Carol, "I guess that's long enough if you're going to go native."

The two patients are a pregnant lady, and a baby with history of diarrhea (which she proceeds to prove with action) for an undetermined time, and with an undetermined weight loss. We take them on board. There is a local doctor here, we hear, and he's the one who owns the brand new Cessna Skylane RGII that's tied down on the strip.

Again, the runway is only just long enough to coax the Navajo into the air, with the stall warning horn bleating this time. Oh-six-oh degrees course brings us straight over Ayer's Rock again. I lean back and close my eyes. The drone of the engine is like a lullaby. Then, I'm waking, and look to my left. John is snoring gently in the pilot's seat. The plane is holding oh-six-oh degrees, and we're still at 9,000 feet. It's as calm as a pond. I let him sleep for about another fifteen minutes, and then he wakes himself up. That's comforting! (Wandu Hills is also known on the maps as Warribrei.)

The desert is just beautiful. Everything is gray and green and brown and red. They say that this is the wet season. I guess it runs in eleven-year cycles, like sunspots. They say that in the dry cycle, there's sand blowing everywhere, and the desert looks entirely different. I like it this way.

The radio comes alive with the story of a pilot in a Cessna 210 by the name of Bartel who is on a charter with a passenger from Adelaide to Curtin Springs. He was going to land at Curtin, but the dumb gear won't come down.

"I've done everything I can think of to fetch it down, but it's stuck tight, for sure," he informs the Alice tower.

"Did you try cranking it down?" asks the Alice.

"Right-e-o, but it won't budge."

"How about diving the plane and doing a snap pull-up and see if increasing the g forces will make it right?" queries the Alice tower.

"Tried it five times, and nothing happens positive," answers the apprehensive pilot.

"Well," muses the Alice tower. "it could be that you're low on hydraulic fluid. Can you check the level?"

"How do I do that?" asks Mr. Bartel.

"Just to the right of the console is a little plastic door. Take off the little door and you'll see a fill spout with a dip stick in it. Check it out."

"To the right of the console?"

"Yes, over by the glove box on the panel and just below."

"Got it!" A few minutes drag by. "It's really low!"

"Do you have any kind of fluid in the cabin?" asks the Alice tower, calmly.

"Only two cans of Coke."

"Put in one can," advises the tower, "but be careful if you have a watch or rings on."

Several minutes go by then, "No use. She still won't come down. I guess I'll head on up to the Alice for an emergency landing."

They change frequency, and we hear no more. "Landing at 1700 hours," John had said when we left Wandu Hills, and sure enough, it's 1658 hours when we touch down. But as we come over the end of the runway at Alice, we see the 210 on the runway of the private airport strip; prop tips bent back, but looking surprisingly unharmed otherwise. Mr. Bartel did a good job. So much for another day. The sisters at Amata are going to ask the Council if Laura can come back with me. Mich is one of the best artisans they have there for the *woomera*. We'll have to see what he has next time.

19 March 1981

The days are getting shorter, and there's a pinkness to the hills on the drive out to the airport. But the temperature is about in the low seventies, Fahrenheit, and it looks like a great day to sit on the bench and read some cardiology. The flies are again all pervasive; jillions of them! They want to get into any moist opening that there is, no matter what the consequences. It's not a good day for trying to read. I make a phone call to the base dispensary to tell sister Di about Allen Harding's admission to the hospital with a bleeding ulcer. Sisters Carol and Pauline arrive. The pilot is suave Darryl; the plane is the Navajo; and we're off the ground at 0815. Darryl flies a ways east before making his right-hand turn, and I see some of the desert out that way that I haven't seen before. Then we backtrack parallel to the runway, but just south until we come to the railroad tracks. Then 204 degrees to head us for Fregon. I read my cardiology in silence with half a cup of coffee from sister Carol's thermos on the way.

Then we're going by Ernabella, and starting the let down for Fregon. Sister Beth meets us there. She's new to the area, having arrived in the last few weeks. The lad that she brought up to Ernabella with the spider bite is fine. Sister Beth is so apologetic for everything that it gets a tad cloying. She means well. It's a small clinic. Classic old man in a hair shirt and felt hat. Bobby is the name. Wish I had a picture of him!

Then it's tea time. Sister Beth has a husband who is a publisher in London. Her youngest son is with him there. Her older son is in engineering with the RAAF out of Sydney. She seems like a lonely person. She has a little dog that has been attacked by camp dogs this morning and sustained a bad bite on his right front foot before being rescued. It's kind of pathetic here. Pauline is giving all the school kids BCG (Bacillus Calmette-Guerin) vaccine because of the exposure that was secondary to Ivy's tuberculosis some time ago. So, she's all tied up. Sister Carol and I visit the school. Christine is the teacher. All the little preschoolers are singing songs and clapping hands ("If you're happy and you know it clap your hands!"). Some have clothes on; some don't. Two Europeans are in the group (they have their clothes on, and kind of clean, at that!). Cute! Then to another class. The kids are watching a video tape of *Sesame Street*. I'm asked to take a picture of them by the headmaster, Ncil, who is an aboriginal. Gladly. It's an unusual request since generally the aboriginal does not care to have his picture taken. It removes part of the spirit, I've been told.

Sister Carol and I take a dozen of the kids in the utility to Shirley's Well. This is a mud and straw ruins of a house from the early thirties. The family that used to live here were dingo hunters. They had their bedroom in the basement. A huge cloudburst came along one day, and the house caved in on top of them. All were dead but one little boy. The grave is there and the aboriginals approach it gingerly. That's dream-time stuff; the aboriginal "happy hunting ground," and they don't want to mix with the spirits. The kids range in age from about eight to fourteen. Probably some of them are petrol sniffers. But they're nice, friendly and curious about the gray-haired one. In Pitjantjatjara that word is "tjilpi," and it denotes a wise, old man.

We leave the spot at the suggestion of the boys (sister Carol really does well with Pitjantjatjara), and we drive towards a bore that they know of some five miles west. One of the boys shouts. We stop the car, and there on a hill about three hundred yards away is a dun-colored animal, a dingo, sitting watching us. He's too far away for a picture. We proceed to the bore. There's a big tank about twenty feet in diameter, and a partly filled reservoir beneath it for the cattle. A windmill is pumping continuously, and when the tank, which is about fifteen feet high, fills, there's a spillway for the water to run into the reservoir. The tank water is green. The kids plunge in; some with clothes, and some without. They all know how to swim, it seems. Then, after a good swim, we all jump back into the utility and head back to town. Carol sees it first, loping along through the scrub on the left hand side of the car.

"Fifty kilometers," says Carol. The bird is alternately raising and ducking its head as it runs. Its a "kalkya," an emu. It paces the car for about a quarter of a mile, and then turns away.

Pauline is just finishing up when we arrive back at the settlement. We're airborne at 1530 hours. It's too late to make the mail pickup at the APO. There're thunderstorms over the Alice. We don't have any rain, but it's been here. The air is warm, and the smell is of fresh rain. That's nice. I hasten home to tell Laura about the day.

2 April 1981

Sister Glenda and John are the crew this morning. Two aboriginals will be flying back to the settlement today with us. One of them has a small, FLK (funny looking kid) with her. It's a newborn, but with a funny, flattened bridge of the nose (congenital syphilis?), and a pointy chin, and a tad of talipes (club feet). They are on the way back to Ernabella after checking out the FLK. Pauline isn't with us this week for some reason, and last week we missed Indulkana because the runway was under water again. The road from Granite Downs was also washed out. I guess they had another five inches of rain this last week. It's going to be good for the banana trees.

The Navajo makes short work of the trip, and I do my CME lessons. John makes a swing counterclockwise over the village this time, and I'm on the low side with my camera taking shots of the clinic and the village. It's overcast, and there's a light drizzle at times. Julie and Jessie meet us, and Beth is up from Fregon with a few to see. It's a cordial welcome and a fairly busy day. There's Ronald, again, with the acute myelogenous leukemia. He's not as frisky this time as he was last time, and I doubt that I'll see him again. There's lots of gingival hyperplasia, but no significant nodes. He just doesn't look well.

Then there's Sally Ann, originally from Santa Teresa settlement, who has a paraplegia from some unknown cause, and is developing pre-patellar bursitis from trying to drag her little body around. She was born the 31 May 1978. I'm going to have Dr. Martins, our pediatrician at the hospital in the Alice, see her and determine if there's anything we can do with braces through the RALAC team. She was up in December, and was supposed to be notified, but nothing was done. She's going to lose her legs if we don't do something for her.

Ivy is here again. She always has a smile and a clap on the shoulder for me. She really does think that I cured her of the dread disease.

There's the forty-week gestation patient who went down to the Alice three weeks ago. She absconded, and ended up back in Ernabella. She's dropped, but it's not engaged yet. Maybe there's to be a birth on the Navajo today.

Then it's tea time, and Jessie has made up some nice sandwiches and a carrot cake. We discuss the strychnine poisoning of some aboriginals in the Alice the previous week, and the shooting of Mr. Reagan in the United States. The strychnine was placed in a bottle of Yellow Label sherry, and, of course, five blacks shared the bottle. Two of them are already dead. Everyone wonders who would do such a thing, just like the shooting of the president. Of course, we'll know who shot the president, but no one will ever find the malcontent who poisoned the aboriginals.

Sister Jennie's garden has been prolific, and the girls load me down with butternut squash and cucumbers for the return trip. Then I find that I've been granted permission by the council to take a tour of the settlement. First, out to the garden. Originally it was put together by a young man fresh out of agricultural college, but now not much is being done with it. There's a date palm grove that's about eight feet tall, and there are some dates coming along even though no one is taking much care of it. There's maybe an acre of tomatoes rotting on the ground, and lots of squash and rock melons, and figs on the trees. No one is caring for them, either. There's grapes that look like they could be quite productive, if only someone took care of them. There's even a stand of gum trees in rows, but too close together. There's lots of little seedlings still in their black, plastic cups, but no one is going to plant them. Most of them are already dying for lack of water.

Then to the cemetery. The plots are all protected by reinforcing wire projecting from concrete slabs that cover the graves. I understand that after the casket is placed, they allow the ground to settle for a few weeks, and then come back and do some sort of ornamental mosaic over the grave, usually with a cross. No matter that the corpse isn't Christian. Then they pour fresh concrete, and as it begins to harden, they poke plastic, artificial flowers into the cement, stem first, so that the whole thing begins to look like a flower garden. All colorful and bright, and set in concrete forever. On the older graves the color has gone and they're dead white, but no matter. It was worth a picture.

Next to the dump (the "tip," in Aussie): You wouldn't believe the cars that have been abandoned here, and picked over, and scavenged, along with everything else. The dump is there in all its ugliness. Then we walk up to the top of the hill where the "tank" that supplies the town with water pressure is located. We can look down on the civic center from here. Hope the pictures all turn out well.

Now it's time for the trip home. We have a drizzle yet. John elects to take off down wind, and down hill so that we can fly straight out. Not much wind, anyway. We load in the forty-weeker (pregnancy), and poor, old Yakiti. Remember? He's the old man with the toes amputated from one foot whom I thought I was losing one of his hands to gangrene a while back? We found out he'd burned it in the fire to make it look like gangrene. Well, he's not able to make it alone, so he's coming in to live in the Alice at the "Old Timers' Home." Poor, old Yakiti.

The ride home is smooth, and we break out of the overcast about the Palmer River. Another week is over with the Aeromedical Service of the Australian Royal Flying Doctors.

9 April 1981

It's another one of those spectacular mornings, but the sun is coming up a bit later each day as we swing into fall in the southern hemisphere. The sharp ridge of the other range at the gap is red and rosy in the early morning sun, and there's just a hint of a nip in the air. The new runways/taxiways at the airport are getting their base now. It's been a slow process, but when they are done it will be a safety measure for all. John is checking out things on the Navajo, Graham Pitt this time. Sister Carol has gone on her holiday to Melbourne where her folks live; and sister Glenda is sick so sister Ray Stone, the chief AMS "angel," is going to be in charge on this trip to Amata. Sister Pauline is also coming along so that she can give BCG to the "Ivy contacts" out in the Amata area.

It's just about 0800 as we roll down one-two for take off. The tower has told us to be at 4,000 when we come abeam the tower on track 222 and our altitude today will be 5,000 feet MSL. That's neat, because that's just about 3,000 feet above the desert, and it's a very clear day today. Amazing! From this altitude, I really think I could see a kangaroo under a tree if one were there. (I do see some other livestock, but no kangaroo.) The desert is beautiful: all colors from brown and red on through green and yellow, and even a dusty blue color to some of the vegetation.

About sixty miles southwest of the Alice, as we cross the Palmer River country, there are sand dunes. They look like red sand dunes. They're horseshoe shaped, with the high side on the loop, and dropping maybe fifty feet to the baseline. They're covered with acacia trees, so it must be more than fifty years since they were created. There's maybe a fifty mile patch of this. It must have been a miserable place to be when it was forming, but now, apparently with moisture since they were created, they become part of the sparse forest that I've mentioned to you so many times. We fly past the Henbury meteorite craters.

There are thirteen of them altogether, but only three show silica flour and glass, suggesting that these three were created by an explosion. The glass would tell us that the temperature at the time was in the neighborhood of 1,562 degrees Fahrenheit! Mt. Connor comes into view. This time we're really pretty low, and I think, "I've taken so many pictures of that thing, but then again, I've never been so low." So, I take another slide. We'll see if it adds to the program when I get back home. I finish most of my Core Content Review of continuing medical education program that I buy each year, just as we start to let down for Amata.

I'm glad I had the pictures of the car dump before. They've bulldozed the whole thing under. No more old cars in a heap covering about an acre. Just a scar of dirt showing where they were, and probably heralding the start of another dump. Too bad that the sewage lagoon has sprung a leak. The town is going to be rampant with Giardia lamblia, an intestinal parasite not uncommon to the aboriginal, or, something worse! The fence to the lagoon is gone, and cows and kids swim in the sewage. A few months ago someone had delivered the fencing to protect the lagoon from swimmers, but no one put it up, and there it lies, half covered with drifting sand. Meantime, the powers that be in Canberra have elected to spend thousands to bury the old cars. That makes sense . . . to someone, I'm sure.

Sisters Chris and Jennie are still holding down the fort here. It's a busy clinic. We have more than enough people to evacuate. Two babes, both with enteritis. One is European and one is aboriginal. I think they're both Giardia from the dumb sewage lagoon thing. Then a primip (first pregnancy), who is about forty weeks. That should be interesting.

Then we have another aboriginal, Murray, with no breath sounds on the right. He really is in trouble, his condition having been diagnosed previously as tuberculosis. But he didn't take his INH (isonicotinic acid hydrazide—an anti-tuberculosis medicine), because he was "walkabout" (walking between settlements). Poor sister Pauline will have to come back again now, and track down all the people that have been with Murray. Of course, the two children's mothers will go with them, and then there are two more children who have to go back for reasons such as failure to thrive. Their mothers have to go with them, too, of course. It's too much for the Navajo, and we have to radio to AMS in the Alice and have Darryl come on down with the Baron to take out part of the load. He'll also take sister Pauline because she weighs in at about 110 kg.

Tea time with sisters Chris and Jennie, and we have a nice talk about the disaster that is the aboriginal program established by the do-gooders, the legislators who have never really been out to see what the situation is. It was infinitely better for all but the planners when the station manager hired a "stockman" who provided many jobs, food clothing, and education for the whole tribe. The philosophy was: "you will go to school (and learn it in English, too), and when you go home at night, you will learn your tribal customs from the elders in your tribe!" Then the do-gooders ruled that the station manager must pay all the people that are on the station a minimum wage. With that, the tribes have had to leave, and usually the stockman, too. They've now gone on the dole, and instead of having a continuum the aboriginal is now spaced out doing nothing but collecting his sitdown money, and then wasting it on gambling, or blowing it on booze. Worse, the work on the stations isn't being done. A couple of weeks ago we mentioned the strychnine-laced sweet sherry that had killed the two aboriginals. The bottle has been traced to the churchyard of Uniting Church in the Alice.

Darryl arrives with the Baron and takes his load. We depart at 1430 hours. It's bumpy! Poor Murray is having a tough time. At 9,000 feet on the way back, he's really dyspneic (short of breath). We do have oxygen, and he's on the mask, but it's so rough in the air that he starts to vomit. I sit with him trying to commiserate. It's tough. Back there in the middle of that bucking aircraft, even I begin to feel lead in my tummy. We are finally on final for the runway. We pass on the load of sickies to the St. John's ambulance company, and it's home to details of what's going to happen next.

16 April 1981

I had a call from AMS yesterday saying that sister Carol is still on holiday, and sister Glenda is still not feeling well, so Dave Winding, a medical technologist, is to be my "sister" today on the flight to Fregon. It's an incredibly beautiful morning, and the sun is peeking above the treetops at 0800 hours when we depart. Dave is sitting in the right seat, and I prop myself up on the two aft seats on the port side reading cardiology. We're cleared at 4,000 feet, but first we make a 360 around a smoking pile of debris at a cattle loading station near the railroad. It looks like old tires are burning. Maybe they're disposing of a carcass. It's about 0915 when we land. Les is there to meet us. He's the husband of sister Audrey, who is going to be taking sister Beth's place. He's kind of an all-round jack-of-all-trades, and will be employed there. They have two sons with them; both older and matriculating now. He's a diver. He says he has a diving card.

The clinic is run by rather quickly. Nothing too much. The little guy with a gunshot to the foot is back. He's unhappy with me, but his foot does look a lot better. One of the Europeans (council) gives us the name of David James and forgets to tell us that his last name is Sweet. He doesn't like Dave, it seems. Finally we get him sorted out. He has a healing abscess on his right shoulder that is granulating. We cauterize it with silver nitrate. It'll come right.

Tea time at Les and Audrey's. Beth is here. She's going to be coming to the Alice to work after a couple of weeks holiday. Then it's back to the plane and the trip home. It's bumpy on the way home, so I don't read all that much.

23 April 1981

This is to be quite a day. We're off the ground at 0815, but it's sister Jennie this time, and the pilot is Darryl. We're taking back Mrs. Rowe (she and her husband used to teach at the Iran

American School when we were there). Their daughter Patty is on her way to Indonesia, and wants to take chloraquin for malaria prophylaxis. So, I've brought some for her. Mrs. Rowe has been in the hospital secondary to an acute reaction to penicillin given at the Indulkana mission. Also on board is an aboriginal man from Indulkana who is going home. I never did get his name or what his problem was at the hospital.

It's the Navajo, the Graham Pitt, and we climb out on a heading of 182 degrees. It's clear. I'm reading a bit of cardiology, and then we see Chamber's Pillar ahead. This is an interesting formation, with a chimney of rock rising out of the plain. It looks for all the world like the World Trade Center in New York. I think it's about 1,500 feet high, and about the size of a skyscraper; this morning it's creating its shadow westward. There's a trail all the way around it, and Darryl says that the only way to get to it is by four-wheel drive vehicle, but that even with that, it's a hard journey. I didn't get the picture I should have taken. Well, maybe next time.

Darryl's "dead reckoning" is right on, and we cross the river and find the "home place" and then, quickly find the strip for Granite Downs. It's almost hidden in the high grass that has grown tall with all the rain. Irene Press, the cook for the home place, is waiting for us, and takes us on into the station, along with Mrs. Rowe and her beautiful African violets. There's coffee and biscuits, and I check out Irene who thinks she's pregnant. We take a urine specimen with us, and I place her on erythromycin for her bad cold. She's running a fever of 37.8 degrees Celsius. Then Mr. Rowe arrives in the Toyota, and we're off past the railroad township of Chandler and on to Indulkana.

Sister Ann is the new sister there. She's got things a bit disorganized. She's just asked all the aboriginals if they'd like to see the doctor, and, of course, they all say yes, so there's this clinic with bashful aboriginals sitting on the chairs, and no one knows why they are there, except that they all want to see the tjilpi doctor. We finally get things sorted out about 1430 hours, and have a cup of tea. But now we're supposed to go on to Fregon, because there's a little girl there that got hit in the face with a rock, and she's got a laceration that needs suturing. Darryl does his homework, and we take off, but I do have them contact the

Aeromedical Service in the Alice to let Laura know that we're going to be late. Then they tell us that when we finish at Fregon, we're going on to Mt. Ebenezer to look at two sick kids with enteritis, and see if they need evacuation.

Darryl hits Fregon right on the head after forty minutes of flight. The desert is beautiful; lots of rain has made it lush with grass, and the acacias are all green. It's late afternoon as we roar in over the town. Sister Audrey's boy meets us at the strip. Back to the hospital. The patient is about seven years old, an aboriginal girl. She's got a laceration over the left cheek prominence that's cut on the bias, semicircular, and about two centimeters in length. It's quite near the corner of the eye. It's been cleaned by sister Audrey (kind of), and she's lying on this filthy bed.

There is a sterile suture kit, and I've brought some 4–0 silk suture with me from Indulkana. There's one percent lidocaine, and so we begin. She screams in terror as I approach with the anesthetic, and so we have to have some of the other aboriginal women hold her down while I drip a few drops of Xylocaine on the wound. The light is at the wrong end of the table, but no time to worry about that now. Let's get on with the job. Darryl has told us that if we don't leave the strip by 1730 hours, we won't be able to land at Mt. Ebenezer. I do an infiltration of the wound, hoping that I don't give the child a big hematoma. There's no way to debride the laceration into a straight line. And the flies that want to keep covering up the wound in the first place have to be shooed away, although they do manage to coat my suture. I place five sutures. I think they'll do the job.

Sister Audrey is instructed to put some Terramycin ophthalmic ointment on the suture line. That's the only ophthalmic antibiotic ointment we have. Then, the sister is to take out the first (middle) suture in three days, and the rest on the fifth or sixth day, if she can get the child back. No worry. This child already has five or six significant scars on her face. One more just might make her "beautiful." She really was a pretty good kid, though, after we got her over that first fright.

We are back out to the strip for a take off about 1715 hours, and we head for Mt. Ebenezer. It's on the road to Ayer's Rock, and Laura and I did stop there when we were coming home from our holiday to Ayer's to take a picture of the settlement and its traditional windmill at the bore. We come down over the dry lake country low enough so that I can see where the cattle have sunk into the mud getting to the little water that's still left in the dry beds. I look for kangaroos and emus, because it is getting around that time of the afternoon. I don't see any. The strip at Mt. Ebenezer is almost hidden again by the tall grass. It's about a mile northwest of the settlement.

Darryl makes a smooth landing, a bit downwind, but then it's awfully hard to look into the sun if you land west into the wind. The sun is very low on the horizon now. It's a bit intimidating as the truck load of aboriginals descends on us at the strip. There must be twenty-five of them: men, women, babies. The only thing in common is the filthiness. The flies are atrocious. One screaming (apparently healthy) child is slung over a mother's back; his eyes are so full of flies you can't see them, and I count nine flies inside the external auditory canal on the side that's toward me. He's got a bottle of something that looks like half tea and half milk (maybe it's radiator fluid) that he's clutching in his hand. One of the enteritis babies is listless and apathetic. Exam doesn't reveal much, but a weak cry and a distended belly. He's had diarrhea for five days. The other kid is also wailing his heart out, but his eyes are shiny and alert. He gets the dehydration salts. The other ought to come with us.

"Jennie, will you bring the baby to the hospital?" to the filthy Mom. She nods affirmation, and climbs aboard the plane.

Then there's a foot to look at. A girl about fifteen who stepped on a broken bottle. There's a laceration of her foot just at the flexor tendons of the lateral four toes. I think she got the tendons, but it's pretty puffed up to really see. She hasn't had the "needle" yet (penicillin). We'll give her 1.2 million units of Bicillin mix (it has half a million of aqueous penicillin G with it), and soak it. She can stay home.

Then it's time to take off because the sun is just about to touch the horizon. We button up and it's up and away. We're still about 130 air miles from home, and that's when I get the nice picture of the sun setting on the range, and Darryl turns on the panel lights. It's amazingly beautiful as we approach the Alice. There's the Spyce Byce all lit up like a big city. It's a pretty spectacular place. A nice touchdown by Darryl and we're home.

Oh, yes, I forgot to mention that at Fregon they're having a problem with hepatitis. I did see the son of the headmaster of the school, Neil, who was so haughty on my visit before. But this time his kid was sick, and I looked at him. We'll see if it changes Neil's attitude the next time I come down.

30 April 1981

It's another beautiful morning in the Alice. It's a mite chilly around the edges as we head into winter, but the sky is clear and the sun is coming up to the north, and there isn't a breath of wind. It's too cold for the flies to be much bother this morning. Carl Catlin, my new med-tech, is here and that's going to help a lot.

John is the pilot this morning for the Graham Pitt, and the sister is Ray Stone. Glenda is still sick down in Adelaide with her boyfriend, and I hear that sister Carol is at Granite Downs with Marg and Murray Baxter for the last of her holiday. We're cleared off runway one-two, and a right turn to report at 4,000 feet just west of the south road. So, we're to be low again on this trip down. It's hazy, though, and the view isn't all that good, except to look straight down, and then it's kind of fun, because you can see individual rocks and things like that. We do see some cattle, but no emus or kangaroos. I read a little comprehensive cardiology and then we're ready to let down. Julie meets us, and we head back to start the clinic.

First patient is Gillian who is pg (pregnant)? But there's a question. She's so big that her amenorrhea (lack of menstral period) may be a secondary type, and with 100 kg of fat, it's hard to tell if there's a uterus in there at all. Then we see Ann, who's pg by twenty-seven weeks (27/52, as they'd say it here), and she's coming right. Then Malpiya, who is pg about 18–20/52; and then Alison Troy, the school marm, who has the bad varicose veins, and is now about term. Is she breech? She's at 59.5 kg. So much for the prenatal (ante-natal down under) clinic.

Good old Ivy appears. She's had a touch of jaundice, and it

may be secondary to her INH. They cut her off for a while (she was taking three a day), and she now looks lots better. She fawns around me like I was really the great tjilpi doctor. (I like it! I like it!) She looks right, so I guess I'll start her back on it for one tab a day for a week, and if all goes well, up her dose to two a day for a week, etc.

Then Alec with a bite on his foot (it's nothing), and Nyinguta who looks anemic (we take a blood sample). How does such a black person look anemic? The contrast between the gingiva (gums) and the skin, for one thing; or the conjunctiva (lining of the eye inside the lid) and the eye lid for another, tips you off a bit. Then there's poor little Audrey with an exfoliative dermatitis (scaling skin) that is secondarily infected. She looks terrible. Her face and scalp are masses of running sores. Her peers reject her. Let's try Flagyl. We've used just about everything else with varying success. We can't go too far wrong with a try of Flagyl. Then comes Morris who's had three or four seizures. We could try to get him into town for an EEG (electroencephalogram or brain wave study) and see if he does have a disorder, but his folks won't allow it. So, let's try a quarter grain of phenobarbital q.i.d. (four times a day).

Next is tiny Clara, the FLK (funny looking kid) from last time, when we brought her home from the Alice. She's still an FLK, with a very high palate, but it's not cleft. Her little feet are talipes equino varus (club feet), but the right one is loose, and the left one is stiff. I don't know just what to do because the parents won't carry through with any exercise anyway. Then there's Joslyn who has what looks like tinea versicolor (a fungus infection) on her face, with different sized white spots. She's being ostracized by her peers because she's turning into a European. We'll try a little Lotrimin for her.

Then we see Maxine Capp who is a European who needs a driver's eye exam. Then Marie, another European wife who has honest to goodness chicken pox. She's not too sick. We advise her that she just make sure that the lesions stay inconspicuous. Then comes Harry with his hypertension and hyperadiposity. Next is Roy O'Toole (what a strange name for an aboriginal!) who's been having "fits" (I think it's a petrol sniffing). After Roy is big, heavy Ruth with left hip polio when she was two, and now apparently an osteoarthritis of the hip. Not much to do for Ruth except practice the art of medicine and reassure her. Time to look out the window before we see poor, little Ronald.

He's about done for sure, now. He sits there with his eyes bugging out of his head from the orbits being filled with tumor, and tears running down his face. Poor little fellow! I talk with his concerned father, who speaks very good English. He wants Ronald to die at Ernabella. The sisters will admit him and attend to him in his final time. We discuss what medication to give him when the pain gets bad. Let's try pethidine (Demerol) and pro-chlorperazine (Compazine) and see if that will relieve him a tad.

The last patient is Trevor with a sore throat. Routine treatment will do the job. So much for the clinic. It was well organized, and it didn't take too long to see all the patients.

We have a sandwich and a cup of coffee—the best coffee I've tasted in Australia so far, except what we make at home—and then we're off for the Alice. We take Alison Troy back with us. She says, "Thank you doctor, for taking such good care of me through this pregnancy." That's when I realize that she's spoken the total truth. I've given her all her ante-natal care. That's the first time I've done that since I left Balboa Hospital in San Diego in 1955 . . . twenty-six years ago. How about that?

The trip home is uneventful. We're home early; about 1530 hours, and I make hospital rounds and pick up the mail at the APO. It's fun to get back home!

7 May 1981

It's a crisp morning, but sunny, and no wind, and the flies aren't bothersome. It's too cold for them. This morning it's Mark at the controls of the Navajo, and sister Jennie, with the new last name now. She had just gotten married during the two weeks or so. Mark opts for runway three-zero, since he has the choice, and we're going flying out almost a heading of 270 degrees anyway.

Also, this takes us quite close to the Spyce Byce before we make our left turn, and he likes to look at the golf balls (a group of round, white protective domes on the roof of the JDSRF project). It's a bit hazy at first, so I study my lesson on continuing medical education as the sky gets clearer. Mark is a tad west of Mt. Connor, but we can see Ayer's and the Olgas to the right. We cross the highway just about at Curtin Springs, and have a good look at the dry lakes below. One can see tracks where the animals have been walking out on the salty mud to try to get at the water that's out in the middle of the lake.

Mark makes his usual downwind landing at Amata, but there's almost no wind blowing anyway, so it doesn't matter. Sister Jennie, the skinny sister, meets us. She has a well organized clinic. One of the patients is Puniljaya who had gone in to the Alice two weeks ago for her delivery, but somehow ended up down on the Todd river, and found her way back to Amata. She's now forty weeks, and the head is engaged, and she'd better come back with us for sure. We hear by the grapevine that little Ronald, up in Ernabella, had a massive nosebleed this morning. Raymond, his father, is such a nice guy. I also heard that their older son had a motorcycle accident some time ago, and had such a severe fracture of the femur that he subsequently developed gangrene and had lost his leg.

After the clinic we have tea at sister Jennie's house. Chris had taken her baby, Pita, up to the Alice a couple of weeks ago, and they did a femoral stick and sent the blood in for a thyroid hormone level. I still think Pita looks like a cretin. Now we'll see. I think Chris is more fearful now, too. Well, we'll see. We have a good discussion about the aboriginal problems, and then we're off. But then we're diverted to Ayer's Rock to see Mr. Bob Allen, the accountant for one of the hotels. He had a sudden loss of a portion of his vision; says a cobweb dropped over his vision. He says it seems to stay in the same place all the time. On examination, he has what looks like a vitreous floater that's stuck to the back of the lens in the right eye. The fundus otherwise looks okay. I reassure him, and then I see another patient who had a lintel board drop on his upper lip. I think he fractured the spine of the maxilla. Boy, I'll bet that's sore!

Then the takeoff, and we're on the way straight home. This

is over the area of the great sand dunes again. They look like frozen ocean waves, about a kilometer apart, but all covered with brush now. It would be hell to walk in that area. It would be a continuous up and down trek with nothing to really look at, and no water in sight for maybe forty miles. I wonder how much mineral wealth there is under those dunes?

Mark greases the plane onto runway one-two just about a quarter to five, so there's still time to get into town and the APO before it closes.

14 May 1981

It's a beautiful morning again! Sister Carol is back from her holiday, and the pilot for Fregon is Mark. The Navajo is on its best behavior, and we're off the ground on runway three-zero at about 0810 hours. The mountains are crystal clear in the crisp morning air, and casting long shadows, because at this time of year the sun is just about at the northeastern horizon at 0810. The Spyce Byce is a tempting subject for an early morning shot, and so it's done. We track out on a 204 degree heading. I watch the ground for a while, but we're at 6,000 feet and one doesn't see anything as small as a kangaroo from that altitude. It's amazing, though, how much water has dried up in the pot holes. But things are still pretty green.

An hour or so later and Ernabella is on the starboard quarter. We continue on by. It's about thirty-five miles south of Ernabella to Fregon. I've been reading my lesson on cardiology, but now sister Carol produces the thermos and we all have a cup of coffee. Those mountains ahead sure don't look familiar. There aren't any mountains at Fregon. But we're sure cruising right over those mountains. Mark starts a gentle turn to the right, and that's when I begin to understand that we're lost. That's the first time we've ever been lost coming out this way, or any way for that matter. Mark admits that he doesn't have his sectional map. Looking back to the mountains of Ernabella, it's my guess that we're about twenty miles too far south. We track west for a while, and then there's the river. Okay! Somewhere on that dry river is Fregon, but it's awfully winding to follow it all the way back.

Mark gets on the radio and asks the Alice for landmarks of Fregon. Almost at once they come back saying that there are two small hills, "pimples" is the word the radio uses, that are about three miles west of the runway at Fregon. We look ahead, and sure enough, there in the flat are two "pimples." Mark drops on down and even lowers the gear, and we make a straight in approach to the strip. Barry Bean is there with the mail plane. He had left half an hour behind us in his Cessna Skylane, but we've sure seen a lot more territory than he has!

Les takes us in to the clinic in his utility, and sister Audrey is her usual nervous self. Raymond has gotten his certificate for completion of his correspondence course. One of the patients is little Jeffrey with the gunshot wound through his foot. He's racing round like nothing had ever happened. The foot is dirty, but intact, and there's a bump where the scar is on the dorsum of the foot. The sole has healed well, and the scar there is invisible under all the dirt. Then there's Tali, who is twenty weeks pregnant; and the strange case of Karen Munser, a European, who is a case of pseudocyesis, I think. She really thinks she's pregnant, but it's in her imagination. Nothing convinces her that she's not pregnant, including a recent D and C (dilation and curettage) in the Alice. Next patient is Bill Townsend, the transport driver, who will get an ECG in Alice on Monday. He's having chest pain, but I think it's all muscular. He's sure it's a heart attack.

Andrea is a visitor from Germany who "talks funny." She doesn't have a German accent; she has an American accent. She sounds all right to me. Beverly has a strange lie to her fetus, and I can't hear any fetal heart tones. She's about twenty-six weeks. I don't know what that means. I think she should go up to the Alice and have Dr. Cahill do a pelvic on her. Dr. Cahill is a fine female specialist in obstetrics and gynecology, and is allowed by the council to do pelvics on aboriginal females.

Then we get the call that we have a threatened abortion in Amata. A pregnant woman is bleeding vaginally. We'd better go over and see her. This time Mark heads us west, and we come out right on the money! It's a lot hazier now that the afternoon is coming on. He sure has his little hand-held computer doing its thing well. We land, and sister Jennie meets us. She's worried. Poor sister Chris has been up all night with Millie. Millie had come in saying that she was bleeding. Over the radio, the girls had been instructed to start an IV (intravenous fluids), and Millie has been restless all night. Sister Chris stayed with her, and she's now sleeping. Millie is lying there with her eyes closed. I begin my exam, and start to talk with her, and she opens up her eyes and answers. She's playing possum! She's about twenty weeks, I'd guess, and the belly is soft around the edges of the uterus. Bowel sounds are normal. Of course, I have to take her word for the bleeding. I can't do a pelvic on a pregnant aboriginal. Not a male European doctor. That would be against tribal law. I imagine such action might result in my premature demise at the hands of Pompey Harding, her daddy, who is standing bedside with his ruminous eyes streaming. I think he has glaucoma. He should really be seen in the eye clinic. Pompey holds a territorial position in the government in Canberra. He's not a man to trifle with.

We bundle up Millie, and away we go to the airstrip, and depart for the Alice. Back over Mt. Connor, and I alternately doze, and watch the sand dunes below slipping by. Then we're home, and Mark greases the plane onto runway one-two in penance for his early-on navigational boo-boo. There's still time to get to the APO before it closes.

We hear that Ronald died at Ernabella today.

25 June 1981

Indulkana had been scheduled for the May 21, and that would have been the day before we were to depart for our medical meeting in America. We were really scheduled to go, but that morning it was cold and rainy. I did drive out to the airport, but Darryl was there and said that they had canceled the trip because of bad weather. I'm not sure whether I was disappointed or not, but I did head for home and made good use of the time.

I understand that while I was gone there were other docs who made the trip for me. Generally, says sister Carol, they were unhappy and disappointed with the service. Most of them said that they really didn't care to go again. I guess Dr. Franklin went on one expedition, and wanted the "health worker" to do blood pressures, urinalysis, etc. on the patients before he had seen them. By the time the first hour had gone by, he'd seen only two patients. So, they changed the plan. Anyway, it was a spectacular sunrise this morning with the sky all pink and orange, and when I drove by the school on the way to the airport, the sprinklers ("rainbirds") were doing their thing. There were sheets of ice on the fence and the grass. I was told that the reason the rainbirds were on was to keep the hoses from freezing and splitting. I hear it was a minus four degrees Celsius this morning. Mark is the pilot. Sister Carol is the sister, and she gets there a little late. We have one little girl going back to Ernabella. I never did find out what she had been in the Alice for.

As we get past the Palmer River, the sky lowers, and then we're in the overcast with a little bit of rain. I'm doing my AAFP (American Academy of Family Physicians) journal quiz, so I don't pay that much attention to the navigation, but once when I look down, there's Mt. Ebenezer going by the starboard wing tip. Mark mentions that he'd rather let down if they'll let him, so that we don't have to descend in the overcast over the mountains to the north of Ernabella. They give him permission to descend, and we have the strip in sight. A good stiff crosswind is blowing as we come in, but Mark does a fine job, and we're down. Sister Julie is there in short order.

On the west side of the church in the village is a new grave with two fences around it. One is the short fence that we usually see, and the other is much taller. It looks like it's meant to keep people out instead of animals. It's about a meter wider than the usual grave, but the artificial flowers are there in profusion. Not only that, but the concrete slab is bordered with a brilliant red cement, something that I've not seen before. I'm told that it's Ronald's burial place. How they ever managed to get it there just at the side of the church is a mystery. But there it is. Poor Ronald.

I wonder if I should have hugged him the last time I saw him, when his eyes were all bulging out, and he looked so sick.

The Clinic is busy. Sister Ann from Indulkana is here. Sister Jessie is on holiday. Sister Julie in charge, and is wearing a big blue and white stocking cap against the cold. It's drizzly cold with the wind blowing across the runway. Mark does a good job. The "cabin door open" light has been on all the way. It still doesn't work properly. There's no cabin door open. Some new babies and some that are just in the playpen dot the floor of the clinic. There's a Peyton Place thing going on between two sisters and two brothers, and neither couple is married. But there are offspring on the way.

The usual babies with draining ears, and Gordon, who is drawing about $500 a month in pension for his wounded (amputated) right leg, and is also earning about the same amount as a settlement worker. Here's Emily, his wife, who is also drawing salary for working. Between the two of them, it's almost $1,400 a month Australian. There's a question as to whether he really needs the disability pension money. I check him over. He's going to be mad at me when the government reads this report. But really, he does get around just fine. I heard that his amputation was secondary to an infected spear wound way back in 1955. Hmm! Heard that Mrs. Troy is back in the hospital with a breast abscess, but that the baby girl is just fine.

Yilipanya is thirty-nine weeks pregnant. We'd better take her back with us, and then there's another who is having some problems. Dr. Cahill wanted to have her back with us this week, but after she sees me she goes "walk about." Dr. Cahill will have to wait another time. Sister Julie has hot tomato soup for lunch, and then we're off and away.

It's rainy, and we have to take off to the south, with the crosswind just angling a bit across the starboard bow. It's a rather stiff wind, too. At 2,000 feet MSL, we're in the clouds. Mark sets it up for heading 030 degrees and 9,000 feet, and we stay in the soup all the way home. It's amazing! The autopilot holds the course and the altitude and the roll of the plane, and the DME keeps showing us getting closer and closer. I keep on with my lesson in the book. The heater is on full, and it really does get quite warm in the cockpit. I don't say anything, though. It's sure gloomy outside. Then, about the time we're 40 miles out on the DME, we let down to 6,000 feet, and then 5,000 feet. Suddenly we're out of the stuff with scattered clouds overhead, and we're just where the new railroad comes through the mountains on the south side of the Finke River.

Another day is over for the RFDS/AMS. I hear that there's one new Navajo been bought with the money so far collected for the new planes. It's going to be named after Mr. Oliphant, who was once governor of South Australia. Can't you see it now? A flying Oliphant? You know what the wags are going to nickname that airplane: "Dumbo!"

2 July 1981

Rather a strange set of circumstances for the trip out today. Actually, sister Di had rung up sister Carol last night and told her that the doctor (me) would not be able to go "bush" today because he happened to be over in "cas" (casualty—the emergency room at the hospital) trying to pass a kidney stone. And that was true. He had driven himself there about 2200 hours. It only seemed fair that the doc should let them know that he was indisposed, so that if the plane and the pilot and the sister had some other urgent mission to perform on the morrow, they could attend to it, and not, for the sake of one indisposed physician, hold up the whole of an aeromedical team. The doc found out that sister Di's call had been held in confidence at the aeromedical service, and not relayed to the settlement, because it came "too late," and there would be no reason to call it off until later in the morning next day.

Therefore, after receiving excellent medical attention by Dr. Stephen Charley, chief surgeon in the "cas" at the Alice Springs Hospital, the doc had gone home in Dr. Charley's car, been solicitously handled for about half an hour by the good doctor, and then checked on by his own staff by phone. It was a cool, cloudy night with some rain, and the fireplace was going, and the doctor eventually awakened on his sofa in front of the almost dead fire, took his shower, and went to bed about 2130 hours. He awakened once about 0230 and marvelled that he had no pain, and promptly retired again into the arms of Morpheus (actually, Demerol; pethidine, locally). He awakened again at 0430 in the morning, bright eyed and bushy tailed. He listened to a discussion on ABC (Australian Broadcasting Corporation) concerning the findings of the World Council of Churches regarding the racial bias found in Australia against the aborigines, and then rose, shaved and showered and made his bed, and his breakfast (a mandarin orange, a cup of coffee and two pieces of toast, and a small lamb chop), wrote a letter to his sweety who had remained behind in America to attend a reunion of her family in Langdon, North Dakota, and then set out walking the mile and a quarter to the hospital to pick up his car.

On the way he stopped off at the aeromedical service office, and found out the time of scheduled flight departure for Amata, and the mission was on! Mark is the pilot and sister Carol carries the paraphernalia. We arrive at Foxtrot Delta Quebec about 0845, and by 0700 we're lifting off runway one-two in a rather overcast, drizzly sky. At 4,000 feet we're between layers, and at our cruise altitude of 6,000 feet we're in hard driving rain. It's comfortable inside, and I proceed with my quiz in the *American Family Practice Journal*. Mark sets things on autopilot and reads his book (I novor did scc what it was, but it was well-thumbed). When the DME read thirty miles, we passed from clouds into brilliant sunshine and unlimited visibility! It was so good that I took another picture of the Olgas and Ayer's Rock as we went past. Then we were down and sister Jennie met us with the Toyota at the Amata strip.

We had about twenty-five patients. Muna, who was supposed to come in with us last time for Dr. Cahill to check her pregnancy, was the first. She had a hard time with her last delivery. She was at Ernabella last week but "absconded" when we were to take her back with us. So, today we just checked her (and her baby girl born last August), and drew several tubes of blood from her. (Later, back in the Alice, I just happened to run into Dr. Cahill, her obstetrician, and told her the story.) Then there was Sarah with the head lice. The excoriations she'd made scratching the things had given her a fungus infection of the back of her neck and her shoulders. Then came Joey, one of the really bright aboriginal boys, age eleven or so, who had recurrent ear infections, and now his teacher says he doesn't seem to hear anymore, and she feels badly, because here's a really bright kid, and he isn't getting the messages. I look in his ears. The right one has no eardrum at all, and the malleous seems to be gone, but the rest of the anatomy seems intact. There is no current evidence of infection. The left ear looks like I'm looking right down the Eustachian tube. There seems to be no middle ear bones there at all, and certainly, no eardrum. I try a tuning fork, but when he's asked "we–ah" (no) or "oh–ah" (yes in Pitjantjatjara), he just looks blank. Sister Carol speaks Pitjantjatjara to the mother, and she'll ask Joey later if he heard the sound, and then it will be reported back to sister Beth.

Then there's Monica, ten weeks old, with congenital syphilis. She's had proper treatment at the hospital for the disease, but they'd like a serology on her. That means a femoral stick for 10 ml of blood, and I refuse (again) to do this. I just don't like the idea of doing a femoral stick on a baby like this, then having the child go off "bush" with its mother, and not be seen again until the baby is moribund with a huge femoral hematoma or worse! They can bring her in to the Alice.

"No," argues sister Jennie, "Dr. Martins, the pediatrician, is going to be out this next week. He can do the femoral stick if that's what's indicated. Or else he can break out his little bottle (I know they have them) that collects enough from a heel stick to do a serology."

Next is Ajax. He's been one week now with a sore foot. He was "inspected" by the doctor on the radio last week, who tried to determine if he was hearing about a deep thrombosis or a cellulitis. He had prescribed fluoxacillin from sister's description of the problem. Well, it's a cellulitis, all right. It's resolving nicely, but complete with inguinal nodes. The lymphangitis is gone now. There's quite a bit of swelling on the medial aspect of the foot just below the malleolus, and there's no way to tell if there was trauma or not. The half-inch thick, fissured skin of the sole of the foot is covered half an inch thick with mud. Ajax is about forty-five years old. My thought is to continue the cloxacillin, but they've just run out, and there was supposed to be more on the plane today, but there wasn't. What can we substitute? They changed to just plain penicillin V. I decide to add 500 mg of tetracycline four times a day for five days until we get some more cloxacillin. The only other alternatives are erythromycin and Septra.

The clinic is over. We have some yogurt nut bread with bananas, homemade by sister Beth. And, of course, a cup of tea. She also had homemade bread with cheese, but I don't think the calcium in the cheese is tempting because of the recent bout with kidney stones, so I turn it down.

Then we're off. Brilliant sunshine! Unlimited visibility! And as we depart we get the message from the Alice that they are no longer on VFR (visual flight rules). They have clouds down to 1,000 feet. We climb to 9,000 feet and tool on at heading 030 degrees. It's just beautiful. About forty-five miles out by DME we hit the first edge of the clouds, and we begin our descent. Down Amata way the wild hops cover huge areas of the landscape with red blossoms that from above look like huge splotches of blood. Jennie had a bowl of them on her table today for decoration. They look just like sweetpeas, except they're only about half an inch in diameter, and all red. No white. No pink. Suddenly we're in the open sky. Five miles from the Alice the clouds end, and it's beautiful sunshine! We land, and I make hospital rounds. I buy a can of Pet dog food for my adopted dog-friend, Tess, and stop by to mail the letter I'd written to my best friend in North Dakota. There's no mail for me, says postman Jack. There's a strike on in Sydney. I believe him.

9 July 1981

This morning, Dr. Tom Hanson is to accompany us. He's visiting from Washington, having arrived only yesterday. He's going to have a busy schedule, but sister Carol has worked in a visit for him, so that he can see part of the value of the aeromedical service provided by the American doctor to the Spyce Byce.

We arrived at the airport at 0755, and Mark is there looking around for the airplane. It seems to have disappeared. I guess we'll have to take the Baron, Foxtrot Delta Charley. Sister Carol is just a tad upset. She thinks they've taken the Navajo off for service early. We also have David Musgrave, sister Audrey's son from Fregon, to go back with us. Seems that they've rolled a 4-wheel drive vehicle again at Fregon. That's the second one! David suffered a fracture of the right clavicle in the accident. That's why he's been in the Alice. So, we submit to his obvious burning desire, and Tom and I sit in the second row, and David gets into the right front seat. In no time we're rotating from runway three-zero. It's kind of a hazy day, and although we're at only 6,000 feet, we really don't see that much scenery. Sister Carol is in the back seat, and comes through at the appropriate time with the call "who wants coffee?" She proceeds to provide as ordered, plus biscuits. A new sister, Julie, is waiting when we land. This time Mark has found the strip straight away, and we don't have to radio for landmarks.

The place looks just the same as always. There is the usual trash strewn around, and the natives are moving just a little slowly this morning; kind of clinging to the wood fire behind the corrugated metal shield. Nothing much is noted to be cooking, but I suppose they've had their damper (bread of flour, water and soda, cooked in a skillet) and tea already. The clinic starts off with the usual gaggle of runny ears and noses, and then there's Jolyne, about two and a half years old, with long, straight, blond hair, and all dressed up in a really cute outfit, with calf-length black leather boots! She's got a belly ache. I examine and she cries. I think the diagnosis is all the damper that she's put away this morning. I guess we must be just about "between checks" (sit down money). I reassure Mom, and Jolyne stops crying and scampers out.

Next is Fred Tapa-tapa with an atrophic right leg. He fractured it some years ago, and then fractured it again. He has very little movement in the right knee. There's a lots of muscle atrophy. We're to fill out the form for disability money. Tali-tali is next. She's about thirty-nine weeks pregnant. Her husband is Pompey, who is featured in a full page photo in one of the books of Central Australia. Tali is fine. Pompey has been taking Motrin for chest pain for about the last three months. I examine him; a beautiful specimen of manhood, but he's about fifty-five years old. I really can't find anything wrong with him, but sister Audrey says he's been taking away an awful lot of Motrin, and she doesn't think he's using it all for himself. That's easy; just give him two tablets each time when he fronts up. He won't be in that often, and that will limit the use.

Then a few more runny noses, and runny ears, and we see Millie Harding. She's pregnant about twenty-four weeks, but she looks like she's got twins; one above the other. It's a rather nasty gastric dilatation; probably damper again. No treatment this time. She'll digest it, and it'll go through. I should give you the recipe for damper. One takes a skillet, greases it with mutton fat, and pours in a mixture of water, flour and salt, with a little baking powder. Heat it in the campfire or an oven and add a little jam, and chew. It won't look like bread, but it will sit heavily in the stomach long enough to take the hunger pangs away. There's also a recipe of similar ilk, but with no baking powder. This is called "buckjumper." A buckjumper is also a wild and untamable horse who will do his best to unseat his rider. Theory goes that the damper is heavy enough to insure the rider a permanent seat on the bramby (wild horse). Anyway, Millie has good fetal heart tones, and all seems well, except for the big belly.

Next is Thelma with a severe bronchiectasis. She's had one lung almost entirely removed for this. She's only about fifteen, but she's been in trouble since she was about three. It's a classic, with clubbing of the fingers, even the toes. There's nothing, really, to do for her but watch her. She's got 0.9 liters forced expiratory volume in her pulmonary function studies, and only 0.45 liters in one second! She looks a tad dyspneic (short of breath). I learned two new Pitjantjatjara words today. "Wiltja" is the habitat they live in, and the local spelling for "Charlie" is "Tjali." That figures!

Next we have Milyika. She's the one who has visions, and that's why she has no husband. Not even a chance of getting pregnant, because the males are all afraid to approach her. Poor thing! She takes Tom on a tour of the school. When he comes back, he goes to the craft shop and buys a few things. One is a batik skirt for his wife, and some other knickknacks. Sister Carol borrows a dollar from me to pay for a loaf of bread she's bought at the bakery. I visit the bakery, too. The bread has just come out of the oven. It smells all yeasty and good. So, I buy a big loaf of hot bread, too.

Then to sister Audrey's for tea and some Spam and cheese sandwiches, and some really hard cookies with an almond in the center.

Then it's time to leave. Back through the village in the brilliant sunshine, and FDC is ready for takeoff. This time Tom gets to ride the right front, and the haze has cleared enough so that we can see Mt. Connor. In the distance Ayer's Rock is visible. Tom really does want to get an "up close" look at that. We'll go to Ansett when we get back to the Alice and arrange that for him for Sunday. But in the Baron it's dreamtime. I try to read, but just can't resist the warmness of the sunshine, the smoothness of the ride, and the drone of the engine. Then we're on final for one-two. Another day of payment in kind.

Next week it's to be Indulkana. Addendum: On leaving the clinic, I noticed a small child sitting in a dusty depression in the yard of the clinic—sans clothing. It took me a while to mentally redress the blond-haired youngster with the blouse and skirt, and the calf-length black leather boots, and sure enough, it was Jolync. She wasn't crying and she didn't appear to have a bellyache. She is enjoying the full rays of the sunshine, protected from the chill breeze by the walls of the dusty depression; a pathetic little human animal.

16 July 1981

This is looking like one of the "not so good" days, as we arrive at the airport at 0745. John is there with a new haircut that almost fools me at first. It just doesn't look like John with those ears showing, and the back of his neck, too. He's running up the Baron, Foxtrot Delta Charlie, but the starboard engine sounds awful. Lots of popping and knocking, even at full throttle. Plugs? Mag? Something sure is wrong with it. I hope he doesn't want to take that one. FDQ is sitting on the line, but looks a little forlorn, too. John taxies FDC to the Connair hanger for maintenance and walks back.

"No," he confirms, "FDQ won't be flying today, either. Last night Darryl was running it up, and the primer on the port engine stuck open, and suddenly there was a ball of fire in the engine. Darryl cut the mixture and opened the throttle wide open, and sucked the ball of fire back into the carburetor. I don't think we want to take her, either, until the maintenance people have had a look at her."

I agree, totally. That leaves the RFDS with one airplane left; Foxtrot Delta Echo, also a Baron. But we can't take that until we have a back-up airplane for emergencies for the base. Sister Carol has just arrived, and she makes a phone call to sister Kay. That's taken care of. They'll have a charter on standby. At 0845 we're off on heading 182 degrees for Indulkana. I didn't notice Chamber's Pillar go by this time. Guess I was reading. It's kind of hazy. Then, there's Kulgara, and we've crossed the border into South Australia. Chandler is up ahead just before the airstrip at Indulkana, which is now opened. John greases Echo onto the strip, which is being dragged intermittently by some lethargic aboriginals in a utility (pickup truck) that looks like it has seen better days. Glad they weren't dragging it as we decided to land. Sister Julia is there. Julia the younger, I guess we'd call her. Sister Victoria, the other sister, is down in bed with a severe vertigo.

The clinic is a bit disorganized, but not for lack of patients. First there's European Leigh Ann with history of an abortion in Adelaide about four weeks ago with subsequent fever and bleeding, and re-hospitalization. But no further instrumentation. Now she's had another episode of bleeding that has stopped spontaneously. What to do? I guess she'd better go up to the Alice and see Dr. Bankroft; not Dr. Cahill—Dr. Cahill won't have anything to do with abortions. Then another European, Sharon, with a Bartholin cyst. She's going to have to go up, too. I sure don't want to get into anything like that in a remote place like this. Next is ante-natal Lipsey, an aboriginal with breech presentation at thirty-four weeks. We'd better get her off in the next fortnight for Alice.

Cathy Martin is a European of 60 kg, 124/70, 13/52 (thirteen weeks of gestation), doing fine. Julia is aboriginal, age eighteen, and had a Cu–7 intrauterine device placed in Adelaide a month ago with the admonition from the GYN man down there to take a look after a month and make sure it's still in place. We do this, with one of those funny little plastic speculae that don't want to close after they're opened. But we manage, and the string is right where it's supposed to be. The next two patients are newborns. Michelle and Anne Myra, both cute as buttons with no problems. Then European baby Adrian with a cough, says Mom. The baby is fat and drooling around one of the biggest "dummies" (Aussie for a pacifier) I've ever seen. Adrian's chest is clear, but she's teething. That's all.

Next funny little Lynette, a European from the railroad gang at Chandler, with blinking eyes, and migraines, and a big tattoo on her right shoulder that says "Lynette loves Robert." That's her husband's name. I don't see any neurological deficits. I guess we can treat her with aspalgin. Do you remember Robyn Warner? She was the one that we had on the temperature chart six months ago. She's thirteen weeks pregnant now, but never did go up to let Dr. Cahill see those temperature charts. Then another old friend, Eileen, the aboriginal girl who can cough up blood on request. She's got a cough again. This time I don't ask her to cough up blood. She does have some rales in the right posterior chest. I'll just give her some Amoxil (antibiotic). She'll take it for a day or so, and then go walkabout.

Next is Edie with the right pyelitis (kidney infection). I think she's pregnant. Better for her to go up and see Dr. Cahill. We draw antenatal blood on her. After that it's Claire and Adele Starkman. Mom has a check up, and Adele has her head measured because she has been told that the head is in the tenth percentile. It's 43 cm today. Not bad for the age. Next is aboriginal Judith Mimili with pain in her hip. I can't find anything much here, and she isn't talking to anyone today. I guess a little aspirin might help. Then it's Lorraine, thirty-seven plus weeks pregnant. She'd better start for the Alice this next week.

John is Biddy's child. She says he has a "knot" tummy, whatever that is. I suspect he may have a right inguinal hernia, but it won't come down today, even when I make him scream. Then we have Topsey (that's right—that's her name); a newborn who's growing appropriately. Ah! And then just to keep things mysterious, we have Nellie next with the "different belly." She's about twenty-two weeks along, but there are two lumps in this abdomen, one above the other. I think one is the uterus (the lower one), and the other is a stomach distended by damper. Nellie's not talking today. On the other hand, one wonders if it might be twins. There's something different about this one. It will probably sort itself out by the next time I come around.

Roger is a ten-year-old aboriginal boy with an abscess under his chin that's resolving. No history of trauma or other reason for onset. Thyroglossal duct cyst? Well, it's resolving. We'll just let it go. Terry is a thirteen-month-old aboriginal baby with pneumonia in the left lower lobe. Bicillin for him, but it's not really Bicillin; it's 300,000 units of Bicillin and 300,000 units of procaine pen G. We'll give him that today, and another one in two days. No use giving him oral medication. Mom would stop it tomorrow anyway. This way, he's got it in his little butt. Lastly is Teddy with a foot burn that's coming along. He'd been up to the Alice a month ago and had some skin grafting. He's going to be first-rate. The last few of these patients arrived in a truck from Mimili just as we were finishing the clinic. Then I visit sister Victoria, and Julie generously provides us a with a cup of tea; no lunch, although it's 1330 hours.

But we're not off for home, either. We're on the way to Ayer's Rock; a fifty-four minute diversion. Some guy with a work injury. The Baron is sky-hungry, and climbs out at 1,500 feet a minute. It's a beautiful, sunny day with almost no wind. John must have a slow thyroid, though, because the plane heater has it about 140 degrees Fahrenheit inside the cabin. Sister Carol sleeps. I watch roads meander around the bush; some water holes, but mostly mulga (wood and wattle tree) and spinifex. Past Ernabella, and there's Mt. Connor and Ayer's in the distance. We home in on it, and sister Phyllis meets us at the strip.

It's Richard Mann, with a foreign body in his left hand; the lateral side, just about at the level of the metacarpophalangeal joint (first knuckle). It's been festering there for four days. He's been on Amoxil. It sure looks sore. There's no small forceps to work with. I'll have to make do with a larger one. But first, I'll need a little more room to work in. So, it's 4 cc of one percent

Xylocaine to block the nerves, and then a longitudinal slit through the wound to make it about a centimeter long. It's bloody for a bit, but pressure on the wound stops that. I reach in with the big forceps. Bump! I can feel it, but I can't get hold of it. I look up at the ceiling and fervently request help from the Lord; then back into the wound with the big forceps. I feel it! I've got it! I draw out a wooden splinter, blackened from four days of sepsis, about three quarters of an inch long and a quarter of an inch in diameter. I irrigate the wound with the remaining Xylocaine.

"Are you going to suture it, Dr. Rutten?" asks sister Phyllis.

"Heavens no! That would mean that we'd be sewing all that poison right back into the wound. We'll let it heal from the inside out. But we will continue the Amoxil." Richard is delighted!

Then, Forrest Duval comes in, a hiker who has an abscessed big toe. We I&D (incise and drain) that for him. Elaine Welch has a possible ectopic pregnancy. She'd really better get into the Alice. Julie Field has an eye and ear infection, and she's pregnant, too. Helen Parton with tinea versicolor, and John Mills with a costo-chondral syndrome on the left from being hit by a car.

Then we have another cup of tea, and we're off for the Alice. The sun is making long, horizontal shadows to the southeast in the sparse forest below. The ancient sand dunes cast ridges of shadow so that it's hard to determine which is the dune and which is the shadow. The sun colors the tops of the hills red; then the color fades except for that on our own wing tips. John turns on the panel and navigation lights.

"Foxtrot Delta Echo," says the radio, "Call Alice tower at 30 DME (distance measuring equipment)."

The Spyce Byce comes into view with the whiteness of the bubbles almost glowing in the twilight. We're on final for one-two. It's been a good, busy day. John says we've covered 542 miles today. Next week we'll be going to Ernabella again. I'm glad I have the opportunity to serve these people.

23 July 1981

What a different day this week than last! It's been windy the last few days, but almost cloudless. This morning when I rose, the sky was almost solid overcast, and it was surprisingly warm. That should have warned me that the warmth was probably due to "compressional heating" of the air. Sure enough! The wind began to blow from the west; then north at a fair clip by 0730. Darryl was waiting and had preflighted the Navajo, so that when sister Carol arrived with Bob, we were all ready to go. The runway had been divided and the western half closed as the ground crews were just finishing the new taxi way. No matter. Half the runway was plenty this morning, and we were off and climbing out by 0810.

Darryl is a fidgeter. He adjusts the prop speed until both needles on the tach are absolutely even; then adjusts the throttles so that the manifold pressure from both engines is exactly the same. Of course, this changes the R.P.M. a bit in one engine or the other, and so he goes back to the prop control, which throws the manifold needles off dead center. Ad infinitum! Then he reaches over and adjusts the cabin heater. Then the altimeter needs to be adjusted to 1009 from 1012. Then, switch from main petrol tanks to auxiliary. By this time I'm engrossed in my *American Family Practice Journal*, and we're tooling over the desert with Mt. Connor already in sight. The sky is not quite overcast, and here and there are shafts of sunlight making like spotlights on small areas of the desert floor. But it's also getting a bit bumpy.

We descend from 8,000 feet after passing Mt. Connor, and suddenly the plane is skittering around like a restless stallion. We make a fly by to look at the windsock at the Amata strip, which is standing straight out from the pole, and almost directly crosswind. That's probably fifteen knots with gusts to thirty. Then the bottom drops out and even with a snug seat belt, I hit the overhead with my head. It doesn't hurt; it hit quite flat on a lot of my skull, and a padded overhead. Still, the thump is considerable, and there are cookies scattered all around. We had, fortunately, just finished our coffee, and the tollhouse cookies, which I had brought this morning, had been well accepted. None-theless, we did make an extra tour of the strip just to let things settle down a bit. The landing had us crabbing about twenty degrees until just before touchdown when Darryl straightened things out, but dipped the upwind wing so we slipped on a straight line toward the runway. As expected, just at the last minute the bottom dropped out again, and we were firmly planted on the runway for our roll-out.

Sister Julia Dorn was waiting for us with the vehicle. The clinic this morning is rather helter skelter, since they didn't have much time to organize it. I'm really not due here at Amata until next week, but this week had just seen Dr. Martins and Dr. Stapleton at Ernabella, and Ernabella really didn't have much for me to do. So, today was supposed to be an "off day." Since Laura is returning to the Alice from her family reunion in North Dakota next Thursday, I didn't feel like I wanted to take off two Thursdays in a row, and this was the way to do it.

One interesting patient today was Cheryl Nelson, an unlikely name for a black, aboriginal girl, who had me fooled into believing she had an acute abdomen. I really thought we'd better take her with us to the Alice, except that she hadn't any fever, and she had only vomited once, she said. And now she was lying quietly with her legs extended and her ankles crossed, and only went into her "act" when I tried to feel her belly. She did have bowel sounds, but she sure was guarding that belly. She also had a suprapubic scar from an operation that she said was done in Adelaide. Sister Carol told me aside that Cheryl had been active and breast-feeding her two year old baby just before coming into the clinic, and that she sure didn't look too bad doing that. No evidence of a belly ache at all, as a matter of fact. I deferred to this bit of history and ordered up three grams of Amoxil with a gram of probenecid stat. After all, I don't want a p.i.d. (pelvic inflammatory disease) to get out of hand.

Another interesting patient was sister Julia Dorn, herself. She's got shin splints from jogging; a right peroneal tendonitis, the way I look at it. I don't know what she thinks it is, but she doesn't agree with my diagnosis. I really think that stopping jogging for a couple of days, and some Indocin will make her well. She's disbelieving. That's okay, with me. It's her pain.

It's really a rather small clinic; maybe fifteen patients in all. Then, it's "cup of tea" time, and then we're ready to depart. The wind is blowing fiercely. I take a couple of pictures of the mountains almost obscured by blowing sand. On board the aircraft, Darryl runs us up well, and holds the Navajo on the ground until she's well over 100 M.P.H. Then, we're off like a shot into the sky, and climbing for 9,000 feet. It's rough! No reading on this trip! We're now into the clouds. Darryl asks for and receives permission to go to 10,000 feet from traffic control. But we're still in the clouds, and it's still bumpy.

Finally we clear the clouds, and it's quite a sight. Dust storms, with dust going much higher than we are. It reminds me of the dust storms that I've seen in Afghanistan. The rolls of dust rising from the desert floor on a front of maybe fifteen miles to an estimated altitude of 25,000 feet! Not just one or two, but maybe a dozen of these scattered from horizon to horizon. It's a real duster!

The approach to the Alice is uncomplicated, and the wind is right down the pike for runway three-zero. There's a Cherokee down in a paddock to the north of the road at the airport. Seems a student pilot that was practicing "touch and goes" got caught in the wind and ended up tangling first with one of the high trees that spun him around. Thanks to the stability of the Cherokee, it just pancaked into the pasture, with considerable damage to the plane but none to the pilot, except for his ego.

We're back by 1445 hours. It's been a fun day again. Not as pretty as last week, but not as busy, either. It will be Fregon in a fortnight!

6 August 1981

We didn't fly last week because Laura was coming home from her family reunion in North Dakota, and I sure wanted to be there to say "g'dye" to her. It was a neat homecoming with her journey sandwiching in between transport strikes in Australia and the air traffic controller strike in America. This week we have Fregon as the settlement needing our attention.

The Graham Pitt isn't ready to fly when I arrive. It seems that they made a "quicky" run down to Finke for a lady that was going into labor, and so, we have to refuel before we set out for Fregon. John gets everything on board, and we taxi over to the fuel pumps. It's 0830, but the Shell crew won't pump petrol until 0845, so John opts to pump his own. I disembark, but sister Carol sits in the plane doing her paperwork. John hooks up the static line, cuts his finger rather bloodily on the nozzle, and proceeds to fuel the port side main and auxiliary tanks. The heat convection is apparent over the hot engines, and so are the petrol fumes as John pumps in the stuff. He manages to run about a litre over onto the wing and down on the tarmac. Then the starboard side is fueled in a similar manner. Amazing! There's no fire! We're ready to go.

Scattered overcast, as we leave on runway one-two, but the air is clear and not hazy. I become involved in my continuing medical education tests until there's an increase in cabin noise, and I look up to find that we're in a rain squall. Sister Carol is there with a half cup of hot coffee and a biscuit, though, and everything remains cozy. The temperature drops noticeably as we head south. Ernabella is involved in a shower as we go by, and then we're letting down for a smooth landing at Fregon. There's lots of activity at the strip as the mailplane is also due. Julia picks us up, and Audrey greets us as we arrive.

It's a busy clinic today, about twenty-five people. But today is a varied lot. There's Noah and Rosie, both with draining ears. Nothing very unusual about that, except that I can't get used to looking in and seeing no drum and no ossicles, just a snotty hole in the skull. Yet, these children seem to be able to hear. Melissa is something else again; she has maggots in her ears. I pick them out, but learned later from Dr. Hauptenhausser at the hospital in the Alice that he irrigates them twice a day with three percent peroxide cut half and half with water. He says the maggots are anaerobes, and they die with this treatment. It also washes out the substrate for them to feed on. So, it looks like Melissa will be back to normal like the other kids and just have snotty ears for a while.

I'm asked to check over Errol. He's been "crook" for a while, and his parents have taken him to the nungkari (witch doctor) who has extracted the evil that was causing his distress. There is a doubt with sister Audrey as to whether there's any evidence of illness in the child, whom the parents state is now "getting better." Audrey shows me the "spirits." One is a small stone about a half inch in diameter, dark and rough. Another is a small piece of glass with sharp edges, squarish in shape, and about half an inch on each side. The third is a piece of the bottom of a bottle; it even has some printing on it in raised glass letters. It measures about two-and-a-half inches by an inch, but has part of the right angle of the bottom and the side of the bottle on it. I'm told that as recently as five years ago these "spirits" were beautiful works of art; well polished wood in teardrop shape, but that the state of the art—like everything else in the aboriginal community—is declining in quality. The nungkari extracts these spirits in a ritual "bloodless surgery." I don't find anything wrong with Errol. I guess the nungkari has done his work well.

There's discussion about a diet for the diabetic husband of the baker in town. Not much point in getting involved with that too much. It looks like for certain, his diet is going to be mostly carbohydrate.

Then there's Millie Harding who has had quite a beating from her boyfriend. Seems that they were to a show in Yuendumu this last week, and Millie had gone off with a group of folks to a barbecue and left "boyfriend" behind. He thought she had jilted him, so when he had her alone next, he seized a metal bar and beat her on the arms, the back of the head, the chest and the legs. He did a fairly good job of it, too. She has a large, swollen area on the left arm, about halfway down from the elbow, with a large ecchymosis and abrasions. I don't think there's a fracture. She can pronate and supinate it, but it sure is a nasty bruise. Her neck is also swollen over the right trapezius. I don't look at anything more. She's just bruised. But "boyfriend" is in for tribal trouble. I'll probably see him around with a spear wound in his thigh next month. Millie had been with relatives of her family, not just anyone. "Boyfriend" should have found this out before he set on her.

Audrey's son, Ray, tells about being eyewitness to tribal justice in Yuendumu during this same show. Seems that there was a female who had killed her husband there last fall. I don't know the reason, nor did they, but she did it, and according to tribal law, that means that she must die slowly. Of course, after she had killed her husband she split, but after seven months away from Yuendumu, she had the poor judgement to return for the show. The relatives of the husband seized her and beat her with "nulla-nullas." Ray was witness to this. He said that they didn't really hit her full force, but hard enough to keep knocking her down. Blows across the head, the shoulders, the chest, and the legs, and still she kept getting back up and trying to get away. They'd knock her down again. After a while, she was a bloody mess, but they kept on her, until finally she couldn't get up anymore, and then they finished her off. That's right! They killed her! And no government authority stopped it or arrested anyone. It's pretty primitive out here yet.

John was hoping to get back to the Alice before the banks closed. He's leaving for Darwin in the morning, but doesn't have any money. His plan is wrecked by a radio message from the Alice asking us to divert to Amata to pick up an antenatal in the thirty-ninth week who's spotting. So, the Navajo is off the ground, and across the back country to Amata. It's a beautiful ride. The trails on the ground seem to run in remarkably straight lines from one water hole to another. Patterson's curse is the name given to the little red flowers that I mentioned once before that make the outback look like huge pools of blood from the air. They actually look like little snapdragons, but there are thousands and thousands of them: the blooms of wild hops.

Then we touch down at Amata. The lady is waiting and shifted aboard, and we're off for the Alice. Over Mt. Connor, we fly, but I doze a lot. Then we're on final for the Alice. It's a most interesting diversion in a hectic week. John greases the plane onto the runway, and this time there's no backtracking. They've finished the new taxi-way that takes us right to our hangar.

13 August 1981

Sister Ray Stone flew with us today. First, we would stop off at Granite Downs to look at the finger of Ray Saltman, and then to check the blood pressure on Maggie, but before that, we had to get off the ground. The Graham Pitt has been having trouble ever since Darryl had the fire in the port engine. Seems that the engine was reluctant to start now. At least, that's what Mark felt, and so he started the starboard engine first, so that the alternator could supply the power to the starter on the other engine. It would alternately begin to run, and then quit. After about twenty minutes, it started as though there had been nothing wrong with it at all. It seemed to be in the fuel injector system, because sometimes Mark would be looking out his window and announce that we were pouring fuel overboard from the primer. That's probably what caused Darryl's fire. Not too comforting a thought. When it started we hastened out to the end of "three-oh" for takeoff. The big old M.A.C. Starlifter is squatted on the runway with its droopy wings. We heard that the crew had a nose wheel failure while taxiing. Seems double strange that the casino had just opened, and that the M.A.C. flight had never been stalled in the Alice before.

"Track 181 degrees at 55, report 35 miles DME," says the radio. I mentioned to Mark that this time I'd like to get a picture of Chamber's Pillar as we go by. The pillar is a tall stand of rock, much like some of the pillars that one sees in the New Mexico desert, with the base sloping from debris that has eroded from the shaft of the pillar. Chamber's is off the beaten track by a hundred miles or so, although I have talked with some hardy souls who have made the trip out there in a 4-wheel drive vehicle. I guess it's pretty spectacular from the ground. It's pretty spectacular from the air! It's just sixty miles DME from Alice (distance measuring equipment—an instrument in the plane that measures the time it takes for a signal to leave the plane and be returned by a receiver transmitter on the ground at the Alice airport), and just south of the Charlotte Range and west of the Maryvale Hills, and a tad (five miles) north of the Finke River, just in case you might like to go there some day. I snapped one picture of the whole area as we approached. The morning sun was low enough so that its shadow seemed to be a mile long. It does stand up to 1,632 MSL (mean sea level) so it does cast a pretty long shadow! The second picture I took just as we came up to it, and when I went to take the third picture directly down on the summit, I found I was out of film. I changed in a hurry, and thought that Mark might make a circle, but he didn't. I'll have to get that shot next time we go out.

We follow the road south of Kulgera right to the station. Mark makes a circle around this, and we have a beautiful picture of the station from the north this time. Then we fly south east to the strip. This one is smooth, but tufted with desert grass, making it visible from the air, but blending it in with the other desert plants from the surface, so that one wouldn't know there was a strip there at all. That's why when the big, old Navajo is sitting there in the open, next to the road to Oodnadatta, the tourist buses all stop, and everyone piles out to take a picture of the Royal Flying Doctors on the job!

I suppose it does look impressive. We were really just enjoying the crisp morning air and the warm sun rising on our backs and making small talk while I examined Ray's "tea-drinking" finger. He had almost amputated it in the equipment of the bore he was fixing. I think he did get the flexor tendon, fifth finger right, at the proximal IP (interphalangeal) joint. But it was stuck back together by the sisters at Indulkana, and it's going to be right, even if a might stiff. It won't be much different from the other fingers on his weather-beaten, misused stockman's hands.

Maggie's pressure is up a bit, probably due to the two "stone" (an Aussie unit of weight equal to about fourteen pounds) that she's put on since the spring, and mostly secondary to eating the leftovers from the VIP entertainment that she's had to do this winter. They (the Baxters) are the people that are giving their station back to the aboriginals on request of the government. I think I mentioned them to you some time past. It's not the biggest station in South Australia, by far. It's only about a million acres. The largest station is about 12,000 square miles.

Then we're off to the delight of the picture-taking tourists, the Navajo rising like a phoenix from the desert grass into the morning sun. I'll bet there was a lot of film wasted on that takeoff!

We stay about 500 feet altitude for the ten miles past Chandler following the railroad and the parallel "south road" that take us to Indulkana. A big road train (huge tractor truck with multiple semi-trailers) is northbound on the road, leaving a tower of dust almost as high as we are, drifting slowly eastward in the calm morning air.

We're met at the strip by sister Kay, who looks to be about twenty-two. She's the senior sister. The other sister is Ann, who is maybe twenty-one; and visiting is sister Vivian, about twenty. All in all, they look like they should be in high school instead of taking care of all medical problems alone in an aboriginal settlement almost three hundred miles from the nearest doc. It's "check" day in the settlement, so there are people sitting in the dust all along the main street of Indulkana. Looks like all the dogs in a hundred miles have gathered with them. It's a way of life for these people, who are unmindful of the criticism heaped on the Australian Commonwealth government by an uninformed World Council of Churches. Somehow the label of poverty and filth must be mitigated by the fact that these people really enjoy this way of life.

Robyn Warner is 55.5, 120/70, 1+ protein in her urine, 16/52 weeks pregnant, and had some spotting on the sixth of the month. We advise. Little Adele Starkman is there to have her head measured again. This month it's 42 1/2, a net gain of half a centimeter since last time. She's nine months now, and still no teeth: happy as only a microcephalic can be. Maybe that's the better diagnostic criterion than the head size, the happiness. Then there's Dorothy, who had a bad fracture of her left leg in an accident years ago. Her foot is numb. This makes walkabout difficult for her. We advise her.

Next there's Larry Prince; *gorked* in 1979 in a vehicle accident. He needs a renewal exam for his pension. Now we have Nellie Wilson, 77, 140/90, 26/52 and doing fine. Lippie is 39/52, with her fundus (uterus) right up to her xiphoid (breast bone), and the stretched scar from her previous C-section. We'll take her back in with us. And so the clinic goes. Mark is feeding his "Joey" (Aussie for baby kangaroo). He just took possession of a six-month-old baby red kangaroo the other day. He's feeding it soya milk from a bottle, and the baby (he's named it Skippy for some reason) hides out in a pillowcase contained in a woven purse. The children of the village are quite taken with it, and reciprocally display their baby emu. Poor little thing. It doesn't look like much yet.

Then it's tea time, and we're back to the strip. Not as much trouble with the port engine this time, and we're off and on the way home. Seven thousand feet, 001 degrees, and that intermittent "pop-pop" in the engine is a bit unnerving. We'll just have to have that fixed before we go out again. I don't mind the engine quitting in the air as much as I don't like the thought of a fuel leak and fire. But now we're letting down and the day is over. I think I'll see if I can take Laura along next week to Ernabella again. That would be fun, since we also have reservations at the casino for dinner and the floor show that night. It will be our thirty-first wedding anniversary!

20 August 1981

Now, this is the way to celebrate a thirty-first wedding anniversary—fly off to Ernabella! That's exactly what we do, too. Laura has permission from the aboriginal council to come to the settlement with me, and so at just about 0800 hours, John, sister Carol, and Laura and I load ourselves into the Graham Pitt, whose port engine has been repaired this last week, and, with Laura in the right front seat, me riding backwards behind the pilot, and Paula from Fregon sitting on sister Carol's lap in the seat facing mine, we lift off at just 0815. The air is clear, and we have flight level four (four thousand feet), so we are low enough to really see what is happening on the ground. There is a layer of clouds at about 7,000 feet, and on the way out to the airport, we see a strange rainbow: a shaft of sunlight filtering between two layers of clouds just managed to catch a rain shower, so that a triangular shaped rainbow, with the crust side of the pie upward, appears just over the mountains.

We mention it to sister Carol and she exclaims, "Ah, what are they doing at the Spyce Byce this morning?"

No matter what natural phenomenon occurs, the locals always seem to feel what the space base is involved in the explanation. Shafts of sunlight illuminate areas of the desert ahead and to the side, like heavenly spotlights on a stage. Mt. Connor is visible in the haze to the right, but the rock at Ayer's is not. John complains to Laura that we are heading almost into the teeth of a wind of about thirty-five knots, and it does take a long time to cover the ground to Ernabella. But then we are over the salt lakes, and it's soon time for coffee and peanut biscuits that Laura bought at Coles Market. She had wanted to take some more of her homemade tollhouse cookies, but this time I was a little selfish, wanting them for myself. That is why we bought some. We also have some "lollies" (candy) along: Tootsie Rolls, the little ones that Laura brought from Santa Barbara. Paula palms everything that she is handed, instead of eating, saving it in case it rains, I guess. She stays just as sober as a judge all the way. She's been in a plane before, so isn't scared; she just doesn't have much to say.

The circle to the right over the settlement gives us a good look at the community, and John makes a wide approach coming in heading due south to the strip. It's a smooth landing, and not much of a roll-out, since we are into the teeth of a pretty good gale. Sister Julie picks us up straight away, and we are taken into town. Laura has Brian direct her to the craft shop and other sights in the town, and I dig into a clinic that turns out to be bigger than I had anticipated.

First is Johnny Tjapura, sitting is one of the back rooms of the "hospital" where he has slipped in. Johnny is going through his initiation rite, so to be seen by a woman would really undo him. He does manage to get in with Brian's help. That is the first time I have seen the genitals of a male undergoing initiation. Johnny has lymphogranuloma venereum, with a chain of huge nodes in the groin that have suppurated into masses of red, stinking proud flesh, stretching along both inguinal ligaments. The penis is a scabbed, suppurating mass that seems plastered against the belly, with pubic hair matted into crusts of old pus. Johnny says it isn't too painful. He allows me to touch it with gloved hand. It isn't as hard to the touch as I had thought it would be. More like a squishy sensation over the granulation tissue. Brian will try to stick close to him and give him a gram of tetracycline four times a day for twenty-one days, but I doubt that we'll really get a whole course into him. He can't be evacuated. He still has a month to go in the initiation rite, and to leave now would mean that he'd never be a tribal man. So much for Johnny Tjapura.

Then there's Nyarulya, who is forty-two weeks pregnant. She went up to the Alice two weeks ago, but went A.W.O.L. and reappeared in Ernabella. She'll go on the mailplane on Tuesday, if she hasn't delivered yet. Remember little Matthew with the stitch in his tonsil a few trips back? Well, the stitch came out okay all by itself. He's in today for his cough, and for Mommie's achilles insertion tendonitis. Then poor little Allison Troy; she's had big festering abscesses of the left breast. She sure had trouble with that last pregnancy. It looks like the abscesses are all drying up now. She had to go back to the Alice last week and have them drained under general anesthesia. What a mess! Next is Robert Nelson; a funny name for a black man, but he's had a draining abscess of his left lateral thigh for some years now. I thought maybe he'd been speared there, but they say that's not so; that it was just an accident. There must be some foreign body in there, though. He's had it explored in the Alice, but nothing was found. It looks like it might be drying up with cloxacillin, but he'll probably stop taking the medicine now since it's looking better.

A few runny ears in between, and then it's Athol Blyton . . . really! That's his name! Poor bloke has had an unusual accident. He was working in the power plant, and was on his knees under a machine, when a 55 gallon drum that had been cut in two, rolled off a saw horse landing sharp edge down on his right achilles tendon; severed it right through! He'd had to go up to the Alice to have it sutured. He's doing fine, but there's a little stitch abscess forming. We dig around it and find a piece of silk suture. Maybe that will cure it.

Remember one other time when I told you about the FLK (funny looking kid) syndrome with the talipes (club feet)? Well, they finally gave her a name, poor little thing. She's called Clara. Poor little tyke is just failing to thrive. Not because Mommy doesn't love her, either. She just has such a hard time nursing, what with her face all pushed in like that. The guys up at the hospital at Alice call it a mid-face hypoplasia because the maxilla just didn't develop. She doesn't have a cleft palate, though.

And then there's Santa Claus; at least he looks like Santa Claus: Tjilpi Jackie. He's about eighty, they think, and he's confused and wanders around a lot. They're worried about him getting hurt. He's also a bit cantankerous at times. We suggest a little haloperidol (called "Serenese" out here). Jackie seems to be in good shape with 2 + sugar in his urine and a blood pressure of about 180/100. He's dressed in about three shirts, and a brand new pair of bright blue "stubbies" (bermuda-like shorts). More about Jackie later.

Next there's black Brian. He's fifty years old and wants a pension because most of his contemporaries are drawing pensions. This is just about the most virile man in the settlement with bulging biceps, a chest like a weight lifter, and more hair on his chest and back than the average aboriginal—all gray, of course. I can't find any reason to give him a pension. He's upset with me until I tell him that I'll re-examine him next time and see if I can find anything wrong. We look at Baby Wynmarti with laryngeal stridor (croupy) next. He's getting better after a half dose of Bicillin IM (intramuscular). After the baby we look at good-looking Dale who's about 15 and who is a congenital deaf mute. Isn't that funny? His ear canals are clear as can be, and there's no pus at all, and the tympanic membranes are intact. He can't hear. He's going to Adelaide to be re-evaluated. Maybe he can benefit from a hearing aid. I understand he had one years ago, but that peer pressure (they laughed at him) kept him from wearing it. Maybe now that he's older.

How about Aliscan, born in 1925: She's got the mumps. She's miserable. Another classic next. Maringka was born in 1913 with the deeply sunken eye sockets made famous in all the paintings of aboriginals. She's an old tuberculosis, and has been coughing up blood. It's a bit hard to get to her shrunken, bony chest to listen. She's wearing her whole wardrobe: five dresses. I think her blood is on the basis of old atherosclerotic vessels giving up when she coughs. I don't think there are any acid-fast bacilli here, but we'll get a sputum to look for them. Then there's the antenatal clinic, and the guessing game by feel as to when each should be sent up to the Alice to deliver. It's been a long clinic.

Tea time over at sister Julie's, and then Laura displays her new possessions. Three wooden goanas of varying size. She did pretty well with her bargaining. She says they didn't have any boomerangs at the craft shop, so she stopped Tjilpi Jackie, and actually bought his trusty old boomerang right out of his hand! What a merchant! It's a real collector's item. It's been around a long time, and is obviously handmade. You can tell it's a hunting boomerang—not made to return—because it has the angle far towards the end away from the throwing hand. It's supposed to cartwheel along the ground and the heavy angle is supposed to hit the animal on the head, killing it. I'll bet this one has killed its share of game, and dogs, too. I guess they practice on camp dogs that are in the way. The very distal end is burned; apparently used to stir up the fire at times. It's a real treasure. I'd like to hear the story that goes with it. Maybe next time I'm out I'll have a chance to ask the old bloke about it. He might be in a good mood, what with that Haldol (Serenese) coursing through his body.

And then it's time to go. The plane fairly leaps into the air against the strong, gusty wind. Our flight level this time is nine (9,000 feet), and it's terribly bumpy even up here. As we cross the Finke River, though, there's the end of the front. The clouds of the Alice are there, and it does smooth out a bit just as John is told by approach control to start descending. The landing is on runway three-oh, and just as we're about to touch down, John pours a burst of power on . . . windshear! It almost got us! He's a good pilot, and the landing is otherwise uneventful. Sister Carol promises Laura a trip to Fregon soon; we've also been talking about asking the Amata council for permission for her to come there. It's been a really fun day!

It's not quite over, either. That evening we celebrate by dressing up in our finery. Laura even wears her mink jacket, and we take in the show and dinner at the cabaret at the casino. It's really a good show with lots of songs and dancing, and a magician, and girls with nothing on their boobs! Wow! We both have a pepper steak. We were going to have an appetizer with our drink, but the little waitress wouldn't bring us just one order of Tasmanian trout with horseradish sauce. By the time we decided that we'd like a half dozen oysters on the half shell to go with it, she told us she didn't want to bring either of them, since our dinner was on the way. Oh, well. We ordered a bottle of Seppelt claret to go with the meal. It was fun. I still can't get over the great serratus anterior muscles (chest) on those girls!

27 August 1981

I was thinking that maybe Laura would have permission from the council to go down with us to Amata this week, but it didn't happen yet. Probably just as well, too, because we have Blind Mary going back with us, and her daughter, and the daughter's baby. So, the Graham Pitt is pretty full anyway. This time again we don't have fuel on board, and Mark has to taxi us over to the fuel pumps and fill it up. I stay on the plane this time, because he has opened the door beside his seat, and also there are so many people in the plane that it would be difficult to walk past them in the narrow passage between the seats. The engines on the Navajo start quite easily now. I heard the cylinder head on the port engine had been cracked when it wouldn't start. Good thing we didn't have a blowout. That could have messed up a whole day. But it's not "crook" anymore. It's "right" now.

Mark tops them all off, and we proceed to runway one-two. John has a short, little trip up to Papunya today, and Darryl is taking a kidney failure patient all the way to Adelaide. He says he thinks he can make the round trip of almost 2,000 miles today, if weather and traffic hold up for him. That's a long ride in the Baron. They really have some pretty good pilots in the aeromedical service.

We climb out, right turn, and heading 222 degrees at 6,000 feet. It's a bit overcast; kind of a buttermilk sky with high strato cumulus, with the shafts of light making spotlight patches on the desert floor. No rainbows today. A little hazy. The Graham Pitt drones over the Waterhouse range, which is actually a double range with a hidden valley in the middle. Next is the Hugh River. It's amazing how rivers wander through the mountains, finding a bed that runs downhill all the way. Then the James Range comes into view, and it has rounded protuberances stretching out into the flat desert. The protuberances almost look like the feet of the gigantic elephant. Across the Finke and the Palmer Rivers, and the Seymour Range, and then the road just west of Mt. Ebenezer. Straight over the top of Mt. Connor, we cruise, and there's Amata ahead. The desert is still bloody with Patterson's curse (wild hops), and the paddy melons on the airstrip are of all sizes. I guess they don't dry into gourds that can be used. There are a lot of them lying about at the airstrip, and when they dry up they just shrivel away. Nothing in them good to eat, either. I don't know why God made them, but there has to be a purpose.

Sister Jennie greets us at the strip. Jennie's last name is Markam, I've learned. Chris' surname is Halpin. The clinic is a busy one. Antenatal clinic first is Kaye who is 34/52, 69.2 kg and doing just fine. Then little Lisa with pneumonia. Priscilla has diarrhea, and Lorna, who is thirty-seven weeks has a fetal heart of 172/minute. I think we'd better take her back with us. I don't know where the fetal distress is coming from, but that's a tad high for a pulse, and the fetus is hypoactive. Then eight-year-old Andrea with a big belly, but she's well-fed. It's not kwashiorkor; it's just a bloated tummy. No masses here and normal bowel sounds. Damper syndrome, like as not. Lots of ENT (ear, nose, throat) infections in between these interesting patients, of course. Runny noses are universal in the kids. Yellow, sticky, thick discharge that accumulates on the upper lip is the rule. There must be something protective about it. Maybe it keeps the flies from entering the nose. There're always plenty of flies on their upper lips. Funny they don't wipe it away, but maybe it's because the kids don't have sleeves.

Nita is seen next with condyloma lata. This is diagnosed by history, because I don't usually visualize the perineum of the females. I leave the room and sister Carol looks at Nita's bottom. Carol advises that Nita see Dr. Cahill (a female gynecologist) when she comes up on the bus next week. Then there's Mary with a lump in her breast. I think it's fibrocystic disease. There's no puckering or dimpling and it's movable, but I can't really tell and I think she should have a mammogram. Jane and Kathleen are epileptics that we check out back-to-back. They're both well controlled on Dilantin, but they won't take it on a regular basis. If they're well, they figure they don't need it. And so it goes.

Finally, the clinic is over, and we have a spot of tea at Jennie's place. She's really kind of political. She has signs all over her place; posters like "Soweto Lives, Apartheid is Death," and stuff like that. She tells us that the young man that gave the program with her at the Alice Springs Hospital Staff meeting that Friday was named Cliff Younger. I tell her that I admire his knowledge of the aboriginal people and their language. We also have a look at the father of Chris's child. He's European (mostly), but I think he's lost his brains in some disaster or another; maybe petrol sniffing. Anyway, he's not all there.

Then the radio tells us that they want us at Ayer's Rock to pick a piece of metal out of the eye of one of the carpenters at the hotel. He was grinding a piece of metal and a piece flew in his eye. They do have goggles, of course, but they're only for the "sissy" types. Mark lifts the Navajo off the runway at Amata, and trims it out about fifty feet over the trees, and points it at Ayer's Rock forty miles in the distance. And there we stay. It's exciting! We skim by some outcrops of rocks that are actually higher than we're flying. We look for game on the ground, but besides the gallahs disturbed by our noise and scattering out of the tops of the trees, we don't see anything moving on the ground. Too bad I didn't have my movie camera along. That would have made a good sequence.

The landing is smooth, and sister Debbie meets me. Mark and Carol and Lorna stay with the plane. I meet Alex at the dispensary, and under tetracaine anesthesia, I spud out the offending fleck of metal that is buried tightly in the cornea of the right eye, just almost at the lateral limbus. Hard to see, kind of. Alex has one of those irises that have lots of little brown flecks in it, and they all look like flecks of metal. My spud? It's a nineteen-gauge needle. They work really pretty well. Sure would help to have an appropriate magnifying loupe, though.

Then, back to the plane, and off and away at 7,000 feet across the Cassuarina forest towards the Alice. The weather is beautiful.

Mark turns on the heater for the folks in the back. It's a bit hot
for me, but they like it warm, so. And before long, we're descending, and watching the new areas just west of the airport
and the Spyce Byce where they're planting more of the desert to
grass. Some of the areas are circular, about a quarter of a mile in
diameter, but not as big as the circles that we see in the western
United States.

Mark touches down easily, and we roll out and to the tarmac
at the Royal Flying Doctors' hangar. It's a fun way to spend a
Thursday.

Oh, yes. There was a sad note in the clinic that I didn't
mention. I saw a little old blind lady who had been seen back
in 1966 and again in 1973 by the doctor. Both times she was
judged to have a cataract that would be too dense to do anything
about. Why that decision was made, I don't know, but anyway,
there it is; a big, dense cataract in the right eye. The left eye is
atrophic; maybe injured or destroyed by trachoma. The See International organization, funded by the Lions International,
hasn't been around in almost two years to see these people. They
had a program going on with the school children on trachoma,
but no one has been around to follow up.

Pompey Harding was one of the aboriginals that I had seen
way back in June with what I thought was a possible acute glaucoma. They had assured me that he would be seen that same
month by the "See" people, but it seems that the doctor who has
been appointed by the aboriginal council to take care of such
programs had informed the doctors down in Adelaide, that the
airstrips weren't safe, and that the mountains were often shrouded
in fog, and that he'd advise that they didn't come, and so they
didn't. I saw poor old Pompey today. He's apparently developed
a fistula in the anterior chamber of that eye. It's collapsed, and
Pompey says the pain is now gone, but he can't see. What a
shame. I think I'll talk with Doug Richey about this.

3 September 1981

It's a brilliantly beautiful morning again. Lots of early morning sunshine, but still quite nippy around the edges. Almost no clouds, except for a few little cirrus wisps toward the south. John Everett is out on the tarmac, has checked out the plane, and is quite upset with Mark, who had used the Graham Pitt yesterday. Seems Mark came back from that trip and left the plane empty of petrol, low on oil, and just generally dirty. John accuses him of having left the plane because he had a date with his sweety.

Sister Carol comes to Mark's defense, though. Seems that she was with him yesterday. They'd flown down to Curtin Springs on the Ayer's Rock road to assist with the evacuation of a family that had a terrible misfortune. On the dusty road, they pulled out in their compact to pass a road train, and in the dust and sun, they didn't see one coming head on. The impact demolished the car and killed the husband outright. Sister Carol said that the little boy was dying when they got there. I think it was Dr. Eisman that went out with the plane. They got an IV into the little fellow, but he died on the ground there. Two daughters aged about eleven to fourteen were injured, too. One had both arms broken, and sister Carol said the one was compounded and sticking out at a gross angle. The mother had some broken ribs, but seemed to be in better condition than the others. Carol said that it was after 2000 hours when they arrived back in the Alice. John still grumbled, but not with the same vehemence.

"Runway one-two, cleared for take off, right turn, 204 radial, report 6,000 feet west of the Stuart Highway," said the ATC (air traffic controller) in the tower. The Navajo lifts off easily into the morning sun. There's more new planting of desert grass south of the airport. This is a type of grass that is good fodder for cattle, and will grow on the sparse soil and water afforded by local conditions. If the plantings are successful, they could transform the whole outback into a pampas like our own midwest cattle country. At 6,000 feet as we approach the Finke River and the James range of mountains, I see a curious yellow, round object framed against the blue of the mountain backdrop. It's moving slowly; it's a hot air balloon! There's another just west of it, sailing about a thousand feet over the mountains, and about three thousand feet below us. There's still another, spread over the desert floor in a little valley between the east-west directed chain of low mountains. I don't see a support vehicle or a road, even. I wonder out loud where they could have come from.

"There are tourist agencies who make trips like that available," John responds. "They fly along for a few hours each day, landing at night, and camping wherever they happen to be. Radio communication with the home base makes eventual pickup a sure thing. What a way to spend a week! The trips aren't unreasonably priced, either. Like, maybe a thousand dollars for ten days."

Past Ernabella strip. Sister Carol says that poor little Thelma, the girl with the TB-disastered lungs, died. She's the one that I mentioned on July 9 that I'd seen at Ernabella with the classic clubbing of the fingers and such. She'd had part of a lung (most of it, I guess) removed some years ago. Poor little thing. We gaze down at Ernabella, and include her in our little prayer for Ronald of the leukemia fate. In a fortnight we'll be back to Ernabella and see where they've buried Thelma. Not next to the church with Ronald, I'll wager.

Fregon is glinting in the sun. From up here it looks so peaceful, and one can't see the dirt and mess and trash; just a little village nestled beside the gums of a dry billabong. The bore is on the east side with the windmill, and an incongruous concrete basketball court on the west side of town; probably some politician's idea of a community athletic center, I suppose. There's no wind at all. The sock hangs limply from the mast beside the runway. It's a little chilly here, too, and the sun feels good.

Sister Julie Dorn picks us up. She's a little intimidated by the power of sister Carol, and reflects it in a rather deprecating attitude of apology for things that wouldn't be her responsibility anyway. Sister Audrey and Les and the boys have left for the Queensland coast. Laura said that she had seen them at "Woolies" (Woolworth store) earlier this week in the Alice when they were on their way. The new sister that will be junior to Julie is named Denise Smith. I didn't learn much about her background, but will next time. She was properly quiet and seems like she'll be a good sister. She's rather young, but not as young as Ann at Indulkana.

Clinic is the usual. Joe Peters, the diabetic, who is supposed to be taking sixteen units of "isophane" (insulin) daily, has just been up to the hospital in the Alice for evaluation. I don't think he's taking it. The urine is now 1 + sugar, 2 + protein, and moderate ketone. He's lost the left kidney some years ago. We draw a sugar which is later reported as 26.2 mmol/liter. (That's pretty high!) Nyukana, the mother of Angkuna, has just returned from Alice hospital, too. She was hospitalized for a terribly sore throat and fever of forty degrees Celcius. I find out later that her diagnosis was measles. She's about thirty years old. No notes came back with her from the hospital. Then after a few runny ears, we see Christine, who is six months old, and her BCG vaccination is still draining pus. We take a culture.

Murray Minkolu is a tjilpi warrior who professes to have a cough; wants cough medicine—probably for the forty percent alcohol, not for what else is in the liquid. We don't give him his own bottle. He'll have to come to the sister each time he wants a spoonful. And so the clinic drags on.

Then it's time for a bit of tea at Julie's house. She has a pair of "kidochi" boots. These are special shoes or moccasins made by the witch doctor for the purpose of concealing the identity of an assassin. Really! If someone is marked for "the bone," the "spirit" will come in the kidochi fcct and destroy him; actually remove him to dreamtime. The boots are woven of human hair; kind of a macrame thing, and then little double-shafted emu feathers are sewn onto the hair. The idea is that the footprints left by the spirit will have no definition. The shoes themselves are round; almost look like a beret, and aren't even of the same size. The sad part of it all is that women aren't even supposed to see such things (where are you, ERA!), and here some repository of the secrets of the culture is selling these things to a female. Julie says they cost $20 each.

It's time to say farewell again. The Navajo rises easily off the strip and there's the reassuring "thump" of the gear nestling into its well and closing its doors. The rate of climb indicates 2,000 feet a minute. At 9,000 feet we go on autopilot, and soon John's head nods. I watch contentedly as the Patterson's curse on the ground moves slowly backwards, and then the fuel gauges catch my attention. We're on the auxiliary tanks, and they're both red-lining. At eleven gallons an hour flow rate indicated on the panel, it won't be long until we're going to skip a beat. I wonder how John will respond to that? Needn't have wondered. John suddenly comes awake without a miss in the engines, and just reaches down and switches back onto main tanks like he was programmed by a higher source, and promptly nods off again. At fifty miles DME he again comes alive like something had intervened, and reports our position to Alice control. We start our descent. A smooth touchdown, and another day with the RFDS is over.

Oh, yes, almost forgot to tell you. Millie Harding's boyfriend didn't front up on this trip. Either no spear wound to treat, or he's fled, and that will only make it worse. I'll be bound to see him one way or another sooner or later. Remember? He was the guy who beat up the fiancee who had gone with family to a barbecue while at the "corroboree" (show) at Yundamu. Of course, I didn't ask anyone at Fregon what happened to him, nor did anyone volunteer the information. We'll just keep our ears open.

10 September 1981

I thought I was being a bit cagey this time when sister Carol rang and said we were off for Indulkana, but would stop at Granite Downs first and take the blood pressure on Marg Baxter. I said, "Oh, Marg has extended an invitation to Laura to come down to the station some time when we were out that way."

Sister Carol said, "Oh?" And that was that. No chance for Laura to go on this trip. I found out later that we were really supposed to be taking "Crazy Martha" back with us, but Carol forgot her, and it wasn't until we landed at Granite Downs that she remembered. We'll keep trying. Carol can't hurt my feelings.

When we arrive at the Alice airport, the Graham Pitt is all set to go, and it is just the three of us: Carol, me and nervous Darryl. Gee, he really is picky. You can almost hear his brain clicking as he goes through his prestart check list, and everything has to be touched as he does it. The glass faces on all the instruments get a finger print and a "hmm," and even the handle to set the parking brake gets three or four tugs. But eventually everything is in the green, and we move to one-two for takeoff. Almost straight south for the course to intercept Granite Downs. We're at 6,500 feet. I'm getting to know my way pretty well. This time we're just a tad west of Chamber's Pillar, so it passes on the port side, and I don't get a good look at it. I suppose I could have asked Darryl if he'd move it over, but it really wasn't necessary. When John or Mark is along one of the times we go down that way, I'm going to ask them to descend, and maybe we can get a flyby picture. That would be pretty dramatic.

Darryl does manage to hit the strip right on the head. That's pretty good dead reckoning navigation. The station is about three miles west of the strip, and that's about 150 miles over trackless desert. Marg and a new girl, I think she's the school marm but I missed her name, are waiting in the $300 minimoke, a stripped down vehicle that has been declared illegal in the United States. So, you won't see one of them there, but Marg bought it in Kulgera when a fossicker (prospector) needed a grubstake. All he had was his vehicle. Marg's blood pressure is 158/98, so we increased her propranolol to 60 mgm b.i.d., and we'll see where it goes from there.

Then off the roller coaster strip into the air, and Darryl climbs to a sensible altitude of about 1,500 feet on the quick trip to the strip at Indulkana. Strange, the wind is from the west here, and it was from the east at Granite. Sister Vivianne meets us with the vehicle. She's sure a young thing. The clinic is packed. Mimili and Indulkana; everyone is here, she tells us. And it seems to be true. Also, all the Europeans from the railroad siding at Chandler are here. All in all, it's going to be a thirty-two patient clinic. But I didn't know that yet. Kym Borke, ten months with nodes, but I can't find them. Then Tanya, his Mom, young English, I think, and scared to death, says she's having a period with clots. We draw an FBC (full blood count). Next is Raymond Martin with a fever convulsions. He's fine, but Mom's a mess of nerves. She's pg at 22/52 gestation, and has an inferior vena cava syndrome.

Lorraine Parkinson, a kid with infected pierced ears is next;

Rhonda Manapol with a cold, and son Adrian who is also chesty. Newborn Karen is okay, but Rodney Foster has a hiatus hernia. John Shannon has a sore big toe, but there's no x-ray available. How about seven-year-old Linda who is paraplegic? Kaylene Mange is antenatal with fetal heart at 172/minute. Maurene is antenatal and okay. Bill is Kadaitchi Wangapi, born 1907 more or less, and has a blood pressure of 142/80. He's dribbling urine, and having a hard time with it. He also has pain in the back. Maybe a prostatic carcinoma? How do you tell an aboriginal you want to feel his prostrate by putting your finger in his rectum? Even if you have an interpreter? So, before I do that, I ask him if he would be willing to go to Alice Springs to have his problem fixed at the Hospital?

"No." He doesn't "ninti" (to know) Alice Springs. So, he won't go; what's the use of doing a rectal? I ask sister Vivianne if she has a catheter.

She says she does, so we'll just leave old Bill at that. It feels a bit like I've done something immoral; leaving him to get worse with possible skeletal metastases of cancer of the prostate. But I don't know how else to solve the problem. Then Rebecca with bilateral ureteral implants. She's about two-and-a-half years old. She really seems okay. How about Nellie with the fits? She doesn't take her medicine. I guess it's okay to treat the fits with 10 mgm of Valium to keep her off the sister's back. Did you know that "compo" means to urinate in Pitjantjatjara? I didn't either. But that's what it is. It's a problem that Whiskey is having. We do get a specimen for culture and put him on Bactrim; two tabs twice a day, but he won't take it.

Did you know that "ippi" is Pitjantjatjara for breast milk? I didn't either, but I do now. I'm getting educated! James, born 20 August 1981, has thrush and a fever. We have to crush up a tablet of nystatin for him. Otherwise, Mom's teat is going to be purple from gentian violet. Molly has pneumonia, but she's getting better. Angelina is the possessor of a fever of forty degrees Celsius (about 104 degrees Fahrenheit), and she has a right lung that is nothing but a few squeaks and rasps. I'm sure she has pneumonia, too, but I'm not sure what the etiology is. She's a heavy thing, too; about 20 stone (280 pounds, or, in metric, 125 kg; you have to know them all, because someone is going to

inform you in one of the three measures). As I listen to Angelina's
chest, she's looking down on my head and gives a mighty cough
with lots of juice on the back of my head. I wonder what the
incubation period is for that pneumonia. We put her on Amoxil.

Lipsy is James' mother. We get a culture from her too for the
urinary tract infection. Kaylue has a wart (verruca) on the knuckle
joint on top of the right third finger. She needs it surgically
removed next time she's up Alice way. After a few more patients
here and there we get to sister Vivianne, and she breaks into
tears. She's got a temp of 38.6 degrees Celsius and is just miserable. Poor thing. Here she's been running the clinic, taking the
abuse from sister Carol and, I guess, me, and she's sick. Ahh, I'm
sorry! We take a throat culture and put her on Pen-V for ten
days . . . four times a day!

At tea time, sister Vivianne tells us that Tiger Whiskey (the
son of Whiskey, the patient just seen) was one of a group of half
a dozen kids who broke into her flat after coming out of a high
of petrol sniffing. She was pretty scared when they did it, but
she did manage to drive them off with words. She had precious
little else to fight them with. She's not very big. No use complaining to the authorities. They'd have the compassion for the
poor, abused, misused, disadvantaged aboriginals.

Sister Judy is the other young lady who attends to Indulkana's medical needs. She's new, the daughter of missionaries
from the United States to India. She was born in Madras. When
she hears that I am the doctor at Pine Gap she says, "I don't want
anything to do with that place. I joined my friends in Adelaide
in a demonstration against that place!"

"Why?" I ask.

She replies, "It's a bad place run by bad people."

"Gee," I say, "I think there are an awful lot of really neat
people who work there, and we really are trying to make the
Alice a better community by working with people, like I'm
doing."

Gradually she comes down off the soap box and puts away
her prejudices. She spent some time in the Tacoma, Washington
area; chubby, red hair in a long pigtail, and apparently has done
some work (or would like to do some work) in the Indian reservations at home. She's that kind of "dedicated."

As we arrive at the strip to leave, she says, "I guess people are really nice all over the world; it's governments that are bad." I guess I agree.

It's hot. The strip seems long enough to look at, but we use up eighty percent of it to get up to an indicated 100 M.P.H. It's also rough in the air. At 11,000 feet it is cooler, and nice, and I doze as Darryl fiddles with knobs. No chance of him doing like John last week. He taps the fuel gauges a dozen times between quarter and redline. But his landing is smooth. It's been a long day. I hasten off at ten minutes to five for the mail at the APO. Maybe a letter from son Randy? No; two copies of the Santa Barbara *News-Press*. Darned kids! Maybe Monday.

17 September 1981

Today was the day for animals! Mark showed up with Giles, his baby kangaroo. On the August 13, the little fellow's name was "Skippy," but Giles is a very famous Aussie explorer, and, no doubt, Mark felt the name more prestigious than something that might be confused with peanut butter. He really is a funny little animal (he's grown a lot since I first saw him) standing about two feet high, and "pogo sticking" himself around the Graham Pitt and then slowing down to that peculiar "poling" action, as he plants his tail at a right angle on the ground, and lifts both hind feet at the same time; kind of "poling" himself along, like a man in a dugout canoe would move along the mud bank of the Mississippi.

There was a recent article in the *Wall Street Journal* about this; some scientist had actually done studies on oxygen consumption of kangaroos both in the slow motion and in the hopping. Do you know that oxygen consumption drops dramatically when they stop the slow movement and get into the real hop? That forty kilometers an hour doesn't mean that they're jumping more times to the minute; it means more meters to the hop. Well, they still are kind of funny when they're little. Giles gets excited, tries to turn around quickly, and falls over like a drunk on his way to the restroom. He also does dumb things like hopping towards me standing at the front of the plane, and slamming into the wheel cover of the landing gear, making his little brown eyes blink. So much for kangaroos.

We had a Mom and her six-year-old child going back to Fregon today with us. First time I'd seen an aboriginal with a real load. She had apparently been buying clothing for herself and others at Fregon, for she had a big, pink, plastic garbage bag crammed full of new clothing; kind of looked like a *new day* Santa Claus pack, or someone with lots to contribute to St. Vincent DePaul.

The Southwest Airlines "Starlight" was just landing as we taxied out, and the tower asked us to wait for it to go by before lining up on one-two. Then, "Foxtrot Delta Quebec, clear for takeoff; 6,000 on 206 radial, right turn," and the engines roared, and we moved along as Mark advanced the throttles and the mixture and the prop pitch until all were up against the forward stops. Then he gave them an extra punch for good measure. The morning was crisp and clear with a little haze on the horizon. I'd brought along the binoculars this time to see if I could pick out things on the ground. It's enough to make you really believe in the Mark I human eyeball! Without the binoculars, the ground is stable, even if the plane is bouncing around a bit. With the binoculars, it's impossible to hold anything still! So much for the eight-by-forty binoculars from the air! So, I sit back and read the October issue of the *National Geographic* that had just arrived. What a story about Columbia, the space shuttle!

Then we're looking for the mailplane; it's also going into Ernabella, and is just a few minutes ahead of us. It's a Cessna Centurion. Again I use the binoculars, but don't see it. It's not on the ground on the strip ahead, anyway. So, we make a straight-in against a rather brisk crosswind. Mark does a good job, and we taxi back to the parking area. The desert is absolutely beautiful. Small acacia bushes about ten feet high, brilliant yellow, with wild hops adding their crimson stroke of paint to the dusty to bright green foliage of this sparse forest. The red mountains in the foreground fading to purple mauve in the background for contrast. Birds all over the place! Some of the hawks are surfing on the thermals rising from the gravel strip.

Sister Julie meets us. Sister Ann is leaving for Indulkana today. Sister Penny is the new one at the settlement, and her husband, who is an ambulance officer in Melbourne, is also here. I don't know how long they'll be assigned here. Julie has the clinic well organized. First there's a Christabel Mintaya, with multiple complaints, but nothing found. I think she just wanted to look at the tjilpi doctor. Hey, next is good old Ivy. Remember her? She smiles her toothless smile, clucks approvingly at me, as she lays her gnarled hand on my shoulder and looks into my eyes, the white reflection of her cataracts looking back at me. Poor old thing! Now she's going blind! She's taking tolbutamide (oral diabetes medicine), one gram each morning and at night, but she's still showing sugar in her urine. She's been found sucking on the leaves of gum trees that exude a sugar-like sap. I'll have to get the name of that leaf next time I'm out. I missed it this time in my apprehension about her eyes. I don't know just what course to follow with this. She's delighted that I look at her eyes, but I don't think she really wants anything done with them—yet.

Next is our FLK (funny look kid) baby with the maxillary dysplasia, Clara. Sister Carol had invited me to start taking pictures now to go with the journal, since I'd been here a year already, and most everyone on the council knows me and trusts me. "Gee, I'd sure like to have a picture of this child," I said to Carol.

"I'll ask the council," she replied. Soon she came back, "They say no, they already have pictures of the baby."

I think Clara needs assessment at the CDC (Child Development Centre) in the Alice. We'll work on that. Next is Wendy, who has been fainting. She's European; she thinks she's anemic. We draw a blood sample. We'll let her know. Then Nancy, a post measles with fever. And then Louis with the big, old, full, gray beard. He's in early congestive heart failure. He's been taking 120 mg a day of Lasix, a potent diuretic, but still he has pitting edema and basal rales in his lungs, but no gallop. We'd better give him digitalis. They don't have any at the clinic. I'm told. Well, we'll order some.

Ten-year-old Lexie has burns on her legs. Regular pattern, ascending, from just anterior and above the medial malleolus (ankle bone) about every ten centimeters to the knee. Both legs are involved. She's done them for "scars," I'm told. They're self-inflicted, not by the family, and have cosmetic rather than tribal significance. We'll treat them with peroxide and bacitracin. Derek is eighteen months old and chesty. He's teething. His lungs are clear, so there's no treatment. Tjulyata is the young thing we couldn't be sure was pregnant last time. Well, she sure is this time! Weighs 42 kg, about 17/52 weeks, and 110/70. She's happy. I don't hear a fetal heart yet, but I have a rather noisy room.

Baby Jennifer is five months old, doing fine, and cute as a picture, with big black eyes, and little puffed out cheeks of fat that make you want to just take her and hug her. What a beautiful baby! She's plump and contented and happy, and doesn't even have an ear infection—yet! Next is Punki, with belly pain radiating into her right hip, and the side of her leg. She has a urinary tract infection. I don't know why her right hip is hurting; probably because she's carrying her three-year-old child on it. She's not too happy with the treatment of the infection. She's pretty heavy, too. I have to laugh to myself. Punki is wearing a great big steel diver's watch, complete with bezel. What on earth she'd ever want with that! I'm sure she can't tell time.

Next is Kinti. He's about forty-five or so, I'd guess. He has a terrible burn on the inside of his left knee, going around to the popliteal space, and measuring about fifteen-by-fifteen centimeters in size. The girls say they work hard to keep it clean during the week when he fronts up at the clinic, but during the weekends he goes walkabout, and when he returns on Monday the thing is a stinking mess. It has nice, bright granulation tissue there today. I think we'd better take him back with us and see if Dr. Charley or Dr. Parke or Dr. Reed can't put a graft on there, and keep him walkabout. Next is Matthew Webb of the tonsil-stitch fame. But now he has burns on his hands and feet where he fell into the fire. He's coming okay. His brother has a contact rash on his legs. Then there's Brian, who wanted the pension last time. I look him over again. Gee, he's really healthy! I prescribe some multivitamins for him. Now he's happy!

And so the clinic goes. It's time to leave after tea. We go by to pick up Kinti. There he is lying in the dust at the base of the chain link fence snoozing. On the blanket, in the dirt beside him, is a twenty-two or twenty-three-year-old girl, with brilliant white teeth, so rare in this culture, and nursing, or trying to nurse, Clara! So, Clara is old Kinti's daughter by this child bride! What you don't learn out here!

The plane is loaded up; we run to the south end of the strip to take off down the open end of the valley. As we lift off and the gear "klunks" into place, we see dead ahead, a surfing hawk. Fascinated, I watch. He is lower than us, but just a tad! I get ready to duck just in case he finds the thermal at the last minute and comes through the windscreen but he doesn't. We're away into the clear sky to 11,000 feet. It's rough even up here, with "willy-willys" (whirlwinds) all over the desert below.

That reminds me; just as we were loading the clinic boxes into the plane on the strip, I had the adventure of being in the center of one of those whirlwinds. I was picking up two metal cases of files, when I heard this sound like a truck approaching. I didn't look up, because I thought it was just pulling into the strip area, and then I was pushed forward, and then backward, and dropped the boxes and grabbed my hat and held on as the truck went through me! I'd been right in the middle of one of those. I can appreciate the descriptions of folks listening to tornadoes when they say it sounds like a freight train coming through. Even a little one makes noise like that.

The trip back to the Alice was bumpy. I dozed. Mark read my *National Geographic*. Giles dozed in his sack hanging on the edge of the stretcher. Kinti looked at the horizon, lost in his own thoughts, and sister Carol snoozed. Then we land again at the Alice. Another day. What an adventure every day is! I do feel useful to these people.

22–23 September 1981

Well, the trip to Ayer's Rock was supposed to have been for a holiday. We had planned that the weekend of the nineteenth and twentieth was to start the thing, and then we'd have the rented Toyota Land-Cruiser for Monday, Tuesday and Wednesday, and turn it in on Thursday morning just before leaving on the Flying Doctors' trip to Amata. Well, it didn't work out quite that way because an eight-year-old boy by the name of Johnnie Barrett disobeyed his mommy and daddy and decided to ride his bike to the opening day of the swimming pool, against their orders. He collided with a Porsche when he disobeyed a traffic sign, and had a serious concussion, laceration of the forehead, a big gouge taken out of his abdominal wall, and a rather serious mouth injury with both his brand new upper incisors loosened and chipped. Dr. Reed and I put him back together in about two-and-a-half hours in what is called "theatre," including burr holes around the skull fracture that extended in semicircular fashion from his nose over the right frontal area and into the superior ridge of the right orbit. We just put in one burr hole; there wasn't any blood beneath, and the cerebrospinal fluid was crystal clear. I still didn't think we should leave town until Johnnie came to, which he did on Monday.

I did pick up the vehicle on Monday afternoon, so on Tuesday we were all ready, and piled in for the long drive about 0800 hours. Rounds first at the hospital to make sure that Johnnie is okay, and then back home to pick up the hamburger for dinner that night, and off we go! Just past the Finke River we turn off for the quick little jump over to the Henbury meteorite craters. It was probably something to see when it happened, but now there are five or six holes in the ground that look as if a bulldozer could have made them in a couple of hours. It was fun to think about how it must have looked to the aboriginals when the things came down. I wonder if it happened at night?

On to Ayer's Rock. The bitumen road ends about thirty-five kilometers short of Curtin Springs, and altogether there's about 130 kilometers of dirt road that's just awful! It's washboardy, and at eighty kilometers per hour one just skims the top of it all, and it isn't too bad. Mt. Connor is beautiful in the haze. The desert is really alive with color of things blooming. The yellow acacias (wattles, they call them here) are all in bloom, and then the patches of red wild hops. There are trees that look like cedars, and some that look like ferns, and the bull dust is red as blood! And thick! The wind is blowing from the north, and at times it looks like snow used to look swirling across the roads of North Dakota, only this is red, and it's hot outside, and the Toyota isn't air conditioned. The last thirty kilometers is terrible. They're building new roads, and the big trucks are using the tourist road for transport of dirt from the borrow pit to the new road.

We pass two young men on motorcycles who have slowed to about ten kilometers because they don't dare go the eighty kilometers per hour to stay on top of the washboard. That must be a hell of a ride! Finally we arrive. The lady ranger gives us all the information about camping and tours and such, and we pay our four dollars: three dollars for two entries into the park, and one dollar for camping for one night. We do have camping gear that we brought from the base. Did I tell you that we rent the vehicle from the base? One dollar a day. That's right! One dollar a day, and eleven cents a kilometer, and they supply the petrol! It's in lieu of an officer's club, I've been told. They have to have some sort of a recreational plan for the troops.

What with the dust and the noise of the trucks going by, though, we just go straight on through and out to the Olgas. We drive around to the north side, and into the valley of the winds. We park the vehicle, and unload the lounge chairs from our own yard, and relax and just watch the scenery, and the other tourists, and pass the afternoon in the shadows of these unusual moun- tains. Tourists come and go, and occasionally, the wind will sigh in the distance; sounds as though it's an approaching tangible substance, and then the tops of the trees in the distance will be seen to move, and gradually, the advancing breeze will move towards us; then pass us with a refreshing bath of fresh air. Finally, the sun descends behind the mountains to the west of the basin that we're in, and we pick up some brush, and leave for the campground at the Rock. A quick stop to pick up some more wood for the campfire at the Rock produces a scratch from the "mulga" wood on my right arm. I've heard the aboriginal rumor that a scratch from such a wood will produce a hundred years sleep. Gee, I'd enjoy that, but I really don't have time.

At the campground we decide on the upper camp, now "dingo-proofed" with a $15,000 fence and a grated gate; the locking of the barn door, so to speak, after the loss of Azaria Chamberlain, the 10-month-old baby who was reportedly taken by a dingo from this same camp a year ago. We park our vehicle beside the camp table and fireplace, but we don't pitch the tent. The wind is coming up, and we might just opt to sleep in the vehicle. Our camp neighbors are a young family from Blackwater, Queensland, who are on a real outing. They have an eight-year-old boy who is total enthusiasm, and quite friendly. The fire gets underway with absolutely no trouble. This mulga may be cursed, but it sure burns swell!

Sunset at the Rock is beautiful as usual, and we even play a game of gin rummy while waiting for the beans to cook and the hamburgers to fry. We have a neat salad, and a couple of vodka tonics before dinner is served. Delicious! There's a hamburger left over. It's put into a nested aluminum bowl with top and left sitting on the table, along with the lantern, the "esky" (portable icebox) and dinner tools. We spread out the sleeping bags in the front and back seat of the Toyota and snuggle down for the night. The wind blows a gale! About 0230 hours the vehicle is rocking, and a look outside reveals that the bathroom/shower building is barely visible in the blowing dust, although it's only about a hundred feet away! The neighbor's tent is holding up pretty well. I'm glad we're not in a tent.

And then comes the dawn. Beautiful! The wind is still blowing, but not as badly. The container with the hamburger is gone! And there are dog tracks at the table. A cursory survey reveals the container sans the hamburger. So much for the dingo-proof fence. Although, I'm sure this wasn't a dingo's work. It was probably merely an ordinary camp dog.

Breakfast is a little fruit, and we drive over to the beginning of the trail ascending Ayer's Rock. It's awfully windy. We hit the rock, and a ranger tells us that it's too windy, and that they are going to close the trail. We continue on. There are 133 metal posts that are anchored into the ground, about thirty feet apart, with chain between them so that people will be less inclined to fall off that rock. So far, I've heard that twelve have died of heart attacks climbing the mountain, while only four have fallen. I don't know what the time span is for all these accidents. At the end of the chain is a depression in the rock that gives room for a breather. You'd think that there'd be some place in that depression where one could get away from the wind. Not so! The wind is all over that rock. We wait about half an hour for the wind to subside, but it doesn't. We're back to the same problem that we had last December when we were forced to give up the climb because of the wind. We opt to go on. Up the wall, and onto the trail, with our noses close to the little white lines that mark the path, and not looking right or left, because there's a mighty drop-off going either way. Hands and toes clinging against the gusting wind. It's still a good half mile from the end of the chain to the top of the mountain, although the real climbing part is at the beginning. At times the wind is so strong that one just leans against it.

I have on my nylon windbreaker, and the sleeves are vibrating in the wind so vigorously that they make a humming sound. We finally reach the summit. Anticlimactic, after all the wind and effort. There's a young man up there from West Australia who snaps our picture with our camera, and we reciprocate with his camera. We look around. It's too hazy with dust for much of a good view. We sign the book that's hidden under the bronze plaque that tells you where you are, and then we head down, again following the little white lines on the rock. It's been a long hike, two and a half hours, but we have the feeling of elation that goes with reaching a goal. Just like I knew it would, the wind abates now that we've succeeded. On the way down we pass a young man sans shirt on the way up. Before we get down all the way, he's passed us going down, and as we approach the bottom of the rock, he is on his way up again. He's the driver of one of the tourist buses, and before we've even polished off our beer reward for our difficult venture, he's back down again, and ready to load up his bunch of weary passengers who have, with various degrees of success, done what we did, or partly.

Back to the campground. We pick up Laura's shirt that she left in the bathroom, and head back over the long road to home—1,077 kilometers all together! That was a fun trip.

24 September 1981

Next morning I drive the vehicle out to the base, turn it in, and drive my little Falcon company car to the airport and meet with sister Carol and nervous Darryl, who will be our pilot. The brand new Navajo, to be unveiled on the twenty-fifth, is standing there. It will be called the John Hawkins, named after a young surgeon at the Alice Springs Hospital, who died at age forty-five. That's another story, but I guess it was a heart attack that took him. Anyway, Mr. Paul Everingham, chief minister for the Northern Territory, will do the official unveiling of the plane, and I have an invitation! The designators on the plane are Foxtrot Mike Lima. We have clearance from the tower for runway one-two, the 222 radial at 6,000 feet. Poor old Murry Burton is coming home with us to die. Remember? About a month ago Murray rode back to the Alice with us for congestive failure and chronic pulmonary disease. He's lost his pension during that time because no one reported to the computer in South Australia that he was in the hospital, so they have no note that he's still disabled. He sure is, though. He needs supplemental oxygen, even though we cruise at 6,000 feet.

We cross the highway to Ayer's Rock right at the Wallera Road junction, where the bitumen stops, and that horrible washboard road begins, and in forty-five minutes, we've covered what took us 5 hours to do in the vehicle. It's gusting at Amata, and Darryl makes a long sweep for his approach. On take off from the Alice, it was fun to watch Darryl make sweeps with his fingers over the various instruments on his continuous nitpicking check and recheck. I wondered how long it would take him to notice that the flaps were still in take-off position. About the fifth time across the panel, he noticed, and up came the flaps. That's Darryl's way. He did make a nice landing at Amata in a gusting crosswind, though.

Sister Chris meets us. Jessie is away, I guess. The new sister is Colleen, and she's going to be there a few weeks, and then go over to Indulkana. I guess the American sister over there, Judy, isn't particularly appreciated. She's involved with too many "negative causes," and is trying to change the world for the better all at once. Colleen will take her place, and poor Judy will be sent somewhere else where she will adapt a tad better.

The clinic is full. First we see Lorna, 39/52 weeks antenatal with previous C-section, so we'd better take her in with us in the plane. Her daughter, Sara, will also come with us. Sara is about three, wearing a brown knitted stocking cap to cover a weeping mass of secondarily infected allergic dermatitis, weeping over her entire scalp and down her neck and onto her back. She's got it bloody to boot by scratching it all the time. When Lorna brings her in for medication, the girls can get it almost cleared up, and then she goes with Mom walkabout, and when she comes back, it's awful again. I think this is a good time to take her with us. While Mom's in labor, Sara can be cleared up. Next is Nita.

Remember the last time when I told you about the young thing with the venereal warts whom I couldn't examine? I had to leave the room, and I think it was sister Ray who checked her out? Well, they're worse, and I've just got to look and decide what we're going to do about it. So, I glove both hands, and look at this poor little thing, maybe about fifteen years old, scared to death. The warts are fungating; infected, bloody condyloma accuminata, rising in the labia, and extending all the way into the anus. She can't even have a bowel movement without tearing them. There are also huge inguinal nodes. She has to have these seen by Dr. Cahill, the woman gynecologist in the Alice, and treated. Nita's Mom is Ruby, and Ruby says, "No!" Ruby has her own complaint. She has a cough and a pain in her right side. I can't find anything wrong with her. She's just putting me on, and poor little Nita off. Nita doesn't go.

"She doesn't have a dress," is the final excuse that Ruby uses.

Kalkula, Yarsitti and Kay are the next three that are antenatal; all doing well. Then two-and-a-half-year-old Leigh, with worms. Norah is pregnant at 16/52; and then Pita Halpin, whose tribal name is Yaritzi, and whose father's name is David Younger, and whose Mom is sister Chris. Pita has measles. She still looks like a cretin to me. She was born 30 September 1980. Nothing to do. Mom put her on penicillin the other day. No indication for it, but she's on it so she might as well continue for a seven-day course. Then Denine Harbinger, a European. She'd seen Dr. Hardesty in Adelaide and been treated for venereal warts. She's afraid they're coming back. She's pretty tender down there. It's just scars that hurt; the warts have been cleared up. She's not married.

Do you remember Ankona? She was seen by me way back on January 15 when she and her husband, David, were planning a trip to Darwin by bus. We thought she might have rheumatic fever. I had been talking to them in simple English, and they both turned out to be exceptionally fluent in English with a classic accent? Well, she's back, and I had to decide if we want to continue her on prophylactic Bicillin injections for rheumatic fever. She did have it! There's no murmur. I opt to discontinue the shots. They're not getting them that regularly, anyway. She doesn't talk to me at all this time. I even tease her about not talking to me. But she won't say a word. She pretends she doesn't understand English. What a world!

Nellie Nyana has lost her eye to glaucoma. Sister Chris said that the poor thing had been complaining about an eye being sore, and Chris had irrigated it with a little saline and suddenly the lens dropped right into the irrigation bowl. And that was that! The whole vitreous just came oozing out into the dish, and Nellie had eviscerated her eye. Another one that the "See International" was following, when they had clinics out here. That's two that I've seen do that now; she and Pompey Harding. Doreen is a seven-year-old with burns healing on her feet.

Then we drag through a few more, and it's tea time, and we're ready to go home with Lorna and Sara. This time Sara is dressed with the stocking cap and a cute little jumper with a kangaroo stitched to the bottom right side. She's sure a cutie. Colleen drives us out to the airstrip. Darryl fidgets, and the plane roars into life, and we're off and away for home. Five thousand feet, and I'm doping off watching the things go by on the ground, and out of the corner of my eye, I see this flash. I turn forward just in time to find myself eyeball to eyeball with a hawk, who's been surfing. He has his wings folded, diving! I cover my face with my arms! No thump or crash.

"What was that?" Darryl questions with surprise.

"Hawk," I say, with the blood returning to my face.

"Foxtrot Delta Quebec, report Alice control when 50 DME," says the radio.

Darryl fidgets some more, and we cruise on. He's taken off

the autopilot, and is really flying the machine, and we have the fullest tanks on line.

"Foxtrot Delta Quebec, please report DME," says the radio.

Oops! We're at 45 DME. Darryl in his picking had forgotten to let approach know where we were. That's not unusual. But the landing is great. Darryl sets her down with a squeak of tires, and we've done another day with the Royal Flying Doctors.

1 October 1981

I am two minutes late getting out to the airport this morning, but the sun is shining, and it is calm and crisp. Sister Carol has already rung up Laura to see where I am. Usually she's about ten minutes late or so, but today she happens to be on time. Isn't that always the way? There's the new Navajo, with John standing on the step of Foxtrot Mike Lima, the John Hawkins. Boy, that's a nice, new plane! But that's sister Ray standing beside John . . . and Dr. Wilson? That's right! They're taking the new plane to Hermannsburg mission and Areyonga, west of the Alice. So, we have Mr. Richard Warren as our pilot, and he's flying the Baron, Foxtrot Delta Echo, for us. It's sister Carol and I, and we're going to Fregon. That's okay, the Baron is a good, dependable plane. Carol says that all the docs want to fly on Thursday now because I fly on Thursday. She's upset about something today. She has a big picnic hamper with her with a towel across the top in proper fashion. It's runway three-zero for takeoff, and as we hold at the line for FML to go by, I take a picture of her retracting her gear. It's sure a pretty plane.

Our trip goes by rather rapidly. We have a good following wind; over the Ayer's Rock road about fifteen kilometers east of Mt. Ebenezer; past the settlement at Ernabella, and Richard hits Fregon right on the head. A pretty good crosswind, too.

Denise meets us. The clinic is pretty full, and we do have that baby with the spider in her ear. Spider in her ear? That's right. On Wednesday I had taken a call from sister Carol that there is a two-year-old baby with a spider in her ear. The sisters had tried to irrigate it out, but it won't budge.

"What tools would you like to have for extraction when you come down?"

"Well, I guess I'd like a fine ear forceps, and a head mirror for light, and a suction apparatus of some kind, and a very large, strong person to hold the head still."

So, here's Katrina, all ten wiggling, screaming, kilograms of unhappiness. The bug has been in there since September 24. No wonder she's mad! A quick peek in the ear confirms that the bug, at least, is quiet; dead, I presume—I hope! It's barely showing through the white, snotty, chronic discharge in the canal. I decide that I'd better use the suction and try to remove some of the exudate in the canal so I can see the bug better. I'll place the auroscope (otoscope) and try to thread a tiny catheter through it. Katrina will have absolutely nothing to do with this. What to do? They have some Valergen syrup (trimeprazine tartrate) similar to Phenergan. Let's give her two teaspoons and bring her back in about forty minutes. I find that Katrina was born in March of 1980; an eighteen-month-old tiger!

They bring in Tali-Tali's baby, Marelle; two months old and post measles, they say. I'm skeptical. She has some rales on the left, and decreased breath sounds in the left base. She's getting over a pneumonia. I have no idea of the etiology. I think Tali-Tali is an arrested TB. If she runs a fever again, we'll give her a third of a Bicillin. (That's the name they have for the combination that used to be like our Wycillin-600. It's a mixture of three types of penicillin.) Next is Joylene. We've seen her before. She's been vomiting, although she looks okay now. She's about three.

Then we see Karen who is twenty-eight weeks pregnant and doing fine. Amanyi has an abscess to the left of her umbilicus. We've seen her before, too, She's diabetic. She's not taking her Tolbutamide. We draw a blood sugar. Next Joe Peters. You've met him before, too. Affable. He's supposed to be on twenty-four units of isophane, but his sugar is 2+ in his urine, and 4+ protein. He's already lost his left kidney for infection. Amazing! His blood pressure is only 122/84. Then Carol, four years old and chesty with an elevated temperature. Eileen is in congestive heart failure; probably fifty years old or so. We'll use a little diuretic first. They do have digitalis if we need it. No use starting Eileen on it at this point. She'd never take it for more than a day or two anyway, and then go walkabout.

The tiger Katrina is back again, only now she's a pussy cat, sound asleep! We position her, start up the suction apparatus, and the pus comes up the cath and into the bottle. I withdraw the catheter, and there's a fly on the end of the cath! Yeah! I look back into the ear. There's a perforation in the tympanum almost as big as the end of the catheter. There's still pus down in there, and one leg of the little fly lying on top of it. But discretion screams at me! You came away with the problem, don't make it worse. The next suction down there could not only bring up the fly's leg, but all the middle ear ossicles, too. So, we release an increasingly restless baby, and Mommie carries her away. I'm sure we'll be seeing more of Katrina!

Back to the clinic. Nkana is back. She's the one we saw before who had been to the Alice with the terrible sore throat and high fever. We never diagnosed her, really. We check her over, then discover that she has itchy eyes. This complaint has nothing to do with her previous problem. She's all over that. We give her some anhistine-privine eye drops. Gary Silvers, Ann Bartell, Christine Larson and Christopher Beagle are all European settlement personnel who need drivers' licenses for the bus. We sign the forms.

Next is Mintji. She had a terrible auto accident a year ago with two fractures of the right femur. She's in for a pension, but when she came walking into the room she wasn't even limping. She has a scar in the lateral thigh, and apparently has some sort of internal fixation of the fracture. She really doesn't want a pension, but it's so much less trouble to just continue with it than to go through the paper work to stop it, that she's been sent in for my signature. I decline. Let the staff do the paperwork that's needed. Mintji leaves happy. She was a health worker in the clinic some time ago, and it was really embarrassing to her to be on pension when she knew she was well. Kunmanara had a seventeen-day period. She's supposed to have had a tubal ligation. She says that she went AWOL when she was up to the Alice for the surgery, and didn't have it. Well, if it was a spontaneous abortion, she's all over it now. No need to do anything.

The radio has told us that they'd like us to stop by Indulkana on the way home. But first we go to sister Julie's house for a cool drink. Oops! Stop first and see Tjanyinti for the fifth time consecutively for his right chest pain. He's okay. Likes the attention, I guess. At sister Julie's, sister Carol unwraps the picnic basket. She's got the meringue of a Pavlova in there, and the cake, and the whipped cream, and the strawberries! In no time we have a dessert fit for a king! The baked meringue is crusty, and the cake and whipped cream and strawberries go on top of the meringue. (That's what I like about Australia; everything is upside down!) Denise has cold chicken, tomatoes, cabbage salad, and a delicious combination of watermelon chunks with onion slices for a salad. What a feast! I go easy; a little piece of chicken, and try the watermelon/onion salad, and, of course, a piece of the Pavlova. These kids work hard out here, and it isn't easy to come up with these kind of goodies when you're three hundred miles from a proper store! It's a nice party!

Then Denise drives us to the strip. Richard fires up the Baron, and we're off at 1430 hours at 7,500 feet, and a heading of 95 degrees for Indulkana. There's Mimili down there to starboard, where the girl was beaten to death, and just east of that is the white tailings of the opal mines at Mintibi.

Then we're down at Indulkana. Sister Ann meets us. First there's Tiger, about eight months old, son of Arthur Walkabout. He's lost from 7,800 grams to 5,900 grams in the last four weeks. Arthur says it's teething, and refuses to allow us to take Tiger to the Alice. So much for that. I'll send down a little fasigyn and we'll de-worm him. He looks okay. Not dehydrated, either. I don't know what's wrong with the poor little guy. On the graph, his weight is sure taking a nose dive. The other child is Glenn, chesty with fever. Glenn's legs are horribly scarred from falling into the fire when he was about eighteen months old. He's about three now. There's a political problem here. Glenn is from Mimili, and his Mom has a couple other kids there that really need her. So, she can't take care of Glenn at Indulkana, and it's not fair to ask sister Ann to take care of him. She's leaving this next week for Europe, anyway. So, we'd better take Glenn with us. It's getting late, too, and no use to argue.

Glenn has a nasty burn on his right hand. "Malu," says Mom. Seems he was eating barbecue kangaroo last night and picked up a hot piece. But in a kid whose feet have both been reconstructed into walking stumps when his metatarsals were barbecued, he's not going to worry about a silly, little burn like that. Down to the Baron, and we're off. Glenn clutches a toy utility in the burned hand.

It's a nasty headwind, and almost two hours getting back to the Alice. Nice look at Chamber's pillar with the setting sun casting a mile long shadow to the east. Richard has a few idiosyncrasies as a pilot. He's not picky like Darryl, nor hot-shot like Mark. But he does use the gear instead of the flaps to slow the Baron down. One hundred sixty indicated, and down goes the gear with a roar! Then he makes a long, low approach. I don't know what would happen if one of the engines faltered on approach. He does that again coming into the Alice, and we touch down about four inches from the edge of the tarmac. Not time enough after we shut down to get to the APO to see if there's any mail, but I drop by anyway. It's locked. I get home to a neat welcome from a loving wife, and she's already picked up the mail. Tapes from both Randy and Raul! Yeah! It's a great life.

8 October 1981

Another beautiful sunrise this morning! Time to go to Granite Downs first and see Marg Baxter, and then over to Indulkana for the clinic. I wonder what happened to Tiger, the boy we left there last week when Arthur Walkabout wouldn't let him come back to the Alice with us? I wish there were more time to follow up on these patients after we bring them in to the hospital, but with all the duties of the base there just isn't available that sort of perk with this job. On arriving at the RFDS hangar, I find that we are indeed going to be flying in Foxtrot Mike Lima, the brand new Navajo, John Hawkins! Yeah! But what's this? The Northern

Territory flag decal is already peeling off the vertical stabilizer! Horrors! Must we trade it in already? It's going to be Chris Earl as our pilot. He's on charter; flies with Chart-Air, same as Barry that took us in the Cessna 310 that time. Chris is a young man, dressed with captain's bars on his white shirt, stubbies with knee sox, a really proper looking pilot.

Sister Carol has all kinds of parcels, even four liters of ice cream, and we pile all this stuff into the wing lockers, secure the doors and begin to taxi to runway one-two. The plane is a kind of pearl gray exterior with red and white stripes, and "ROYAL FLYING DOCTORS SERVICE OF AUSTRALIA, SA & NT" stenciled above the windows along the sides, and the big (peeling) decal of the NT flag on the tail. It looks fast even when it's sitting on the runway. The interior is done with knobby pile rust colored fabric on the seats, but with the seating part done with beige lambskin. The curtains are off-white with brown stripes vertically at the outer borders, kind of linen-looking material. Those up front in the cockpit are solid beige. There's a partition between the passenger compartment and the cockpit that is faced with wood paneling. There are two facing seats on the port side, and two stretchers on the starboard side. The forward stretcher is at floor level, and would serve for CPR or a delivery. The aft stretcher is elevated about half the height of the cabin. There's room aft of that for storage of the oxygen bottles, and between the facing seats is a small sink, but with no faucet. I guess it's kind of a self-draining emesis basin.

Up forward, the cockpit is beautiful. The engines are Lycoming T–10 540A series of 310 horse power each. The card says the MCV is 76 kias (that's "stall" at knots indicated air speed). Avionics is a Kr–87, JMA 20, two CODAN 2000 HF transceivers, two KX–175 BE's, a DME that registers miles/minutes in digital readings, a King 176A transponder, a KA 134 VHF FM, and even cupholders that swing out from under the panel, presumably to hold your champagne, for who could suffer plain coffee in such luxurious settings? Also on the panel above the ADF are two digital clocks; one starts with the starting of the engines, and the other with the retraction of the gear. Of course, there's also air-conditioning, and the new compass and artificial horizons and localizer/glide slope readouts have orange and yellow bars that make the whole thing look real as outside. It's lovely! I was busy looking at all this and didn't hear the tower clearance, but we're off and climbing at 1,200 feet per minute. Chris is a good pilot. Not fidgety, nor casual either. He's wearing his headset that looks like it could do justice to a real high-fi fan, so he doesn't hear well if I talk. He's looking at his sectional (map) with attentiveness that makes me wonder if he's flown this trip very often.

Sister Carol is making the seat aft reclining, puts her feet up on the other seat, and is quite comfortable as she reads her book. We level out at 9,500 feet. It's smooth and there's the Charlotte range already, and the Finke just behind. I don't think FML is any faster than good ol' FDQ. I take out my book, *Breaker Morant*, and begin chapter one.

There's the Kulgera strip off to starboard. Chris taps off the auto pilot. It really hasn't been on all that much. He likes to fly the machine, but I think he wanted to just work a little. It's a neat package. Not as messy looking as the one in FDQ. The fuel selection system isn't on the floor between the seats as in FDQ, either. It's on the forward side of the wing beam that separates the floor of the cockpit from the passenger compartment. Chris hits the "station" right on the button, makes a circle to the east, and drops the gear at appropriate air speed.

Marg and Douglas and Liz Fitch are waiting for us at the edge of the strip, with the $300 moke. Chris applies the brakes sparingly, so we have to taxi back the whole length of the runway. The ice cream is for Marg, I discover. Marg's blood pressure is holding, but we increase her propranalol by 40 mg. Liz has an abscess in her right axilla. We prescribe Amoxil. She'll come right! Laura receives another invitation from Marg to come down to the station anytime. She really means it! It's up to sister Carol to say when.

And then we're off easily from the country strip, and the short ride over to Indulkana, and the wind has shifted 180 degrees. We land to the west. Sister Vivianne is waiting for us. Sister Wendy from the health service is also there. Wendy has been going around giving BCG. Then, there's sister Judy with her long pigtails, and still dedicated to the negative causes of the world. Our first patient is Gilpin Ward, about fifty. He speaks excellent English when he forgets, and has a massively swollen right knee. Says he was chasing bullocks with a Landrover; "mustering" is their word, and when he jammed his foot down on the brake, he felt something snap in his knee, and now it's really tense with fluid in the knee. Blood? Hemarthrosis? I just don't dare aspirate it out here. He'd get an infection for sure. We'd better take him in. I don't think there's anything broken.

Then Kaylene at 56 kg, 35/52 with fetal heart at 152, and she has a VDRL of 1:4 (positive for syphilis). She's been getting her LPG (long acting penicillin G); probably doesn't need anymore. Then Judy's baby. Judy had a C-section her previous pregnancy, but went AWOL when sent in to the Alice and came back to the settlement, and had her baby on the floor of the dispensary. The baby is fine. Judy is fine. Then Linda with COPD (chronic obstructive pulmonary disease), Jamie who is chesty with pus in his eyes. I don't think it's trachoma. He's two years old. Pompey Pearson, who looks like cancer; lost two kilograms in two weeks and has sugar in his urine. He has a lot of arthritis in his large joints. We draw an FBC and a glucose, and recommend brufen for his joints.

Adele Starkman is the microcephalic that you've met before, a European from Chandler. She looks fine; ten months old now and walking, and she has three teeth now. Her head is 43.5 cm now; up from 41.6 on August. She's alert and really fine. Nillis is 85 kg, 37/52 and fetal heart is 132. She's fine. Cathy Martin from Chandler is 26/52. Her pain in the leg is gone now. Lying on her side helped. But she's gained 2.5 kg since last visit and is up to 64.5 now. The other baby of hers had a shot of penicillin a couple of weeks ago for "chest," and he has a lump in the lateral thigh now. I reassure her. Irene Flint, 83.5 kg, 30/52, FH 136. She's okay.

Ian Giddings fronts up with a purple heel. Thorn in it for five days; really painful, he says. It looks like a purple hole to me. He can soak it in soapy water for a while until the clinic is over, and I'll take another look when I can see something. Then the club hits me in the right flank. Involuntarily, I say, "Oh!," and my hand goes to my flank. I continue with the clinic. I've been having trouble with the stone in the pelvis of the right kidney now for almost two years.

Rhonda from Chandler says that six-year-old Danielle is having headaches. What an unhappy looking child. Rhonda is skinny as a rail (has a filthy mouth, too, says sister Vivianne). She verbally abuses the child constantly. That's the problem, I think. School is the only escape for Danielle. I check her over. She looks down at the elephant on her tee shirt without trouble. No nuchal rigidity there. Eye grounds okay, ENT okay. Too late to change Mommie. I guess we'll encourage Danielle to spend more time at school. Trevor Parkinson is European with a frontal headache. Sinusitis. Amoxil will fix it. The balloon builds in my right lower quadrant. I call it a balloon, because it gives the sensation of an almost unbearable fullness in the belly, as though there were a balloon there that someone keeps blowing larger and larger to the point of bursting.

Helen Sevanlab is a loud-mouthed European. She's the school teacher. Maybe Danielle really has no place to go! Helen has a script from her doctor down in Adelaide for griseofulvin, 500 mg. #28, TDS, it says. I write her a new one for the Northern Territory; for the micro crystals, 125 mg, and we'll give her one a day. She has a tinea circinata (fungus) on her neck. It's about six centimeters in diameter. She's been using Whitfield's ointment on it, and she's really burned the skin, but hasn't seemed to damp out the ringworm at all. We'll also script for some Daktarin (miconazole 2%) for the stores of the dispensary for such things. Better than Whitfield's ointment. The balloon is so big now that it feels like someone has kicked me in the groin, and the nausea begins.

Little Troy Nelson is aboriginal, about four, has a "blood nose" for the past week. Looking in there, it's a mess. All kinds of blood and pus there. I just know there's a foreign body up that left nostril, but there's no suction available. I try a cotton bud (Q-tip). Troy starts to cry and the nose starts to bleed. He'd better come up to the Alice tomorrow or soon on the bus. There's a daily bus. It's going to need Dr. H. to take that out of there.

Little Martin Tine comes in and has a pinpoint meatus on his penis at the end of his phimosis (tight foreskin). He sure needs a dorsal slit to open up the foreskin. I'd do it, but there's no sterile probe. I guess he'd better come up to the Alice for that, too. He's only about three months old. I wish we'd had the tools. It sure would save Mom a lot of hassle. Then Roy Wallatina, temp at 39.7! He's hot! Pharynx is injected, and he really looks sick. I suspect this is strep, but he's almost too black to see a rash. I'll give him Bicillin shots, times four, two days apart. We take a throat culture.

Then Ian is back, walking on the toes of his left foot. The purple is gone, and now with a little probing, one can see the tip of the foreign body. It's black; looks like mulga, the local name for the acacia wood that grows in the outback. Proper Betadine prep, and a #11 blade; What? No #11 blade? A #15 will have to do. We put in about a cc of one percent lidocaine. He's sure jumpy! A minute or two of conversation to let the anesthetic work, and to subdue the nausea in my stomach. A slit is made on either end of the point of entry, and the thorn fairly leaps out of the wound! It's a piece of mulga, all right—about an inch long and a quarter of an inch wide. He'll be happy that's out. We prescribe Amoxil, three times a day for five days anyway.

Over to sister Vivianne's, and they put me in the bedroom to lie down while they have tea. The pain in my groin won't go away. I'd stand on my head if it would help. It's been seven weeks since last I passed a stone. It does seem to ease up for a while, then the nausea returns. I don't want to mess up the room, so I have to make my way between the folks eating biscuits and tea, to the bathroom. Lots of retching, but my stomach is empty. The girls leave to get Gilpin into the plane. Then they return for me. I try to act nonchalant. Into the right seat; I really don't remember much about the farewells, and the beautiful, new plane roars to life. After getting everything on the instrument panel into the "green," Chris lifts her off, and we're on the way to 9,000 feet. I'm retching into the "burp bag." It's terribly bumpy. I can't find any position that's comfortable. I'd like to put my head down between my legs, but the control wheel is right there, and if we hit a bump, I'm going to knock my front teeth out. We'll have to correct the design of this front seat to allow proper space for vomiting. It's finally too much. I turn around and sister Carol is already there.

"You need to lie down," she says. Wendy is with us, too, I notice for the first time. Wendy takes my seat. Carol helps me to the aft stretcher. I lay myself prone, with my burp bag right in front of me. Carol places the straps so that I don't fall off the stretcher. My stomach is sore, my balloon is huge, and my flank hurts, and then the smokey smell and I open my eyes. The feet of Gilpin are right below me. He's not really very clean.

"What do they give you?" It's Carol; she's offering me pain medication.

"I can make it okay," I say, surprised at the strength and confidence of my own voice.

"We don't have any heroes in this organization," she reminds me.

"Really, I'll make it, Carol," and she leaves me be. It's a long ride.

"When we get in, I'll drive you home."

"Okay."

"Shall I ask them to ring your wife?"

"No, that's okay."

The plane bounces on. She's taken off my glasses, but I can see the Finke River bed going below us. We're thirty-five miles from home.

"I'm going to take you in your car to the hospital when we land, okay?"

"Yeah. Would you have them ring Laura and tell her to pick up the mail?"

The marker beacon goes "beep-ccp-eep" and then fades away, and Chris lands her pretty hot on runway one-two, and we taxi over to the hanger area, and he shuts down the John Hawkins. The ambulance rolls up.

"I'll get out first," I offer and crawl off the stretcher, and ease myself down the steps onto the tarmac.

"This way," says the ambulance officer.

"No, I'm the doctor; the patient is back there."

"No," sister Carol says, "You're to come with us." I can't even resist. I'm put into the ambulance.

"My glasses, and my camera, and my hat," I request, "and my book." The things are put in with me. Then Gilpen, in the stretcher on the other side, and the ride into the hospital begins.

"Do you have funds?" asks the ambulance officer.

"I'm employed by the government of the United States," I tell him.

"Oh, Pine Gap?"

"Yes." He takes my name and address, but doesn't say any more about a bill. At the hospital I walk in hunched over. The pain, the balloon and the nausea are at a peak. I'm laid on a gurney, then wheeled into another room, and rolled onto another gurney. Mrs. Glenn's familiar face appears.

"Oh, Doctor Rutten! It's really bad, isn't it?"

"Do you have my camera and my book and my hat and my glasses?"

"Yes, they're all here. Dr. Ashlett will be along soon, or else Dr. Carter. Ummm . . . Do you have $15, or shall we open an account?"

The Alice Springs Hospital is run efficiently and in a caring manner by the staff. After handing Mrs. Glenn $15, she had given me the Maxilon, buscopan and pethidine in separate shots in the right bumm. I agonized with the pain of the kidney stone for about fifteen minutes. In the meantime, Laura had been notified, and arrived to sit patiently in the chair by my gurney. In only a quarter of an hour, I could feel the pain dulling, and the warm feeling of well-being begin to take over. A drowsiness that is of similar quality to waking in the morning on a weekend and knowing that you don't have to go to work comes over one, and it would be so easy to close the eyes and drift off into good dreams. I've learned not to do this, though. I had Laura bring Mrs. Glenn.

"I'm feeling a lot better, Mrs. Glenn, and the pain is almost gone. I think I'll have Laura take me home, if that's all right with you."

"Oh, I'm so glad, Dr. Rutten. Wait until I talk with Dr. Ashlett to make sure it's right with him. I'll be back straight away."

Ten minutes later Mrs. Glenn returned. "Dr. Ashlett says for you to go home and try to stay quiet for the next couple of hours, and to let him know if there's any recurrence or any other symptoms or signs."

Laura drove me home, and I followed my doctor's orders to the letter. The pain did subside, and we had a nice supper, and then after playing one game of gin rummy and one of cribbage, I took my shower and went to bed. I made a promise to myself that when this tour of duty was over and I had my five years of overseas duty completed and my retirement assured, I'd submit to surgery and have this fixed once and forever.

15 October 1981

Yesterday sister Carol rang me at the Community Health Centre, and said that, although our clinic was to be at Ernabella this week, we were going to Indulkana first. Marg Baxter would be coming over there because she had a lot of anxiety about her throat.

"It's really quite sore, and she does smoke a lot, and doesn't want to quit," advised sister Carol. "Then there's another European gal from Chandler who has a terrible pain in her back that is requiring pethidine for relief, and they don't know what's the matter with her."

"Sister Carol, I'd like to have that head mirror that I had for the fly in the ear episode at Fregon, and also a dental mirror about 1.5 cm in diameter for the exam on Marg," I requested.

"Rightie-o, Doctor. Anything else?"

"No, that should do it, Carol. Thanks a lot."

Murray is warming up the FML as I arrive on a spectacular, beautiful morning. I'm happy that I have no balloon in my belly today. Last week was initiation enough for the plane. The plane really looks nice. I think for a moment about how neat it would be to have a tape of the sound of that airplane, but then, it would only be that much more hassle to put together. Murray shuts the engines down, and Carol arrives with sister Margaret, who is going out to Fregon; no, Mimili.

Both of them are carrying black babies; cutest little things. One was born in June; she's the smaller of the two, and has huge, black eyes, and a knowing look, and is happy and quiet. Not a peep. The other is larger but fussier; born in July, dressed in a little yellow dress that's new (it's clean). Murray taxies out reading his check list, and I'm a little nervous as he rolls from one side of the runway to the other, but he always looks up in time to correct the direction before we run off the side of the runway. It's one-two we're cleared for, but no wonder I didn't hear the clearance last week. There isn't a sound in the cockpit. It's all in those big ear muffs that Murray has on his head.

Then the throttles come slowly forward, and the acceleration pushes one back into the seat, and at eighty-two knots indicated, she rotates and we're off the ground. The gear makes an awful clunk when it seats into the wells, but I guess that's okay. The green lights go off; the amber comes on for a moment, and then fades. The clocks are running, and we make our right turn to 180 degrees heading. Murray is wearing white socks and brown shoes. He has a baseball type cap on, like I do. Murray has a bald spot on the cowlick, and a salt and pepper beard. An infectious grin shows a need in adolescence for orthodontia, but they are his own.

More about FML? There are 38 HF channels and 700 VHF. Both props swing counterclockwise. Murray says that there is a theoretical disadvantage to that, in that it torques the fuselage in the opposite direction, but it reduces the number of parts needed by half, and increases the spare parts by two, since the engines can be used on either wing. And "out bush," that's practical! Did I tell you that the KR–87 is the ADF times two? The KX–175 is the VHF times two, and the KT–76A is the transponder. The autopilot is made by King. It can couple onto the ILS (instrument landing system), or it can couple to the flight director (the gyro horizon) or any component separately, and the display for what is coupled is mounted right in front of the pilot. When anything changes, a warning beep lets you look and see what's happening.

Murray spends a lot of time looking at his sectional, but I notice that he has the plane headed right for the "surf" at Mintibi opal mines. The "surf" is the white tailings that come from the mines, and from a distance looks exactly like waves breaking on a distant sea shore. At the appropriate moment, he takes off the altitude hold, and we start down. Murray is a classic "old school pilot." The flaps slow us down; the gear comes down at an appropriate time, and he "leads" the runway with lots of altitude, and a rather steep glide slope.

Sister Vivianne is there, and she still doesn't look well. She's so young! She has two aboriginals with her, and another plump European lady, and, of course, Marg. We take Marg first. Sitting in the plane, I just can't get the head mirror to find the sun, so we get out, and standing behind the nacelle of the port engine, with Marg's back to the sun, I get things ready. She has a well-fitting upper denture that I don't ask her to remove. She really has a quick gag reflex. I find the sun with my head mirror and reflect its brilliance into Marg's throat. With her tongue sandwiched between layers of a cotton four-by-four and held between thumb and three fingers of my left hand, and the mirror held "just so" in my right hand, she says the "eeee" for about a fifth of a second before the "wauuchh" of the gag reflex, and I've removed the mirror and closed my eyes for the "instant replay" of what I saw in just that split second. The "eeee" will bring the vocal cords together tightly, and I don't recollect seeing any tumors or other lesions on them, and they did come together without any evidence of paralysis. Were they red? Let's look again.

Same procedure with the split second look, and, no, I don't think they are red, but they're not the ivory white that I'm used to looking at, either. Maybe they're stained with tobacco smoke. Let's take a third look. The instant replay says that the other two looks were the same, and I don't see any lesion; just a funny color, and they do come together. I think we'll let Dr. Geoff Hauptenhauser look at them next time Marg comes up to the Alice.

Then Susan Meier, and the history of the terrible pain. It's kind of out on the top of the hip bone and the upper portion of the rather substantial buttock on the right side. Feeling it brings pain on gentle finger touch. I don't even push down to make it hurt. It's not the pain of pyelitis. Let's have a look. She ups the dress and downs the panties, and there's a redness in a radicular pattern. She's coming along with shingles! No blisters yet, but I'm pretty sure that's what it is. We'll give her half the doses of pethidine that she's been having, but give her a little Phenergan or Valium along with it to ease the distress.

Then we see the aboriginal. It's a fifteen-year-old boy. The other female with him is his mother. He's a petrol sniffer, says Vivianne. His belly is soft. His lungs are clear. His throat is, too. No koplik spots, but I think he has measles. He's just too black to show a rash. We'll treat him for measles.

Then we say bye, and I tell Vivianne that she should have liver function studies done the next time she's in the Alice. I think she might have hepatitis, but I don't take a blood here. We have too far to go yet today. The Navajo is off by the time we're abeam the wind sock, and we turn to 300 degrees, 5,500 feet, and it's 1037 hours. About thirty-five minutes and we're circling Ernabella, and making our approach.

Sister Julie meets us at the strip. Rounding the church and little Ronald's grave, we note the benches sitting in the horseshoe shape under the trees outside the church. They had a rally here the other night, says sister Julie. Lots of folks showed up; the singing got really loud and lots of hand clapping, and a real "praise the Lord" corroboree. The benches fashioned into a kind of grandstand came tumbling down with the enthusiasm. Nobody was hurt.

We unpack the boxes from the Toyota for the clinic. Oh, yes. Troy Wilson, the kid at Indulkana with the blood nose last week? They didn't have to come up to the Alice. Troy blew out a piece of foam rubber about an inch long. He'd forgotten that he'd stuffed it up his nose. And Pompey Pearson had a blood sugar of 24.4 moles/liter; about 474 mg/deciliter. No wonder he was losing weight. He was peeing out all his calories in the sugar in his urine. We put him on Diabinese, an oral antidiabetic agent; 750 mg a day. He won't take it anyway when he starts to feel better.

Our first patient is Thelma; not the one who died a few weeks ago from COPD; this is the other Thelma, and she's dying from the same thing. She's thirteen. Her finger tips are twice as big as the rest of the finger: real "clubbing." She was put on Vibramycin in the Alice. I'll give her a month of Bactrim, too.

Here's little maxillary dysplasia Clara. She's now got a bad bronchitis; reflux aspiration and tracheitis, I suppose. Clara looks like a rag doll with too little stuffing. She can't even hold her head up now. She's also having seizures. She was put on 30 mg phenobarbital at bedtime in the Alice. That's good enough. I can't think of anything else to do. I don't think she'll be around too much longer. Her Daddy had his skin graft to the burn on his leg, and Mom's beautiful teeth are all hidden under the brown filth of her "mincobah," her tobacco. I'm not sure what all is in the mincobah, but it's a mixture of herbs, probably real tobacco, cannabis and whatever. They hold it in the side of their mouths like a cigar and chew on it, and I think, swallow the juice. It is not something that they smoke. Sometimes it just stays in the corner of their mouth like a brown "dummy," their word for a pacifier.

Next is Tyulyata; 43 kg, 20/52, with FH 138/minute. Okay.

Nyalapantja is 60 kg, 100/70, 18/52 and FHH not heard. Blood is taken. Then good old Punch Johnston for his driver's pe (physical exam), and Brian Reagan for the same thing. Brian is the European who took Laura around when she was here. Brian is a good guy! He also has a dermatophytosis (ringworm), and we put him on Daktrin.

Here's Robert with that persistent left thigh abscess. I'm going to send him up to the Alice and have the surgeons cut it out. That's the only way that's going to clear up. There just has to be a piece of something in there that's organic, like a foreign body. Margaret Inpiti is 30/52, 45 kg, and HB of 10.4. We'd better recheck that. We draw another "milkali" (blood). We re-inspect the healing ulcer of Athol Blyton. It's coming right. He had two of them last time; now he only has one. It's on the area of the surgery for repair of the achilles tendon, and he has a lot of varicosities that are compromising the circulation of the area.

Rodrick has a blood pressure of 164/102 at 87 kg. He's supposed to be on thiazide (diuretic), but I don't suppose he takes it when he feels well. Melissa is fifteen months old with diarrhea. Marlene is five and has a fever of forty degrees. Yurpia is about twenty-one and has had months of abdominal pain for which she was sent to the Alice, but she absconded from the hospital. Her pain is vague in area and intensity, and her belly is soft. She has a 4+ urine protein, though. Porphyria enters my mind. I don't know if aboriginals can even have that disease. We draw an FBC and an ESR (erythrocyte sedimentation rate).

Matthew is Robert's son, and won't eat. He's about nine; has been to the Children's Health Unit at the Alice just this last January. He weighs 17.3 kg. He takes "lollies" (candy) with alacrity, though. And to polish off this clinic, sister Julie Peters has scabies on her neck.

We enjoy a cup of tea at Julie's house, and then we drive out to the strip. Julie tells us that at the time of the Christian service that we described before, the congregation went out to where Tjuntakali died last month, and walked through the house and declared that it was now free of spirits, and, by golly, a family has moved into the house! Julie says that has never happened before.

About 1600 hours we're off and heading for Amata. Remember poor old Murray Burton whom we brought home with the terrible lungs not too long ago? He had been in the Alice at the hospital but opted to die at home? Well, we're going to bring him back. They've run out of oxygen at Amata. Strange. He's never been on digitalis at all. About a half hour run from Ernabella, and we're touching down in Amata. Chris has him in the Toyota waiting at the airstrip. We load him aboard. He sure is dyspneic (short of breath).

Then we're off for the Alice. It's been a long day. Murray estimates that we've flown 632 miles today. Our total elapsed flying time is three hours twenty-seven minutes. That's a lot! Now the port engine on the FML won't stop, even when it's full lean. Murray turns off the petrol at the shut-off. I hope they remember to turn it on again before they start to take off next time. But that's another story.

22 October 1981

Nothing is supposed to be unusual about today's trip. It's to Amata, and it's pretty straight forward. At 0745 I'm on the way out to the airport in the little Falcon. It's a beautiful, sunny day, but not too hot, and there are some "mare's tail" clouds way up high that seem to show that there's a lot of wind blowing down from the "top end" up in the stratosphere. It's also a bit hazy towards the horizon. I've brought along my super-8 movie camera, in addition to the Pentax this time. I think there might just as well be some movies made of these trips as slides. Who knows? For sure, don't forget the Pentax at home, or sure as anything, there'll be something you'll want a slide of.

John is just finishing up the preflight on Foxtrot Mike Lima. He found it short of fuel and messed up this morning, and had to go over and fuel it first. But it's ready, and here comes sister Carol and Bob Worthing, and Murray Burton, going home to

Amata again. Only this time he looks a lot better. This time some "registrar" got hold of him instead of Dr. Franklin, and he's on Digoxin. He still uses oxygen like it's going out of style, though. He's going to be a terror to wean off the oxygen. Then there's little, fat-cheeked, big-eyed Fred, going back from the Children's Health Unit, where he put about twenty-five percent extra weight onto his little frame. Nothing wrong with Fred at two years, except that he had too big a burden of parasites to share his nutrition with. Now that Flagyl and Vermox are through with the menagerie, he can start a whole new zoo in that GI tract. Meantime, he doesn't have to share his intake with worms.

The loudspeaker comes on with the taxi instruction, and I notice that John isn't wearing the earphones. So, the option is there to let the rest of the crew know what's going on, not just the pilot. John likes to share because he knows that I like to hear. "Foxtrot Mike Lima, runway one-two for line-up. You may use taxi intersection for takeoff start if you wish. Fly radial two-two-two, right turn to 8,000, but stay east of the new railroad until 5,000. Barometer is reading thirty point sixteen inches of mercury."

"Swell!" exclaims John, and we whip eastbound on the runway about a third of the way down where the taxi way intersects, and in half of that we're off the ground and climbing. The gear comes up with a "thunk." John retracts the take-off flaps, and starts the right turn. We don't even have to parallel the new railroad. John is at 5,000 feet before we get to it on the 222 radial.

Sister Carol hands me the reports that have accumulated since last time. It seems that Nita had granuloma inguinale, and was placed on erythromycin because she's pregnant. Dr. Cahill didn't want to use tetracycline. It didn't really make that much difference. Two days after Nita was placed on medication she went AWOL from the hospital. She's probably back in Amata already spreading the "good news." She's eighteen. Lippsie is older; she's nineteen, and she was started on Amoxil and Flagyl for gonorrhea, and whatever else, but that's academic, too, because she's AWOL.

All the way down it's clear to hazy, and there's Mt. Connor ahead. I opt not to take any movies of that yet. It's too hazy, and the light isn't just right, and I'll get a better angle and lighting later. There's an axiom I always repeat to myself, and then forget: "Take it while you can get it." Naturally, I'm talking about movies and slides. I ignore my own axiom, and then we're approaching Amata. It's hard to keep the movie steady when the plane is bucking like a bronco in the hot desert thermals.

The approach has John doing everything just the way I was taught to do it; high prop at twenty-six inches manifold pressure, drop the flaps a little to slow down to 140 M.P.H., then drop the gear, and hold her at about 120 until final. Then full flaps and carry about 100 M.P.H. to touchdown. That's the way John does it, too. There's almost no wind on the strip.

Sister Chris meets us, and another car with family of Fred, who are joyous, and so is he! That's fun to watch. The drive in to the settlement prompts me to ask. "When was the Amata Gran Prix?" There are cars here and there abandoned on the road.

"Oh, they just broke down this morning," says Chris, as she briefly loses control of the Toyota in the soft sand of the road. She slides the car three quarters broadside through the space between the abandoned vehicle and the shelf of red bull dust that the grader has pushed up as a margin of the road through the wattles. We all suck in our breath, and wish that we had lap and shoulder harness on. But then we're at the Clinic and things start.

Frances is a cutie, with fat cheeks and runny nose and ears. She's fine; has been an Amoxil for two days. She has four teeth at eleven months. Next is Nora; antenatal, 58.7 kg with 1+ protein in her urine, 80/44, 26/52, FHH 142/minute, and she's fine. Then Kaye who is 76.5 kg, 110/58 and term. Then Lena, her daughter, who is positive serology for syphilis and also term. Kaye had twins first and then two normal deliveries, and she's refusing to go to the Alice. She'll deliver on the floor of the clinic when she's ready. We'll give her three shots of LPG to wipe out the treponemes (Treponema pallidum, the spirochete of syphilis). I wonder if the granddaughter will be born before aunt?

Next is a sad story. Ivan is in the back of the hospital. He's 16. The girls think Ivan has a tinea cruris (jock itch) or something. His father says it's in the groin, but of course, the girls can't see it. So, I go back. Walter, his father, says that Ivan has a lot of problems with both his penis and his anus. Ivan timidly drops his filthy trousers, and there's an awful mess! All this is happening back in the hospital part of the clinic, and of course, we're all alone. I have a disposable glove and peel back a bit of the prepuce. Ivan isn't too badly scarred up from his initiation rite, but the glans and the prepuce are oozing a gray, thick, sanguinous exudate, and the anus is excoriated and macerated, and there's feces mixed with the same pus.

What a mess! I suppose two weeks of tetracycline, 500 mg four times a day might solve things, but he won't take that kind of dosage, so better make it a single dose. I guess I'll give him 500 mg of probenecid now, and in about forty-five minutes let's give him three grams of Amoxil in a single dose. Then get a serology, and if that comes back positive, we'll hit him with three doses of LPG. Sheesh! What a mess!

Back to the regular clinic. Yerritti is 66 kg, 20/52 with a clear urine (for now). Blood pressure is 106/66, and FHH 152/minute. Craig is nineteen months and probably asthmatic. He's taking Bondecon, but objects to taking it, and it's almost impossible to get any theophylline in him. We'll go with suppositories, even if they are unreliable. I'd like to see if it helps. Janet is six, and has a fever. She's on Bactrim. Paniny is one you'll remember. We saw her in April for about the fifth time with vague pain in her chest. She's got it again. Let's try Motrin (brufen, they call it), instead of Indocin. The Indocin works, but the Motrin will look different and she'll think it's something new. Hadelai is five months with diarrhea. He dropped from 7.49 kg to 7.36. He's had Bicillin for this, and is a little better. "Tjuri" is Pitjantjatjara for diarrhea, and "uru" is watery in the same language, and that's what he has.

Kerry Tracor is European. She wants an oral contraceptive pill (OCP). She's never had one before. She had a Pap when she was in the Alice about eight months ago. We go over the side effects, etc., with her, and put her on Nordette 21. She's living with her boyfriend when she does go into the Alice. She's the school marm. Her birth date is 17 October 1960. I remind her that the OCP is not an "after the fact" remedy.

Marion Simm is another European. She looks sick, too. She's been on Amoxil for two days. Her temp is thirty-nine, and she does have a cough. Iris is black; she has lower abdominal pain.

She has a history of the same thing in 1979. At that time she was given Amoxil and aborted. She thinks of it as cause and effect. Okay, let's try Bactrim this time. Nyurpaya has a uti (urinary tract infection) too. It's funny. She can talk perfect English, because I've heard her in the front of the clinic with the sisters, but she won't in front of me. She had a tubal ligation a year ago. We'll treat her with Bactrim, too.

Then William. Condylomata? That's what Chris says she was told. He's twelve years old. The girls leave, and William drops his filthy jeans. Shades of Ivan! It's the same mess! William pulls up his jeans and leaves. I tell him sister will give him some medicine. When Chris comes back in I tell her what I've seen. "Do you have any homosexual activity here? This looks like the tip of an iceberg, what with Ivan and William!"

"Oh, yes! That's quite common, and they are so reluctant to talk about it that I don't know how we'll ever cure it," says sister Chris, rather matter-of-factly.

Golly, maybe we should write a note to the World Council of Churches asking them how to handle this. Meantime, we'll prescribe the same medicine we gave Ivan, and from now on, when the parents come with something wrong with a bottom on one of their kids, they are to be asked by the sister if it looks like the problem that William and Ivan have, since the sisters won't be allowed to see it. Then treat it accordingly. Thank goodness, we don't see any (or very little) penicillin sensitivity among these people.

Next is Muna (pronounced "morna"). She has a weird looking mess on her legs. They are wart-like, black, sessile eruptions; in groups and some places like they'd been seeded in rows, mostly on the inside of the legs, and terminating suddenly at the ankle and about mid-thigh. They've been there for years, she says, and they are not "wyawyanie" (itchy). She says she doesn't "pirini" (scratch) them. She has them nowhere else. She's quite sensitive about them. Do you suppose they could be molluscum contagiosum? Well, for sure, if they are, we'll never get them removed. There's just too many of them, and she won't be in one place long enough to get them done. If one took her to the hospital (if she'd go in the first place), one would have to graft her to make up for the lost skin.

In dismay, I just tell her that I'll ask my colleagues back in the Alice what they think. Then sister Carol comes up with a wonderful idea. "Why don't you take a picture of them?" And so, I unwrap my flash unit, put in the battery, set it all up, assure Muna that I'm not going to take a picture of anything but the lesions, and she agrees. There it is on film for y'all to see some-day!

Disappointment! Chris says that See International did come through a couple of weeks ago. Pompey Harding does not have glaucoma, they said. And with poor old Unpulyaru with the terrible corneal scarring, they think she has only a five percent chance of sight if the surgery were done, and so they left with nothing done. So much for See International. I guess it is a hard area to cover, though.

Then over to sister Chris' for coffee. She has fried a chicken and has salami and all kinds of goodies. I have a cup of tea and a peanut butter cookie that is really good. Sister Carol is feeling crook. She has a cold and an eustachian salpingitis. She does give in enough to take an Actifed when I remind her as she once reminded me as she drove me to the hospital, "There are no heroines in this organization." Colleen is the other sister here with Chris. Jennie has been on holiday and is due back on the fourth.

Then we get the word that we have to be stopping at Ayer's Rock on the way back. It seems a young man burned his hand with a welding torch. So, we're off and away. John brings us around the west side of the Rock so I can get some neat movies, and a couple more slides, and we land and have a look at Alistair Gannet and his hand. He has two cute little chicks with him. Wendy isn't around anywhere.

It seems Dr. Harberth had been down here yesterday and opened up this wound, but after I've looked at it and mentally decided on a course of action they hand me his notes. It pretty clearly says that if there's still infection, he wants him brought in to the Alice where he can explore surgically under general anesthesia. Well, there's plenty of infection left, so Al will have to leave the nymphs behind and come along with us. He's not unhappy, I think. And we're off again.

John thinks he'd like to practice an ILS approach when we

get to the Alice. He's going to be flying his biennial check ride tomorrow. So, at about seventy-three miles DME, he contacts Alice approach and they set it up for him. He doesn't like the hood. Tunnel vision. He arranges his side of the cockpit windows with sectionals, and I can still see out. He uncouples all the autopilot goodies, and takes the pedals and wheel in his own hands. There's that initial fishtailing and porpoising, and the plane settles down to fly the Simpson Intersect. It's interesting. I've never been on this side of the Spyce Byce before.

We cross below it about twenty miles west, and there's the Alice up the valley where the road goes past Mt. Gillen, and out to Simpson Gap. There's the gap and the chicken farm. I take some extra movies and slides. John nudges FML around onto the approach, and handles everything quite neatly. He lines right up with the runway without seeing it, and there's the outer marker. The gear is coming down, and the glideslope stays right on center and the localizer on the vertical. The radio says, "Foxtrot Mike Lima, clear to land." Then the middle marker says, "beep-eep-eep," and John flings away the sectionals from the windows just as it's time to flare out for landing. Hey, that's good! Sister Carol's ears are hurting, though. Next day I hear from Maurie Killarney of the Commonwealth Police that they were wondering about that plane. Usually the tower will tell the base that there's a bloke on ILS practice, but this time they didn't. I guess there was a bit of hell to pay by someone.

But they didn't shoot us down. I'd joked with John when I was looking at the base from the plane. "John, don't worry, you just watch the instruments, and I'll watch for contrails." I wonder if they'd really do that?

29 October 1981

Well, I was supposed to have been in Fregon today, but then Atjungka, a fifty-six-year-old aboriginal woman died in Ernabella, and the last notes on her card with the Aeromedical Service had been mine for last November, so I had been asked to sign her death certificate. "I'd better have a chance to talk with sister Julie first," I said. "Maybe on the way down to Fregon we can just stop at the strip and I can ask Julie about the details of the death so that at least I'll be partly right. I don't know if she came in beaten with a nulla-nulla or if she had pneumonia again, or maybe an m.i. (myocardial infarction—heart attack). Or maybe it was congestive failure." The partial story that I have is that she just came in from walkabout and went into a coma and died. Maybe it was petrol sniffing and lactic acidosis. Who knows? One thing for sure, no one is asking for an autopsy. Isn't that racist? If she were European, they'd sure want one.

But the point became moot about 1830 hours when Carl (Bud) Webster, a sixty-year-old engineer from the base, rode his motorcycle off a twenty-foot cliff in the Temple Bar Creek wash, and suffered a fracture dislocation of the third dorsal vertebra and total motor and partial sensory loss below that level. It seems that Bud was riding with Neal House just west of the Alice and south of the Hermannsburg Road in an arroyo with bike trails from previous riders. Bud said that he had come to this little seven-foot rise on a well traveled trail, gave it a little kick so that he'd be airborne briefly at the top of the rise, and when he came clear of the ground he realized that there was no bottom. He had just sailed off a twenty foot cliff!

He said he remembered the front of the bike dropping down, but can't remember if he rode the bike to the ground or if he came loose. He can't remember if he landed on his head or his tail, either. When the cobwebs came loose he tried to get up to get his bike, and he couldn't move. Neal got to him shortly after that, sized up the situation, and hurried back to the Diorama in the Alice to phone the St. John's ambulance people. He said they arrived in about ten minutes, and had about a quarter mile hike carrying Bud back to the ambulance on a stretcher.

At about 2000 hours I received a call from Ken Clairborn at

the hospital. His wife is in for delivery. He said that he had heard that Bud Webster was in cas (Casualty—Aussie equivalent of the emergency room) with bike injuries. Did I know about it? "No, I haven't heard a thing about that."

When he rang off, I rang the cas, and sure enough, he was in x-ray. I went on over, and there it was; the films showed a real mess at the T–3 level, and possibly a C–6 lesion as well? Not a scratch on his elbows or knees. No evidence of abrasions, but there were a lot of dark subcutaneous spots around his fore-head where it looked like his helmet had really been jammed down on his head. Sure would be nice to have a lateral view of that T–3, but we don't dare turn him on his side. He complains of pain in the T–3 rib distribution when we try to bring his arms above the level of the head. That's where he hurts the most; right in the chest about T–3 level; just above the nipples. To light touch below the waist he has a spotty distribution. He can feel the soles of his feet, and the lateral and anterior sides of the left leg. Not much at all in the right leg, and no motor function at all. He can tell if his toe is up or down, though. Funny. Certainly not a picture of a transected cord.

Dr. Trambell has put out a call for Dr. Charley. Hal Barker is sitting with Leota, Bud's wife, and Gwen Terry and the Houses in the cas waiting area. I stop briefly and tell them what's hap-pening. But I don't really want to say too much until Dr. Charley arrives and we decide what's to be done. I tell them that until he's stable, we won't move him. Bud's pressure is in the neigh-borhood of 80/40, but then comes up a bit. He's hurting, but not in shock. His mentality is clear, and he has a sense of humor in spite of the chilling reality of the situation. He's to be admitted to ICU (intensive care unit).

I try to contact Merle, but no answer. Later I find out that he's in Adelaide. Good old John Brandywine is contacted. John takes over the administrative side of the problem. Try to reach Bill Miller. No answer. Dr. Charley arrives. He confirms what we know. He begins plans to evacuate ASAP to the spinal unit at the Royal Adelaide.

Bud gives me instructions on some things hanging fire at the office that he wants passed on the Marty and Rita. The plan gradually unfolds. It's to be AMS (aeromedical service) of the RFDS (Royal Flying Doctors' Service) taking him to Adelaide. The plane has never gone beyond Oodnadatta; usually the South Australian St. John's ambulance plane picks up the patient there, but this time it will be AMS all the way. Sister Virginia Gretchen will be going down, and Dr. Rutten will accompany. Mrs. Webster will fly in the right front seat. Mr. Miller arrives on the scene. He's most anxious about the evacuation.

"Should we ask TAA (TransAustralia Airlines) if there's a plane we can rent? Is it safe to send him in a little plane?"

The plane to be used is the John Hawkins good old FML. "Yes, that's a very good plane, and well suited for such an evacuation."

"But the weather people say there are thunderstorms at Oodnadatta."

In the visitors area of the ICU, Gwen is going into great detail about the diet restrictions for her children who have many, many allergies. The Houses are sitting quietly. Leota is lost in her own thoughts, but making small talk answers to Gwen's rambling. Gwen is a sister at the hospital. She knows a little about a lot of things. The ICU sisters are wonderful. "Would you like some coffee? Tea? Anything we can get for you?"

"The plane will be ready to depart at 0100 hours." Gosh, it's already 2345! Gwen will go home with Leota and help her pack. I'll go home and pack and pick up Leota. St. John's ambulance will bring Bud out to the airport. Dr. Stephen Charley has been in touch with the team at Royal Adelaide, and that end is all set up. There's going to be headwinds, so we'll have to refuel at Leigh Creek. And it's all set. Home for me; throw a few things into the suitcase. A call to John Brandywine. He's going to ring Tom Clayton in Adelaide, who will set up the Adelaide end for Leota; a place to stay, and for me a return trip on the Ansett flight on Friday. Tom will meet us at the airport. Leota is short of money, and worried. No problem. There's help available.

Laura helps put things together for me; makes sure that I take my medicine with me. At 0030 hours I'm on the way over to Webster's house. It's spitting a little rain. It's cloudy. Gwen has Leota packed, and we head out to the airport. It's pleasant weather. Not too hot, and no flies at this time of the night. A few stars are poking through the cloud cover. The FML is running up on the tarmac, then taxies off around the other hangars to be fueled. A while, and we hear it start up, and it comes back. It's Darryl. Fidgety Darryl will be the pilot. He's dressed in his white, short sleeve shirt, with the captain's bars on his shoulders stubbies; a proper looking pilot. He's sweating a lot though as he removes the extra seat, and gets the plane configured for a stretcher patient.

Then the patient arrives. Officer Kevin tells me that there's word that Neal tried to lift Bud to his feet after the accident. We all help lift Bud from the ambulance to the stretcher on the ground beside the plane. He's on a proper spinal frame. No problem. He's not that heavy. He's now in the plane and secured. Sister Virginia takes the backward facing seat to attend to the head of the patient. I'm in the aft seat near his feet. He's to be on oxygen all the way, says Dr. Charley's notes. He's had 10 mg of morphine intramuscularly and five mg intravenously at the hospital. Bud's in good spirits. Leota takes the right seat, and we're ready.

The panel lights up with reds and greens and the plane looks beautiful. Taxi instructions; runway three-oh. We're underway at 0147. Bud's IV is glucose/saline. We're to add a Hartmann's solution next. His BP is 112 systolic by pulse, and the pulse is 92/minute. Respirations are 24/minute, and he has 75 ml of urine in his foley bag. I notice that his feet are on the frame with a pillow under his heels. Darryl heads it out at 150 degrees, and we're to fly at 7,500 feet. The sky is clear now. The stars are bright. There's not a bump in the sky. We watch Bud; occasionally I find that I've dozed off, but when I wake I note that the elapsed time on the clock on the panel has moved ahead by only about ten minutes, yet I feel rested. Sister Virginia does the same. Gradually the sky pales in the east, and miraculously, there's a big, lighted strip down below us. It's Leigh Creek. You can turn the lights on from the plane with the transponder. Isn't that something? Like Grandma would say, "Isn't it wonderful? Just when they needed to refuel, there was that nice airport right below them!"

Darryl hit it right on the head with the help of a few thousand dollars worth of avionics in the plane. Time to stretch the legs, empty the reservoir, and Bud says that he thinks he could use some medication for the pain. We give him 10 mg of morphine IM. We touched down at Leigh Creek at 0445 Thursday, with the elapsed time showing 2:55. We're underway at 0505 hours with a spectacular sunrise. It looks like waves of surf breaking red, from the parallel rows of altostratus up there. The sun rises like a red ball, then there are the square tilled fields instead of the desert below us, and the water off to the west and the east. We're across the bay from Adelaide, and start the let down at 0620 Alice Springs time. It's daylight savings here in Adelaide.

They're an hour ahead of us. There's one tiny patch of stratus (fog) right on course for our straight in approach. The auto pilot handles it beautifully, and we touch down at 0643. The ambulance is waiting for us. Here comes Tom. The patient is transferred to the ambulance. Tom takes Leota's suitcase. I leave mine in the plane. I've opted to return with the plane at "mid-day" as Darryl puts it.

It's a nice ambulance. The driver, the med tech officer, me, Virginia, Leota in front, and, of course, Bud. I don't remember much about the ride in. Soon we're at the "casualty" like in Alice. They're waiting for us. Into the "ESS" (Emergency Surgical Station). Solicitious people. "Can I get you a cup of tea? Coffee? Would you like some breakfast? The cafeteria is right upstairs. I'll take you there."

After Dr. D.E. Mercer takes charge of the patient we go up and have something to eat. I have a cardboard egg, and a greasy sausage, and a piece of toast and coffee, but like in India, I forgot to say, "no milk; coffee." But already I have a cup of white coffee. It's hot. Then, back down to the ESS. They are getting those lateral films. The team has moved Bud onto his side. He'll be going to "theatre" (surgery) about noon. No additional neuro return, but no further loss on Bud, either. I phone Tom. He and Merle are coming by at 1100 hours [1000 Alice Springs time]. We meet them. Leota has a call from the States. Just as we were leaving the parking lot this little aide came running out with that message. Leota will wait here until I've been dropped at the airport. I wonder if such a special attention by the staff would have been forthcoming had we been at a large hospital in America.

At the airport, Darryl and Virginia are waiting. Darryl is going to file his flight plan. I buy a *Time* magazine, and a bottle of Kaisserstuhl cabernet sauvignon, and a bottle of Maxwell Mead. The plane is ready. It's quite a walk from the terminal, but it's a refreshing morning. Virginia will take the first leg in the right seat. I can recline in the back seat and snooze. At 1140 hours we're off the ground. At 1325 hours we're at Leigh Creek. This is coal mining country. In the daylight we can see the open pit mine, with huge piles of coal laying on top of the ground. Torrens Lake is just to the west. It's a huge, dry, salt lake. On the map it looks like it might once have been connected with the Spencer Gulf. The Flinders Range is to the east. The fuel attendant is a big woman, poured into a small set of coveralls. She's just finishing refueling a 182 Cessna that had a pod underneath as big as an extra fuselage. We're next. Time to walk about a bit. Sure wouldn't want to argue with that lady. Those bulges in those coveralls aren't all fat. There's a lot of muscle under there!

We're off at 1357 hours. I'm in the right front seat now. There's Lake Eyre ahead of us. It's fifty-two feet below sea level; the same elevation as the Caspian Sea. From 8,500 feet one can't see the north shore from the south shore. Of course, there's no water in it right now, but there is a big line of thunderheads way up north. It's getting downright bumpy now. Sure glad we didn't have this kind of turbulence when we had Bud on board. Off to the west is Lake Cadibarrawirracanna, but it has to be a big map to know which dry lake that name goes with. Then as we cross Lake Eyre, we see the Neales inflow bed, just south of Oodnadatta, and then, the Macumba, as the delta of the Finke is known, as it enters the dry lake.

Virginia's head is lolling about on the headrest of the reclining seat. She's dead to the world. Ahead are the black and gray streaks of rain beneath the thunderheads. Some of them are the real "anvils," with the tops blowing off to the east. Some are "dumplings" with rolls and rolls, but only about thirty-five thousand feet or so high. Darryl picks a few of the shorter ones to fly under. Lightning strikes in the black rain veils; cloud to ground. Don't ever believe anyone who says lightning doesn't strike more than once in the same place. Almost every strike is followed by a second strike in the same place! And don't believe that old wives' tale that whirlwinds are always clockwise in the southern hemisphere. That might go for the bigger storms like the cyclones or for the large water movements in the ocean, but the willy-willys that I count are moving just about fifty percent clockwise and fifty percent counterclockwise.

We're just about 500 feet above the base of the thunderheads. Darryl asks for and gets 7,000 feet. It's been a little hairy flying through those. Never really sure which might have hailstones in them, and the big water drops are hitting the windscreen with explosive force as it is. It's like swimming off the coast of Goleta, California with scuba gear under kelp. Sometimes it's gray when the kelp isn't too dense, and other times it can get downright black. Same with flying under thunderheads. You can tell when you're under a real biggy; it gets black!

Intermittently we find ourselves in between clefts in the barrier of buildups, and that's when we see spectacular rainbows! Gee, I wish I had my camera. It did occur to me to take it, but I didn't do it in those early hours of today. We dodge about a bit, but the good old avionics don't forget which direction is home. Now we're descending. "Foxtrot Mike Lima, make a short base for runway one-two." Darryl whips FML in close, pours on the flaps and back on the throttle for a descent of 1,500 feet a minute to make the ears pop. Out east here comes a dust storm cloud, and there are two 727s from Ansett and TAA in the pattern, and we're going to be number one! We touch down, roll out and turn in to the RFDS hangar.

There's John and Carl waiting for me. Isn't that funny? I climb out of Darryl's door. I never do that! I always wait for the main door to be opened. I'm not thinking very fast. It's been a long day. We say goodbye to those really fine people. I pick up my *Time* magazine. "Can we get to the APO before five?" We touched down at 1640 hours.

"Yeah, I think we can make it." I'm in the back seat. Carl and John in the front. We stop by the post office at fifteen seconds before five. Jack, the postmaster, has it closed up. There's no mail in the box anyway. They drive me home. Carl will keep the car and take the call tonight. It starts to rain. It rains a downpour! It's a wild storm. I'm glad we're on the ground. Damn! I left my wine in the plane. Oh, well, the AMS will have it tomorrow. It's good to be home. Laura has a nice steak ready for the broiler after a good double scotch! Yeah! It's good to be home. I'll have to make up for missing Ernabella and Fregon next week.

Later I learned that the surgery had been successful in decompressing the fracture in T–3. However, twenty hours after surgery, the patient still did not have motor function, and there was rising apprehension in the spinal team for "significant loss of function."

5 November 1981

Sister Carol rang on Wednesday, and told me that we were scheduled for Indulkana, and that she had heard that we were to have thirty patients! Good grief! Sounds like the whole of Chandler is going to be there as well as Mimili! Well, the little sisters will just have to sort them out, because twelve minutes to a patient, that will be six hours of constant work, and I don't imagine it would be sorted out well enough to see them in twelve minutes each. We'll just have to do what we can. Also, sister Carol is going to a wedding down in Adelaide, so she won't be along. It will be someone else.

It's a beautiful morning. I'd delayed just a bit with one thing and another, and so left the house about a quarter to eight. Carol has also asked me if I'd be willing to leave at 0700 hours instead of 0800. I'd said, "Sure, if it means that we got home an hour earlier, but I can't see leaving at 0700 and still getting home at 1700 or 1800 hours." So, we're ready to leave at 0800. I arrive at a minute and fifteen seconds past eight. I learn later that sister Ray has already rung Laura to find out if I'm coming. It's John at the controls of "Foxtrot Mike Lima." Clearance to 8,000 feet, 179 radial, runway one-two. John takes it all the way to the end of the runway, and pours on the petrol. The Navajo leaps ahead. It's a bit hazy on the horizon, but there's hardly a cloud in the sky.

We follow the railroad towards the Finke crossing. We're a bit west of Chamber's Pillar this morning. I'm studying my "ECG

Interpretation" book, and sister Ray offers coffee. It's nice and hot, but there's no biscuit like Carol offers when she's on board. Don't look a gift horse in the mouth is the old saying. John tells me that he enjoyed flying the Navajo on a "flyby" for the twenty-fifth anniversary show at the Alice Springs Soaring Club that was held at Bond Springs last Sunday. He says he made a slow flyby with gear extended and stuff, and then wheeled it around and made a fast flyby, bringing her up and rolling it out on a wing-over, apparently to the delight of the crowd. Unfortunately, Laura and I missed it because we had blown our radiator hose out there, and had limped home a bit earlier than the 1430 hours that John made his flyby. But that's another story. I extract from gentle John that his girl friend was in the right seat during the flyby. I'll bet she was impressed!

Then John reaches behind his seat and brings out my red, white and blue nylon windbreaker. I'd left it on the plane when we came back from Adelaide. I hadn't even missed it. I'd been thinking only of the wine, and I'd already retrieved that. So now we really have it all together again. Thanks, John. The South Road comes in from the west to meet the railroad as we cross just east of Kulgera. What's that funny dark patch up ahead there about at Indulkana? Why, it's a burned area, almost a square mile, it looks like. We lower the gear, and drag in for our approach. There's a Piper Seneca on the ground, too. The police. Wonder what's up? Sister Vivienne meets us.

Susan Meier never did break out with the vesicles of shingles, but the medicine we gave did give her relief. Gilpin Ward had a septic arthritis in that knee. Pompey Pearson swears that the Diabinese that we gave him last time is the most wonderful medicine in the world, and for the first time in more than a year, he feels spunky. He'll probably father a child, he feels so good! Martin Tine never did get up to the Alice for that tight phimosis, and Helen Sevanlab's tinea is clearing up fine with the griseofulvin. So much for the answers to last month's problem.

The Parkinsons from Chandler are our first patients. There's Adam with a big bruise on his forehead where he's fallen down some time ago. But this time he has a tinea on his left volar forearm. Hey, aren't we glad we ordered up the Daktrin last time? We'll just put some of that on, and it will begin to go away straight away. What? You don't have any? But I ordered it last time. You didn't send in the order? Well, I guess that's why you don't have any. How about diluting out some Whitfield's ointment with petrolatum and using that? You don't have any Whitfield? Anything for fungus? How about some undecylenic acid? No? What do you have? Some Kenalog and some suntan lotion and some calomine lotion? No, none of that will do. Well, let's just be sure to have it sent down, and when you get it, start Adam on it. Adam goes back to exploring the examining room, climbing on the tables and chairs, and generally getting into things, while we listen to the next problem.

Little Lorraine has had a temp of thirty-nine. She had a messy urine, says sister Vivienne, and they had her on Amoxil, but she's still got the temp, and her urine is still 3 + protein and 2 + blood, and she's still running 38.4 degrees. Okay, let's try her on Bactrim and see if that won't relieve some of this little one's problems. You don't have any Bactrim? What do you have? Tetracycline? No, I don't want to use that on a four-year-old child. Oh, you have Bactrim in the big tablets? Okay. One tablet crushed up with some jelly twice a day for ten days, and don't tell me you don't have jelly.

Rhonda herself is next. She has a backache (what with lugging Adam around on her hip, that's no wonder). I look over her notes. She saw me about that a couple months ago. Indocin was prescribed. Did it help? You didn't take it? Why? Oh, they were out of it. Do we have any now? No? We'd better order some of that, too. Meantime, maybe we can try two aspirin four times a day if the back pain is really bad. You what? Not really! You're putting me on. You really are out of aspirin? That's incredible! I guess you'd better order some of that, too.

The floor trembles as two-year-old Adam comes backwards off the examining table access step right onto the back of his head. There's a deathly moment of silence, and then a shriek, and we know that Adam isn't dead, anyway. Only three patients seen, and we've been half an hour. We're ahead of schedule if there are to be thirty of them. But we won't have anything to treat them with, that's obvious.

Baby Selena is a newborn. She's okay. Peter Russell is an old man. His eyes long ago clouded with the white scarring of trachoma, and his sight is gone except for light and dark. He has a walking stick of well-polished mulga that's very beautiful. Laura might be able to buy it away from him, but I can't. He really needs something to feel his way along the ground. Poor old guy. It says on his paper that he was born in 1897. He's really dyspneic, with thick and scraggly yellow hair hanging to his shoulders. The shirt must have been red and green checks once upon a time. Now it's the same color as the bull dust. Pants the same. Thongs on his feet. That's a step up, anyway. His notes say that he was on Digoxin in 1979. None since. By golly! We have some Digoxin, but they're 250 microgram, and not scored. Oh well, give him one tablet every other day, empirically. His chest reveals a few rales in the bases and a third sound gallop. A closer look at his eyes reveals the granular blepharitis on the upper lid that goes with ongoing trachoma. Sheesh! He's blind with the disease and it's still ongoing. How about the tetracycline and some of the Bactrim. I know we have that. He probably won't take it for a full course of twenty-one days, though. Do the best we can.

Little Nelson is fourteen months. That's really his given and surname (English). He's just back from the Alice hospital with pneumonia. He looks okay. Then there's Maisie Parker from Wingelina. She's about sixty; asthmatic. Sister gave her some neulin the other night, and she thinks it's magic. It really worked. That's fine. Might give her a shot of Ventolin, too, if she really gets acute. Then she tells the health worker that she's been numb on the right side; arm and leg. TIA (transient ischemic attack—like a ministroke)? When we get the aspirin, let's have Maisie take an aspirin each day.

Irene Flint is next. Irene is the cook from Granite Downs. I saw her on one of my very first trips out there when she had become pregnant. Well, she's 34/52 now; 82 kg, 130/80 and FHH at 160/minute. She's leaving for Adelaide on the Ghan on the thirteenth. The Ghan is the train that runs from Adelaide to the Alice. It's called the Ghan because the first means of transport across the outback was by camel caravan, and the camels were driven by camel drivers from Afghanistan. The wild hops of Patterson's curse is also due to the Afghans. They stuffed their sleeping bags with wild hops, and it has since spread cross the outback.

Next is four-year-old Hazel from Fregon. She's chesty. Amoxil should clear her up. William Pitts is about four, too. He's Danielle's brother, and there's skinny Rhonda. William looks like a classic strep throat; circumoral pallor, the whole bit, but no rashes . . . yet. We take a throat culture. Erythromycin for him. Yeah! We have some of that! Katherine is next. She sure looks like measles; the conjunctivitis, fever, she has a fullness on the right upper quadrant of the belly that she's sure tender about. Liver? Let's treat her symptomatically and see what comes up next.

Ken McClelland is the fifty-two-year-old engineer from Mimili. Ken was over about two weeks ago with severe pain in the right flank and abdomen, and sister Vivienne says that he hadn't voided in almost two days. He was in real trouble and also complained of back ache. He's coming along better now. He thinks he may have passed a kidney stone. But I think Ken is knowledgeable enough to be aware of cancer of the prostate. He's "Pohme"—an acronym for the original Brit settlers to Australia— "prisoner of Her Majesty's Empire." His blood pressure is 128/72. Everything feels okay in his belly. We explain about a rectal exam to him. Yes, that's what he really wants me to do. He wants to be sure there's no cancer in that prostrate. Hurray! His prostrate does feel normal. No nodules, and no masses in the rectum. I don't have the wherewithal for a stool for occult blood. We should really carry some of those with us. He's really grateful.

Sister Ray has some papers for me to sort out. Athol Blyton is going to have his veins done, and needs the paperwork for referral to the Alice. Joe Peters is back for his pension papers. But that's from Fregon. Sister Ray just happens to have the papers with her. Also, Murray Burton from Amata's papers are here to be filled out for his pension. Then we are done with the clinic. Gee, that was only about twelve people instead of thirty! "Well," says sister Vivienne, "I guess the rest of them didn't want to wait."

Judy from America with her pigtails is still here in Indulkana. She's mellowing. Not nearly as activist as before. Colleen is a big girl; placid, quiet. Vivienne had cooked a chicken for tea time. "What's the big burn?" I ask.

"Oh," says sister Vivienne, "There was a corroboree here two weeks ago, and in their enthusiasm, someone threw a little fire around, and they got that thing going. I thought the whole place was going up in smoke, but they got a ring around it and stomped it out. It burned a little over a square mile. No harm, though. It was all ceremonial ground anyway. But while the fire was going on, two young blokes sneaked back to the settlement and knocked over two of the houses. But they got caught, and that's what the police are here for.''

''Police?''

''Yes, they came in the Seneca, and they're having court across the street there. I guess they're going to convict them. They'll have to take them up to the Alice. That's Northern Territory.''

Today is the day that the government of South Australia returned a huge amount of territory to the aborginals; a parcel of land that pretty much encompasses the area of my responsibility for the Aeromedical Service. All the million acres of Granite Downs, clear through to the western border with West Australia, and from the Northern Territory border about sixty miles south, and including all my settlements. It's an area twice the size of Tasmania. ''Will it make a difference in our flights?''

''No, they wouldn't dare undo the medical service. That would be racist. Did you know that Dr. Barker and Dr. Buroin are here?''

''No! Gosh, I'd sure like to meet him,'' I said. Dr. Barker is the Southern Australia director and regional medical officer of this area. I'd been told about him before, but never met him. Sister Vivienne takes us outside, and at the garden fence we meet Dr. Barker. Sandy hair, receding and thin. He's about sixty, I'd say. Nice older fellow. With him, Dr. Buroin, heavier, younger, and wearing Franklin half glasses. We pass the time of day. He's happy to meet me, too. Then the troops go back inside.

Ken says, ''I'd like you to meet my friend, Wally. He's from Mimili, too. He feels fine, so didn't come to the clinic today.''

Wally is a Yugoslavian; short and stocky, about forty-five or so, I'd guess. He's wearing a green canvas pork-pie hat, and with weather beaten hands, says, ''G'dye.''

''G'dye to you!'' Wally's a miner. He works at Mintibi, but headquarters in Mimili. We talk opals. Yes, he's had fair luck, but has not made the big strike. He reaches into his pocket and pulls out a small plastic envelope with the ubiquitous red, linear closure. Inside, an opal about a centimeter long and half as wide, done in oval cut, shining with red and green in its milky matrix.

"Eighty dollars for this one," he offers. "I used to send them to Melbourne to be polished, but this bloke down there didn't know how to do anything well except cheat me." says Wally. "He'd cut them and polish them, and then send me back substitutes that weren't what I sent down. Made me mad enough to kill him," admits Wally, and with the look he had in his eye, I'd hate to be that jeweler from Melbourne closer than fifty feet.

"Now here's a proper lot," says Wally. "Cut and polished by a bloke up in the Alice. He does a proper job and charges me ten percent of the value no matter what. Can't really tell what's in a rough piece. Might be cracked and not worthy anything after you've put in a lot of time cutting and polishing. But he still only charges me ten percent. He told me of another miner who struck it right a few weeks ago, $2,500 for a single stone!"

Wally's eyes gleam with that same look that one would see on a gold fossicker (prospector). It must be inborn. In his little bag there are about fifteen stones. Wally opens that bag and pours the contents into the palm of my hand. My, how they gleam! Beautiful! Odd sizes and shapes, most of them smallish, about 8 mm to a side on the average. But the reds and greens refracting from the surface are beautiful to behold. A few of them are dark; most are like a milk matrix.

"It ain't really the color that's important," says Wally. "It's the size of the color. The smaller the better. Looky here! This one is worth $220!"

And with that he pokes a small, milky stone around in the palm of my hand with his dirty, cracked fingernails. The stone is about 8 mm long in a triangular shape, with the base being maybe 5 mm. No brilliant greens or reds here, but deep down in the milk there are little silver scintillations; myriads of them. It's like looking at the Milky Way on a dark night. So that's what they look for!

"Do you ever sell them, Wally?"

"Well, we're not really supposed to retail them for ourselves, but I reckon we can give them away. I can sell you the bag they come in."

"Wally, I'd like to make a deal with you. I'd like to have a $500 bag. Could I do that?"

"Sure. Do you want two or three stones in the bag? Or more? Or less? I can put as many as you want in the bag."

"Okay. Give me about five or six stones in the bag. Is a check on Anzed bank okay? I'll be back in four weeks, and can just leave the check here with sister, and she can give me the bag. Is that Okay?"

"Sure, but it's the lot for the bag for $500. You can't take some of the stones out, and then try to bargain with me. Or even bargain at all on the price of the bag. It's $500 or nothing. You have the right to refuse the whole thing, but not to break up the lot."

"Fair enough!" I'd entered the strange world of raw opals. "How about uncut, unpolished?" I asked.

"Sure," said Wally. "I sell them in a jar. You can buy the jar. The stones are in it. Would you like some like that?"

"No, not this time, Wally. Let me just see what comes up this first time. I'll be here for another ten months, and I'm sure I'll get a chance to buy several more bags from you before I leave." So, now you'll have another facet of this life in the outback to follow.

It's time to load up the plane and head for home. Sister Ray makes herself comfortable in the recliner chair; fastens her belt. John goes through his preflight check. I sit in my seat in the heat of the day, daydreaming about opals. The engines roar into life. John taxis out to the strip slowly, letting all the gauges come into the green. Then we roar down the dusty strip and lift into the air.

"Clunk-clunk-kabunk!" goes the gear. The radio says, "niner thousand," for the trip home. That's nice. The air conditioner isn't working yet on the John Hawkins, and neither is the gyro horizon in front of John. We have a good tail wind. We hustle home. I'm still in the depths of a milky opal as we approach the middle marker for our landing, and the end of another interesting day. Who knows what next week will bring? We're scheduled for Fregon for the twenty-sixth. That's Thanksgiving Day. I'd told sister Carol that it's an American holiday, but that I'd be willing to fly that day. But I couldn't bear the thought of leaving my poor wife behind on a holiday. Sister Carol has already said, "That'll be no problem; we'll just bring her along!"

19 November 1981

Last week there was no trip, since we were in the midst of one of the coldest Novembers on record in the Territory. On Tuesday the seventeenth the temperature didn't rise above 9.9 degrees Celsius! (50 degrees Fahrenheit.) The previous coldest on record was 14.8 degrees and that was in 1941. The average temperature at this time of year is 33 degrees. It was rainy, besides. So, the trip to Ernabella was washed out. Well, we were told that the new assignment of the land of the area to the aboriginal tribes by the government of South Australia was also responsible for calling off the trip. It seems that there were certain number of corroborees that had to be held. So, there just wasn't that much enthusiasm for the trip.

It was still a memorable week as Laura and I had the fun of making our first flights in a sailplane! That's right! We went out to Bond Springs strip north of town, and were lofted into clear, blue skies (the only day it hadn't rained in almost a fortnight) by a cable of fence wire attached to a winch on a truck. Now there's an experience! The initial "whoosh" as the machine is jerked into the air in about ten meters by the winch, and then the steep climb that really doesn't feel as steep when you are inside the machine as when you're watching from the ground.

At about 1,500 feet there's a dropping of the nose, and a "clunk" as the tow is released, and then a sensation that you could sit up there forever and not have to come down, except that there's no engine sound. The sensation is more like sitting in a drifting boat than hitting the waves with a power boat. That's the difference between a sailplane and a powered craft. Laura was lucky. Her pilot, Ron Russ, found a thermal and got her up to 6,000 feet. They had to dial in the radio to the tower at the airport and get a clearance to go that high.

My pilot, Geoff, didn't find a good thermal. Our ride lasted only about fifteen minutes. But it was most enjoyable. I did take a lot of movies and slides of the scenery. We'll see how they come out. I think my bumm was too heavy, and we came down right on the dime, so to speak. Geoff let her roll right back to the hook-up point for the next launch. Rather remarkable. I'd like to do it again.

On the nineteenth, the weather had cleared from the rain. It was still cold. I didn't really know if we'd go or not, but I was out at the airport at 0750 hours. There was FML and FDQ both standing on the tarmac, buttoned up, and no pilot in sight. Well, I thought, they forgot to let me know that we'd been cancelled. But it was nice, so I stood there and admired the view and some of the activity that is always on-going around an airport. Then came along the little utility (pick up truck), and it was Mark with Giles, his baby kangaroo.

"Look how much he's grown!" exclaimed Mark, proudly, as he dumped the marsupial from his cozy sack. To me Giles looked like a skinny waif, about 18 inches high if he stood up straight. Weighed about five pounds, if you soaked him down with water. A Fokker Friendship was warming up for Ansett on the apron, and as the turbines whirred louder, the joey looked uneasy at first, and then bolted straight east, away from the noise, with Mark in hot pursuit. Eventually, Mark came back with the sack bulging from his right hand. Apparently, kangaroos don't like the high frequency turbine whine.

"We're taking FDQ today," says Mark. "The avionics have all failed on FML." What he's saying is that the beautiful console of locking on the controls to the "flight director" is all washed up in the new plane. Isn't that awful? Six hundred thousand dollars worth of unusable machinery. That's O.K. FDQ is a good, faithful airplane. Then sister Carol arrives; out of sorts. The sisters at Amata hadn't told her until this morning that the strip was open. Dr. Hugh Wilson and Barbara, an aboriginal woman, are coming along with us. They're scheduled for Docker river, but Mark will drop us off at Amata first. Back into the right hand seat.

"Foxtrot Delta Quebec, line up runway one two, cleared for take off, the two-two-two radial from Alice at six thousand," says

the controller, and Mark pushes the throttles open, and away we
trundle. Half way down the runway we rotate, the gear comes
loose from the tarmac, and we're climbing out at a thousand feet
a minute. Clunk clunk go the gear doors, and we're all delighted,
except that Mark can't get the take-off flaps to retract. He pushes
the switch for flaps up. Nothing. Push the switch for flaps down,
and the flaps come down some more. Push it up again, and the
flaps come up a little more. After the fourth or fifth flip of the
switch, the flaps are all the way up. Now, if they'll come down
again when we went them, we're in!

Ground speed is good. I read my journal. Mark carries on a
clandestine conversation on a VHF frequency prearranged, with
a friend who is going in a different direction. I don't thing they're
discussing a pleasant week-end, either in the past or coming up.
I don't pay that much attention. We arrive at Mt. Connor, but
about two miles west. Sister Carol chides Mark for being off the
track. It's a clear day. A little haze on the horizon, but one can
see a long way. The Peterman range is visible way out to the
west, and the Musgraves are coming up, with the strip at Amata
quite plainly visible even from twenty miles away. That's good.
It was getting kind of grown over. Chris is waiting for us at the
strip. Mark and Hugh and Barbara are off and away again, and
I get some good movies of FDQ on take off.

The power is off at the settlement. The first patient is Billie;
about twenty-nine. He's been to the Alice for diagnosis, but there
was a death in the hospital and Billie fled. There's the thought
that he has a tumor, or maybe it's just cirrhosis. He's thin, not
feeling well, but not jaundiced, either. I think he has a mass in
the right upper quadrant of his abdomen, but I don't know what
it is. Gallbladder? Something about eight centimeters in diameter
is there, just below the ribs. I don't know what it is. I guess it's
academic anyway. Billie won't go back to ASH (Alice Springs
Hospital) until the "spirit" is gone.

After Billie, we see Myintiryiri, a new born with a positive
serology for syphilis. She was born on 27 October 1981. I'm not
going to do a femoral stick for a blood sample. I guess the lesser
of the two evils is just to treat her with LPG. Barbara is next.
Barbara is 15. This isn't the same Barbara that was on the plane.
That Barbara is on the way to Docker River. This little girl is sick

with a huge abscess in her right groin, says sister Chris.

"Barbara, can I look at the lump?" I say gently.

Barbara turns her head away. That means, "No." She understands English, obviously, but won't voice the "No."

"Barbara, we'll just have you lie on the bed like the ladies do when they have the doctor look at them for their baby," says Chris.

Barbara looks at Chris. There's just the slightest raising of the chin. That's "palya," or "Okay." So, I busy myself at the notes, not looking up, while Barbara gets on the bed, and Chris pulls a dirty sheet over her, and Barbara lifts her skirt. Examination reveals a huge abscess, but not as red as one would think it should be, and about twelve-by-five centimeters. It's rocky hard! No fluctuation at all. It follows the inguinal ligament to the symphysis. There's nothing on the other side but some enlarged nodes. Chris tells me that there's no involvement of the labia with the lesion. We'll put her on Amoxil.

"It would be better if I could make a little opening in there and let that pus out," I tell Barbara.

The head turns to the left just a tad. That's "No."

"Well, when the clinic is done with, you come back, if you'd like me to make that feel better. Otherwise sister will give you some medicine." Barbara leaves.

Next we have Kaye; she had her baby. All is well. She had it on the floor at the clinic in Indulkana. She's involuted (the uterus had contracted) well. Next is Yaritzi, 106/60, 23/52, 67 kg, FHH 152. She's okay. Next is Monica, 22/52, 90.5 kg, 124/60. She has protein in her urine. FHH 144. We'll give her some Bactrim for the uti (urinary tract infection). Then, there's Lorna's newborn Stephen. He's a fine, bouncy baby boy. Cute as a bug's ear. Lorna is involuted well too. Then Millie, who is Monica's Mom. She has a uti (urinary tract infection). She's on Daonil for her diabetes, had 3 + sugar in her urine, and is AWOL from ASH. Her pressure is 154/84. Riva was born at ASH 10 September 1981 with a positive VDRL (flocculation test for syphilis). We'll give her LPG treatment.

Malpiya had involuted okay after her baby. Nakara is 120/68. She has substernal pain. She's diabetic. Her pain is on the right side. She was seen by me in March, May, August, September and now with the same complaint. Maybe it is gallstones (kukia).

Next is sister Bailey. She's gray haired, down from Adelaide on some mission, and has laryngitis, and is on Amoxil. She's rather haughty; condescends to let the doc take blood pressure. It's 192/112. She's taking half a tab of dichlortride when she thinks about it. I advise her that she's the victim of a significantly elevated pressure, and should really have it watched more closely. She advises me that she has a physician in Adelaide whom she sees periodically, and he's not unhappy with her pressure. That's the close of the discussion. It's kind of like she moved her head sideways, just a tad to the left; like Barbara.

Brenton has a right biceps bursitis. Little Craig Strong was the child that we've seen before with asthma. The aminophyllin suppositories weren't accepted by him. But the sweat test was done and was negative. Not to worry about cystic fibrosis. We'll keep him on the brondecon. At least he takes that. Kerry Tracor is back. The chemist gave her only one pack of nordette, an oral contraceptive, so I rewrite the script for her to have six months worth. Another Monica? This one was born on 6 April 1981. She has a primary chancre of syphilis just above the pubis. I've never seen a primary on a baby before. She also had tinea capitis (ringworm of the scalp). I'm not sure which will be the biggest problem for Monica. We don't have anything here but Whitfield's ointment for treating tinea. We do have LPG for the chancre. Poor little thing. I wonder where she got it? The chancre, that is.

Kunmanara is antenatal. 126/62, 20/52. And that ends the patient part of the clinic. Sister Chris says that Ivan's serology and FTA (fluoresceine treponemal antibody, a test for syphilis) came back positive. So, they are giving him a course of LPG.

Now it's time for lunch at sister Chris'. She had homemade bread rolls, whole wheat, spread with butter. Yumm! And a cup of hot tea! She has some anemic looking fatty sausage that I decline. She also has some cheese, but again, she's worked hard to get that, and I don't need it at all. There's another Chris here who is a linguist of some sort. I don't know what she's doing. She has a cute little chihuahua dog that had had recent surgery for something. I didn't ask that much about it. Then there's Gina Dinnell, an aboriginal health worker who is program director for the South Australia Health Commission, and then we're off for the airstrip.

Back into FDQ. Mark turns things on; the fuel boosters are

inoperative, say the warning lights. Well, so be it. The main boosters still work, but we hope that the engines will kind of suck up their own petrol as they need it. The runway is all smooth and clean; the grader is just finishing up the job. FDQ roars down the runway, lifts easily into the sky. I glance out the window as we cross the village. Gee, there's a beautiful swimming pool just on the other side of the school. I've never noticed that before. Next time we're down here, I'll have to walk over there and take a look at it. I read all the way home. It's bouncy as the devil for about twenty miles near the Finke River, but then smooth after that. Mark gets a right base for one-two, and puts it smoothly on the tarmac. We taxi up to where Bob Worthing is waiting for sister Carol. Time to get to the APO yet if I hurry. By golly! I just remembered! Barbara never did show up to have that abscess opened.

26 November 1981

It's an American holiday, and I had told sister Carol that I'd be happy to fly that day with the AMS of the RFDS, but hated to leave my wife alone on a holiday, and sister Carol had said, "That's no problem. We'll take her with us."

That's why we were out at the airport at 0745 this morning. It's a lovely day. There are some high clouds, and we've had a lot of rain. Everything is kind of drippy, but the air smells so clean, and there's almost no wind here at the Alice. John is here. He's upset. He had to get up this morning because no one could find Mark. It's supposed to be Mark on duty, but at 0515 Darryl had called John and he had to come out. He had to move FDQ out of the hangar, and then the little tow machine had run out of petrol, and so they had to move the big Navajo out with man-power. It's pretty heavy to push very far. Then he had to fuel it, and the flaps haven't been fixed yet, and the booster pumps still don't work, but FML is totally out of it, so I guess it's got to be FDQ.

Anyway, there are two aboriginal women waiting with two babies. The one, thinner girl is Judy, and her little girl is about three or so; Winmarti. Then there's a fat lady, whom I do not know, but her little boy, maybe about nine months or so, is Dudley. The kids have been to the Child Health Unit to be de-wormed and such, and are now on their way to Fregon. Chartair is upset. They claim that they lose $150 by us taking these people to Fregon. Sister Carol isn't too happy about it, either, but we're going to be all going. It's going to be a full plane. Laura is in the right front seat. I'm in the one that faces backwards. Carol is in the "Recliner," and the ladies are sitting on the side seat, holding the babies. I have my GP journal to read, and do the lesson for CME. John fires up the plane. He has the earphones on so I don't hear the tower clearance, but we roll out to the taxi strip, and head down for "three-oh." It's amazing how one feels the accel-eration when you are sitting in the backward facing seat. That Navajo really has the power.

We come unglued from the strip about half way down. It's hard to turn around in the seat with the belt on, so I just read my magazine and look out the window at the world retreating. Things are sure coming colorful. The dusty gray of the leaves of the wattles are coming green, and there seems to be an unusual amount of water lying around. Over the highway we fly, and then back again as John listens to what his earphones are telling him. We're to fly at 6,000 feet.

Sister Carol hands me a sheaf of notes from patients that have been in hospital. Let's see. Here's on Robert Nelson from Ernabella; had the abscess in his left thigh? Well, they did a superficial I and D (incision and drainage), and were going to undeck the whole thing, but Robert went AWOL. It seems that someone asked him for money, and, since he didn't have any, he didn't bother to explain that he was "disadvantaged," and therefore didn't have to pay. He just took off. Well, we'll have to get him back again. Kinta's graft on his leg is fine. Remember him? He's Clara's daddy. Billy Nelson's blood count is back. Billy is from Amata. Remember last week? He was in Amata, having fled the hospital when someone died? Well, he has twenty-four percent eosinophils, a white blood cell associated with parasitic infections or allergy. I wonder if that lump in his belly could be an amoebic abscess? Oh, yes. Here's one about Sharon, mother of Nellie from Indulkana. She's four, and has reflux in her left ureter. She's going to need surgery in Adelaide.

Tanya, mother of Kathleen from Mimili has SBE (subacute bacterial endocarditis). She's scheduled for a cardiology consult next year. Gilpin Ward did have uric acid crystals in that swollen knee (gout), but Dr. Franklin put him on Indocin. I wonder why? Would you like to hear what they've found in the gut of some of the kids coming to the children's Health Unit? Well, I'll tell you anyway. There's been Giardia, Entamoeba hystolitica (amoebas), Hymenolepsis nana, Chilomastix mesmili, and Trichomonas hominis among other things. What have the kids been treated with? Well, gentian violet, iodine, dry mop of the ears, Bactrim, Yomesan, Flagyl, Minterol, and Sofradex for the ears, among other things.

There's the strip at Ernabella way up ahead. Laura has already spotted it. Then John slips off the autopilot and we start a gradual descent. The babies have been good as gold. We have a couple of pictures of them with Laura holding the little one just before we boarded the plane. They sure are cute little kids. Strange, Dudley has a bottle for his nine months, and Winmarti has the teat for her three years. It's a strange culture. It's a little bumpy as we descend. On final, Laura is caught by the illusion of the shortness of the strip because of the hump in the middle. It really does look terribly short when you're on final. John does a superb job in spite of a little cross wind, and the shear calls for just a tad of power at the right time to keep from ballooning.

Sister Julie Dorn is there to meet us, but has a strange Land Rover that I've never seen before. I guess they've rolled another vehicle. Fregon is sure a tough place for vehicles. In to town with Laura on my lap. The vehicle is pretty full. The road comes past the craft store. Things are awfully messy. Then Julie tells us that a couple of weeks ago they had a big, black cloud, and at 1500 hours, a wind came right through the center of the town. It tore part of the roof off the craft building, bent the radio tower right in two, and broke down some huge trees. The big white cedar in the middle of the town square has been literally ripped apart by the force of the wind. Miraculously, no one was injured. A dog was killed. It must have been quite a wind. Hard to tell, though, how much of the junk that was there was just re-distributed. The place looks just as messy as ever.

Beverly, age twenty-four, is our first patient. She has a backache. Seemed at first like she was saying that it was in the left sacroiliac joint, but later turns out that she was pushed down, and it's really her tail bone that's sore. Let's try some Indocin for that. Next Sammy wants his driver's test. We do it for him, all official, although the land we're on now is tribal land, and the state of South Australia has no jurisdiction, and he really doesn't need a license at all. I wonder what happens if one of the ab-orignal drivers, now without a license, should run down one of our sisters out there? Who's liable? Who pays for the sister's hospitalization if she's busted up? I guess none of the politicians thought of that. It figures. Sammy has a blood pressure of 152/94. Sister Julie is asked to follow up on that. He also has a mitral murmur.

Fiona is six. She has microscopic hematuria (blood in the urine). She's had it for a couple of years now, but never had a work up. Mom has had tuberculosis. We attempt to palpate the belly, and are greeted with shrieking and struggling. Forget it. I'll ask Dr. Martins about it when I get into the Alice. We do take a urine specimen with us. It looks clear.

Did you know that since the tribal takeover, the name of Fregon has been changed to Apparawatatja? I didn't think you did. Well, it is. Next patient is Mantuwa. She was seen before, about a year ago, with complaints of pain in the side of her head. Today she has the same complaint. She has a hard node in the posterior cervical triangle on the right. As I feel around, my fingers find a cystic mass in the scalp just above the node and into the hairline. My fingers trace this clear around the occiput, and down on the trapezius muscle behind, and almost around to the left ear. Is it a cystic hygroma? I don't know what it is. Mantuwa is reluctant to go with us in the plane to the Alice. She wants to talk with her husband, she tells sister Carol. Sister Carol says a few words ending with a question mark in Pitjantjatjara to Mantuwa, who drops her face into her hands giggling, and if the black skin would show a flush of blushing, you'd see it on Mantuwa. One chuckles at the reaction to what sister Carol must have said. They're a shy people. Mantuwa will come in on the mail plane on Tuesday. That reminds me, I'll have to write a letter for Dr. re-referral. Mantuwa's thirty-seven.

There's another Mantua whose mother is named Robyn. When two offspring in the same settlement have the same name, whichever dies first will have that name, and the survivor will have to change her name. This Mantua is pregnant, and is nineteen. About 22/52, 120/60. FHH 142/minute. By golly! Here's funny, little Clara. Julie Peters has brought up a couple of patients from Ernabella for us to see. History from the Mom (Kinta's wife with the pearly teeth and the "mincobah" sticking out the side of her mouth) is that Clara had a seizure the other night; right arm and left leg were twitching. Clara's taking 30 mg of phenobarb at night. Examination today reveals a poor, little waif who just looks awfully funny. She has a peculiar lack of tone in her neck muscles. Her head lolls back and forth like a rag doll with too little stuffing. I don't know what to make of it. I guess I'll just leave her on the phenobarb, and reassure Mom.

Next is Tjunjilya. She's twenty-eight. She has tinea corporis all over her body. Just all over! I've never seen anything like it! I guess I'll put her on Grisovin tabs, two twice a day for a month and see what happens. Next is Katherine; 64 kg, 120/70, FHH 144, I think. She's only 17/52. She's okay. Next is Tjalora, also known as Priscilla. She's fourteen months, and is really chesty. She's breathing really fast. Let's put her on Amoxil. Amany is a diabetic, but she's not taking her Daonil regularly. We draw blood for sugar just to see how far off from control we are. Nellie is also diabetic. Blood pressure is 150/100. We draw blood on her, too. Jill Burns is a European; has an ear ache. Her birth date is 8 November 1949. Examination shows nothing much. She's also asthmatic and needs some ventolin. I think her husband landed one on her ear. There's no evidence of blood. The TM (tympanic membrane—ear drum) is intact. I'll do nothing more.

Then we take a walk over to the school. Laura has already had a couple of exposures to the school. Neal, the headmaster, is his usual diluted, aboriginal self; alternating from aboriginal mentality to European mentality each five minutes. It's schizophrenic trying to follow his thinking. He's nice, then put upon. He does invite me to visit the school library, then leaves me in the middle of the books with no reference as to what I'm looking at. I thumb through a few basic readers. It all looks like "numanumanuma" to me. But then, I'm uneducated. Sister Carol is picking up a couple of copies of "readers" for her own library.

Then over to sister Julie's. There's a big crowd for lunch today! There's Noel and Pat and Rudy who are up from Adelaide on an inspection of the settlement. I don't know what their report will alter, but they're here to make a report to someone down there. They have their own "draft" with them. I don't know if Fregon is dry, but I think it is. John Tapp is also here. He's the chief administrator for the council. He's awfully young for that kind of job. We find out that Barry Ferrel is the director of the Health Commission, and Elliott Carter will be taking over that post now that the land has been given back, but they've changed the name now to the Pitjantjatjara Homelands Council. That ought to make it better!

Mark and his friend are here from Indulkana. Mark is sitting next to me. He's eliciting information like he's writing a book. He wants to know where I'm from and what I do. When I mention the Spyce Byce he clams up; never said another word to me the rest of lunch time. There's a big spread. Chicken that's from Cole's that sister Carol brought, and a salad, and lots of things. Laura and I have a cup of tea. The rest all munch out.

Then it's time to go. But we have to stop by Amata. Yeah! Laura will get to see Amata. Out to the airport in the ute (utility—pickup truck), and John fires up FDQ. G'bye to Fregon . . . er, Apparawatatja, 'til next time. I'm facing backwards again, so don't see much coming up; just what's going away. It's almost too bumpy to read. There's the valley to the right (south) and the mountains to the left (north), as we head west. Laura and John are chattering away up front, but I can't make out what they're saying. Carol has her recliner reclining, and her eyes are closed. She's sleeping—like a fox. I try to read.

Then we're over the Amata strip. It sure looks nice and neat now that it's all been graded off. I don't see the pool just south of the school. I'll have to make a special trip back that way next time I have the chance. Is there or isn't there a pool at Amata? Oh, boy! A real mystery! Then, we're touching down and rolling out. Laura remarks that there are a lot more trees here that Fregon . . . er, Apparawatatja, and for sure, there are a lot more paddy melons! Sister Jennie is there, and she has a new health worker with her now.

Margaret is a huge, African, Black sister; tiny voice and hand shake, but her head has close cropped hair to hide the curls, contrary to the black skin of the aboriginals and their blond hair. I wonder if Margaret will give her hair an experimental try with a little 20 peroxide? We're there to pick up Billy Wilson! He's been vomiting and just having a terrible time. The lump in his right upper quadrant is a lot bigger. I'll bet that really is an amoebic abscess. Well, we'll soon know.

That's all there is at Amata. John cranks up FDQ and we head back for the end of the strip. What's this? Two large pieces of corrugated metal roofing forming an "X" at the end of the strip and held down with two huge rocks! Good thing we didn't hit that when we came in! I didn't even see it from the air. That's the universal sign for a "closed" strip! None of us saw it from the air. That's scary! Maybe the grader operator put it there when he was working the strip and then forgot to take if off. We're on the ground now, and John keeps us just to the left of it as we start our take-off runs. Now we're up and away for home. Back over Mt. Connor and the dry lakes that have a lot of water in them this week. I'm riding backwards and can't see it all that well. Then we're tunneling through the bases of some neat thunderheads, and I turn forward. Laura's head is fixed, but her eyes are closed. She's snoozing!

The autopilot carries on, alternating with shadow and brilliant sunshine on the desert floor, and the total fog of the clouds as we sail through them. Then we're letting down; runway three-oh again. John sets it down neatly. We give our thanks to John and sister Carol for the fun time. Now Laura's been to three of the four settlements. I still want her to honor the invitation from Marg Baxter for Granite Downs. That will be fun; another time.

Oh, yes. Another detail. While we were on the ground at Amata, John had talked with RFDS on the low frequency radio; our VHF had gone out and we couldn't let traffic control in Alice tower know where we were. He was able to get through to RFDS, though, and sister Kay had phoned the flight service to let them know that we were on the ground at Amata. Then, when we left there, we had sister Kay call them again. But the radio seemed to work okay as we got nearer to the Alice, and John was in contact with the tower as we made our final approach. I wonder which of the planes will be airborne next week? Well, I won't be here, so it won't matter. It's to be Indulkana the week after that, and I wonder if Wally will be waiting with his opals?

28 November 1981 (Saturday)

I made a visit to the hospital to see Billy Wilson, but it was futile. Sister says he refused to take a shower when he first arrived on Thursday, and when she looked around for him half an hour later, he had absconded. So much for Billy Wilson. I wonder when we'll see him again.

29 November to 6 December

It really does have a business purpose. Once a year it's nice for me to have the opportunity to travel south to Adelaide to visit those doctors that I most often refer patients to when I'm in a bind up at the Alice. I did it last year at almost this exact same time, and I did get permission from by boss to do it again this year. Now the air fare, economy, return (round trip) is $282 Australian. That calculates to $327 American at today's exchange rate. But if you buy the ticket far enough in advance, it can be quite a saving. So, we bought Laura's ticket in September for $181 Australian. On Sunday afternoon at about 1600 hours, Carl Catlin, the medical service officer at the base, picked us up and took us to the airport. It was a really nice Ansett Airlines 727, and it was right on time. No strikes yet. They'll come around Christmas time when it will disadvantage the most people.

Mr. Dolan is the head of the ACTU (Australian Council of Trade Unions), and although he's not elected by the people, he's really the one who runs the country. I might say, that from my point of view, he's running it straight into the ground. One of these days, the Australian currency will have to free float on the world exchange, and it's going to be like Argentina. I wouldn't invest any money in Australia right now. I'd wait another year or three.

Adelaide is on the "summer" time, so they're an hour ahead of the Alice. It's about a two hour flight, and it was as smooth as could be. We came in over Port Augusta right on time, and began the descent that brings us over some of the Barossa Valley, the wine country of Australia, after crossing the Spencer Gulf to the Yorke Peninsula. From the Yorke Peninsula, we picked up the approach over the Gulf of St. Vincent into Adelaide airport, which is right adjacent to the beach in the western side of the city; LAX on a wee scale, if you will. Progress being what it is, they are talking about making Adelaide an international airport, so that they can land the jumbos here, and if they do, it will call for enlarging the present airport, and it's going to be a mess. But . . .

It's just sunset time as we touch down. There's supposed to be a rental car at Budget, and so there is. It's a nice, little Holden Commodore 4-door, white outside, blue interior, air, radio, but no power steering. It's nice. Then to the counter of Ansett. "If someone told me to pick up something left at the Ansett counter, where would I look?" I ask the chick at the desk, who is busy preparing her nails for a coat of shocking orange.

Without looking up; "The message box," with a sideways toss of her head to the right. Yes, there's the message box, clear plastic boxes with the letters of the alphabet under each pigeon hole. There is a message under "R" for Robertson; nothing else.

"It's not there," I tell the little thing who is still working on her right nails.

"Then there isn't anything," she announces, without looking up.

"Maybe it's under the door mat or some other unlikely place at the flat," I suggest to Laura. We take the luggage out to the Commodore, start the engine, figure out the lights and other panel items, and off for town, about fifteen kilometers away. After about five kilometers, Laura points out to me that the petrol gauge is on zero, and so it is.

"We'll find a petrol station," I predict. But on Sunday anywhere in Australia, they roll up the sidewalk, and there isn't going to be any petrol station open. I understand there are some that are coin operated, but I don't find any. Well, we can get some in the morning, and we finally arrive at the flat. There are series of flats that are maintained by the U.S. Government for employees who TDY (temporary duty assignment) to Adelaide. They are booked through housing at the base. No key under the mat. No mat, as a matter of fact. There's not one on the ledge over the door, either. Another tenant in the upstairs flat allows me to use his phone to call Joint Defense.

"It's at the airport," I'm told. So, back into the car with the empty petrol tank, and back to the airport. The little chick still has the fourth and fifth nails of the left had to finish, so I don't go to her. I go to a young man who looks intelligent. He walks over to a box in front of the chick with the nine-tenths of a finger manicure job done, and picks up the keys to Flat eight. Did she look up at all? Was there total disdain on her face? No matter. She's probably married to the boss' son. Poor guy!

Back to the "Budget" counter. "It's empty," I enlighten the girl behind the desk.

"It's empty?" She's shocked. "How could that be?"

"Well," I reply, "I haven't been gone long enough to burn it all out."

But she's a sweet young thing, and calls a service boy. We rode with him to the service area, since all our things are in the car, and he really does fill it right to the brim. We drive him back to the terminal. She apologizes again.

"It's okay. It's really good service!" We're off for the second time for the flats in North Adelaide. We really do know our way around pretty well by now. We've done the route before. The flat is nice. Two bedrooms, and a bath; kitchen, living/dining area, and a color TV with more than one channel! But it is getting late. A bit of unpacking, a shower, (the water looks like diluted mud), and into bed. It's cool; maybe fifteen degrees Celsius and this just has to be the best mattress I've slept on since the round bed at home. Good thing, too. Today started at 0100 hours, with a huge balloon from a ureteral stone trying to find its way to the bladder, and it didn't go away until I presented myself at CAS at the hospital in the Alice at six this morning and had received my pethidine and Maxilon to make the spasm go away.

Monday was lots of fun. We saw a lot of old friends, re-acquainted with a lot of friends, and even met a few new ones. Adelaide is an extremely easy town to find one's way around in. We bought thirty dollars worth of groceries, and went home for a steak dinner. Laura had been with me all day on the itinerary, so was happy to have a chance to kick off her shoes, too. It was fun shopping. Lettuce is reasonable at forty-five cents a head, compared to $1.29 in the Alice. And zucchini at eighty-five cents per kilogram compared to $2.69 in the Alice. We watch some shows on color TV, eat a superb steak dinner, and hop into bed. So much for Monday.

Tuesday is just a beautiful day. The sun comes up clear and warm, but not too warm. Today is the day that our son, Randy, is to be sworn in as a lawyer (pardon me; attorney-at-law) in Los Angeles. Well, really, since today is yesterday in America, it will be tomorrow that's today. But, anyway, you know what I mean. We do spend the whole day getting around to nice doctors, and we also see a lot of friends. Yesterday we stopped in at the Royal Adelaide Hospital and saw Bud Webster, our friend with the smashed T–3 vertebra, who is paraplegic. Bud wasn't feeling well; lots of pain, and he was on his way for x-rays. Today he's feeling much better, and a bit out of the doldrums. He sure has had a rough time with this thing. He hasn't gotten anything back for movement or sensation at all. His prism glasses for viewing TV from a supine position are broken, too, and he hasn't found anyone to fix them yet. We'll take care of that! We tour quite a bit of the town, see lots of interesting doctors, and have a chance to discuss patients. Then it's time to head back to the pad. It's nice to get the shoes off. Laura has a superb "chopped topside" (hamburger) with all the trimmings, and then a couple games of cribbage and a show on TV, and it's time for bed again.

Wednesday is a good day. I've seen Dr. Deringer, my urologist, and he thinks we can sit still on the kidney stone for now, but that it will have to come out some day. He talks about a muscle-splitting technique that he's done that gets the patient on his feet the next day. He also talks about scuba diving in Tahiti, etc., and I wonder if I'd catch him at home if I really had a problem. Tonight we're having dinner at Eric and Pat Clay's house. Maureen and Ahmed Belt are there, too. Eric is the father of Jonno Clay. Jonno and his wife, Jean, are personal friends up in the Alice. He is territorial police officer in the Alice. Ahmed is a pediatric urologist. We sit for cocktails in the yard under a beautiful variegated boxelder tree. It's just lovely. Then, in to leg of lamb dinner, which follows a tasty gazpacho, and is served with an excellent Barossa Valley wine. Eric is a horticulturist, historian, and professor emeritus of the pediatric department of Flinders medical centre. They're just delightful people, and have had six weeks tour of Europe on holiday this year. It's a great evening.

Another beautiful day greets us on Thursday. There's time to walk a bit in the mall (the Rundle Mall) in downtown Adelaide, and also to look around a bit on O'Connell Street in North Adelaide. Passing a fish shop, we see "crayfish—$8.80/kg," and they're there! We buy one! We were going to go out to Benjamins tonight. It's a lovely restaurant down on the Torrens river, where it's dammed up to make a little lake, but this looks so good. Then we've committed ourselves, and have a bug in the bag, with some fresh broccoli, and some garlic toast, and melted butter. Not as fancy as Benjamins, but with butter on your hands and around your mouth, and those big, white chunks of lobster going down the hatch, it doesn't have to be really fancy. That was fancy at Eric and Pat's last night.

Naturally, we've kept up our itinerary for the day, and a bit more besides. We even found our way back to Bud's hospital room, and found him encouraged after a good day. He's going to be going to the rehab centre for training a week from today. That's when I find that Leota, Bud's wife, has to see a doctor, too. I make an appointment for her with Dr. Adams. It'll be okay, I tell myself. We did find time to stop off at Henley Beach for a while today, too. Beautiful sunny day, about twenty-five degrees Celsius and the water is warm and clear. No tar, no seaweed, just a beautiful beach with very little surf, and the wind-surfers are out in force. I read. Laura soaks up the rays. We had about two hours there just enjoying! This is a beautiful spot!

On Friday, another beautiful day. We finish about noontime, and head out for the Cleland National Preserve. It's about thirty kilometers out of town, up in the mountains, with lots of trees around it. The admission is still only a buck for adults. We visit the aviary, and see the kangaroos and the dingoes. Then it's feeding time for the koalas. There is a group of "Brownies" there, all lined up on the wall of the enclosure, and the rangers are passing two koalas around between the kids to let them pet them and feel the softness. Laura places herself at the end of the line of kids on the wall.

"Wait till the kids have gone," whispers the ranger-lady. "Then you can hold one!"

Laura is delighted. The session with the Brownies ends, and they depart for another part of the park; each delighted to have felt a real, live koala. Then there are about a dozen "grown-ups" left, and "Beau" and "Angie" are passed from ranger to visitor.

"Let the animal do the work," says the lady ranger. "They get nervous if you try to take them in your hands, and those claws are very sharp."

They have two fingers of the hand that oppose, like two thumbs, and the nails of the first and second digit of the hind foot are combined to make a comb that they groom themselves with. There's a small spot just beneath the chin on the upper chest that is their scent gland; they mark out their territory with that. They really are as soft as they look, and since they are a nocturnal animal, they don't fuss much with people during the day. I was told that they make a screeching sound at night, though, not unlike the beginning screech of a wild donkey braying. It's amazing! I didn't hear it, but it sounds like it would be strange to hear that kind of noise from one of these teddy bears of real life.

Back to North Adelaide, and we'll go to the Pink Pig, or the Fish Manse tonight for dinner. That was the plan until we were walking down O'Connell street and saw the Greek shop with "Yiros" advertised. It's a vertical barbecue, done with slabs of pork, and as it does on the outside, the man slices off well done chunks with an electric knife, and adds seasoning. Yummy! We cave in and buy half a kilo, and a barbecued whole chicken, and some wine, and retreat to the apartment. What a fun way to picnic; right in front of the TV! But what's this? Someone is trying a key in the lock of our front door. Laura is frightened.

"Not to worry," I reassure. "If the key doesn't fit the lock they won't get in, and they have the wrong apartment. If they do come in, it will be someone we know from the base."

The door opens. It's friends who have been on R&R (rest and relaxation) to New Zealand, and have returned two days early. He's scheduled for a surgical consult on Monday, but wasn't to arrive until Sunday night. What to do? With dinner in the oven, we can't just move out. They have two small children who are at that stage of absolute fatigue from two hours time change, and a day of travel, that they are just super alert! They're also into everything! Oops! The little one almost got my cocktail! A quick phone call confirms that we are to be in the flat until Sunday. Never mind. If we can find a place for them tonight, we'll move out tomorrow; a day early. So be it. We find them a room at the Grosvenor Hotel.

Saturday is another beautiful day. We've been blessed with beautiful days. The family arrives back at the flat at 1000 hours. We pick up and move to the Grosvenor. It's a lovely hotel on north terrace, and only fifty dollars Australian a day! We move in, then back to see Bud one more time, and finish up with a few more phone calls to friends and doctors. Then we go down to the Mall again. We find a book store, and finally find the book on the Great Barrier Reef that we've been looking for almost a year. Well, not really the one we want, but close enough to take it. It will be under the tree for Christmas! Also, we buy a soft ice cream cone, then some towel/calendars that will make neat presents, and then some more shopping.

Then we find ourselves back at the Torrens river, and the little paddle boat concession. This is on of those delightful places where they have the little boats that one makes move with pedals, like a bicycle. Only they are really streamlined, and make one feel like one is in a boat; not way high up. Three dollars for half an hour, and when you come back they give you one dollar back.

Back to the hotel room. Another trip to see a doctor out towards Flinders, and stop at the beach again on the way back to town. The yacht races are on! We sit and watch. Almost no wind. They aren't moving fast at all. At the near buoy, they try to cut it close. The challenger to the leader tries to cut it too close. He capsizes! No problem. It's calm water, but by the time the poor bloke has his craft righted, he's just at the end of the line. Then comes a helicopter, and just shortly after that the surf patrol vessels come along and shoo everyone out of the water. It seems there's a school of four-foot hammerhead sharks tucking napkins under their chins and grabbing utensils! So much for the beach. But it was fun to sit there for a while. Back to the hotel again.

Sunday morning it's off to the airport. We turn in the little car, board Ansett for the flight back to the Alice, and another lovely ride on a 727; smooth and comfortable. Two hours, and we're landing at the Alice. Carl and Audrey are there to greet us when we have claimed our "ports" (suit cases). Carl handles them into the "boot" (trunk) of the car and slams the lid. He fishes in his pocket; no keys! He's just locked the car keys in the "boot." There is no other set.

Margaret Fee offers us a ride into town. We accept. Carl and I grab his tools and two coat hangers and head back for the airport. It's almost deserted now. Not too many cars in the lot. I try my luck at snaring the lock post on the left side. Carl works on the posts on the right side, through the rubber insulation of the window. Carl wins! The door is open. Meantime, this rather well dressed younger man is leaning against a lamp post about ten meters away calmly surveying us, but with eyes darting to right and left on occasion. Then he moves behind two other cars at the far end of the parking lot, and I can see him watching us through the glass of the windows. What a suspicious looking bloke he is! But he doesn't say anything, and Carl and I have removed the back seat with his tools, and have the keys, and we drive away. That's how it is. Everything is under control. It's been a good holiday, and I did get a lot of things done! Hope my successor can continue this annual trip down there to see other doctors.

10 December 1981

Today is the first day of the 0700 hours departure. Even at that, when I leave the house at 0640, the sun is already up about 22 degrees on the horizon. It's a bit hazy this morning, and a few high clouds, but there's been rain lately, and it's also been up to forty-three degrees in the afternoons! Darryl says that he's taking a group off to Docker River; he'll be in FDQ. Mark is driving FML, and, yes, the avionics have all been repaired and in working order. FML is running up with Mark at the controls, so while we wait, I sit with Darryl on the bench just outside the AML lounge and chat. Darryl is relaxed. "Is Giles with Mark?" I ask.

"No, I think Giles has moved on," says Darryl.

"Oh," I kind of murmur, wondering if I should say anything at all to Mark. No, I guess I'll wait until he tells me about it. Bob Worthing arrives driving the Ford, with sister Carol beside him, and the conversation ends. Mark has finished the run-up, and shuts down FML. We load the notes and stuff into the plane, and a small talk conversation never does mention the baby kangaroo.

"Foxtrot Mike Lima, line up for runway one-two, 6,000, take the 207 radial, report to control at fifteen DME, clear for takeoff, right turn," says the tower. Mark pours on about two thirds power, until the needle comes off the post on the airspeed, then pours it all the way on, but he doesn't push and push at the throttles like Darryl does. He just keeps his hand on them, and lets the mixture and prop alone.

He becomes preoccupied with something else, like maybe the Cessna turning left ahead that took off before us. I don't say anything, and as we begin the right turn, he retracts the gear. I didn't notice before, but the left gear comes into place with its "thunk-thunk" before the right side.

It's not good enough visibility to look around all that much, so I turn to my continuing medical education booklets from the Connecticut and Ohio Chapters of the American Academy of Family Practice that I purchase each year, and find that I have twenty-two out of seventy-five questions answered incorrectly, but the correct answers are there in the answer booklet. It's not really because I'm dumb. It's because medicine has changed, and it's no longer first choice to do a cystoscopy and retrograde pyelogram on blood in the urine. Now one does an IVP (intravenous pyelogram—an x-ray study) first and then something else. Progress is getting with the latest ideas. Did you know that the "battered child" is no longer "in?" This suggests that the parent is always wrong. Now it's called "PITSS," which almost seems ironic. "Parent Infant Trauma Stress Syndrome," now suggests that some of those babies are really abominable!

Then we're descending for Ernabella. The elapsed time clock shows 1:04; an hour and four minutes since the engine started, and it was 4:13 when we lifted off; four minutes and thirteen seconds. So, it's just about an hour exactly since we started. Mark drops the gear at 160 indicated, and then the flaps! Who has he been flying with? But the rest of the approach is flawless, and we don't even have to "back-track;" just turn in to the parking area. Sister Julie Peters is along in the vehicle in short order. She's got a terrible cough; bronchitis. Remember? It was just a year ago that she had the bad infection that we had to bring her back with us? Thought is was mastoiditis then. She had fainted twice. Well, she's on Amoxil. We'll listen to her chest later. Now it's into the clinic.

First patient is Mantuwa from Fregon with the node and the hygroma or whatever. She had gone in to the hospital, but the letter I'd written didn't get there with her, and she was seen by a registrar (intern) who did nothing and sent her away! We'll have to send her back. Her letter is still on the desk of the surgical clinic! She's from Fregon, though, and, sure enough, here's sister Julie Dorn. She's brought up about six patients to be seen! Ray is one of them. He has pain in the right upper quadrant of his belly, she says. Not so, really. He has some sore ribs from trauma. Let's try some Indocin.

Next is Stanley from Fregon. He has low back pain. Let's try some Indocin for him, too. Then Tungku. He fell off his horse a week ago, and has pain in the paracervical muscles. Let's try some Indocin for him. Sounds like sister Julie should have used aspirin first, if she has any. Roderick has been taking Clotride, one a day, for his blood pressure. It's 158/90. He's 85 kg. Let's just keep him on his medicine. Next is poor little Clara again. Imuna, her mother, is really concerned. Clara had five seizures yesterday. Julie saw one of them. They were all just about alike. The child gave no cry; just suddenly rolled her eyes back and began to have a clonic seizure. She didn't stiffen out; no consistent incontinence, and, after the fit, she dropped off into a deep sleep. She had been seen by registrar, Dr. Mann, on October 6 at the hospital, and he thought they were just febrile convulsions. Actually, on the Harvard Standard Chart, she's in the eightieth percentile. She's been worked up for T.O.R.C.H.S. (a mnemonic for toxoplasmosis, rubella [measles], cytomegalovirus, herpes simplex and syphilis), and all were negative. Poor little Clara. Imuna, with the beautiful teeth and the mincobah in the corner of her mouth, is really worried. "We'd better take her back with us; okay (palya), Imuna?" She dips her chin just a tad.

Roland is next. He's with a foster mother. He's about nine, and he's breathing with a strange, grunting sound; expiratory with a sharp inspiration, and a rate about thirty-six per minute. When I listen, I think I hear decreased breath sounds in the right apex and middle lobes. Foreign body in the right mainstem bronchus? He's not febrile, but he's in trouble with his lungs. We'd better take him in too. "No," he says; not "We-ah." It's "No!" He speaks English, and he doesn't want to go to the hospital!

Foster mother says, "Ohah!" He'll be on the plane! He also has a lot of nodes in the cervical triangles, but none under the arms or in the groin, and the spleen and liver aren't palpable.

Good old Robert Nelson of the left lateral thigh abscess fame is here. Robert had left the hospital when we took him in before for his excision of the abscess, because some social worker told him he had to pay for it, and, gee, you can't spend money for something like an abscess when there's grog to buy in the Alice. So, he did the logical thing, and after they'd done the initial incisional drainage of the abscess, he fled; "absconded" is the word they use. By golly! The skin is healed over the incisional drainage site, and there's no induration beneath it. "Yes," says sister Julie, "but I've seen that before, too. And then it comes back up, and is a mess again in about six weeks." So be it! It's not there now, so there's nothing to do. I tell this to Robert, and he shows me a brilliant smile, except the right upper incisor and lateral teeth are missing, secondary to his initiation rite.

Remember Punch Johnston? Punch is the person who has

his picture in the brochures of the Tourist Bureau for the typical outback aboriginal? Punch's pressure is 128/92. He's really taking his medicine! He does have headaches at bedtime. How about an aspirin? He grins. Next is Morris; mother Kalkulya, born 23 October 1981 He's a beautiful baby! Edward; mother Lorraine (Laryn) is 3 months old. His left ear is full of pus, and he has a strange, transverse adipose roll just at the lumbo-sacral junction, but otherwise, a beautiful baby! Mellissa Thompson; mother Carlene, 21 September 1980, with diarrhea. She's teething. Let's try some elixir of benedryl. Then Jowis; mother Muyura (what a strange name, even for an aboriginal child), 17 September 1981. He's also a beautiful baby. Didn't you think all those antenatals would be producing something for me to look at? Isn't it funny? I don't have a single antenatal exam this time? Maybe there's a religious "no-no" about the time of the spring equinox. That would be September down here. Hmm! I'll ask around and let you know.

Next is Yvonne, 9 March 1981. She's spotted like an Easter egg with gentian violet, but it's all outside of the red ear on the right. How about that? She has a real myringitis (inflammation of the ear drum). Let's nip that in the bud with a big dose of penicillin. She's a fine baby. Patrick is about ten. He has had a nasty laceration of the right big toe, just at the MP joint dorsum, and it's infected. He has big, tender nodes in the groin. He's already got a bit of pubic hair. Maybe he's older. He's visiting from Finke. Mom is Lexie. I'll give him a Bicillin today, and another on the twelfth. He speaks English very well, but reluctantly.

Alison was born about 1925. She has a right biceps bursitis that is really swollen. Gosh, I'd love to put a needle into that. I'd bet I could get two hundred cc. of fluid off that. But I'd better not do it out here. She'd likely get an infection. Better if I put it in a sling and give her some Indocin. The sling will make her a discussion topic, and she'll be delighted! Still, it would be fun to drain that and put in about a mililiter of appropriate steroid!

That's about the total of the clinic. Then we look at sister Julie. She's on the Amoxil that she prescribed for herself. I wonder if she might have a mycoplasma? Maybe we'd better be wary, and put her on erythromycin as well as the Amoxil. Maybe it's a legionella? Well, that would be interesting to work up. She's not really well, though, and two antibiotics might do the trick. We'll try. She's not alone out here like last time, anyway. Patrick Markam is the new sister now. Patrick is from Adelaide. We get into a good discussion about medicine when we first go to Julie's for lunch, but then he learns that I'm "Spyce Byce" affiliated, and he kind of clams up. So does his wife, Jennie. We don't talk much about Adelaide.

We are taking Clara and Roland back with us. They do show up at the airstrip just at the right time. Mark puts everything into the plane, and we all take our places. Poor little Clara. I wonder how long she's going to last? Mark puts FML through its paces, and we race down the runway and take off into the hazy veil over the desert of the outback. Sheesh! It's really rough! I don't look back. I study my lesson. It must be pretty bad back there with the turbulence. The kids don't seem to mind. Carol is nodding as she reclines her seat. Mark sets the "flight director," and picks up some magazines. What is this? *House Beautiful? Better Homes and Gardens?* Yes, he's bought a house! It's at 156 Stuart Highway in the Alice. He's looking at Franklin stoves and all sorts of exotic furnishings! Does he have a friend that he's going to set up housekeeping with? Was Giles expendable? I'm invited to help move him in on Sunday the thirteenth at 1700 hours. I'll be at the COF's at that time. Too bad. I'd really like to find out. I'll try to remember to let you know in the next week or so.

Mark gets approval to descend from approach as we get to 20 DME. "Airforce 309, clear to land," says the tower, as we make our base leg, and a neat little Lear jet touches down and turns into the Ansett service area. We land behind. Mark does his usual great job, and the tires squeak a little, and we roll out and turn into our taxi way. As we come abreast of the jet that's disgorging two neat-looking men who are pulling suit coats on in the heat, I notice that there's an American flag on the tail. Gee, we're getting VIP's to the Spyce Byce! We taxi in to our usual place, and the ambulance is there, with light flashing, to pick up Roland and Clara. So, another day is almost done.

I find out later that the VIP's on the jet had been assigned to our parking area for security reasons, and when we landed right behind them with medical people, they had to make way for us. Sorry about that. I guess we did cause a bit of anxiety for the security people. But it's a lesson they should learn. Wonder who they were?

17 December 1981

It's Thursday again, and so it's time for "out bush" with the Aeromedical Service of the Royal Flying Doctors. Sister Carol Evans rang on Wednesday, says it's to be Amata for this week. That's good. It will be fun to find out what has happened to some of the patients from out there that we're curious about. It's to be a 0700 takeoff again, since it is the middle of summer, and the days are so long. I wake again at 0430 to hear the news; 1900 hours Greenwich. Mostly news about Poland and Azaria Chamberlain; slain by a dingo, and the fact that I learned today that the Northern Territory is broke. Not just the Health Department; the whole schmeer! Isn't that something? Sounds like the U.S. of A.

But Laura gives me a good breakfast of a hamburger with salad (for breakfast? . . . yeah! we didn't have any chelokabob left). The sun is up nicely, and it's not yet hot, but it's going to be a hot one! John is waiting at the airport. It's going to be FML today. FDQ is all bundled up. I guess it's not going anywhere. Giles did die. John said so. He said it was "lung congestion." Mark did move into his house. It's nice. They initiated it proper, says John. Someone sat on the Esky, and it broke and flooded the new carpet. But it was only pure water. Then someone else dropped a bottle, and it broke, and so there were a few shards of glass in the new carpet. Mark's getting married next June.

I don't hear the tower today. John has the earphones on. We line up on three-oh. It's a twenty-four second run to rotation and take off. I was watching the elapsed time clock. We're heading straight up the valley at the Spyce Byce, then the slow right turn, and we're at about 217 heading. Would you believe? It's clear enough to see Mt. Connor when we're only eight minutes out of the Alice! There's an awful lot of water in the series of dry lakes parallel the road to Ayer's Rock, and things are green. Really green! Oh, there's a lot of brown around, but the hills and dunes are covered with green, and it looks beautiful.

We're at 6,000 feet so it's easy to see all the water puddles lying around, and almost all of the rivers have water in them near the ox-bows. I've learned to recognize the windmills in the morning by their shadows. You can't see the mills themselves, because you are looking almost straight down on them, but the shadow is so distinctive, that one can pick out the shadow, then the mill, and then the tank, and sometimes, even the cattle. I'm going to miss this when we leave. I had the word last week that my next assignment is going to be Washington.

It's been calm. John clicks off the autopilot. There's the usual little porpoising, and then John has it controlled, and we're descending at 210 knots TAS (true air speed). John does everything proper. As we pass the village, he brings the nose up to kill off some of the speed, then drops about 15 degrees of flaps, then the gear as the IAS (indicated air speed) drops below 120 knots. There's almost no wind. John lines up from south to north. The corrugated metal X that was at the end of the strip last time is gone. It looks awfully nice; almost like cement, the white desert floor. There's a Cessna parked in the parking area. John holds it two inches above the runway until the stall warning horn beeps, and the plane settles on in a perfect stall landing.

The plane is the Pitjantjatjara Council plane. They are in the second day of their conference here, I learn. Philip Crane is the pilot, says John. He's worthy of a nickname that surprised me when it comes out of placid John. John doesn't care for him, either as a person or as a pilot, it would seem. On the vertical stabilizer is the flag of the Council; a square, black on the top and red on the bottom with a yellow ball in the center. John shuts down FML, and almost at the same time, sister Jennie is there.

Jennie says that Billy Wilson had come back, but he hasn't fronted up at the clinic. She says that she's been told that he's losing weight and looks terrible. She hasn't seen him. Murray Burton, God rest his soul, is "deceased." That's a word you can use, but don't say "dead" or "passed away," and don't mention his name to anyone anymore. Poor fellow. He died (oops) "deceased" at Alice Springs Hospital. Maybe that's what Billy fled from the hospital about; maybe it was Murray. We hurry into town. Some of the skeletons of the "Gran Prix" that I mentioned a couple of months ago are still sitting half in the bush and half on the road. It's that same exciting ride into the village. Some of the time the car is racing its own back wheels in the loose sand. The clinic is waiting.

Dr. Walton, ophthalmologist, who has been to the Alice for about two months and who is leaving this next week, has been by. He looked at both Mick and Pompey Harding. Pompey is a candidate for surgery when his other eye gets a little worse. So! That's good news. But Mick is beyond hope. I guess he's been looking at the sun. He has a macular degeneration that has left him pretty hopeless as far as corrective surgery is concerned. He's been given dark glasses to wear. Also, last week's curiosity about what happened to all the antenatals is cleared up. Nothing as exciting as a taboo that keeps them from being seen at this time of year. Dr. Cahill from the Alice Hospital has been around. More about that later. But that's why I didn't see anyone at Ernabella last week. Sister Carol has nothing nice to say about Dr. Walton. It seems that he commandeered an AMS plane last week to go to Docker River just to see one patient. He just wanted the ride. It seems he managed to overnight at Ayer's Rock, too. That really set sister Carol off. She's not unhappy that he's leaving.

First patient is Norah. Remember from last time? She's antenatal. Dr. Cahill says that she's breech presentation. I exam. I think she's LOA (left occiput anterior) presentation, but the fetal heart is heard loudest at the left upper quadrant. She's 34/52. We'll know before long.

"Take her to the medical center in the Alice and let's get a sonogram," I advise sister Carol. Everyone laughs. Next is Rosemary Plane; also seen by Dr. Cahill. Dr. Cahill has written on the chart that she doesn't think Rosemary is pregnant at all. She sure has a big belly, about 22/52 size. I thought I heard heart sounds before on November 19. Maybe there's more than one in there, and the parts are just little. I listen again. I really do think I can hear a fetal heart, but only one, and it's about 158/minute. Well, we'll see along about May.

Then little Fredrick. He's about 18 months. He has decreased breath tones on the right, and he's not very active. "Crook, all right!" Let's get him on half a Bicillin today, and half again on the nineteenth. Felix is about twenty-two months, and almost the same thing as poor, little Fred. He's already on the Bicillin. Let's give him half again in two days. Kukika we saw last time. She's still having some pain in the right upper quadrant of her belly that is also felt in her shoulder and sometimes by her shoulder blade. She denies light stools or dark urine, and I think she knows what I'm saying. I guess we'll have to get a series next time she goes up to the Alice. Also, her plasma glucose in September was 12.6 mmol/l, and she's been on tolbutamide (anti-diabetic oral agent), a gram twice a day. She's 144/80. Let's draw blood for sugar.

Now there's another Kukika, but she's twenty-six, and she has pain in her back and belly, and headaches, since July. She's 124/76, urine is NAD (no abnormal data). She has a C-section scar on her belly. She's tender suprapubic, but I don't feel any masses. I think she might have a PID (pelvic inflammatory disease). We'll give her a gram of probenecid stat, and then in about an hour, let's give her three grams of Amoxil, and just see what happens. That's not a very professional way of treating a patient, and I'm sure all the journals would berate me for such a decision. But it's practical if not professional; and it might cure her.

The next patient is really interesting. Paniny is forty-eight. She gives a history of two weeks of having episodes of bloody diarrhea, with normal stools in between. Not much for cramps, she says. She's brought in two specimens; both are bright red blood, but without stool. Gosh! I just have to feel in there. I tell Jennie what I want. Jennie calls in Myanyika, the health worker, and tells her what I want to do. Myanyika tells Paniny, as I bend over the notes, trying to appear disinterested in the conversation.

Paniny said, "Oh-ah," almost in a whisper. Carol puts her on the bed facing the wall. It's going to be a left handed rectal exam. On with the glove; lubricant; gentle! She's really tender. She has big external hemorrhoids. She's really tender inside. Maybe it's a fissure. There certainly are a lot of hemorrhoids. I don't feel any masses, but then I'm only about five centimeters when I decided I really should give up. We'll try to get a stool specimen. Meantime, some hemorrhoidal suppositories and some Metamucil. We'll try to get a stool and O and P (ova and parasites).

Kayana is a nineteen-year-old primip (first time pregnant). She also answers to Karma. She's 26/52, FH is 152, and blood pressure is 104/60. She's 49.2 kg. Janet is twenty-nine years old and has a messy ear. They won't do a tymnpanoplasty until the ear stops draining, Jennie's been told. I look in the right ear. It looks just fine with a nice light reflex. The left ear has a large posterior perforation. But the head of the malleus is intact, and showing through the intact portion of the tympanum. There's no pus here; just a thin transudate that looks like what I've come to call a snotty ear. The word is the same in American or Australian, and in Latin you'd probably call it "rhinorrheotica." Her blood pressure is 118/102. That's strange. I wish I hadn't taken it. It complicates things. I was going to give her some Sudafed for a couple of days before she presents herself. If the pressure stays up, she's to contact me through the AMS radio service. Then she tells us that her belly is tender at times, too; paraumbilical. Palpation reveals that she's only tender when I come down on a very palpable abdominal aorta. She has good peripheral pulses. I wonder what her serum creatinine is? Sounds like Janet might have an aneurysm of the aorta above the renal arteries! She's going to be an interesting patient.

Next is Henry Stanley, and I'm going to come back to you later on with his story. I spent about twenty minutes with him, and no one else in the room because he had his problem on his penis. I'll come back to him soon; I promise.

Manyungha is 176/108 hypertensive; thirty-three years old. It's hard to get a pressure at all on her in the left arm. She's taking 500 mg of Aldomet twice a day, but no HCTZ (hydrochlorothiazide—a diuretic). We draw glucose, and an FBC, and we'll add 50 mg HCTZ in the morning. Jennie will let me know what the readings are next week by radio.

Yariti is 30/52. Dr. Cahill said 28/52. She's fine. We'll see if she delivers on the floor of the health centre going by Dr. Cahill's dates. Probably not. They are usually a couple of weeks behind what you think they're going to be. Kathleen is eighteen months old with wet ears and lungs. She's febrile, too. Let's give her half a Bicillin now and half again on the nineteenth. That should take care of that. Iluwanti was seen just about a year ago. She had the big lump on her left tibia, and we sent her in to the hospital. She still has the lump, but it's smaller now and asymptomatic. She is complaining that she's lost her vision the last two weeks. Near vision is particularly poor, and she can't thread a needle anymore. She's only about twenty-two years old. She says her eyes itch, too. Well, there's not any blepharitis that I can see, and not even much conjunctivitis. But what's this? The right cornea is like looking through frosted glass! She has corneal ulcerations! The iris looks okay, and everything seen behind looks okay. But it sure is a messy cornea. The left one is a little involved, but not as much. Wow! Let's give her some chloroptic drops. She was a health worker a couple of years ago, understands English quite well, but wouldn't admit it. She knows what I'm saying. She'll put the drops in every two hours! We'll patch the eye, too.

Tinami is fifty. She's having headaches. She has a cataract forming in the left eye. It looks like it's central; kind of scintillating as you look in. Her blood pressure is 122/80. I don't know what it is. She's Janet's mother. Let's try some brufen (Motrin) for her, just on the off chance that she's having some kind of inflammatory response. Isn't that dungeon medicine? Sure is a long way from the Ivory Tower, I'll tell you that! Now the clinic seems to be over, and now I'll come back to Henry.

Henry was apprehensive. He has a lesion on his penis, and he isn't sure what it is, but it is a lump, and he knows that lumps are bad news, particularly on the penis. There's a vein on his penis that seems to be pretty prominent. What is it? Examination reveals that it's just a little sebaceous cyst; just behind the corona on the dorsum of the penis, and it's causing a little interference with one of the local veins. which appears just a little dilated. He has no inguinal nodes. I check each testicle in turn. No lumps, and look up just in time to see an ashen faced Henry start to pop with beads of sweat on his forehead. He's going to faint! I get him onto the chair and his head down between his knees, and have him push up with his neck muscles against my hand on his occiput. Pretty soon the strength comes back into the neck muscles, and I sit on the other chair and again reassure him. I won't try to take it out here. They have a forceps with teeth that's about eight inches long, and I'd like to have a little Adson forceps with very fine teeth to hold the skin of the prepuce away from the area when I do it so that I can pop the thing out whole. I'll bring them along next week when we go to Fregon on Christmas Eve, and then we can divert down and do this thing for Henry.

Henry wonders how an American doc got down to Fregon. I tell him that I'm really in charge of the medical care at the Spyce Byce, and he wonders how come then the attachment to the Community Health Centre and the hospital. I remind him that the Aussie docs in the Alice had said that no way were they going to add 1,500 Americans to their work load; that if the JDSRF (Joint Defense Space Research Facility) came in there, the least the Americans could do would be to provide their own doc. Since the Northern Territory provided the rooms at the CHC (Community Health Centre) for no charge, my Thursday trip each week with the AMS of the RFDS was payment in kind for the use of the rooms at CHC. I told him that I only spent one day a week at the Byce, and that was mostly just to make sure that my medic followed through on public health programs that were instituted at the base. I also told him that I had been in private practice for over twenty years, and that my wife and I were enjoying the fruits of a second career. He thought that was a pretty neat idea.

Then he told me that he had been in aboriginal work for a lot of years, too. He said that he was becoming the victim of aboriginal flame-out not burn out. This was flame-out like jets in the airforce, and he was going to have to go back to Sydney soon and get his wheels back on the track. He said that the cultural differences that he had seen were such that often he wondered whether the European invaders of this huge, wealthy land hadn't done the wrong thing by exploiting the black man. I suggested that such was the way of the strong conquering the weak all through history, and that it was perhaps futile to try to change the nature of such things. I said, "Perhaps the fact that they have no written language makes it difficult for them to compete in a contemporary society."

And with that, Henry insisted, "But they do have a written language! They just don't show it to the white men!" Henry says that he's been privileged to watch many of the sacred ceremonies, including the initiation rite of young men. What a fascinating man to listen to! He said that about every ten years or so, the tribe called all their men together for a corroboree that might last for as much as four months. At this time the elders would draw the "mosaic" grand descriptive paintings into the sand; each representing a different period or event in the forty-millenium history of the aboriginals. Rather like laying out the whole library, I thought.

"The Shinto religion in Japan does this same sort of thing," said Henry. After the information is all transmitted to the space between the men's ears over the four months period, the drawings and painting are destroyed! The heritage is in the mind. "Think on it," says Henry. "There are civilizations like the ancient Egyptians and the Mayan culture in Central America who have left their monuments for other men to see, but no one remembers what they were all about. Here the civilization destroys their monuments after they've served their purpose, but retain the entire culture in their minds to transmit to future generations. It's all in how you look at it," repeats Henry. "Think on it." And as I think on it, it seems that he must be perfectly correct. It's a way of thinking of the aboriginal culture that I hadn't paid attention to before. It's kind of mind boggling.

An attention-getting triple rap on the door, and the voice of sister Carol. "You about done in there?"

"Oh! Oh, yes. Sorry about that. Do we have more patients?"

"Lots of them. Let's get on with it." So we finished up the rest of the clinic that I've already told you about. But Henry's words are haunting. It's food for laying on your back at night when all is dark and quiet and contemplating in those few minutes before one falls asleep. I'll really have to think on that.

The equipment is put back into the 4-wheel drive, and we proceed to Jennie's flat. "Soweto Lives—Apartheid is Death," announces a poster on her wall. There are other issues, and a picture of Walt Whitman, and posters that shout her activism. But she does say, "I want to thank you for spending so much time with the people and showing them that you really care."

For her to say that to an employee of the Spyce Byce is something else, and to an American besides, is almost sacrilege, I'd think. She has a nice, little spread; some rye-crisp, cheese, tomato slices and salami, along with a cup of coffee. There's a lot of small talk. Margaret, the South African black sister, has been silent all day. She just stands there taking everything in, but she hadn't contributed a word to the clinic all day. We're talking about Billy Wilson. Maybe an amoebic abscess of the liver took him? I mention that once in Karachi, I had watched as an amoebic liver abscess was percussed out in a skinny Pakistani, and then the doctor at the Holy Family hospital had stuck a needle percutaneous into the cyst. He drained off about a hundred cubic centimeters of tawny fluid, and instilled about fifty cubic centimeters of emetine right into the cyst. Margaret's eyes got bigger and bigger.

"Did he really do that?" she asked in amazement. Her English is perfect. It doesn't sound African at all; rather quite like Oxford. The ice is broken. She joins in the conversation from there on.

Back to the plane. It's hot! No wind. FML fires up. It doesn't take long for the gauges to come into the warm zone. This time it's a thirty-seven-second run on the clock for the wheels to come clear of the strip, and with only about fifty meters to go at that! It's bumpy coming home. I read a little. The temperature at 9,000 feet is a neat 14 degrees Celcius. I nod off thinking about Henry's story. I wake just as John is letting FML down through 5,000 feet for a right base for runway one-two. Darn, I forgot to ask Jennie whether Barbara had ever had that big, inguinal abscess drained; the one her mother had refused to let me do anything with about eight weeks ago. I'll have to remember to ask.

14 January 1982

I'll bet you're wondering what happened in the flights with the AMS of the RFDS since December 17. Well, I was interrupted by a trip to America. It began at 0400 on the morning of the nineteenth here. The phone rang. I picked it up on about the third ring. "Jack?"

"Yeah?"

"Jack, it's Vernon. Can you hear me?"

"Yeah, Vernon. I can hear you just fine."

"Jack, your Mom's dead. Can you hear me?"

"Oh, my God! Yes, I can hear you just fine, Vernon."

"Jack, she was down at your sister's place in Carlsbad, and she just didn't wake up this morning."

"Oh, my God! Let me get my thoughts together for a minute, Vernon."

"Jack, your sister is getting everything together down there with a funeral company, and would like you to call her. Do you have her number?"

"Yeah, I have her number, Vernon. Gee, it was nice of you to ring me and let me know."

"Jack, you know if there's anything we can do from here, just let us know. You have my number too?"

"Yeah, Vernon. Gee, thanks a million. I'll give Nonnie a ring right away. Thanks again."

"O.K., Jack. Remember, if there's anything we can do, let us know."

"Yeah, yeah. Thanks again, Vernon. Bye."

"Bye." And that was that. Vernon is my best friend, diving buddy, co-owner at one time of the sweetest, little Beech Bonanza in the world, and our family doctor back in Santa Barbara. I rang Nonnie, my sister, and she answered straight away, and announced the "Eternal Hills" mortuary people were there just then, and taking Mom's body away. I almost laughed out loud at the name of the mortuary, but felt it wouldn't be too appropriate with Nonnie sounding just a little upset. Seems that she had gone up to Santa Barbara on Monday, the fourteenth, and picked up Mom and brought her down to Carlsbad for the holidays. They had been out to dinner the night before, and had a good talk till almost 0130, and then gone to sleep.

In the morning when Nonnie awakened, Mom was still "asleep," so Nonnie went down and made coffee. When she came upstairs again, Mom was still asleep, and when Nonnie touched her, the body was already cold. It was quite a jolt for Nonnie. I opted not to ring my boss until a better hour, since it was already Saturday here in the Alice, and there wasn't much that could be done until 8 o'clock or so anyway. But at 0800 I rang Merle.

"Sure, Jack, you should go home."

"Merle, I don't have the faintest notion how to go about it."

"Don't worry, Jack. Just ring John, and he'll take care of everything."

And, so it was. John was very solicitious. "When do you want to depart?"

"Gosh, soon as possible, I guess, John."

"We'll have you on the 1700 plane today. How's that?"

"Gee, John, that sounds great."

About three o'clock, John came by the house with my passport, my tickets, my reservation for layover at the Travelodge in Melbourne for Saturday night, and even some greenbacks.

"Just in case you didn't have any, and didn't want to bother fooling around with exchange at the airport."

I did have some of my own, though, so I didn't have to use his scarce supply. At 1700 hours, Laura had me at the airport, and I was on the way. The Travelodge in Melbourne airport is horrendous! Very lovely room with all the amenities, but $69.35 Australian per night for a single! That's $79.87 American! I was up to catch the plane, Continental's flight 2, which departed at 1000 hours. Our first landing was in Honolulu; a bit over eleven hours nonstop. It was just after midnight, but it was a brand new Sunday; two of 'em! I arrived in LAX at 0908 hours Sunday morning. Isn't that amazing?

It was "Statesman" class on Continental. They really treat one nicely. There were a number of superb meals with cocktail service first, at no charge, and then wine with the meal, at no charge, and then after dinner liqueurs, also at no extra charge. Then, when the movie came on, one had the option of travel into oblivion with booze or movie. I did watch the movie.

It was *Arthur*, with Liza Minnelli and Dudley somebody or other. That shows you how many movies I watch. I'd rate it just a tad below a good B movie. Randy met me at LAX, and that day we spent at his place just puttering around. We went to a dandy supper of barbecued beef ribs at a little place near his apartment. Then, in the morning, after he had seen Dr. Baker for his dermatology appointment, we headed north.

Mom had everything in good order. There was a minimum

of fuss and bother, and my two sisters had contacted Mr. Tracy at the Welch-Ryce-Haider mortuary in Santa Barbara, and everything was in perfect order there, too. It was a little difficult to get much of the estate work sorted out, because of the season, but a trip to Solvang on Monday the twenty-eight sorted it out quite well. Christmas was delightful. Both Randy and Raul were there, and Raul cooked a twenty-two pound turkey for us. It was absolutely delicious!

Vernon and Annie Freidell had me to the club with them one night, with George and Mary Spencer, for dinner and cocktails. We tried to get George and Mary to talk about their latest cruise, but they were more interested in the next one than the last one. I was at Freidell's for New Year's Eve supper, too, and that was done by Annie, and was absolutely delicious: oyster stew, small, sauteed scallops, and a delicious lobster chunks on lettuce leaf salad, with some Korbel's champagne. Not too shabby for New Year's Eve.

I did watch the first half of the Rose Bowl game on their TV before I had to depart on New Year's Day, on Golden West, to LAX, with two hours layover there. Continental flight #1 this time to Honolulu, with forty minutes there. (Just enough time to buy a turquoise ring for Laura's birthday.) Then, forty minutes in Sydney, and two hours direct flight home. I was met by Laura with the big Cadillac, and that was that. Oh, yes. Breakfast that morning on the plane of filet mignon with mushroom omelet, two spicy sausages, a blueberry muffin, half a papaya with pineapple chunks in the middle topped by a banda orchid, hot coffee, and all the champagne one could drink. Not bad at all! As I started to say a while ago, business continued as usual when I returned, and now I'm writing about the trip to Amata on the fourteenth. Oh, yes. Ernabella last week was cancelled, because all the folks were still "walkabout" from the holidays.

So, about 0400 hours again on the fourteenth, I woke with a balloon punching me in the right kidney. "Oh, oh!" I thought, "It's going to be one of those days." I waited for a few minutes to see if it was really there. It was! I got up and went to the bathroom, took a 50 mg Talwin from the medicine cabinet, and a glass of water. It's a rather smallish pill; pink, but bitter as can be. It went down. I went back to bed. The pain subsided. Maybe my kidney stone wouldn't give me trouble today after all. Usually those that I wake up with like that, though, are disasters. I didn't eat much breakfast, but did take two extra glasses of water, and was at the airport at 0645 hours. John had FML all ready to go, and sister Carol arrived bright and chipper. We loaded the paraphernalia into the lockers on the wings and in the nose, and at 0710 we were lifting off runway one-two. The balloon was back in my right flank! John had the earphones on, so I couldn't hear the tower directions. We headed off towards Mt. Connor, cruising at 6,000 feet. At 0720, I decided I should take another Talwin. I had brought a little baggie in my hip pocket with two Talwin and a half-grain codeine with Tylenol. I feel like a small-time junkie carrying a packet like that, but I sure would like to finish out this tour of duty. Nine more months to go. Then I'm going back to CONUS (Continental United States) and have that dumb thing taken out of that kidney. No water to swallow the pill with, but I do have a small piece of gum in my mouth to generate some saliva, and both the gum and the Talwin slide down the tube together.

John is lying against his window with his eyes shut. The flight director is doing all the work—autopilot. I notice that when the autopilot is coupled to the flight director, the plane tends to search for its direction, and there are tiny banking turns almost with the regularity of waves on a ship. I mention this to John, but he has his earphones on and doesn't hear me. Finally, he does notice the dipping, and I mention it again. He lifts his earphone on my side, and I repeat it again.

"Yuugh," he grunts and switches to three-axis autopilot and the dancing stops. John looks at me. I'm struggling with my balloon, which isn't going away.

"I don't feel good," I tell him. "I'm passing a kidney stone."

"You don't look too good," he agrees, and then adds, "I don't feel too good, either, but mine is self inflicted."

John has been up late with his buddies. He's had a few too many beers. But John isn't that kind of pilot. I'm sure he's sober enough; he just doesn't feel good. He's an honest man, anyway. Sister Carol brightly asks if we'd like our morning coffee. John and I gaze into each other's eyes just for a moment.

We both whisper, "No thanks."

Carol comes forward. "What's the matter?"

"I'm passing a kidney stone," I say with anguish.

She forgets about John's problem. "Do you want to come back here on the stretcher?"

"Yeah!" I move back, but it's only good for about thirty seconds. The pain is monstrous. I put my head in my hands; knee-chest position on the stretcher. It's no good. On my side. No good. I stand up. No good.

"I'm getting sick."

Carol produces a burp bag. Four or five good retchings, and things come up. The nausea fades, but a cold, clammy sweat comes on, with a weakness that is overwhelming. I hand the bag to Carol and collapse on the stretcher on my side. The balloon is going to explode!

"What can I give you?"

"Oh, God, Carol. Do you have pethidine?"

"Sure." She busies herself at the plane locker. "I asked you last time if you wanted some," she says, "and when I asked it I could have bitten my tongue off, because I didn't really have any with me. After that trip I put some into the kit just in case it should happen again. So, now I have some to give to you."

"Thanks."

She expertly filled the syringe. I loosened my trousers and lowered my shorts on the left side. I didn't even feel it go in. It was about 0746 hours. Maybe there's something psychological about it, but that pain started to subside almost immediately. The balloon decreased by half. Sister Carol sat in the front seat with John. We were descending for Amata.

"You'll go to sister's house and lie down for forty-five minutes," she commands.

John made his usual, skillful landing on the dirt strip. Sister Chris was there with the Toyota. I climb out of the plane, feeling quite a bit better. The hot summer sun beating down turns my legs to jelly.

"I'm going to faint," I tell them, and place myself as close to the dirt of the strip as I can. "It's an antagonist," I think to myself.

Pentazocine HCL and meperidine HCL are antagonists. The Talwin and the Demoral were fighting it out in my body. I was a chemical demolition derby. It's like being cut in half, or turning into a jellyfish. They took me to Chris' quarters. I laid on the bed while they went to sort out the clinic. I had not unpleasant hallucinations, finally dropping off to sleep. I awakened, looked at my watch. Twenty-five minutes since arrival. I felt better. I got up and sat at her table. The troops were back. A cup of tea, and it was time to start the clinic. We have twenty patients.

By this time, I really do feel pretty good. Claudia is twenty-eight months old. She really should go back to the Children's Health Unit at Alice Hospital. She's been losing weight too fast. We'll see that she gets back. Next; Ngingi, age forty-four, Parkinson's disease. He's taking Sinemet, two tabs a day with quite good control, and also Daonil, two in the morning and one at night for his diabetes. Kenneth is nine years old. He has runny ears and nose. Routine treatment for that.

Then comes Tommy. Tommy is forty-six years old. The young, male sister from Ernabella, Patrick, has persuaded Tommy to come and see me, and Patrick has brought him by car all the way. Tommy has some kind of trouble with his penis. Let's see. Tommy lies on the bed; same one we use for the ante-natal exams, of course. Patrick encourages him gently. Tommy opens his dirty trousers, and lowers them to reveal what looks like a massive post-operative purulent infection of an amputated penis! The sore is about fifteen centimeters in diameter, and extends to about the middle of the scrotum, anteriorly, and about where the base of the penis should be on the abdomen! There are no inguinal nodes. There is no history to go with it. Tommy isn't saying anything. I'm lucky to just get a look at it! I guess I'll give him a course of probenicid, and then, in about forty-five minutes, three grams of Amoxil by mouth, and we'll draw a serology for syphilis. No use asking Tommy to come to the Alice. He wouldn't do that anyway. But we do ask, and he says, "No."

That's that. Next is Nyinytja, who just happens to be Ivy's sister. Remember Ivy? She's the lady from Ernabella that I saw more than a year ago with miliary tuberculosis. Nyinytja has a sore eye. Examination reveals that she's enucleating her left eye. That's the third one I've seen like that now. It's awful to watch. Cursory exam of the right eye shows that she has almost complete loss of vision there, too, with a huge cataract. Well, we'll let Dr.

Barker know, and see if we can't get her to Adelaide for some sort of treatment. She probably won't go, though.

Manyungha has a blood pressure of 182/104. She's not taking her blood pressure medicine. She's to be on Clotride, one a day, and Aldomet twice a day, but she feels well, so hasn't taken it for some time. We encourage her. Janet is twelve; has a wet ear. We'll treat it in the usual manner. Leigh has the same. He's just two, though. We'll give him half a dose of Bicillin, and half a dose again in two days. Hector is Leigh's brother. He's six. He's lost the anterior incisors, upper, and laterals, to caries. They've rotted right down to the gums. He has marked caries on other upper teeth, too. Curiously, the lower teeth look pretty good. We'll have to try to get him in to the Alice for dental care.

Now the antenatal clinic. Yantzi is 32/52 weeks. FHH 156/minute, 90/52 and 70.3 kg. She looks good. Jilian is 33/52, no fetal heart is heard. She's diabetic. She has a big tummy. 104/62, 76.9 kg, and she's thirty-nine years old! Rosemary is 24/52 weeks, fetal heart at 144/minute, BP 90/50, 68 kg, and she's sixteen years old. Karma is twenty years old, 32/52 weeks, fetal heart 148/minute, 52 kg, 96/58, and she has a recent RPR with the time of 1:1024! That's positive for syphilis. She's being treated.

Next is Henry Stanley. Henry had a sebaceous cyst on his penis, and decided he wanted it removed. The dumb thing went and broke spontaneously, so we don't have any surgery to do. Darn!

Veronica is two years old. She has rales in her left lower lateral chest. I guess we'll treat her pneumonia with penicillin. Ruby is about thirty-seven or so. She has an obviously displaced fracture of the left humerus. She was kicked by her husband two days ago. She's in quite a bit of pain.

"Ruby, you should really come back with us in the plane. We need an x-ray of that arm."

Ruby at first says oh-ah (yes). Later when we went to find her, we had a hard time. Finally, we were told that she wasn't coming because, "she didn't have any money." That means her husband had said we-ah (no).

Tjulyata is forty-three. She has an acute iritis in the right eye. We'll take her with us to the Alice. I patch the eye. Alma is tired. 152/104. I can't really find anything else wrong with her.

We take an FBC (full blood count). Maureen is twenty-seven. She has an infertility problem. She's had no period for two months. Her BP is 132/98. We'll get a urine for HCG (human chorionic gonadotropin–the hormone of pregnancy), and also an FBC. The last patient is Leigh, who is twenty-seven, and has left lower quadrant abdominal pain after drinking a can of beer.

I don't find anything wrong. I wonder what's really the story with Leigh. He seems satisfied after my exam. Then we have one more little lady who is at Ernabella with a traveling inspection group. She's been vomiting for two days. She's not really sick; just vomiting. John had gone over there with Patrick to pick her up and bring her back to Amata. She'll be going in with us to the Alice. I think she might have a carcinoma obstructing her. She looks like it.

Back to sister Chris' mobile. There's tea again. I still feel pretty good, although there is a little balloon still there. Then we return to the plane. It's hot. We have the Ernabella lady with the obstruction, and Tjulyata with the iritis. Ruby would have filled up the last seat, but her husband won't let her go. We take off at 1400 hours. It's 38 degrees Celsius. Amata is 2,260 MSL (mean sea level–altitude), but the strip is plenty long. John gets us off with plenty of strip left. But the air is turbulent! We climb to 9,000 feet, then on to 12,000 feet. It's pretty smooth up here.

Then the balloon is back. I try to ignore it. It won't go away. I lay my head against the window. I'm sick. I take a burp bag. The damned control wheel is in the way. I thought we were going to re-design this plane. It's a long flight back. Carol taps me on the shoulder. There's a patient history card with the following message printed on it: "Dear Sir: I will drive you home, and Bob will pick me up from there. O.K.?!! PS: don't argue, 'Cause you're not feeling well. That's plan A. Plan B. I can take you to the cas to be seen, if you want. Plan C. Plan A, plus another 'shot' in the rear at home. Signed: Carol."

I turn around with a grin on my face in spite of the pain. "I'll opt for Plan C," I tell her.

John has us on the ground at 1515 hours. The ambulance comes for us sick patients. Carol drives me home. I am absolutely in agony. I try to joke with Laura. It's no good. I really can hardly make my way to the bed. I lay on my belly. The needle goes in.

It could have been a crow bar. I really didn't feel it. The pain again begins to subside. In an hour, Carol is long gone, but the pain has subsided. I stay in bed. No supper. At 2000 hours, I take a half grain codeine for the remaining balloon that's there. It's enough. I sleep until 0100. I wake. I feel fine. I'm hungry. Half a bowl of ice cream tastes just great! Back to bed for a good night's sleep.

21 January 1982

Sister Carol can't go this morning, 'cause sister Kay is crook, so it will be sister Fran, a diminutive lady with a lot of go. Mark is the pilot, as I arrived at the RFDS hanger at 0645. Kathleen is coming back to Fregon with us. She's been at the ASH (Alice Springs Hospital) for something or other, but she does have a small baby back at Fregon that she's anxious to get back to. "FML" is fueled and ready to go. It's a cloudless sky already thirty degrees!

"Runway one-two, Foxtrot Mike Lima, fly the 204 radial at 6,000. Hold at 4,000 east of the Stuart Highway until cleared. Right turn."

At 0704 Mark has the engines at thirty-nine inches of mercury, 2500 RPM, and we rotate at a little less than ninety knots indicated. "Klunk, klunk, kabunk." and the gear is in the wells. The Alice is 1,700 MSL this morning. There's another plane inbound; that's why we were told to hold east of the highway, but then the control gives us clearance to proceed to 6,000. I read a little, but it's more fun to watch the desert unfold. No niggles of balloon at all. Matter of fact, since about 2000 hours last week, I haven't had any. I think last Thursday was enough to make up for a whole month of kidney stones. Mt. Connor is a purple, hazy bump on the southwest horizon. There are some little alto cumulus up there that are purple on the bottom and silver on the top, and it almost looks like a painting by a poor artist, it looks so typical.

It's 38 degrees when we land with a stiff cross wind from the east at Fregon. That settlement is 1,600 MSL. It's 0835. Sister Julie Dorn is there, and seems her usual, slightly disturbed self. The clinic is waiting. Julie has flushed out everyone under the bushes to see the doctor. I think it's because she likes to purge her mind of all responsibility; kind of like a mental housecleaning, as it were. We start with Tjangana/Kalkulya; born 1908 or so. She's hypertensive; Clotride one a day with Inderal 40 mg/d. She's still running 238/108 today. She's fat, too. We'll give her some Minipress. That's about all we have except for some Aldomet. But the tabs are two milligrams. We'll cut them into quarters; quarter tab three times a day, starting, and then we'll go up to half a tab bds (twice a day), and see what happens next time. Calion is about nine years old; temp of 39 degrees with decreased breath tones and dullness in the left lower quadrant of the chest. She's on Amoxil, 250 mg tds. Well keep her on that. It's a pneumonia.

Carol is five; failure to thrive. She only weighs 15 kg. She almost looks cretinoid. Actually, she's the bottom of the pecking order for some reason, and is passive enough not to fight enough for her food. We'll give her a trip to the Alice to the Children's Health Unit, to fatten her up. Lena is four years old. She has a fracture on the distal radius and ulna on the right; a Colles. Julie has plaster, but no roller bandage. We have to use webril for the base and the top of the sugar-tongs. So be it. It's done. Lena is happy with it, and I didn't hurt her very much. We find out that Julie is out of aspirin and most of the other routine meds that make a clinic like this function. "There hasn't been a truck in a long time." I wonder why they can't bring stuff like that down on the mail plane?

Brendon is next. He's with a temperature of thirty-nine degrees, but he's on Abbocillin. I can't really find out why he's running a temp like that. He doesn't look sick. We'll just keep him on the medicine. Munatji is Brendon's Mom. She has a big abscess in the lower eye lid of her left eye. She smiles shyly when I suggest we can open the abscess with a #11 blade. She's unwilling, says a miniscule turn of the head to the left and back again. We'll put her on Chloromycetin eye drops and Amoxil tds. Munatji is twenty.

Hartley Alan is seventeen months, screaming; has diarrhea, says Julie. Exam is NAD (no abnormalties discovered). I'll leave him alone. Norman is two. He has a "grotty" sounding chest. We'll put him on Amoxil, too; for seven days. Then sister Jennie from Ernabella. Jennie has brought down seven patients for me to see, but she's first. She's been coughing. She's raising yellow sputum with blood flecks, and her temp is 39 degrees. She's thirty-six years old. She has decreased breath tones in the right base. She has placed herself on erythromycin. That sounds good. We'll give her 500 mg qid . . . for today, and then back to 250 qid . . . for ten days. She won't have to go back to the Alice with us. Violet has a breast abscess. Her right breast is sore and tender. She's been on Bicillin injections; has had two of them so far. Examination reveals a resolving abscess in the right breast laterally. She can nurse on the left breast for a few more days, and then if there's no pain, she can start with the right breast again, too.

Payula is twenty-four. She has multi-complaints, but a history of previous mitral valve disease. She hurts in her joints. She's running a temp of 37.5 degrees. she has a grade II/IV (two of four—four being the loudest) mitral murmur. Maybe she's having an episode of SBE (subacute bacterial endocarditis). We'd better give her some good doses of Bicillin, and then aspirin, tabs II qid (four times a day). That's when I find out that we don't have any aspirin. I don't know if we can use any of the other non–steroidal anti–inflammatories. Maybe a little Motrin (brufen) might give her some relief from the joint pain. No use giving her oral penicillin therapy. She'd never take it anyway. We'll take an FBC, too. Somehow, Payula gets away from us without the blood being drawn. Smart chick. "Cheeky" chick, too.

Tjinkuma is eleven months of amenorrhea (no menstrual period). She's a para one (she has had a baby), so we know she has had ovarian function in the past. Pregnancy tests have been negative. She's twenty years old. Let's feel her belly. Sure enough. There's a mass, about ten centimeters in diameter, right lower quadrant, but almost up to the umbilicus. It ballots (resists finger pressure like a balloon). Sister Julie feels it. So does sister Jennie. So does sister Fran. It's a good day. She has a serous cyst of the ovary, I think. We'd better make arrangements for her to go to the hospital, but not until Dr. Cahill returns from her holiday.

Next is Keith with an ear infection. He's five. We'll try to dry it up with erythromycin. Next is Yurpuja. She's twenty-one. She was seen by Dr. Cahill on the December 9, and a Cu–7 (intrauterine contraceptive device) was placed. She's had pain in the pelvis this last week, and now has a fever of thirty-eight degrees. Her note card from Dr. Cahill shows when the IUD was placed, Dr. Cahill had to clear thread worms from the fornices—the gutters of the vagina around the cervix. That's a new one. I suppose it might account for the fever, all right. I'd sure like to have some Keflex, but with this place not even having aspirin . . . ! "You do?" How about that? Julie just happens to have an unopened, unexpired bottle of a hundred 250 mg Keflex. We'll start her on qid (four times a day) dosage, and get her up to the Alice to have the Cu–7 removed.

Then comes Peggy; antenatal and twenty-one years old. 24/52, 47.5 kg, 100/65, but I can't hear any fetal heart tones. There's movement, though. We draw her bloods. Mantuwa is 20. 59 kg, 140/62, 24/52, and fetal heart at 148/minute. The baby, James, is three months old; a "juicy" kid, but I can't find anything wrong. Mom is reassured. Albert gives a history of pitting edema, and "itching" of his legs for the last four days. I don't find any pitting edema, but he does have a skin over his legs that looks indurated. He's 103 kg, 135/96, and forty-two years old. No tenderness in the calf, and he does have good peripheral pulses. What's this? He's tender in the groin. No nodes; just tender. This is through his clothes, because he won't take down his trousers. His ocular fundi are clear. Let's guess this one. I'm going to give Albert a gram of probenicid now, and we'll give him 3 grams of Amoxil in an hour and draw blood for serology for syphilis. What would you have done?

Hudson is Albert's son. He has impetigo over his whole scalp. He's nine years old. That head is a gooey mess; looks like his head has been dipped in honey, matting his hair all together. He's had this before, and it never really cleared up. He's also been treated for trachoma in the past. By golly, Julie has some coal tar shampoo. Let's get at this mess, and we'll also give him Bicillin; a whole ml. in the bottom today, and another one on Saturday. Jim Blanton is a European; works in the school. Jim has a sore throat, he says. I think he just wanted to see what the doc looked like. We'll give him some salt gargles. What? You're out of salt? You're kidding!

Amonia is in again. She's diabetic. You met her a long time ago when she had the big abscess just to the right of her umbilicus. It's all cleared up now, but she has an infected foot, says Julie. Examination reveals a seven cm. abscess in the plantar part, medial, of the right heel. There's pus exuding from an opening. There's an awful lot of tenderness here, and it's hard. There's a foreign body in there; probably a piece of mulga wood. It has to come out. She's rubbed mud into the mess to take away the pus. The skin is thick and cracked from walking for forty years barefoot. I really don't dare do it here. We'll take her with us. She nods her head a tad up, then back down. She'll go!

Nola is thirty-one. She has low back syndrome. No radiation of the pain. That's easy. Let's give her some Indocin about 25 mg tds. Ancona is age twelve. She has a sore throat. She's had a fever for three days, says Julie. I think this must be the end of the clinic, 'cause Julie seems to be running out of sick people. Exam on Ancone/Nguniwa is NAD, and her temp is 37 degrees. No treatment is indicated here. Then there's Joe Peters. I've already filled out Joe's papers for permanent disability. He's diabetic; you've met him before, too. He's had a nephrectomy, and the urine from this man always shows 2 + protein and 3 + sugar. He has some low back pain. I don't dare give him much medicine because I'll bet his serum creatinine is 3.5 or so anyway, and he's apt to go into a kidney shutdown at any time. "One more," says Julie, and in comes Sandra. She's PG, 37/52 weeks and she's got a urinary tract infection. Fetal heart is 136/minute. She's twenty years old. We'll treat her "uti" (urinary track infection) with Ampicillin.

"Would you see Cordula?" a hesitant query from Julie.

"Sure, Julie, what's her problem?" It turns out Cordula is forty years old, and has leg cramps, but just at night, and not very bad. I look her over. Good peripheral pulses. No evidence of deep vein thrombosis. Let's suggest some stretch exercises before retiring.

"Umm, Pete just came in. Can you look at him?"

"Sure, Julie, what's his problem?" Pete I've seen before. It's the same problem he had last September. Pete gives me a bit of a history of pain in his left neck, and down his left ribs. It's exactly the same story that he gave me before. I didn't find any-thing wrong with him then, either. There's no treatment. Pete goes away happy. He just wanted to eyeball the tjilpi doctor again. And that really does end the clinic. We'll have a cup of tea at Julie's.

Fran has been helpful all this time, but she really doesn't know how to find the patient's cards in the system. She doesn't draw bloods very well either, and they save the disposable ear specs for the auroscope. But she's a good girl. Mark is lounging at Julie's with his book. The three of them have tea; salad with boiled eggs. I enjoy my cup of tea and piece of home–made cake. It's good, too! Then out to FML and load up. Good grief, it's sure hot! Inside the plane is like an oven! It's 44 degrees outside air temp. Mark fires up the engines. The air conditioner sure feels good! Not much wait for the engine temps to come into the green. We're racing down the runway. Mark pulls her off again at less that ninety indicated. That's a lot less than single engine per-formance, and would be sure death if we lost one. At about 3,000 feet the light comes on the panel that says "nose storage door ajar." Mark notices it at almost the same time that I do.

"If we lose one of those cases of patient cards, sister Carol will have you crawling around the desert on your hands and knees recovering every one!" I warn Mark.

"Yeah, I bet she would." Mark rolls FML up on her starboard wing to try to put the door on the high side. The light stays on. Mark undoes his belt and stands on the seat, but he can't see the nose door.

"Nuts, we'll have to set down at Ernabella." It's bumpy, too. I can just see one of those forty pound metal cases coming out that door. Mark shuts down, and we make a smooth landing at Ernabella.

"That'll make the town wonder what we're doing," Mark offers.

"Not really," I suggest. "They'll probably think you're just picking up a bale of pot."

Mark shuts down both engines while he checks the door. It's okay. Apparently one of the boxes had shifted just enough to touch off the warning light. Mark fires up the port engine. The starboard won't fire. Mark starts to taxi back to the end of the runway on one engine. The right one just won't fire at all. Mark lets it rest while we taxi. At the end of the runway, he turns us around, and tries the engine again. It comes to life. That's the thing I had worried about before. What if that engine had decided to quit on take off? We roar down the strip again, and lift off; again less that ninety knots indicated. There's plenty of runway left; I wonder why he does that?

We climb towards 12,000 feet. It'll be cool up there and not so bumpy. Right here at 6,000 feet the jolts are enough to make the seat come up against the stops on the track. Mark switches off the fuel pump booster. The starboard engine dies! Now, that's an experience! Mark switches the fuel pump back on.

"In the heat like this, the darned thing has a bad habit of vapor locking," he says quietly.

The engine roars back to life. My heart slows down from wildly thumping to about 160/minute. The thunderheads are building up. At 12,000 we're just below the bases. It's a beautiful trip back. Amonia sits in the back, stoic; she's going to be glad to get that piece of wood out of her foot. Mark starts the let down over the Finke River. This is a fun world. I really do enjoy this. It's a rare opportunity. I'm glad that I've been able to see this part of the world with the RFDS.

28 January 1982

Carol, Darryl and FDQ were ready and waiting this morning when I arrived at the Alice Airport at 0650. Bob had brought Carol out a little early "cause she had to get up to answer some radio messages at the AMS anyway." Douglas was coming back from a trip to the hospital for a nasty herpes ophthalmica. The distribution of the ophthalmic division of the trigeminal nerve on the right had been infected by the same virus that causes shingles (and very similar to the viruses that cause herpes II that is the venereal [now called STD for "sexually transmitted disease"[so deadly to newborns). It's also related to the virus of chickenpox. It had spread around the forehead and even into the eye. They've done a good job with it. They used Stoxil, the report says. He's much better, but really should have stayed in the hospital for a while more. His Mom, Lucy, has other things to do back at the settlement, so took him out early against the doctor's advice. Oh, well. Douglas is about eleven or so.

Oh, yes. FDQ is being used today, because they found some other problems with the starboard engine on FML. No one said what it was. I guess the fact that it was stopping in flight last week was reason enough to bring it in and have a look. It's kind of nice to have a ride in the old beast of burden again. No one has really said where we're going today, so I guess I'll just keep my mouth shut. I did take a blank check with me today, just in case it's Indulkana way, and Wally should happen to have some opals in sister's cabinet for me. Remember when I said on my last visit to Indulkana (a long time ago) that Wally was going to sell me a packet for $500 Australian, and it would contain five or six nice opals? Well, I hope he hasn't forgotten. I'd love to see what he comes up with. Did I tell you that Laura and I have already purchased five lovely gems? Two of them are solids; one about thirteen carats, and the other three are blacks. One is almost a "harlequin" with big squares of color. I'd sure like to see what Wally has to offer. Darryl had run up FDQ before I arrived, and apparently has all the numbers for takeoff, because I just hear him say to the tower, "Alice ground? FDQ. Taxi to runway one-two?"

"FDQ, Alice ground. Clear to one-two." And we taxi out.

"Car fifty-four, hold for the Navajo," the tower tells the little yellow car that is proceeding from the commercial terminal to the Chartair terminal on a road that runs just past the end of runway one-two. The little car stops.

Darryl fidgets with the handles on the door, the safety belt, the latch on the window on my side. Then, he puts his finger on every instrument on the panel, and even runs down all the circuit breakers on the panel at this left arm. Sheesh! He'd drive a saint up the wall with his pickiness! But I guess I'm glad he's that way. It doesn't hurt anything.

We make the turn at the end of the runway. "FDQ ready for takeoff," Darryl announces.

"FDQ, clear for takeoff, right turn," says the tower.

We move away as Darryl gradually advances the throttle. He finally has everything as far forward as it will go. He puts his hand on the throttle, prop pitch and mix, and looks like he's trying to break them off just to make sure he has them all the way forward. FDQ has no digital read-out clocks, but I notice that the airspeed comes well over the "Vce" (single engine capability) mark on the dial before Darryl lets it leap off the runway. He retracts the gear almost at once.

It's 0707 hours; the sun is just up enough to make the trees on the ground cast long shadows almost straight west, and in such parallel lines that it makes the whole desert look like it's been lined with a draftsman's rule. Darryl turns to heading of 204. It's going to be Ernabella. Incidentally, did you know that the "new" name for Ernabella is Pukatja? That's because of the recent "give back" of the tribal land in that area. Darryl begins to turn left just slowly. He's following the highway to the east. Maybe he had that word from ground control before I got there. At 6,000 feet he turns to 192 degrees. We're going to Indulkana! Darryl begins fiddling with the power settings, trying to get all the needles absolutely on the mark.

I read my *National Geographic* for February 1982. I also hand sister Carol the travelog of the Amata trip where I had the kidney stone come down. At 0722, Darryl reaches for the microphone to let Alice control know that we're at thirty-five miles DME. As he puts the mike away, he inadvertently hits the autopilot switch on his control wheel, shutting off the gyro. The nose drops suddenly. Everyone comes out of their seat just a little, and heart beats stir just a tad. Darryl grabs the wheel, and we start the whole process over again of getting all the needles right back on the mark. About the time we're passing over Chamber's Pillar, it is just about to his liking again. At 0820, we're circling Indulkana. The landing will be east to west. Darryl does a beautiful job. We hardly feel the touchdown. The airstrip is teeming with gallahs, the gray-backed, red-breasted parrots that are so numerous here. Sister Ann is waiting for us with the Toyota.

She's had quite a trip to Europe since I last saw her, but she isn't talking about that. She's telling us that we have a large clinic. Most of the Chandler people are going to be there, and again, they have lots of problems. Vivian is there, too, and of course, Margaret, the South African black sister from Lesotho. A full crew at least. Maybe things will go along better today.

First patient is Maxine who is thirty-three and wants to have a baby. She gives a good story of tries, but no successes. I guess we should send her in to ASH to be seen by Dr. Cahill for an infertility evaluation. But we can't do that until Dr. Cahill returns from her holiday. We'll set it up, anyway. Maxine is happy with that. I notice that the chart for visual acuity here is made up of egg-shaped ellipses with the sharper end of the egg cut off, and pointing in different directions. I've never seen a chart like that. Usually they are "E" pointing in different directions. Nupi is nineteen, 51.5 kg, 110/60, and is about 31/52 weeks. Fetal heart is good at 156/minute. Her hgb (hemoglobin) is 10.1 grams. I guess she should be on a little iron supplement.

James is only three months old. His Mom has been a health worker at the clinic, and is worried about his left foot. The doctor at the hospital wasn't worried about it. James does have a bit of a talipes (club foot). I think he should go back for a plaster on that foot, particularly since the Mom is asking for it, and eager to take care of it. Usually an applied plaster for something like that will be off in about twenty minutes after the hospital. But James' Mom would leave it on, I'm sure. I think we'll arrange for James to go in and have that done.

Tommy was born in 1935. He's very proud of a large nodule growing on his neck from just about where the left submaxillary saliva gland should be. It's about four centimeters in diameter and has a small ulceration in the edge of it. It's freely movable, and not particularly tender. It's soft rather than hard. There's no abnormality in the floor of the mouth. Tommy wants to know whether he'll be in dreamtime when it's taken out. I suppose he'd have to be given a general anesthesia, because no one could guess where the base of that thing would be. He'll be going in to ASH for that. His blood pressure is checked. What's this? Irregular pulse! Blood pressure is 138/78, but he's in atrial fibrillation. Adam Walker is from Chandler. He's twenty-two months old and has had intermittent fever to 39 degrees Celsius, but only for four days. I don't think we'll use anything but a little

Panadol (Tylenol) until we really see what's going on.

Martin Tine (you've met him before) is nine months old now, and when you met him before we were going to send him in to the Alice for correction of a rather severe phimosis (tiny opening of the foreskin to allow the urine to escape). Mom says that the doctor on the east side saw Martin and rang up a specialist, who said that it should be left alone. So nothing was done. Martin is into that stage where he crawls from here to there with great speed and manages to get into just about everything. A look at his little penis confirms that there is just a pinpoint opening here. I can't see the meatus at all. He's going to have problems with that somewhere down the line before he's more than a decade old. I tell Mom that I'll bring back the tools and we'll do it here next time. I'll just make a little dorsal slit and then with a smooth probe, release the adhesions till I can roll it back over the glans. I tell Mom that it won't be a circumcision. That's when Martin pulls the rubbish bin over on his head. He lets us know with a yowl. It's one of these kind of bins that has a plastic trash bag hanging from a circular frame of metal. Martin has just managed to catch the edge of the metal frame right on the upper outer corner of his left eyebrow. Even as we look it's swelling. He's going to have a real shiner here. We put a little pressure on it. He stops yowling. Rosemond is Martin's Mom, and she was born on the last day of May in 1960. She wants to change from Microgynon (oral contraceptive pill) to Noridal. That's easy. We write her a prescription. One like Martin every two years is about right. Closer together would be chaos!

Tanya is twenty. She has right upper quadrant abdominal pain. In October you met her on the plane when she had shingles. This time she has a temp of 36.9 degrees Celsius, but is really tender suprapubically, more than the right upper quadrant. Probably a p.i.d. (pelvic inflammatory disease). She's menstruating. We'll just put her on five days of Ampicillin. Little Kym Borke is eleven months old and has a really sore looking right arm in the deltoid area. It's his BCG (Bacillus Calmette-Guerin for tuberculosis) vaccination. Mom says that it does exude some pus every once in a while. Not much to do for this except give Kym a little Panadol when it hurts. It will get better with time, but that's one of the reasons that I don't care for BCG.

Riley is Whiskey's brother. He's been on a disability that has been renewed for so long that no one knows really why he's getting the pension. Just more hassle to undo it paperwork-wise than to let it keep coming. In the interests of good government, we'll undo it this time. Examination reveals nothing much wrong. He does have a few complaints that suggest peripheral lower extremity neuropathy. Maybe 50 mg of thiamine each night might help that out a bit. Considering his brother's name, there's probably a reason for his problem. Nginti is twenty-eight. She has what seems to be a p.i.d., but we'd better check out her urine just to make sure it isn't a uti (urinary tract infection). She "nicks off," and we just don't see her again. Guess she wasn't sick enough yet.

Now come the Pitts from Chandler. You've met Rhonda before, Mrs. Pitts, and there's Bill, and little Elizabeth who is eighteen months. Bill is having insomnia. It's not a new story. Rhonda is having a hard time coping with the kids. They're really good kids, but this family's story would make any person uptight. They've been in Chandler two years. Bill has applied for transfers at frequent intervals since they finished the first year. The oldest child is seven, Bill tells us, but can barely write her name. There just isn't competent schooling, he says, and he wants to give his children something better than Chandler. Rhonda, skinny little thing, has tears in her eyes. She tells how it's hard to be a good wife when neither she nor Bill is happy with their situation. Bill says that he did write to the Union down in Adelaide, and that he's to go for an interview somewhere in New South Wales in a fortnight for a new job, but if he does, he's going to lose his holiday time just in moving the family. On top of that, he says, there's the overdue account at the company store. Bill says that his grocery bill runs about $600 a fortnight, and that's just about his wage. On written complaint to the Union once before, he did get about a $200 refund from the store for "gross overcharging."

"That's going on all the time," he volunteers. "Doc, for two years I've ridden a section car 250 kilometers up and down the track every day. After two years there's nothing to see that's stimulating, and I come home and there's no use trying to fix the yard or a garden in this bull dust. I work on the car, and it runs well, but there's no place to go. We just have to get out of here.

Maybe if you'd write a letter for me, they'd listen if you said that it is a medical necessity."

Isn't that a shame? I tell Bill that as long as he's going for the interview in a fortnight, let's just let things be, and if his new job doesn't pan out, I'll write a letter, although I really don't think it would do much good. Bill and Rhonda seem satisfied. I think it was good just to let him ventilate. I prescribe some diphenhydramine hydrochloride, 50 mg at bed time for Bill's insomnia. He doesn't know it's just Benedryl, but the white capsules with the red bands look impressive, and will probably help some.

Nyunima was born in 1942. She has abdominal pain. I don't find anything on exam. Maybe it's parasites. Mylanta seems to make her feel better. Then I discover that Nyunima's husband is Whiskey. We could start a television series call it "All in the Family." Peggy is 50 years old; has high blood pressure. It's 152/92 today. She's taking Aldomet, two bd, and Clotride. If she's happy with that dosage and taking it regularly, who am I to change it?

Next is Mauna Whiskey. See? What did I tell you? Mauna has just turned sixteen. She thinks she's pg. She's 52 kg, 105/70, but I can't feel any fundus (uterus). Guess we'll just have to wait for the next time. Amanda Flint is a newcomer. She was born the first of December in 1981. She's doing fine. Her weight is 5,390 grams. That's pretty good. She looks fine. A good, alert baby. Her Mom, Irene, had a Cu–7 placed by Dr. Cahill after Amanda was born. She wants to be sure that it's still there. No problem. Irene is European. We put her up and a spec exam shows the strings right where they should be and a normal looking cervix as well. That's good. Mom's reassured.

Suzie Presley (no relation to Elvis) has a rock in her right external auditory canal. The sisters tell me that they've tried to get it out, but can't seem to move this one. Yes, they've taken rocks out of Suzie's ears before. I look again. It's about the size of an early June pea, but stippled. It doesn't look like an opal. I guess we can leave it there. She'd probably just fill up the canal with something else if we did get it out. "Not to worry," as they say out here. Suzie is thirty years old.

Snowy was born in 1927. He's diabetic. blood pressure is

128/82. He's had a recent road accident; tried to mow down a tree with his auto. He got a bump on his head, and now has a headache. That's the fifth car that he's had trouble with. His fundi are clear; not even any neovascularization (new vessel growth seen in the eyes of diabetics). We draw blood for sugar. Maisie is fifty. She had a fracture diagnosed by x-ray at ASH of T–12 (twelfth thoracic vertebra) when she fell off a truck a month ago. She still has some pain. We'll treat her with aspalgin. Then comes along white-haired, full-bearded John Rowe. He's sixty-two and has a cough. You met John a long time ago. John has had surgery for cancer of the right colon, and subsequently surgery of the left colon for carcinoma. He's due for sigmoidoscopy again this June. John is going to the U.S. for a holiday; up to Maine where he has some family. John was in Iran about the same time I was. The last patient of the day is Margaret from Lesotho. Poor Margaret has a terrible time with dependent lymphedema. I think it's a family thing. She gives a good history that it is. She's thirty-seven, and depressed. She's really homesick, it turns out. But she is going home in three weeks. She's used Ponderax, 20 mg t.i.d. for this before. We'll give it to her again. I listen as she has a good chance to ventilate. Poor thing. She really is homesick!

Tea time at sister's. Darryl is reading my *National Geographic*, the article on Napoleon. Ann provides canned oysters on a square biscuit. It's good. The mamma cat has five little, brand new tabby kittens in her cardboard box. She licks them all, in turn, proudly, as each fastens onto its own faucet. A gentle move to pet her is greeted with turned back ears and rapidly changing pupils. I withdraw the hand. It's time to get back to FDQ. What's this? There's a coal black mare and her coal black colt beside her, grazing on a little spinifex-looking stuff beside the plane. Sister Vivian tries to muster them back through the gate, but they go charging down the strip.

"I can't do it with the Toyota," she admits. "I'll go back and get some aboriginals to drive them off the strip."

"Not to worry," says Darryl, quietly. "Let's see what we can do with the plane."

The engines start up with no problem. Darryl cautiously taxis toward the horses. The mare turns abruptly and heads east down the strip. Now she's really trapped at the fence at the perimeter. The colt follows her. She heads toward the north edge of the strip. Darryl turns FDQ that way so she can't slip behind us. She turns for the south side of the strip. Darryl heads her off again, although he's a little apprehensive about the softness of the strip right at the edge. The mare races eastbound again, but this time the colt is in front of her. She must have told the little filly something, because the colt keeps running, but the mare stops, whirls around and confronts the Navajo, with ears laid back, and murder in her eyes!

Darryl stomps on the brakes, shoves the throttles clear forward, and retracts the prop pitch. "Rowrrr," roars the Navajo. The mare turns on her front feet and lashes out at the plane with both the back ones. Fortunately, she's far enough away that she doesn't make contact. She races back eastbound, catching up to the colt. We taxi slowly behind them. We're almost at the end of the runway now. I look at the outside air temp. It's 39 degrees Celsius. That's pretty hot. A glance at the windsock shows that this is going to be a downwind takeoff. Darryl whirls FDQ around, leaving the astonished horses behind. I don't notice him try to break off the throttles this time. I've been capturing this whole episode on Super-8 movie film, and that includes the takeoff. One doesn't really remember what one's seen when looking through the view finder, but I imagine looking at this film is going to be a little hairy. I can remember watching the windsock go by, and then a glimpse of the Toyota on the port wing-tip just as Darryl lifts it off. In retrospect, that means that we had about ninety feet of runway left. Yes, that will be an exciting movie sequence.

The trip home is smooth. No kidney stones. Not too bumpy, and the temp stays in the upper teens and low twenties. What's this? As we approach the Alice, there's a black layer at 4,000 feet. It is twisting over the desert from near the gap. Someone is burning old tires at the "tip" (sanitary fill). There's smog here! That makes a fitting finale to the movie sequence. Smog in the Alice. What next? Be sure to be with me next week when we visit Ernabella.

Oh, yes. Just as I was leaving sister's place after tea, I asked Vivian about Wally.

"Gee," I said, "I have the check right here. Did he leave anything?"

"Yes, but he came back last week, said that he needed money, and took them away. I told him that you'd be here this Thursday, but he said he needed money right away."

"Were they nice?"

"Oh, yes! There were some really nice ones there."

"Five or six?"

"Yes, five, I think. Some had really nice fire."

"Heck, well, tell him that I did have the check and that I'll be here in four weeks again. Maybe we can try again." So, you'll have to wait a month now to find out that part of the story.

4 February 1982

From the very start, this promised to be a day of surprises. It wasn't sister Carol going with me. It was sister Ann. Ann used to be the sister at Ayer's Rock, and remembers me making one of my infrequent visits to that settlement for the man with the foreign body in his eye. Ann is pleasant, but doesn't seem to have much idea about what she's going to do at the clinic today. The pilot is Richard. He's a rental from Chartair. Mark is just coming in from a trip out with FML to Fregon. Seems they had a "first light" emergency out there. A youngster with a fit. Did hear later that it was a case of meningitis. At first when I arrived, the boxes of patient cards were sitting on the tarmac, but there was no plane in sight. I assumed that it was being fueled, and so it was. It's to be FDQ again today.

Richard had the numbers from the tower. It's to be runway one-two, and it's to be the 207 radial at 6,000. There's a hawk on the runway. After we're cleared for takeoff, Richard advances the throttles just a little, and we move towards the hawk until he elects to abandon the runway to the Navajo. Last week wild horses; this week hawks. Something different every week.

I study my continuing medical education lesson. Richard isn't nervous like Darryl, nor does he take off without proper Vce, like Mark, but he does talk. He's on 124.10 mhz and 124.80 talking to every pilot in the air, it seems. He has lots of friends. Ann sits in the back reading. It's about an hour and ten minutes to Ernabella. Richard is just a tad west of where he should be on a straight line. It's a clear morning with only a little haze. There's quite a crosswind blowing at Ernabella. The altimeter says we're at 2,120 feet when we're on the ground.

Patrick meets us. Jennie's up in the Alice. She did get over her bronchitis okay, says Patrick. The clinic isn't too well organized. There are some people drifting in and out, but the first patient is Simon. Simon is forty two, and has had rectal bleeding. He's reluctant to discuss the problem, and I become aware that he really doesn't want Patrick around. Then there's the second complicating problem of Adrian. Adrian is a medical student from Adelaide who is up here for a three week stint as medical officer. I'll bet he learns things in this three weeks that they won't teach him in school!

Simon is persuaded to have a bowel movement. He speaks English, but it's his body English that is more important. He comes back to a quiet room in the hospital. Patrick and Adrian step outside. I explain that I really want to feel for the source of his bleeding with my finger. No problem. Simon lays on his left side and I perform a proper rectal exam with a gloved finger. The prostate is smooth. There are no masses, but I do feel the fullness and ballottability of some large, internal hemorrhoids. That's where his bleeding is coming from. We'll use some HC (hydrocortisone) suppositories and see if it improves. If not he'll have to come up to the Alice. He nods his head just a tiny bit. He'll do it if it's necessary. Then it comes out that he owns a house in the Alice, and plans to go up there on Saturday, anyway.

Brian is fifty. He has a letter from Dr. Parker from the aboriginal medical service down in Adelaide, as a matter of fact. Brian was seen down there on the January 15, and Dr. Parker thinks that he might have Crohn's disease (colitis), and wants me to refer him to the appropriate specialist in the Alice. Brian has a two-year history of rectal bleeding. Well, how's that for a specialty clinic? Maybe we'll have all rectal disease this time.

Ann does find his notes, and I find that I've seen Brian before for this; once in August and once in September of last year.

Brian has strange antecubital fossae (the fronts of his elbows), like he's had both arms broken. It's not easy to find the artery for checking blood pressure. He's 148/82. Patrick is advised that we should send Brian up to the Alice about the first of the month when Dr. Finley, the radiologist, is back from holiday. Then Dr. Charley can do whatever he thinks needs to be done. He's our specialist in any event, and will have to double as whatever specialist is needed.

By golly! It's little Clara! Imuna has brought her to the clinic along with some papers that say that Clara has now been diagnosed as microcephaly and epilepsy and squint. That's Clara, all right! She seems fine today, and even smiles at me. Imuna is grateful that we've given a year of attention to Clara. Esther Yanyi is nineteen. Esther had been on thyroid, but taken herself off about three months ago. We'd kept her off and had TSH (thyroid stimulating hormone) and T4 (circulating thyroid hormone) drawn last time, and we have a TSH of more than sixty. Yup! She's primary thyroid deficient, all right. We'll start her back on fifty micrograms a day for about a week, and gradually increase until she's asymptomatic. Pyula was seen at Fregon a couple of weeks ago with the SBE (subacute bacterial endocarditis). Her blood pressure is 102/68, and she still has that mitral murmur.

Nuuitja/Harry is fifty two and wants her IUD out. We'll send her up to the Alice when Dr. Cahill returns from her holiday. Tjulkina is thirty two and "all over sore." Examination doesn't show us why she's sore all over. Her blood pressure is 121/80. We'll try a little Indocin for her. Maybe that will help. Phenone is here from Fregon. She's brought up a carload of people to be seen. She's new. She's French; dresses and looks French, and sounds French. She's brought Ruth for a driver's license. That's easy. Ruth is a health worker down in Fregon. Nyalpantja is twenty, 71 kg, 110/80, and Adrian does a masterful job of examination, rattling off the numbers above like he's in a classroom. He doesn't hear a fetal heart.

"She's 36 weeks," he announces. I write everything down but the last numbers. I can see from the desk that the fundus is only a little above the umbilicus. I have a feel of her tummy.

"Let's call it twenty nine weeks," I suggest. That will keep Nyalpantja from arriving at the hospital in the Alice two months ahead of her delivery date. Wanatjura is eighteen, 100/70, 50 kg, and she's also about thirty weeks. It's bedlam in the clinic with kids screaming and people talking. No wonder Adrian can't hear fetal hearts. I mention it to Patrick.

"Oh, they're just having a social time," he laughs. I hold my tongue. I'd like to suggest that they can have a social time under the tree outside, and not in the clinic where I'm trying to practice medicine. But then I opt not to upset Patrick. Never know the tenderness of these male sisters.

Here's Tommy, the man we saw two weeks ago in Fregon with the amputated penis? He's infinitely better! The pus is all gone. It's just red flesh now, and it's true. That penis has been amputated, but from just in front of the corona on the dorsum, slant-wise downward and posteriorly, so that the urethra has been cut off about half way down the shaft, and the fleshy part lies against the scrotum. That keeps it moist all the time, and probably is why he had the infection in the first place. It's been a ceremonial thing, I think, and probably was done early on in pubertal rites. We'll give him another does of Amoxil; three grams. Tommy smiles. He's plenty tickled that the mess is cleared up.

Heather is 82 kg, 110/70, 27 weeks. Fetal heart is 146/minute. Her surname is Hess. She's European. Hilda is from Yalata. The notes say that she's a problem mother. She didn't want anything to do with her baby back in 1976. She's 118/72, about 24/52. I don't hear any fetal heart tones on her, either. Christina is two. She has a "grotty" chest. Temp is 39 degrees. We'll give her half a Bicillin now and half again in two days. Tjitayi is twenty two. Mononucleosis? We'll draw an FBC (full blood count). I can't find anything wrong on physical exam. Audrey has left flank tenderness. She's thirty. She denies dysuria (painful urination). Her blood pressure is 122/80, and her temp is 37.6 degrees. Her tummy is soft. I think she has a uti (urinary tract infection). We'll treat her with Bactrim for two weeks.

Angkuna was born in 1938. I'm sure I've seen her before. She says, no. She has right-sided distress. The whole right side, from the side of the head to the little toe. Just the right side. Exam is NAD. Wasn't she the one I saw a long time ago, like a year ago, that was in the trance? Ann can't find her card, either. There's a lot of cards that haven't been written on today, but I do have my own notes for this. Maybe sister Carol can figure it out later from them.

Judy Morton wants Nordiol 28 (oral contraceptive). She's thirty two and doesn't want another baby. We give her the script. Actually, I write the script, and the AMS (Aeromedical Service) will fill it in the Alice when we get back and send it down to Judy on the mailplane on Tuesday.

Matthew Troy has a periscrotal rash that looks like poison ivy. Mom says it's been there a long time. Matthew has an undescended testis on that side. Patrick says he's used steroid cream and Mycostatin on it, but it doesn't go away. I don't think he's been really treated, but I don't want to hurt Patrick's feelings. Matthew is two. We'll try alternate miconazole and steroid, but for two weeks. Maybe that will do it. And, a little talc to keep the area dry.

Mantuwa is thirty-seven. No period for two months. She's awfully heavy. It's hard to feel much through all that adipose tissue. Maybe she has a p.i.d. (pelvic inflammatory disease). Let's give her three grams of Amoxil and see if she has a period next month.

Then the last two patients, Jackie Mutjuri and his wife Ruringkukuno. Jackie we've seen before. We thought he was tabetic (tabes dorsalis—a complication of neurosyphilis) a year ago. Now he can't walk at all. But when he makes the try, he watches his feet closely and tries to put them down with an exaggerated slapping motion. He can't see very well, either. He's totally aphakic (no lenses in his eyes). The lenses have been removed for cataracts. The glasses he's wearing are so scratched with time and dust that they look opaque to me. Jackie wants to go to the Old-Timers' Home in the Alice. Ruringkukuno is a classic aboriginal facies, with the eyes sunken in, toothless, born in 1906. She's had tuberculosis in the past, and has the big scar that looks like it would be from a lobectomy, but actually is from a lipoma that was taken out years ago. She'll have to go with him to the Home. I'll fill out the papers and have Dr. Whitehammer sign them. (Later Barry tells me to go ahead and sign them; then tells me that syphilis was unknown in the aboriginal community until about fifteen years ago, so he thinks that Jackie's thing could hardly be tabes. I've drawn a serology anyway.)

That's the end of the clinic. We gather at Patrick's for tea. He puts on quite a spread. Phenone and Richard, Ann and Adrian, and Patrick, all dive into sausage and pickles, bread and cheese. I have my cup of tea, and wonder at the large flag that Patrick has pinned to the living room side of the kitchen divider.

"It's the Eureka flag," he announces. It's a flag on a blue field with a white cross. The horizontal arm is maybe twice the length of the vertical arm, with eight-pointed stars at the ends of each arm and in the center.

"I burned the other flag," he boasts. Later I learned the story of the gold miners in New South Wales who rebelled against the government, and for a time, had their own anarchic government. This was allowed to run its course by the proper authorities, until it died out in self-destruction. Patrick is a member of the young, activist culture espousing negative causes.

On the way home, Ann sits in the right front seat. She's delighted to be the copilot. I finish my lesson in the back. God, it's really bumpy! There are scattered cumulus at about thirteen thousand feet. We're below them, and it's still bumpy. We're home by 1515 hours. Now for the meeting with Dr. Hugh Wilson of the N.T. (Northern Territory) Health Department, who is trying to enter 15,000 aboriginals into a Wang computer system, and has found out that I did that sort of thing in private practice. It's another story. I'll have to tell you about that some time.

25 February 1982

I bet you wonder where I've been since last I sent a travelog about the outback. Well, Laura and I have been on a Newman's Coach Tour of New Zealand; the Value Pak one at that; the cheapie, and it was a total success. But that's another story. I'll write a separate travelog about that, and try not to let it get too long. New Zealand is a wonderful country; so diverse and interesting, and such friendly people. But, like I said, that's another story.

This morning I arrived at the airport at 0745. I had been told that since sister Carol is still on holiday, or again on holiday (whichever) that sister Ray would be going with me, and Ray likes to sleep in, so we won't be leaving at 0645. When Bob Worthing arrives from the limousine service, Ray is slouched down in the seat, still catching about the fourth of forty winks. She's been out at the casino during the evening last night, and the wee hours of the morning, and she isn't quite all with us. It's to be Mark flying. When I arrive, he's standing on the tarmac talking with a very pretty, brunette, well proportioned, young lady whom he introduces as Margaret, his fiancee. She's lovely! Mark looks justifiably proud. She's taking the car back into town. Mark has FDQ ready for travel. We're going to Indulkana, but since the rains have washed out the strip again, we'll be landing at Granite Downs, and motoring over.

That's fine! We'll also be seeing Marg Baxter, and she'll be coming back into the Alice with us. "Runway one-two," says the radio, "fly the 160 radial to 5,500, then the 179 radial to 7,000. Report 5,500. Clear for takeoff, right turn."

The desert is emerald green. While we were away on holiday they've had something like 140 millimeters of rain. That translates into something like 5.5 inches! It looks more like Kansas in the spring than the red center in summer! I've brought along my *Family Medicine* journal to study, and take the two hour quiz for continuing medical education. That's one way to keep up with what's going on in my profession. I mention to Mark that it's such a clear day. We'll be flying over Chamber's Pillar today, but I have plenty of pictures of that.

"Funny thing," I mentioned to Mark. "For all the pictures I've taken of things around here, I still don't have any pictures of the Alice from the air."

"You don't?" He's amazed.

"No, I've always taken off heading south, and come in only as far as the airport."

The Alice lies north across the first range of the McDonnels from the airport. Ray is already asleep in the double seat in the back of the plane. Landmarks are altered by the green and growth in the desert. I never did see Kulgera as we approached the South Australian border. But there's the tailings "surf" at Mintibi, and the hills of Indulkana, and the shining metal roof at Chandler, so that place where the green creeks come together must be Granite Downs. I've never seen it look like that before. Mark spots it about the same time I do; he's letting down. We cross the station buildings at about three hundred feet, and head east to the strip. There's a Toyota there now. Mark drops some flaps; slows us down. Then the gear comes down, and Mark kicks FDQ around in a left turn. Full flaps. Our ground speed still looks a little much. We touch down. The strip is roller coaster rough. We use up the whole runway. On turning about to taxi back, the sock is pointing at us at about forty five degrees. Oops! We've done it downwind again!

Vivian is waiting. Ray wakes up long enough to move from the plane to the Toyota 4-wheel drive, then lapses back into coma. It's an exciting drive over the rough and rutted track for the thirty kilometers ride to the settlement. Vivian is so tiny that it's just about as much as she has strength for to hold the vehicle on the track. But we are keeping ahead of our own dust.

There have been a few changes in personnel at Indulkana since last I was here. Jennie and Patrick have come over from Ernabella, and Ann has gone from here to there. Vivian is in her last month of service. She doesn't know what she's going to do, but she's not going to stay out bush. We'll probably know when she knows. She's going down south and will just rest for a while, she says. Mark and I discuss Randy and Raul, my sons, and their careers on the ride over. Then Vivian tells us that we have a rather difficult first case today. We're going to be seeing an eight-and-a-half-year-old girl who was seen in Ernabella on the sixth of the month with a copious, thick, foul-smelling vaginal discharge. The sisters made a smear of it, and gave the child, Wendy/Maylene of Tiny and Biddy (birth date 24 April 1973), an injection of Bicillin. Maylene came right, but the slide returned as positive for Neisseria (gonorrhea) and the parents were outraged. The girls at Ernabella gave her an additional half gram of probenecid on February 23, and then an hour later gave her a gram of Amoxil. Now there are police from Oodnadatta at the settlement who are demanding the doctor do an examination of the child. Apparently there have been other cases of similar nature, and the cops really want to get to the bottom of the things, so to speak. Vivian says that Tiny and Biddy have given their consent for me to examine the child.

We arrive in the settlement. There is trash in the street, and against the fences, and under the bushes; soft drink cans, and crushed fruit boxes, paper containers for cordial, mangy looking dogs, old parts of cars, assorted empty bottles, broken and unbroken, a part of a broken screen from a window. Graffiti on the empty buildings carries no recognizable message, but in some cases, is colorful. There's a sunshield composed of six wooden poles, about eight feet high, with a woven mat roof that would measure about five by four meters if it hadn't fallen in on the eastern side. Beneath this shade are a baker's dozen assorted men and women of the settlement; assorted ages, their clothing not particularly colorful, since it is mostly dun colored from mud and grease and dirt. About the same number of children on the street, too. Mostly no clothes for the younger ones. One wonders what on earth they do day in and day out. No different than any of the other settlements that I visit, though.

Sometimes one is surprised to see someone dressed in something new. But not in Indulkana today. No time to speculate more. We unload all the things into the health centre. Two police officers are there; Mark Borgnine, and another officer whose name I didn't get; stocky build and blond. Mark is tall, well muscled and dark. First, says Vivian, would I look at Rosemary Marsh. She was working in her kitchen the night before, and the hot water hose from the washer had popped off the machine and sprayed her with scalding water. She's been in an awful lot of pain, and awfully worried about scarring. She's European.

Rosemary is lying on a cot in the hospital portion of the dispensary. She is covered only by her panties. She has a nasty looking second degree scald burn about 8 cm in diameter over her right costovertebral angle area. It looks clean. The sisters have been treating it with silver sulfadiazine cream. She has a second area in the right axilla, but it doesn't involve the breast. It looks clean, too. I reassure her. It will be pretty red for a while when it heals, but by the time six months has gone by, it will be hard to see. It might be either more or less tan than the rest of the skin around after it heals, but it really should be okay. She is reassured. She's grateful. She thanks me.

Back to the dispensary part and officer Borgnine. I explain to officer Borgnine, his partner, Ray and Vivian, and Tiny, the child's father, about the course of gonorrhea and its incubation period. Seems that Maylene had been with her parents in Port Augusta until about the first of February. Then they had come north, and the first night in Ernabella, the child had stayed with the minister's family. The second and third night she had stayed with friends. The next night she had the infection. Biddy and Tiny want me to look at the child.

"I will if you want me to," I tell them, "but if Maylene is really against it, I won't." They feel that's fair.

"Will you be able to tell if she was assaulted?" asks officer Borgnine.

"Probably not, but I will be able to tell if she's not been penetrated; if the hymen is totally intact. It's not likely that it will be intact in any event. There are so many things that can rupture the membrane in a child this age. Like falling from a push bike or a horse."

"Not many kids ride horses and push bikes out here," challenges officer Borgnine. "You can tell my partner and me what you find after the examination."

"No, I can't."

"You can't?"

"No, if you want any information from me about the findings of the examination, they'd be available by court order only. I couldn't tell you what I find."

"Well, that's a lot of nonsense! You go ahead with your examination, and then you can ring Sgt. Hardesty of the S.A. police at Oodnadatta 5 and tell him the results if you don't want to tell me."

He's really upset with me. During all this conversation the room has been filling with cigarette smoke. I'm almost nauseated already. Four of the six people in the room have been puffing away. There's no ventilation, no air conditioning. It's pretty bad! Maylene is helped onto the examining table. I scrub diligently while Vivian gets things ready. Both hands are gloved. The light is placed. Ray wakes up from her drowsiness to witness. I gently separate the labia. There is a perforated hymen, but it's only about a centimeter opening. The edges don't appear traumatized at this time. There is no discharge. The tissues appear pink and healthy. There doesn't seem to be any significant scarring. I don't have a child's speculum, so nothing is introduced into the child. I do not carry out any kind of digital examination. As far as I'm concerned, the child has been examined. I see no sign of current infection. She needs no treatment. I really think in the best interest of the child in this case, the less said about it the better. I think the officers should carry on their investigation from some other direction. But that's all that I could ever testify to anyway. Before I terminate the examination, I call Ray over.

"Look, do you see any sign of infection or recent trauma?"

"No."

"Good." Maylene is surprised and happy that this trauma is ended. So am I.

Maxine is back. She's thirty three. Last time she had told me she was pregnant. I didn't feel a fundus then. She's 63 kg, 120/70. I feel. I don't feel a fundus now, either. Next is Mona Whiskey, age sixteen, 55 kg. Last time I couldn't feel a fundus. This time she's 15/52 weeks. Amunari is twenty years old. She's 20/52 weeks, but there's a big, left lower quadrant bruit. I don't hear the fetal heart. She's 42 kg, and 95/60. Peggie is fifty years old. She's about 95 kg. She has a marked, lumbar lordosis (swayback), and she has a backache. She has no limited motion, though. Her blood pressure is 120/80. Let's give her some Indocin for her pain. Hughie is fifty. He has a backache, too. He also has a tachycardia (fast pulse). On August 23 last year I saw him for the same thing. Let's try Indocin again. It seems to keep him away for five months.

Dorothy is sixty-two. She has headaches and vertigo. I check her out closely. Blood pressure is 108/60, and the eye grounds are clear. Oh, yes, she remembers now that she has stomach cramps, too. We order some Stemetil for her. Katherine is five. She has swollen eyes, and about three weeks ago she was hit on the bridge of the nose with a metal pipe and had to have some stitches. The nose looks fine. There's going to be only a little scar. She has a "fly" conjunctivitis. We'll treat her with Chloromycetin drops. Carlene is eight. She has sore eyes like her friend, Katherine. This is truly a case of sympathetic conjunctivitis. There's nothing wrong with her eyes. We'll give her some Visine drops to make her happy, though.

Now the Pitts family again. They're on holiday now. They didn't go anywhere. They stayed in Chandler for their holiday! I wonder if this is a catch-22 for real! Who, in their right mind, would stay in Chandler for a holiday.

No money, they say. Later Vivian tells me that's nonsense. They've bought a new stereo and have money for those things. Rhonda had an appointment for today with Dr. Franklin for a checkup for her cachexia (weight loss). She didn't go because she didn't have the money, she says. It's hard to be sympathetic with a family like that. Bill tells me his father has Paget's disease. He also urinates on his feet to keep from having athlete's foot. He's been doing it for years, and has never had it. We draw an FBC on Rhonda. I don't really know what to do for this family. They take up about half an hour of time.

Tanya is back. We saw her for shingles once, and then a couple of times after that. She's European. She's twenty. Dr. Eisman saw her and gave her some medicine. It was Amoxil. "He says it's a p.i.d.," she explains. She's still in pain. We'll put her on two weeks of Bactrim. Little Kym Borke is next. He has a subconjunctival hemorrhage in his left eye. Mom is reassured. Examination of the eye is NAD other than the blood.

Archie Fabian is a brand new one. He was born at thirty-six weeks, though, and was in the hospital for quite a while struggling with hyaline membrane disease. His respiratory rate is still almost 60/minute, but I don't find anything really wrong on physical except that he's using accessory muscles of respiration and retracting his chest. He was born on 12 February 1981, and left the hospital on 15 January 1982. He's 5,105 grams today, a 40.5 cm head circumference. I guess he's all right. I reassure Mom. Joan Rowe is next. She's just not feeling well. Joan is fifty-nine. You met her husband last time. He'd lived in Tehran for a while and has had two surgeries for rectal and colon carcinoma. Joan's BP is 152/94. I reassure Joan. She's happy. Cathie Polokon is thirty-two and has a low back ache. We'll try some Indocin.

Martin Tine is back. I've plumb forgotten to bring along the instruments to treat his phimosis. Sister Carol wasn't with us. Sister Ray admits that she never did her homework before coming, and I sure forgot. Mom is pretty irritated. She's been sitting out there for an hour.

"I'm sorry," I repeat, "I promise I'll bring the tools next time." I really am sorry. Poor little kid. That phimosis should have been taken care of a month or more ago.

Next is Tilly. She's thirty-two; has diarrhea and some epigastric pain. On examination, she has a big belly. Tilly is pregnant. She hadn't bothered to check with the sister before. Vivian didn't know. Tilly is about 30/52! Fetal heart is fine at 152/minute. We draw her first bloods and start an antenatal chart for her. Her bowel sounds are fine. I'm glad her belly ache wasn't labor pains!

Next is Kelvin; about nine. He's laughing. He's put a marble into his right ear. Big joke, Kelvin! You can keep your marble in your ear. It will come out by itself, but it might make a sore ear for a while. Then you won't be laughing, and you won't be apt to put anything back in your ear for a joke.

"Look, it's almost two o'clock, and this clinic is getting to be a joke," I complain to Vivian.

"There's Sadie," says Vivian. Sadie is thirty. She has a rash with itching. It comes and goes, and it's gone now. Swell. Next time it comes up let's try a little oral antihistamine.

"That's all," says Vivian. "I sent the rest of them away. They weren't sick anyway. They just wanted to see you so they'd have something to talk about."

So, the clinic ends. We take the Toyota over to Patrick and Jennie's. They have their place really fixed up nice. It's salami sandwiches and tea and cordial for the troops. I do have one of the salami sandwiches; well, a quarter of one. It's good! We discuss Maylene and officer Borgnine. Everyone agrees that he came on awfully strong. I'll discuss the case with Dr. Whitehammer when I get back to the Alice.

Then, we're off for the drive back to Granite Downs. Marg is waiting. Her blood pressure is 142/82. That's good. We drive out to the strip. Ray is starting to wake up now. FDQ roars into life. Mark checks everything into the green, and we race down the strip and into the air. I finish my quiz in the medical journal on the way home, just in time to note that Mark has started the descent.

"We'll go around the town," he says. And sure enough! We fly on over the Alice in a clockwise, big circle. Good time to get photos with the sun in the west! And it's a clear day. Yeah! That's awfully nice. We land just in time for me to get to the APO and pick up the mail. Ray is chatting with Marg. She's finally awake.

4 March 1982

I didn't get the word at all this week as to where it was going to be, or who was going to be going, but when I got to the airport at 0745 hours, there was Mark running up Foxtrot Mike Lima. Shortly after that, Barry came by. He's taking FDE on a short run to somewhere, and then the car arrived. It's sister Wendy, who used to be at Ayer's Rock, that is going to be the sister for today. Also, sister Jennie from Indulkana is along. Seems Jennie came up for something in the Alice; a meeting or something, and her car broke down as she headed back down the track. So, she's going to ride to Ernabella with us, and then will motor over to Indulkana.

There's also Imuntjana with Dudley, Damien, Hazel and Tcatji; four children (you've met Dudley before) who are on the way back from the Childrens' Health Unit where they've been for deworming and fattening up. It's a full plane! Jennie is happy. She's Patrick's wife, you remember, and they've just shifted over to Indulkana from their duty at Ernabella. While we load the plane, a yellow "utility" drives along the runway firing off aerial bombs; scaring away the hawks and such that have come to enjoy surfing on the thermals off the bitumen runway. It does seem to be effective, and the birds depart. The day is so clear, and things are so green, that it almost hurts the eyes to look at the mountains, they stick out so clearly.

"Foxtrot Mike Lima, runway one-two, clear for takeoff, fly the 207 radial at 6,000," intones the radio.

Mark advances the throttles, mixture and prop pitch, and FML leaps ahead, and soars into the sunny, morning sky. Klunk, thunk, kabunk! exclaims the gear, retracting into its well.

"What's petrol cost now?" I ask Mark.

"It's about forty-seven cents a liter," says Mark. "We'll burn about one hundred seventy-six liters an hour with this ship, and she'll hold about three hundred twenty minutes at standard cruise/altitude. Total capacity is about eight hundred liters."

The digital clock for elapsed time on the dash shows 6:34. There's another plane on the same course for Ernabella; the Cessna 206 mailplane. Mark picks it out to the east just about the time that I'm looking at the Henbury craters, where the meteorites came down a few thousand years ago. There's sure a lot of water in the Finke. Jennie has to light up a cigarette. She does ask Mark first if it's all right. The smell of burning vegetation permeates the cockpit. It really does bother me when people smoke in a plane. Oh, well. The irony is that she's such an avid conservationist and environmentalist. I can't imagine the logic of someone with a philosophy like that polluting their own body. She finishes the butt. The air-conditioning clears out the smoke. Then there's another smell in the cockpit. Dudley has filled his "nappy" (diaper). Ah, well. That is, at least, a natural smell!

My, it's green, and the lakes of salt that line the road to Ayer's Rock are filled with enough water that one could drown in them. That's a first! We cross the S.A. border.

"Aren't those the Musgraves (mountains)?" Jennie asks.

"Yes, they are," I reply. "The site of the 'reef of gold' that Lassiter described. I wonder where it really is?"

"I know an aboriginal in Ernabella who claimed that he had talked with Lassiter," says Jennie, "but he was so full of stories you couldn't believe anything he said."

Lassiter was an ancient fossicker of the area around the teens of the century. It seems that he stumbled into one of the settlements in the early days of the century muttering something about having found a "reef of gold" in the Musgraves. He died before he gave up his secret, it's said, although it is also said that he told the location to a trusted aboriginal friend. Back in the thirties, Lowell Thomas, the world renowned explorer/journalist, headed an expedition that found the desert grave of Lassiter. His body was moved for interment in the Alice, and, as a matter of fact, his grave is just across the street from our house on Memorial Avenue.

That's where the "old" Alice cemetery is. The "old, old" one is up near the railroad station near Billy Goat Hill, and the new one is on the track south of town, half way to the airport. I guess that's why Memorial Avenue is named Memorial Avenue. It's also famous in that the Avenue was also the old runway for the original airport, from whence departed the world famed *Kukaburra* aircraft on its exploratory flights of the deserts of the "red centre" back in the late twenties.

Now we're at Ernabella. Mark circles town, and drops us smoothly onto the strip. A tired, filthy, station wagon is waiting at the strip. It's family of Dudley, Damien and the rest. They really are happy to see the little kids, and the feeling seems to be mutual. There really is a lot of love in these family groups. They usually aren't very demonstrative, and you'd never see a display of emotion like this in the Alice aboriginals. Julie Peters meets us just as the 206 mailplane comes over the village, swings around to the east of the strip and commences its final approach; downwind. There really is quite a wind, too. Both Mark and I reflect on the landing run that's about to take place. I take out my movie camera. But the landing is successful. He stopped short of the west end of the strip. We drive into town for the clinic.

Little Ann, who used to be at Indulkana, is going to conduct the clinic. Ann is rattled straight away, and Wendy doesn't know how to handle the card system. It's a good thing I have my notes. First patient is Imitzala, who hasn't had a period since Christmas. She does have a swollen belly; looks almost like about eighteen weeks of pregnancy, but when you feel it, there's nothing to it. No fundus under the swelling. Pregnancy tests are negative, but I do get the feeling that I'm ballotting something. Her birth date is 29 January 1963. Either we've got a dandy pseudocyesis (phantom pregnancy), or there's an ovarian cyst under that black skin. We'd better have her come in for a pelvic in the Alice by Dr. Cahill.

Makinti is twenty-four years old, 20/52. I take her pressure at 122/70. Ann hasn't done anything preclinical; no blood pressures, no urines, no weights. She just brought in a patient whose name she doesn't even know. I notice that the bloods were drawn in December. The clinic is so noisy I can't hear any fetal heart tones. I'm a little irritated.

"That sure is a noisy clinic."

"They're having a social time;" Ann parrots Patrick's line.

"Why don't they have their social time under the tree outside?"

Ann disappears. The clinic does quiet down a bit. Heather Hess is 83 kg, 110/60, 31/52 and FHH 148/minute. Thelma is only thirteen, but she' dying of bronchiectasis. She's been worked up in the Alice by Dr. Mann. She's also got a heart murmur of mitral valve, IV/VI, clubbed fingers. She's on Vibramycin. Her juicy chest almost drowns out the terrible heart murmur. Tjulyata's Jonathon, born 7 January 1982, is in for a check up. New baby. He looks just fine! He does have tinea versicolor (a fungus infection) on his face. Wendy is twenty-six, 53 kg, 120/66, FHH 152/minute, and she's 21/52. She has a mitral murmur that is unchanged from September last year. She has a sore throat today. We take a culture. I notice that Julie has moved in and Ann has gone to do something else.

The clinic is moving along smoothly now. Cheyne Gregory is a big European. He's been running the road grader, smoothing out the air strip and the roads since the big rains. He's 95 kg, 146/96 hypertensive. He's thirty-one. We instruct him on salt restriction and weight reduction. Then Inantura, age eighteen, 35/52 weeks, 51 kg, 110/70 with a one-plus protein in her urine. FHH 158/minute. Who's this? Why, it's Imuna, with the mincobah between her teeth on the right side of her mouth . . . and Clara! Clara is in a nasty mood this morning. She's just a year and two weeks now. She has two teeth down and four up. She really looks pretty good for Clara. I think Imuna just wanted to say hello.

"How's Kinti's leg?" I inquire.

"Palya" (fine), whispers Imuna; delighted that I remembered her husband's bad leg, and his name.

Louis is next. He looks like Father Time without his scythe. The card says 1917 for his age. He's had a problem with congestive failure, although for a couple of years he was treated for his congestive failure with antibiotics. Since we made the correct diagnosis and put him on Digoxin, he's been a tad hypertensive, but his pneumonia has gone away. I last saw him on the September 17 last year. He's a very proud man. Next is Ampintangu, (Jeannie Ward), age eleven and very skinny at twenty-nine kilograms. She just doesn't eat. She's been to the CHU at the Alice a number of times; always puts on weight there when she's fed, but when it's up to her to fill her mouth and her belly, she doesn't. No use sending her in now. I'll wait until she's sick.

Yipiti is forty-six; asthmatic and epileptic at the same time. She doesn't take much of any medicine for either illness. She has another curious malady. Periodically, just at bedtime, her lips and mouth will swell up grotesquely. It's relieved by Phenergan, but no search has been done for an etiologic agent. She's been doing this since 1979. I guess we can try to extract the problem by elimination. Otherwise, she's fine. Blood pressure is 146/96.

Jackie was born about 1908, says the card. He has lipomas all over his body. One gigantic one is over the right scapula. He's particularly proud of that one. He's also a diabetic. I put him on Diabinese once, but I note that someone (a registrar) at the hospital made quite a detailed work-up on him, and decided that he be given dietary instruction at the hospital, and that no medication would be needed to control this diabetes. It could be easily handled by correct nutrition. That was last August. He still shows an occasional two percent urine glucose, but I'll leave him off the diabinese anyway. He's a little worried about a lump in his left groin. The sisters are made to leave the room, and Jackie lowers his stubbies (pants somewhat shorter than typical bermuda style). It's a bit of a communication problem getting him to lie back on the bed. He finally does. The lump near his left groin is just another lipoma; it's not a hernia.

"Okay, you can get up," is misinterpreted by Jackie, and he takes off his stubbies altogether.

"No," I repeat. "You can get up now." So, he takes me quite literally, gets up from the table and starts to walk to the door in his birthday suit.

"No, no, Jackie!" I beseech. "Put on your clothes first!"

He smiles, returns to the examining table and begins to put his things on. He's delighted about the new lipoma. I think he wanted to show all his friends out in the clinic what he had now!

Ankolya was born in 1940. She's also diabetic. She also has a bad back. She was last seen in April. Dr. Tally saw her on 23 February 1982 at the Alice for the back. He says there's nothing on the x-ray except lumbar lordosis. So be it. Let's give her some Motrin. Next is Jaclyn McElwell at one year for a checkup. She's European. She's fine; two teeth down and four up, just like Clara, but a little sharper than Clara. The next patient is led in by sister Julie. He's totally blind. Billy (Ilpilitja—wife Nyann) was born about 1920. He had a terrible left biceps abscess six months ago. Julie said she was sure he was going to lose the arm.

She had made arrangements for a med-evac, and the plane even came for him, but at the last minute, the men of the settlement said no.

And that was that. Billy stayed in the bush, and eventually came back, like a sick cat, and had healed the infection. The pain he must have gone through must have been terrible. He had a pension for that, though. One wonders if that's why the men wouldn't let him go. Now the DSS (Department of Social Service) wants a letter to continue the pension. There still is a lot of scarring and atrophy of the left arm muscles, but he has full range of motion in it. But he can't see! Examination reveals dense cataracts bilaterally. Billy says he can see the light of the ophthalmoscope, but can't see anything else. Dr. Barker is down in Fregon; supposed to be up tonight. I'll let him handle the evacuation of Billy for cataract extraction. That is, if the men will let him go.

The other side of the coin is Windless; born about 1920. He has decreased grip in his left hand. He wants a pension. He's 95 kg. I saw him on the second of last month for the same thing. He weighed 98 kg then.

"No, Windless, we'll see you next month. That's a good job; losing three kilograms. You keep up the good work." And he leaves, smiling.

Mark Carlson stops me on the way out. Mark is the husband of Fanou, the sister at Fregon. Mark had talked with Dr. Banks, Desk B, Dept of Urology at Flinders Hospital in Adelaide, about a vasectomy a week or so ago. He didn't have time to have it done before they came up here. He wants to know if it can be done in the Alice. I tell him that I'll set it up with an appointment with Dr. Lee next Monday. He and Fanou are coming up then anyway for something else. We'll see that it gets done. He's delighted.

Then a house call to see Ann Kersey; European, who is ten weeks pregnant. Ann began to spot about a week ago, and two days ago had quite a flow. It's stopped down to just spotting again. Julie has kept her at bed rest. Ann is thirty-seven. Examination shows blood pressure and pulse rate and all those vital things to be well within normal limits. There are no abdominal bruits. The fundus is just poking above the symphysis by a little bit. I draw an FBC. We'll see just where the bleeding is. There really isn't much else to offer Ann than bed rest. I think the ride into the Alice might just finish the thing off. It's a hard decision to make.

Back to Julie's for a spot of tea. Jennie's crying when I come in.

"What's the matter, Jennie?"

"Oh, it's Olive," cries Jennie. The story unravels. Jennie and Patrick had a spayed cat for nine years; Olive, by name. About Christmas time when they were still in Ernabella, Olive had disappeared. They had assumed that a camp dog had gotten to her, and after an appropriate time of searching and worry, they had accepted the loss. Last night, Ann had been coming back from the clinic to her house when she heard this faint mewing coming from under one of the buildings. She got down on hands and knees with a torch (flashlight), and looked under the house. Nothing. Then there was this bag of fur hanging from a nail! Ann had crawled under with all the redback spiders and stuff, and lifted this bag of fur and the leather band around it with the bell, off a nail in the joists.

Olive! Eight weeks! She had slipped the collar, but the wrong way. It was under her left foreleg. It gave her a little mobility, apparently, and kept her from choking. With the little mobility, she was apparently able to reach the spot where the drain pipe carried off the morning roof condensation, so some meager amount of water was available. But poor Olive! She had been a seven-kilogram cat at Christmas time; now lucky to make two kilograms. And the skin under that left foreleg had broken down, and the strap had rubbed down into the muscles, separating the fascia so that one could look right into the compartments of the muscles of the humerus. But although it was smelly, there didn't seem to be much infection. The girls had already minced some hamburger, and had given her sugar water, and Olive had swallowed some. Would I look at her?

Sure! It was as I just told you. Jennie scratched Olive between the ears as I examined. Olive purred, but there was no meow. She just closed her eyes, and the sack of fur lifted up and down, as somewhere inside there, some lungs pumped air in and out.

"Dust that foreleg with a little sulfa powder. Don't give her any oral antibiotics. Don't force feed the hamburger. Give her just a little at a time, but frequently, and do keep water available. She must have some sort of a strange nitrogen balance after eight weeks. She'll come right," I said with a confidence that was more of a prayer than a certainty.

Ann gave us a ride to the strip. Wendy was delighted when I said that I'd really rather sit in the back and finish the quiz for continuing medical education during the trip home, and that she could have the right front seat, if she'd like. We departed. My God! It was rough! Those cumulus dumplings up there weren't lying about the thermals that had put them there! Finally we came out over their tops at 11,000 feet, and I did finish my test. Nothing as exciting on the way home as last week when Mark had taken me over the Alice for movies and slides. But FML handled wonderfully, and there are about six more trips to Ernabella for this tour. I feel a little sad seeing this work come to an end. It's been unique as an experience.

11 March 1982

Last night sister Kay Douglas rang from AMS and apologized for not having rung earlier in the day. It seems that the flight is to be to Amata on the eleventh, and John will be the pilot. Sister

Ray will be going with me again, since sister Carol isn't back from holiday yet. There's the chance that we might have to divert to Ayer's Rock, since Dr. Harberth didn't get a chance to attend his clinic there this last week. Would I mind? Heavens no, I wouldn't mind at all. Too bad that I didn't know earlier, I mention to Kay. Laura might have been able to receive permission from the council to go along. She's never seen the Rock from the air.

"No problem, no problem at all," says Kay. "You just bring her along. There's plenty of room, and even if there's no clinic at the Rock, John might just have to stop by there anyway to get some fuel before coming home."

In the morning about 0730, Laura and I are heading out to the airport in the little Falcon 500. The day is cool at this time in the morning. It is getting along to fall, you know. The sun is just about on a level with the eyeballs as one looks through the windscreen as we head down the eastern leg of Memorial Avenue and turn onto Bloomfield. As we arrive at the airport, the Fokker F–27 is loading up with all the tourists who are paying $220 each for the return trip to Ayer's Rock. They fly there, have a tour around the rock with a guide who gives them some of the history, then a bus trip out to the Olgas, and then back for lunch. Then back on the plane for the ride back to the Alice. For $220? And one doesn't have a chance to climb the Rock unless one wants to give up the lunch. Today we're being paid to make the same trip.

But it isn't John. It's Darryl to be the pilot. John is due back this week, but isn't due to return to work until the end of the month. Sister Carol isn't due back either. It's going to be sister Ray. Today she's awake. Darryl has the plane all ready to go. Laura is into the right front seat. Ray sits facing forward. I take the backward facing seat. The plane is FDQ. I hear the radio say, "FDQ, runway one-two, 8,000 feet, fly the 207 radial. Report at 5,000, clear for takeoff. Right turn."

Darryl advances the throttles, and then pushes the prop, mix and throttle against the stops until it seems like they're going to break off again. Then I concentrate on looking through the window at where I've been, rather than where I'm going, since my seat is facing backwards. I have my CME lesson with me. Laura remarks on how green everything is. There's the Spyce Byce. She takes a picture of it. No screen around it today, I guess, like sister Glenda had once claimed. Ray picks that up and volunteers the information that Glenda is pregnant. She did marry that guy, she says, and is expecting soon. Isn't that nice?

The Hugh River is sliding below us. Laura comments on the water in it. Ray starts to fix coffee for us from the thermos. As I look backwards towards the rising sun, it's startling to see how much water is glinting in the sun. It looks like half the desert is made up of water. There's Mt. Connor rising like a layer cake in the haze. There's some smoke on the horizon from Curtin Springs area. Either the abattoir is burning carcasses, or there's a controlled bush burn going on. Darryl pilots us to the east side of Connor so Laura can have it on her side to take a picture of its crown. Then the radio announces that there's another Aztec in our area, coming down from Ayer's Rock for Amata; some school officials of some sort. I've never seen Darryl so nervous before.

The radio says that they are just starting along the mountain range that runs west of Amata. Darryl's head looks like it's on a 360 degree swivel. I begin to range my eyeballs over the horizon as well. Then, there it is! A little gleam along the mountains, about a thousand feet below us, three miles behind at five o'clock. I announce to Darryl. The sigh of relief is quite loud. He turns his attention back to his descent and approach. Smooth landing. The other aircraft is on a right downwind, turning base as we touch down. He really is right behind us.

Jennie meets us with the Toyota. Darryl unloads the lockers, and we stow the things back in the vehicle, and we're off. Jennie says that there's a pretty big clinic today, but nothing that is serious. First we meet Andrew, a sister who is "roving." That is, he moves about on the circuit assisting for a few weeks at different settlements. He's a nice-looking, young chap. He seems to know what he's doing, too. We drive past the wrecked vehicles that line the road in from the strip. It hasn't changed at all, but it sure is green. On past the demolished community building with the colorful graffiti. I sure would like to take a picture of that.

Up to the clinic. Scatter the dozen or so scroungy, skinny camp dogs that lie in front of the clinic door. There's sister Chris with her daughter. Piti has no pants on today, just top. The child is about two now, speaks mostly Pitjantjatjara. Her little, white bottom is in quite a contrast to the other naked children in the clinic area, but her face is just as dirty as any of the black faces we see.

The clinic is about to start. Ray is awake, but doesn't seem to have too good a handle on the card files. Rosemary is 72.6 kg, 80/60, age thirty-two, and the fetal heart is 136/minute. She's 35/52. Then, Veronica, who is two, with runny bowels and juicy chest. Her weight is 10,190 grams. She's not gaining weight as well as she should. We'll order down some fasigyn; dose for age, and see if relieving her of the worm burden will help her gain weight. It might also stop some of the juiciness in her chest. Glenice is twenty-two. She's missed two periods. Her bloods are drawn. I don't feel a fundus yet.

Lulu is 72 kg, 92/54, 35/52, bloods are drawn. FHH 140/minute. She's twenty-nine years old. She's a grav-6, para-5 (six pregnancies, five live births), and has just terrible scars on her belly. It seems that she fell in the fire when she was about six. She had a lot of grafts, according to her notes, but they kept getting infected. She's kind of proud of the scars, I think. From the number of babies she's had, they might be considered a beauty mark by the culture. She's a smiling person. She seems happier than most.

Next is little Ashley. He's eleven months old. He rolled into the fire a few months ago, and had to go up to the Alice for grafts to both his feet. His little right foot was barbecued enough to where the fifth toe and metatarsal have been amputated. There's a five-millimeter ulcer on the right heel where the graft has broken down. Seems like Ashley has a ravenous appetite, but Mom couldn't care less. He's having a weight gain problem, too. I tell Chris that if he continues to lose weight, he'll be in negative nitrogen balance, and the ulcer won't heal. I decide that if Ashley loses another 300 grams, he should be sent in to the CHU at the hospital. Let's save these grafts if we can.

Panyny is Ashley's grandma. She's forty-nine. She has left-sided pain from the top of her head to the end of her little toe, and including the left side of her chest to the sternum, and the belly to the belly button. I notice that in the seventies her pain was all on the right side. Someone gave her a brufen then, and there weren't any notes made for almost six months. I guess we'll get her on brufen (Motrin) again. Cursory exam reveals NAD (no significant abnormalities). We draw an FBC on her anyway.

Impata is sixty-six. Her daughter informs us that she is whining and complaining all the time, and that she's awake all the time at night, and that her bowels are not working, and she wants Impata out of her life. Chris says that the daughter has a reputation of being "evil." Chris has Impata on Mellaril and Mogadon, and has tried Senecot for the bowels, but the daughter insists that nothing is working. Impata is a classic aboriginal. She's long ago enucleated the right eyeball. Her other eye is sunken in; the cheeks are hollow, her hair is stringy, held in place by a filthy, blue head band. She's skinny, and has a curious fontannel right at the vertex of the skull. It feels like the outer table has been eroded away in a circle about a centimeter in diameter. It's hard underneath, as though the inner table of bone is still in place. I wonder what that is? I've never seen that before. Her general exam is NAD. On questioning, she's oriented for place and person, but doesn't seem to have much sense for time. But then, that's not uncommon in the culture. I tell Chris to keep on with what she's doing, and I think that in the absence of any fullness in the belly of the descending colon, she's probably just fine with the bowels.

Reuben is just like Hector was: marked dental caries. It's terrible! Only Reuben has carics on both uppers and lowers; teeth rotted right down to the gums! He's six. He hasn't lost the deciduous teeth yet, but the buds below must be taking a terrible beating from all the pus they're wallowing in. Reuben has an abscess right now in the first molar on the lower right, and quite a swollen jaw. It looks like something from the funny papers, only it isn't funny. Chris has him on Abbocillin. That's good for the present problem, but we'd better get him in to the Alice and have the dental clinic fix up that mess. He's got a lot of kangaroo bones to chew on, and will need his teeth! That reminds me. I've never seen an aboriginal with false teeth, and I've never seen an aboriginal with no teeth at all, either.

I note on my card that it's now 1130 hours. We've been an hour and a half on this clinic, and we've only just begun. I suggest that we gear things up and get moving. I notice that Chris disappears with Ray. Jennie brings me in the next patient; little Nigel. He's twenty months old, and they have a soiled nappie

with streaks of brown, liquid stool streaked with blood. I don't
see any parasites grossly. The nappie is from yesterday.

"Let's get a fresh one," I suggest, "and we'll take it in a
container . . . the stool, that is . . . while it's fresh, and have the
lab see what we've got. I suspect it's amoeba." Maybe the fasigyn
we're sending down will be good for Nigel, too, if given according
to weight and age.

Monica is eleven months old, too. She has diarrhea, says
Jennie. She also has a wet ear, examination proves. But her belly
seems okay. Let's treat the ear with routine ear toilet, and keep
it dry. No systemic antibiotics. Pingku is twenty-three. She has
anal bleeding and pain. Examination reveals peri-anal condyloma accuminata (venereal warts).

"Gee," says Jennie, "That looks just like Nanyntja. Is that
what it is?"

"Right! Let's take a VDRL (serologic test for syphilis) on her,
and then we'll give her a course of Amoxil. If things don't improve, or she gets more warts, or continues to complain, she'll
have to come up to the Alice and have them surgically removed."

As Pingku leaves the room, I stand up and stretch; wash my
hands, take a holiday gaze out the window. Darryl and Laura are
sitting in the Toyota out in the yard. I'm a little upset, but say
nothing to Jennie. Darryl and Laura should have been invited to
stay in Jennie's house. Darryl and Laura seem to be involved in
an animated conversation. I return to my work. Jennie has left.
Ray is back. Andrew is back, too.

Dick is the new patient. He's sixty-six. Ray has to leave the
room. Dick has pain in the left groin. He lies down on the bed,
drops his stubbies, and there's a great, big, indirect inguinal hernia. One can see the peristalsis moving the skin over the hernia.
Dick is trying to move the scrotum out of the way, but carefully,
so that he can hide the urethrostomy. He's had a ceremonial
amputation right at the base of the penis, just in front of the
scrotum. The meatus is about seven millimeters in diameter, and
appears to be red, mucosal type epithelium spreading out about
three millimeters in circumference around the stoma. Dick has
fathered children I'm told on asking. I wonder how? Anyway, I
explain to him what has happened, and that it should be repaired;
the hernia, that is. Dick agrees, then in excellent English, "But

I don't want anything else repaired; just the hernia." I reassure him that is exactly how I'll write the consultation request. Dick is happy. He'll go to the Alice. No one will repair that "ostomy." It looks pretty neat, anyway. I wonder how they did that?

It's noon. We're still dragging. Yuminia is thirty-two. She has swelling on the right side of her abdomen. She has a uti (urinary tract infection). She had an IVP (intravenous pyelogram, a contrast x-ray study) in 1979. It was NAD. She has a keloid scar in the right lower quadrant, that all the notes speculate was an appendectomy. But no one has ever confirmed it. Maybe it's ritual. She also has a suprapubic scar from a Cesarean. Blood pressure 120/86. I can't find anything wrong. Her urine is clear. Maybe she has ureteral colic? I don't know. "Cumpa" is urine in Pitjantjatjara.

Rosie is forty-eight. She has a lump in her breast. I think Chris was thinking it was a carcinoma. I examine. Rosie has been super-endowed with mammary tissue, but there're no lumps in the breasts. This thing is almost up on the clavicle, and is a five centimeter lipoma. I reassure Rosie and Chris. No surgery unless Rosie wants it off for cosmetic reasons. I reassure Chris that there's no malignant propensity in this mass.

Tommy has arthritis in his back when he gets up in the morning. Tommy is fifty. Let's try some brufen for that. Then comes Nellie, Tommy's wife. She also has a back ache. One almost would like to ask, facetiously, if there might be a mattress problem here. Maybe a bed-board would be helpful. But I don't snicker and I don't smile. They probably sleep on the ground on a plastic sheet, or if they're lucky, have a three-inch foam rubber pad they sleep on. She does admit that aspirin helps. She's had no period for a year. She's forty-two. That's kind of young for menopause. Blood pressure is 112/78, and I don't find anything else abnormal on cursory exam. We'll try some brufen for Nellie, too. It's 1230 hours. I look out the window again. Laura and Darryl have left the Toyota. Back to work.

Tyalyata is forty-four. She had gone to the Alice with us last time, if you remember, for the iritis. Well, they treated her with chloromycetin drops last time; said that it was corneal ulcers. She's got pain in that eye again. Examination reveals a steamy eye again. I have a pretty good look at the fundus. It looks okay.

There's some ulceration of the cornea. Maybe that's what it was the first time, but I don't think so. I'll treat this with chloromycetin drops again.

Polly is fifty-two. She's a diabetic, with crutches, and an amputated right leg. The notes don't say how she lost the leg. She's complaining of pain in the right hip. No wonder with the goofy looking Canadian crutches that she gets about on. She's filthy! She's suppose to be taking tolbutamide, one gram twice a day. She has a urine with 2% sugar and 2+ protein. She's probably not taking her medicine. We draw a blood sugar. Her last one was drawn a year ago. Manyngatja is forty. She has menstrual cramps. She weighs 98.3 kg! Blood pressure is 144/92. Cursory exam is NAD. I can't really feel anything in that huge belly. It's 1300 hours. I'm getting tired.

"Do you want to stop for a cold drink?" asks Chris.

"No, let's keep on with it and get it done. How many more?"

"They keep coming in."

"Well, I'm not here to satisfy the curiosity of the aboriginal population," I submit rather testily. Isn't it funny? I do this at almost every clinic.

"I'm sorry, Dr. Rutten," says Chris. "I just don't think that the sister should be prescribing brufen and things like that willy-nilly without the doctor seeing the patient. And besides, this is my last day. I've been out here nine years, and I don't see things are going to change for the better in the next nine years, and I think that I'm going to go somewhere else and do something else with my life."

Shades of Vivian at Indulkana two weeks ago! Did I tell you that I had seen Vivian in the hospital last week with a depression serious enough to require hospitalization? It seems that officer Mark Borgnine is—or was—Vivian's boyfriend, and the case of the eight-and-a-half year old child with gonorrhea, when we were there, broke up their beautiful friendship. Now here's the second case in two weeks of sister burn-out. No wonder! I stop criticizing, look out the window, see that Laura and Darryl are back in the Toyota, and get on with the clinic. Alec is five. He has rales in his chest. His uvula is glued to his left tonsil by fibrin from some previous infection. That's what Chris is really worried about. He's on Abbocillin.

"Don't worry about the uvula," I reassure. "He'll be running down the road one of these days with something in his mouth and fix that."

Michael is thirty-eight. He has had epididymitis, and wants a vasectomy. He's aboriginal. We will send him in, at his expense, for a consultation. And, would you believe? That's the end of the clinic. Whether they sent the rest away or what, I'll probably not know. It's funny, though, how when I start to get tired, the clinic always seems to end. I'll be happy when sister Carol gets back. The clinic usually ends before I get tired. I suppose it ends when she gets tired, and her staying power is less than mine. Out to the vehicle. Ray is mucking around with the card cases; doesn't have the cards filed. I walk out to the Toyota and climb in. Laura and Darryl begin to unfold their tale of interest. They've really seen a lot! Laura has been over to the little church.

"It could be so cute, but things are wrecked!" She's going to change the world! "And the store. I was over there, and I took a picture of the graffiti on the community building! And, Jack, we saw them!"

"What did you see?"

"We saw the kids petrol sniffing! There were about five of them altogether, not in one group; and they have these cans up to their faces, like you hold a diving face mask on when you inhale against it. And every once in a while they reach up with their hands and take the can away, and take a breath of air! We saw a man come by with what I thought was a bird on his head, but it was a charred rabbit! There were other people behind with other things to eat, and I guess they were going somewhere for a feast!"

Those blue eyes of hers were snapping with her amazement. It's good to take an observer along. Here I've been stuck in that dumb clinic all these times that I've been down. I don't even see what goes on in the settlement. But Laura sure did. I'll be anxious to see the pictures she took, although, like I've been warned, she didn't take pictures of people. Too bad. I'll bet those would have been good pictures for later—the kids sniffing, and the charred rabbit on the head.

Later, over at Chris's place, Piti still without bottoms, but with a clean face now, and at tea time, we discuss what Laura and Darryl had seen.

"They can't come in to school with their petrol cans," says Chris. "It's a fire hazard." I can't understand why someone doesn't take those things away from them. "Oh," says Chris, changing the subject, "I have some artifacts for you."

Laura had told me that they had stopped by the craft store, but it had been closed down. Peter Yates is in charge of that part of the community, and has gone on holiday. Chris has two "Kulata" (spears), eight-foot weapons with the barb applied with chewed kangaroo sinew, and the joints of the spear made with spinifex gum. They were two for $15. Then there was a "miru" (woomera—a broad, dried, curved leaf, like a palm calyx, used as a sling to propel the spear) for $25. It had been ochered, too, and had a bit of spinifex gristle on the bottom for skinning a kangaroo (or a rabbit—or a man!). That stuff looked like clamshell sharpened. It's like a razor! Then there was a large "wira," a piti, or wooden bowel-like vessel for $20, two music sticks for $4, a smaller piti for $6, a flat, carved wood turtle for $5, a nulla-nulla (aboriginal shillalah) with a mean looking spinifex razor on one end for $7, and two beautiful "kali" (boomerangs), the hunting kind, for $18 and $15 respectively. These are beautiful artifacts. There were also a number of the ceremonial animals there, but we opted not to take any of them right now. I gave Chris the check, made out to Amata Arts and Crafts, for $115. It was the same check that I'd been carrying to give to Wally for the opals. Maybe I'll get them next time!

Tea time is over. The radio has announced that Indulkana wants us. It seems that Patrick has someone he wants to evacuate to the Alice. Back to the strip. FDQ has a hard time, sitting on the ground, raising the Alice to let them know that we are on the way to Indulkana. Finally, the message gets through. We use the same seating arrangement as on the way down. Laura is in the right front seat. Darryl shoves everything through the firewall, and we're off and heading for the valley through Mimili and just north of Mintibi at 106 degrees. Darryl forgets to retract takeoff flaps until we're almost at 8,000 feet. I guess he was too busy checking everything else in the cockpit.

Ayer's Rock disappears behind us. Maybe next time Laura will get to see that. But then, she's not been to Indulkana yet, either. We've been told that the strip is now open there. Just as Ernabella strip comes into view, the radio comes alive.

"FDQ, Indulkana reports that their need for your visit is not now required. You may return from your present position directly to . . . "

Before the last words are out, Darryl has swung FDQ to a straight north heading. We're on the way home. I finish my CME lesson. Ray is sleeping. Laura and Darryl carry on a lively conversation. It's really not too rough. It's been a good day.

18 March 1982

Sister Kay rang yesterday and said that it would be Fregon Clinic for today. She said that sister Ray was crook, and that Carol was still away on holiday, but that there would be someone to go with me.

"Do you think Laura would like to go?" Well, that's like asking if fish like water or dogs like bones or birds like worms.

"Yes, I think she'd like that, Kay."

And so Laura was all dressed at 0600 in her "world around" blue and white striped slacks, her navy blue top and her little white hat with the bill out front perched on top of her blond curls. Proper looking, indeed, for visiting downtown Fregon. Of course, we weren't to leave until 0740 from the house, but no matter. There were some other chores that had to be done, and then she has a slower husband. At 0745 we passed Bob Worthing on his way back to town from the airport. That meant that he had dropped off the sister for the flight. I wonder who it would be?

It's Debbie. The same Debbie who was to Ernabella with me on the March 4. A big girl, but soft spoken, and she served at Ayer's Rock for a while in the past. No pilot? Who's the pilot? Then Mark drives up with fiancee Margaret. Mark is really supposed to be out an hour ahead of departure to preflight the plane. No matter, he hustles around, packs in the metal cases from AMS, and it's to be FDQ again this week. I wonder what's the matter with FML? Laura wiggles into the right front seat, with me facing backwards again, and Debbie with little Nathan in her arms. Nathan has been at the CHU, but not for malnutrition, I'd guess. He's pretty roly-poly and about eighteen months. It's probably chest. He sounds a little juicy. Mark is telling us that his fiancee is also a pilot; flies charter with Chartair, and such. Mark would like to get on with Ansett or one of the large airlines. Margaret has actually been a pilot longer than Mark.

At 0806, FDQ is cleared for the 204 radial at 6,000, runway one-two, and right turn. We lift off. Debbie is saying that the book *A Day in the Life of Australia* is a super book for photographs of the country. I finish my lesson for continuing medical education, and then turn to my new issue of *National Geographic*. There's a good story or two in here. One about the balloon trip across the Pacific. That must be about the size of my balloons. I've got one again this morning. Already I've taken one Talwin and one half grain codeine with Tylenol. But It's smooth this morning; warm, and there's a lot of moisture in the air. It's going to be bumpy coming home!

It's quite hazy with the moisture. Mt. Connor is just a bump in the haze. I can hardly see the Musgrave mountains ahead. The dry lakes don't have as much water in them as last week, but the landscape is still green. The spinifcx looks soft and lush. Actually, if you're down there, that stuff is sharp and gristly, and mean to man and beast! There's the strip at Ernabella ahead. But we fly right over that. Watch for the two little bumps of mountains, both sacred sites for aboriginal culture, that are just north of the strip at Fregon. Debbie has already served us coffee, and as we come below 4,000 feet it starts to get bumpy. Mark makes a nice approach, with Laura's help, and touches down lightly on the strip and rolls out. It's 0912.

Sister Julie Dorn is there with the Toyota waiting to meet us. She hasn't heard anything about "kitty cat Olive," sister Jennie's cat in Ernabella. Amonia, whom we took back with us last time, had her foot explored for a foreign body, but they didn't find anything, and sent her home. We'll be seeing her today. Hudson's scalp impetigo did clear up with the tar shampoo and the Bicillin shot, and little Lena with the sugar-tong splint last time?

"She was out of that in two hours," says Julie.

What's this? There're the three metal boxes of patient cards, but there's no doctor kit, no medical equipment, and no lab material. Julie will have to provide me with the tools to work with. Sister Debbie didn't even know they were supposed to be in with the other stuff. Someone at AMS didn't wake up this morning. Debbie is having trouble with clearing her ears. She has a bit of a cold. She's not very comfortable. The clinic starts off with Mantua. You've met her before. She's had the big, cystic masses in her neck, behind the occiput. She's thirty-six, and spotting. She has an appointment with Dr. Cahill on the twenty-fifth. Exam suggests that she has a mass in the RLQ (right lower quadrant) of the abdomen. I don't know if it's an ovary or a fibroid. She'll have to wait to see Dr. Cahill. I don't think I should do a pelvic on her out here, and it really isn't that important at this point in time.

Julie is just a little bit disorganized, like she is on most of the visits. She brings in Amonia who has the hole in her right medial heel. But Julie doesn't have the notes out, and if I didn't know the history of Amonia from last visit, I wouldn't know what to look for. The hole goes down deeply into a dull, dead callus that measures about 4 cm in diameter, almost the whole heel. She's really tender over the most medial part of this, but there's no evidence of active infection right now. I still think there's a foreign body in there. I guess I'll see if there's an x-ray when I get back to the Alice. She's diabetic too. Her husband is Bernie. She's born in 1933. I'll look her up, but meantime, let's just keep the thing as clean as we can.

Tyalkuta is a *big* lady. I'd guess her weight at 110 kg. She's got a rash, says Julie. And with that Tyalkuta lifts off her tent (muumuu) baring an acre of black flesh, dotted with small, brownish-red specks. Sarcoptys! Scabies! I can almost feel the little animals jumping across to me; jillions of them! She's thirty-three years old.

"Do you have any gamma benzene hexachloride, one percent?"

"Here's what I have," says Julie, and brings out something from the old days with DDT in it, and some Lorexane (Kwell).

"We'll use the Lorexane. Cover her with it tonight, after a bath under the tap out there. Leave it on all night, and then bathe it off in the morning. And then repeat that in a week."

But there's so much skin there, it's kind of like trying to get rid of the Mediterreanean fruit fly in the San Joaquin Valley in California! Peggy Thompson is antenatal, twenty-two years old, 36/52, 51 kg, 105/60, and FHH 148. It's 10 o'clock, and the radio is saying that they'd like us to divert to Docker River. Hurrah! I've never been there, and Laura would be delighted to have a chance to see that. We'll have to stop at Ayer's Rock for fuel, too. It seems there's a patient there with chest pains, and they want me to see if he needs to come in. Mark comes into the room with his little hand calculator.

"We can be there about 1430, if we get away from here about 1230," estimates Mark, ruefully.

He isn't too happy; neither is Debbie, but I'd be delighted to see Docker River, and so would Laura, I know! It's supposed to be one of the most beautiful settlements in the Centre. It's only five miles inside the West Australia border.

Nyjakana is twenty-four. Her hemoglobin is 10.2. She has headaches. We'll put her on iron, but I'm going to send out some hemacult slides for them. Exam is NAD. Mary has a uti. Her urine has been a mess. She's on Bactrim. BP is 102/70. She has no CVA (costovertebral angle—the flank) tenderness. We'll continue her on Bactrim.

Lucy is on brufen. She's been taking Thyroxin when she thinks about it. We'll draw a TSH (thyroid stimulating hormone) and a T–4 (circulating thyroid hormone) on her. Then comes Mary, a child with an infected big toe on the left. It seems to be coming under control. Julie doesn't have a card on Mary.

"How old is she?"

"I don't know," says Julie.

"Open your mouth," I command. Mary opens. Permanent incisors, first molars, but no second molars yet. "She's about eight," I declare.

Julie laughs. "I've never seen anyone do that before!" she says in amazement.

"Gosh, we do it all the time for sheep and horses. It works for people, too," I laugh.

It wasn't meant as a racist gesture. I really wanted to know how old she was for medication decision. Mary is awfully tiny;

probably second to malnutrition. I'll use Amoxil for Mary. Maggie has tinnitus (ringing in the ears) for the last two months. She's forty-five. Julie says that she's irrigated her ears, but can't see any pathology. I look. The external canals are plugged with dense, mahogany cerumen (wax).

"Try some ceruminex drops for about a week, and then irrigate again." Impara is nineteen. She's 29/52, 126/60/0 blood pressure, with no murmur. FHH 148/minute, but Julie hasn't taken her weight. Samuel is four months old and European. Sam hasn't "poohed" for two weeks, says his mom. Sam looks healthy. Exam shows everything else healthy, too. His belly is soft. There are no masses. The descending colon is soft. A gloved little finger is gently applied to the anus, and slowly ascends with Sam expressing some objection, until finally it passes the sphincter. There's soft stool in there. Sam yowls! The glove shows yellow stool. That's normal appearance for breast feeding. Sam yowls again, and fills the nappy with normal, healthy, soft, yellow stool. Yeah! Diagnostic and therapeutic exam, all at the same time. Mom's delighted!

Lilly is three. She's Joe Peter's daughter. Joe is the diabetic with only one kidney. He's really a nice man. I reassure Joe that, although the baby is chesty, everything will come all right. Then Joe shows me some small lumps on his left upper lateral abdomen. They're lipomas. Maybe secondary to insulin injection?

"I don't give it there," growls Joe.

"Here's Jimmy," says Julie. "He's been in a couple of times with chest pain, and I'm not sure whether it's angina."

Jimmy has a red head band holding back his thinning hair. He was born in 1930. His exam is NAD, except that the pain isn't in the chest at all. It's in his low back. His blood pressure is 120/82. Let's give him some Indocin. Keith is back. He still wants his pension. Keith is forty-five. His friend has a pension. Julie doesn't have his card. Exam is NAD. We draw an FBC anyway. His blood pressure is 112/76. Maxie has a lump on his neck. He's seven. It's a big, hard node, freely movable. No other nodes are found. His mouth and throat are clear. this node is almost two centimeters in diameter. It's probably granulomatous. Maxie feels fine. I reassure. I'm not going to do anything about it.

"Let's have a look at it next time I come by," I tell his Mom.

"Five Sierra Delta Papa," crackles the radio. "Docker River

says they really would like you to come by," says Kay from AMS in the Alice.

"Yes," replies Julie, "they'll be there at 1430."

"Roger," acknowledges Kay. "I'll let them know that it's for sure."

Ann is thirty-two. She has pain in her groin. Her temp is 37.5 degrees. Her urine is NAD. Blood pressure is 100/80. I think she's having ureteral colic. I tell Julie to watch the urine and test periodically for blood. In the meantime, let's give her a little Indocin just to make sure this isn't musculo-skeletal. Next is Manjana. She's 36/52 and is going to be going in with us, announces Julie.

"No way," I reply. "We're going all the way to Ayer's, and that's forty minutes. Then twenty minutes on the ground getting fuel, and then forty minutes on to Docker River. They'll be an unknown amount of time on the ground there, and then almost two hours back to the Alice? No way, she can't come with us. She'll have to come to the Alice on the mailplane on Tuesday."

That's too far to take someone in that condition, and it's going to be rough, too. Every one of those neat, little, dumpling-like cumulus clouds is going to have a bump with it.

The clinic is over. Julie has a pineapple cold drink with bits of herb floating around in it. It's enough to wash down another Talwin and another half grain codeine with Tylenol, as the balloon tries to give birth. That's all she offers, too. I think I hurt her feelings. Everyone picks up their things. Julie takes us out to the airport. Mark cranks up FDQ after he closes the port engine oil filler cap. The dumb thing has been popping open in flight. I guess it won't hurt anything unless the wind gets underneath and starts to left the cowl off the engine. That might be downright embarrassing. It's 1215 hours when we lift off the strip and head out on the 280 radial for Ayer's Rock.

Mark turns on the illicit channel to pick up the gossip. The pilots of the Centre talk on this frequency like it's an open party line. I think it's 123.4 MHz. Mark doesn't join in, but he and Laura enjoy listening. It's still awfully hazy. There's Mt. Connor to our right. And there's Ayer's Rock ahead. Laura is snapping pictures. Mark makes a pattern, and we touch down smoothly beside the monolith.

Richard, from Chartair, is just finishing topping off his Navajo with fuel. He's brought a load of tourists down, and they're currently off on a coach circling the rock with a guide. Mark tops off the petrol tanks in FDQ, fires up, and we're off again. The new construction at Uluru village is getting on pretty well. Soon this area will lose all its old flavor, and become just another tourist attraction. Just north of the Olgas is a huge, dry lake.

"That's Lake Amadeus," I mention to Laura. Debbie is having trouble with her ears. She takes a Dramamine, too. It is bumpy. The mountains fade away for a while. The desert floor is smooth as a billiard table, and almost the same color. Then, ahead, the Peterman range. This is really where the Reef of Gold is supposed to be. The mountains are sandstone with conglomerate and layers of quartz and basalt, it looks like, They must be very old. Wouldn't it be fun to know where that mine is? Ahead in a wide valley is the settlement of Docker River. It's scattered around. A few buildings here, and some over there, and the pile of wrecked cars over there, and one can see the power station.

"That's the hospital," Mark points out. The strip looks like every other one you've seen; about 3,200 feet long, 100 feet wide, and red dirt. Mark touches down smoothly.

"Do you have any water in the thermos?" I ask Debbie.

"Yes, there's some left."

"Can I have some to swallow another pill? This kidney stone is playing up a lot."

Debbie pours out a bit of water into the lid of the thermos. It's still hot. I swallow another Talwin. Mark taxies back to the end of the strip. There's a shelter built up on the poles here, with a thatched roof, and a big sign beside it that proclaims that this is a "dry" area—that is, no booze allowed. The sign reminds you that the first offense for having possession is three months in gaol and a one thousand dollar fine. The second offense is six months in gaol and a two thousand dollar fine. That makes it easy to figure out what the third offense would be. We stand in the shade. It isn't too hot, really. There's also a nice breeze blowing. We're not in sight of town. There's quite a lot of bush here, all nice and green, but not as many gum trees as I would have thought. It's mostly wattles. Then the noise of a vehicle coming, and the cloud of dust like a marker.

It's a Toyota, just like every other one we've seen in the

settlements; a bull bar, brown and white, two spare tires on the roof rack. It's Mary, the sister, Kitty is the aboriginal health worker, and the old patient is Tanara.

"She had a bad pain in her left shoulder for the last two weeks," explains Mary. "She cries almost every night and is keeping her family awake. There's no history of trauma. Her notes say that she was born in 1925."

Tanara is classic aboriginal. She has the sunken in eyes, the right one is destroyed by a combination of trachoma, cataract, and probably glaucoma. The dead, white cornea is pointing to Tanara's right. The other eye is blinking, but it doesn't seem to be seeing. Mary has brought a stethoscope with her, but no sphygmomanometer. I touch the sore shoulder. The biceps bursa is swollen. The chest reveals lots of rhonchi throughout. She's probably had tbc in the past anyway. I don't hear any rales. The heart sounds are normal, with a sinus rhythm. I really think it's a bursitis. I put her through a passive range of motion. She cries out when we stress the biceps.

"Gosh, Mary, I think it's a bursitis. I think if we give her about twenty-five milligrams of Indocin three times a day she'll come good."

Mary nods yes, but her eyes implore! She's had it with Tanara and Tanara's people! She wants this lady out of the settlement.

"I'm leaving tomorrow," she announces. "But Sally will be coming in."

It's that bad. Even though Mary will be getting out, she doesn't want to leave this mess for the next sister.

"You'd like her out, wouldn't you."

"Oh, yes!" and again the eyes beseech.

"Okay, we'll take her with us."

I can see Mary relax on the spot. Tanara is helped into FDQ, up on the aft stretcher. The belt won't fit around her. No matter. She'll be right. We get back to our seats. I'm still flying backwards. My balloon is subsiding a bit. Debbie sits in the aft seat beside the patient. Good-byes are said, and Mark fires up FDQ. The starboard engine is a little reluctant, but Laura pulls it through with her eyes, and it fires.

We are assigned 8,000 feet by Alice control. Mark heads us

almost straight east towards the Alice. At 8,000 feet it's awfully rough. The patient quietly vomits all over the stretcher, and onto the little, black purse that she's clutching. Her whole worldly possessions, no doubt. No luggage for this lady. Just that old purse. Debbie turns white. She looks terrible!

"Oh, Doctor Rutten, I'm sick!" I give her a burp bag. Laura and Mark are chatting busily away up front in the flight deck. Debbie is almost too sick to retch. My stone is building a huge balloon. I move back to the patient. The plane is leaping around the sky like a porpoise on a bow wave! I try to clean up the patient. The odor suggests that both ends of her alimentary tract are open. There's no emergency kit on the plane.

"It's in FML," says Mark.

I can't give the patient medication, and I can't find anything for Debbie, either. There are some nappies in the cabinet that make do for towels that I can clean up the patient with. What a mess!

"I'm pretty sure the patient is not a cardiac," I announce to Mark. "Can we take it up where it's smoother?"

"Sure."

The plane rises from just below the beautiful, little clouds to a point where Mark is flying through the canyons of these ballooning puffs. At 13,000 it's smooth. The patient stops vomiting. I'm sitting in the backseat by the door with a beautiful view of the clouds through the window in the door. The patient is peaceful. She's sleeping now. Her pulse is about eighty, and regular. The chest is rising and falling normally. She's not dyspneic (short of breath). I guess it is a bursitis after all. Debbie lies across the seat up front behind the flight deck. Her face is into the pillow. She's quiet. She's getting a little color back. My balloon is settling down. I guess my medicine is finally taking hold, too. The humor of the situation strikes me. What a zoo! Poor patient! Poor Debbie! The place smells terrible! But it is kind of funny.

Mark starts his let-down about thirty DME from the Alice. As we come below the level of the clouds, the bumps start again. But this time it doesn't seem as bad. There's the Spyce Byce, and all the water in the desert is remarkable. There's the Stuart Highway, and there's the middle marker on the ADF "beep, beep,

beep." That's been quite a trip this week. The ambulance people from St. John's are looking for more than one patient. I really feel pretty good. Debbie is making her way by herself. The patient even manages to get herself down from the plane under her own power, and the expert guidance of the attendants. I put all the cleanup stuff into a large plastic bag. I don't know what they want to do with it, but I think Laura and I will head into town. It's just about 1645 hours and we can still get to the APO for the mail, if we hasten.

On Saturday when I made rounds at the hospital, Tanara was in ward six. She's not talking, but they say she seems better, and that it isn't cardiovascular. We'll keep an eye on her and let you know what the diagnosis is as soon as we learn it. Meantime, next week is going to be Indulkana, and maybe Wally with some opals. Laura has her invitation from Marg Baxter to visit Granite Downs. That will be a good trip, too.

25 March 1982

So, this is the big day that Laura has been waiting for. She has her invitation from Marg and Murray Baxter to visit Granite Downs station, and sister Carol is still on holiday, says sister Kay. We'll be touching down at Granite Downs long enough to take Marg's blood pressure and drop off Laura. Then we'll fly on over to Indulkana for the clinic, and Marg will motor Laura over in the moke after lunch. It's an awfully overcast morning, and cool. Drizzly, but there's enough enthusiasm shining out of Laura's blue eyes to make up for the cloudy day. We're away from the house about 0735 hours. At the airport, sister Kelly has arrived, and good old John Everett is running up FML. Hooray! Laura gets to ride in the John Hawkins!

Sister Kelly is older, square, gray hair, sure and from the auld sod. She's probably forgotten more out bush medicine than most of the sisters ever will learn. I double check to make sure

that we have all the necessary tools for the trip. The doctor's kit
isn't there. It's the black case that carries all the Vacutainer tubes
and needles for drawing blood, etc. Oh, well, maybe they'll have
things at the dispensary out in Indulkana. No time now to delay
for going back to town for it. Bob Worthing has driven sister
Kelly out. I remind him that tonight is the play-off game between
the Alice Springs Cosmos slow-pitch softball team, and the Moldies in the championships for this year. Bob says he'll try to be
there, but the Dodgers are having a hard-ball game too, and he
plays with them.

At 0800 exactly John has FML fired up. I'm riding backwards
again today. Laura's in the right front seat, and Kelly is facing
me. I have my bulletin from the Santa Barbara County Medical
Society to read, and also the March issue of *Skindiver* magazine,
with a dandy article about the salvage of the *Andrea Doria*, and
some young divers, one of whom is named Raul Rutten.

"FML, line up on runway one-two. Fly the 179 radial at
7,500. Right turn, but remain east of the railroad," monotones
the tower.

We're racing down the runway with about ten degrees of
flaps on, and FML lifts off about half way down the runway. The
right turn puts Laura's side down where she can look straight
into the scrub and see the cattle standing under the wattles. No
kangaroos this morning. There's sure a lot of haze around, and
there are wispy clouds at about 6,000 feet, and a much higher
layer that has occasional drops beating a tattoo on the windscreen, and drifting back along the windows, where I am, in
horizontal streaks. Laura's quite taken with the natural beige
lambskin that she's sitting on, and the burnt orange corduroy
around the air vent above her head.

"Keeps you from getting hurt if you hit it in bumpy weather,"
explains John.

The desert floor is multi-green with the strange kaleidos-
copic pattern where the sun finds holes in the cloud cover above,
and shines beams of light onto bright patches on the desert floor.

"Be sure and show her Chamber's Pillar," I tell John.

"Oh, yeah," he answers.

There's the Hugh River, and then the Finke. John points
eastward and shows Laura the pillar, but I don't think she can

really see it all that well. We're about four miles west of it. There's not all that much to see in this weather. Kelly has the coffee service aboard, but fails to get it out. No one says anything. Laura has her own set of flight instruments. On the FDQ she only has engine instruments in front of her, but here in the John Hawkins she has a horizon, airspeed, altimeter, vertical speed, and, of course, the digital elapsed time clocks.

At 1:08 on the elapsed time clock, John kicks off the auto pilot and we start our descent. The station is sure a small dot out here in the desert background that looks almost uniform. There's the surf at Mintibi, just almost out of sight in the haze, and there's the range of Indulkana, so Chandler should be about there, and John makes just a tiny correction to the west. He missed the station by about a mile and a half out of about 160. That's pretty good dead reckoning by anybody's book! A low pass over the station with me on the low side this time. Laura hands me her Instamatic. I click a picture, but I think it's going to be on the bias when it's printed.

Then we're making a sweep over the strip, and a 180 to land a bit downwind, but with our roll-out bringing us up alongside the moke, standing by the strip. Marg is her usual self. She's been on a zucchini diet, she says, and has lost a whole stone! (I find out later from my "spies" that she still smokes like a chimney, and dashes salt liberally over her food at the table.) Her pressure is up; 164/92.

"I've been going full ahead all morning," she explains.

"We'll take it later this afternoon," I tell her. "You're still on the Inderal, 80 mg morning and evening, and HCTZ (hydrochlorothiazide—a diuretic) once in the morning?"

"Yes. Will you be able to give me a script so that I can have about six months supply when I leave here?"

"Sure, Marg."

"Laura and I will take a look around the station, and have some lunch, and then come over in the moke."

"Okay, Marg. We should be done with the clinic about 1330 hours."

And with that, John and Kelly and I climb in with me in the right front seat this time, and fire up FML. John turns it around, and this time the takeoff is appropriately against the wind towards the east. Off the ground at a proper single engine performance air speed, and the gear is tucked up, and John tips FML on her side at about a hundred feet of altitude to make the 180 to get us on track for Indulkana.

"No use going too high," says John, and we level out at that altitude.

I snake out the movie camera. John dumps my side as we go by the station, so I have good movies from low altitude. Then it's Chandler.

"Have to watch that microwave relay tower," says John, as we bank around it about half-mast high, but right in line for me to get a picture of the whole of Chandler, all eight houses, and the stock yards, where it's obvious that they're loading the "finished product" from Granite Downs.

Then we're making a 360 over Indulkana, and John is touching down gently, and rolling out to greet Jennie, who is there with the Toyota.

"How's Olive?" I ask.

"Oh, just fine!" exclaims Jennie. "She's putting on weight, and almost all healed up!"

We notice that the old road onto the strip has been fenced off, and there's now a cattle guard for vehicles. That ought to keep the mare and her colt off the strip.

"We don't have much of a clinic today," apologizes Jennie. "The health workers all quit on us. Said they weren't used to working so hard, so they walked off. We told the council that we had to have health workers to keep the clinic open, but they just didn't get around to doing anything, so we closed the clinic last week. We told them, no health workers, no clinic. They were really upset. We told them we'd take emergencies only. They told us they were going to revoke our permits to be here. I said, fine, it will take Patrick and me about forty-eight hours to pack our things and get out of here. They said, don't be hasty, and about two hours later, the health workers were back, so we're open again. But I don't know what will show up, except for the whole town of Chandler. They're all here already."

Indulkana just has to be the dirtiest of the settlements that I attend. There's a sign on the door, *Wanted—clinic cleaners—$90 a week.* "No takers yet," says Jennie.

"I have the instruments to do Martin Tine's prepuce," I tell Jennie. "Let's give him about 7.5 ml of phenergan now, and we'll do him in about forty minutes."

"Oh, wonderful!"

First patient is Cynthia Brown, age twenty-eight, twelve weeks pregnant by history. She's 65 kg, 120/60, but I can't really feel a definite uterus yet. Then Lucy, who is diabetic, and has had a mess of boils. Patrick has had her on Amoxil, and she's doing well. They ran out of diabinese, but have her on Daonil. Her urine shows 2+ sugar yet, but the boils are clearing up nicely. Let's change her back to diabinese when we get it. Lucy is forty-four years old, 158/72. She feels pretty good. Here's Muna Whiskey again. She's 56 kg. today, 115/70, FHH 158/minute. Muna is sixteen. Better have bloods from her.

"We forgot to bring our things with us. Do you have equipment?"

Jennie walks to a cupboard. That's when I noticed that every cupboard and drawer is perfectly labeled with its contents. No more guessing like the days of Vivian and Ann. No wonder the health workers felt put-upon. They must have really had to work. The place is really neat! Sister Kelly gets the paraphernalia. The tourniquet around Morna's arm; the stick. No blood. The needle is withdrawn but the tourniquet was not released, and the hematoma begins to rise. Kelly sticks another vein. No blood. The needle is removed, and a second hematoma comes to life. I can't just sit here and watch this. Kelly has lost her touch over the years, apparently.

"Want me to do it, Kelly?"

"Yeah, would you? She seems to have bad veins."

It's hard not to laugh out loud, but poor Muna wouldn't think it funny at all, and neither would Kelly, in all probability.

"Oh, we all have days like that when we can't find the dumb things," I sooth. I transfer the tourniquet to the left arm. Nice big vein. No problem. Muna looks relieved, and walks out with a subtle look of disgust on her young face.

Here's Mabel Pierson, born in 1934. She's been taking two Tedral for the last six months. I don't really know why. I guess someone started her on it when she had a cold, and she just felt so good, she's kept taking them, or doing something with them.

She keeps coming back and asking for more, and insisting that she's taking the above dose. She's an ex-tbc. I listen to her chest. I don't hear anything but some decreased breath sounds in the right apex. Let's just keep her on them for another month. I'll see if everything seems all right next month, and then we can take her off them if we want.

Tanya Meier is back. I've seen her every month since I started this clinic. I had told Jennie that we'd see the aboriginal population first, and then the Chandler people. After all, this is a clinic for the aboriginals. Tanya is European.

"We're out of black people right now," advises Jennie. Tanya is twenty. She's pregnant now. She's 66.5 kg, 130/80. I draw bloods on her. I don't even ask Kelly, and she doesn't volunteer.

Here's a strange one. Ammanari, born in nineteen forty-eight. Her blood pressure is 104/70. She's about 18/52. She's a grav VII Para VI. She has dyspnea and chest pain on occasion, that is hand-clenching, substernal, and radiates up into her jaw. It's relieved if she plunges her hands and upper arms into cold water. It comes on about four times a day. Her chest sounds fine. I can't find anything but the pregnancy that's different. What a strange sort of angina? Maybe it's the diving cardiovascular response that's giving her relief from her angina. Isn't that strange? Let's try a little nitroglycerine sublingual next time she has the pain and before she plunges her hands into the water, and see if it really is angina. Next is Dorothy; tough as nails, and a face that looks like it. She was in a fight with someone who belted her on the left elbow with a nulla-nulla. She was sent to Alice Hospital on the bus for x-rays. Jennie thought it was broken. She absconded into the Todd River basin for treatment with ETOH, and then took the bus back. She's better. Looks like maybe it was an olecranon bursitis. Jennie says she put a plaster back slab on it, but it only stayed in place about two days. Dorothy is about forty-two. I guess we don't have to offer any more treatment.

Now comes Martin Tine. He's all over the place! No matter. Let's get on with it. That little, tiny opening in the foreskin is only about three millimeters. The glans seems to slide well beneath the prepuce. I gently slide a tiny, curved, mosquito forceps under the foreskin with my right hand, while pulling some traction on the prepuce to remove it from the vicinity of the glans.

Then, with a little, straight mosquito, I slide one jaw under the prepuce and the other jaw over, about five mm, and clamp it!

"EEEOOOWW!" screams Martin.

I glance at my watch. Let's give it five minutes. He's been prepped with a little betadine that hadn't bothered him, but he also has a bit of a diaper rash. We'll have to give Mom a little Desitin. Martin keeps bellering.

"Ask Mom if she has his bottle."

Patrick brings it back. Martin takes it willingly, and the yowling stops. Martin lays there sucking the bottle dry. I watch my Girard Perregaux that was given to me by my good wife in June of 1954 when I graduated from medical school. It still keeps time to about three minutes a month, self-winding. Not too shabby after all these years. The five minutes is up. I withdraw the mini-kelly. The foreskin looks like paper under the clamp. My baby Metzenbaum scissors slices just up to the last half millimeter from the end of the crushed prepuce. Not a drop of blood! I can see the urethral meatus through the opening quite clearly. No more trouble for Martin. No more worry for Mom, and that foreskin will eventually retract behind the corona when it gets ready to.

"Don't fool with it for the next two days," I caution Mom. "You can keep it clean with his bath, but just pat it dry. We sure don't want any bleeding."

"Can I have some Nordiol?" asks Martin's Mom, Rosemond. I think she's decided never to have another baby.

"Sure," and I write her a script.

Now it's the Pitts family again. Mom wants me to check Elizabeth; born 5 July 1980. She's okay. The family seems much calmer this week.

"We've been transferred to Tarkoola," says Jim. "We'll be leaving in a couple of weeks. It will be good to get out of here. They have a good school for the kids."

He goes into a bit more about his knowledge of medicine when he was "nursing" in a hospital down south.

I ask Jennie, "Is he a sister?"

"No," says Jennie. "He always gives us that stuff. He was a ward orderly down there once upon a time. He knows nothing about medicine."

"The council was going to revoke the privilege for Chandler people to come to see you," Jim submits. "They said this clinic was for aboriginals, and that we didn't have a right to come to it." (I was glad that I had insisted that we take the aboriginals first today. I probably saved myself a bit of unpleasantness.) "We have a big screen down there, and show films three nights a week," continues Jim. "I told them that if they wanted to play that game, we'd stop the movie. There's been no more talk about us not coming up here when you come. Did you know that they stoned the Ghan a month ago?"

"Gosh, really?"

"Yeah, they had some big wig that was supposed to get on the Ghan in Chandler for Adelaide, and about 80 of them came down to see him off. They were told that the Ghan wouldn't stop in Chandler; that they'd have to go up to Kulgera to put him on the train. But they wouldn't listen. The Ghan went sweeping right through Chandler, and they were so mad, they stoned the train. Got about eight of them great, big, double-paned windows on the train. Guess they cost about $300 a piece. The Ghan won't never stop in Chandler again!"

Funny what you learn about when you're out bush.

Next is Rhonda Parkinson, 14 August 1960, who wants her Microgynon refilled. Done. Then Tilly, 63 kg, 37/52, 148/minute FHH. Tilly is forty. She'd better head up for the Alice to deliver in a couple of weeks. Jennie didn't even know she was pregnant. This is her first visit, and she's a grand multip, too! (numerous pregnancies). Then another; Amonair, grav II, Para I, 24/52, 100/70, 42.5 kg, about twenty, with fetal heart at 152, and a loud placental bruit in the RLQ (right lower quadrant of the abdomen).

The next is Tommy from Mimili again. We saw Tommy back on February 10th or so, and he was supposed to go up the Alice to have Dr. Parke take out this great big mass in his left submaxillary area.

"They didn't do nothing," says Tommy in disgust.

Tommy also has atrial fibrillation. He's coughed up blood this last week, I'm told. We'd better send him up again.

Then there's John/Biddy mother. John is a kwashiorkor; protein deficiency with sunken eyes, a big belly, and starving because Biddy doesn't feed him. She loves him, but he's dropped down to about the sixtieth percentile. He's twenty-one months old and weighs 7,850 grams. Biddy has a reputation for this. I remember one time when sister Carol had said, "If that woman gets on that plane to the Alice, I'm staying here!" She meant it, too. Biddy is not a good Mom. Not that she doesn't love the kids. She just ignores them, and at twenty-one months, John isn't able to fend for himself.

"We'll take him up to the CHU and they'll fatten him back up. He can come down then, and in about five months, we'll take him back again. But eventually, he'll get big enough to fend for himself, and then he'll be right."

We finish the clinic, and go back to Jennie and Patrick's for tea. It's 1245 hours. Olive looks wonderful. She has a terrible corneal abrasion that's not going to get better in the right eye. The wound under the left leg in front is almost healed up. Jennie and Patrick have a dog, too. It's a long haired dachshund; looks like a cocker spaniel with sawed off legs. It's a cute little thing, about as old as Olive.

"What did Myntie do when you brought Olive back?"

"Oh, she came near her and sniffed, and tried to lick the wounds, but Olive wouldn't have any of that. They really are friends, though."

That was evident watching the two. Not mushy or anything, but you could tell from the looks they gave each other that there was love there.

"Did you know that Vivian's folks came up to the Alice and took her back with them to Melbourne?" asked Jennie.

"No, I haven't heard anything from her. I did see her when she was in the hospital, and she told me that it was in her head, and she cried, but I didn't know she'd gone back already."

"Yeah, we're packing up all her things, and sending them down. Did you know that Ann had left Ernabella, too?"

"Gosh, no, and Chris has left Fregon, too. There won't be anyone left around here pretty soon."

"Well," says Jennie, "They're going to have to pay us to keep us. It's just awful the way they come around for surveys and such, and never seem to get anything else done. They don't get us supplies, and they never go to bat for us with the council, and I think it's just terrible!"

"Well," I blundered, "I don't think it would make a difference which party was in power, either. You'd have the same
problems with a labor government." Wrong thing to say! Jennie
came alive!

"Not so! The labor party would put the right slant on this
thing. They'd provide the money to do this job right. That's what
this country needs is a powerful labor party."

"Or a dictatorship," quietly added Patrick. I could see that
these two had been over this ground before, and there was just
a bit of a contention bone there.

"Gosh, it's two o'clock," I interrupted. "Maybe we should
get in FML and fly the road backwards to Granite Downs and see
if they're stuck in a mud puddle somewhere along the way."

"Yeah," said John.

I could tell he was eager to go, as the weather had deterio-
rated quite a bit since we'd arrived. We finished up our tea,
picked up Biddy and John from the wicki-up across the street,
and headed for the strip. We loaded the plane, and here came
the moke along the road. Right on time! Too bad Laura didn't
have a chance to poke around the village. Well, next time. Biddy
handed John to Kelly, then turned and walked away. The mincobah looked like a sore on the right side of her mouth. I had
just learned that they burn poppy pod on a piece of hot metal
until it's a white dust, and then roll their soggy tobacco in this
so that there's some drug with the tobacco, which isn't really
tobacco. I thought I detected tears in her eyes. Isn't that funny?
I don't understand the mix of emotions here.

Laura was already in the front seat, and it was muggy. Kelly
was trying to strap little John down on the stretcher criss-cross
with the belts there. That won't work, I knew! I sat in my seat
and picked him up. Poor little guy had a gastro, too. They'd put
a nappie on him, but it didn't fit too well. I folded a sheet from
the emergency kit, and put it on my lap first, then John on that.
Pilot John fired up FML, and when everything was in the green,
we taxied down to the east end of the runway, and came roaring
back, lifting into the sky with the aid of a shrieking John, who
was flinging himself in all directions at once. I just let him fling,
and pretended he was a yo-yo, until he tired and settled back
into my lap. At 800 AGL (above ground level) we were in the

soup. We never did see much of the ground after that.

I asked Kelly to put a big, bath towel over naked little John. He snuggled his head into my arm pit. I'm sure it wasn't anything as fulfilling as Mom's! He put one little hand on my left breast and one on his forehead. I heard AMS talking to Fregon about Amonia and her foot. I'll have to get back to them with what I saw on those x-rays when I get home. FML's avionics tracked us almost to the middle marker on the ADF without ever seeing the ground. A great big ambulance with flashing red lights was there to accept John. Laura and I hastened to the APO for the mail, and then home. Surely they'd cancel the softball game. I didn't go over. The Cosmos lost to the Moldies, and thereby the pennant. Well, can't win 'em all!

1 April 1982

And, you know what day this is? It's April Fool's Day! That seems to be an appropriate day to start out with the aeromedical service of the Royal Flying Doctors. Today it's going to be Er nabella, and sister Carol is back from her holiday and anxious to get on with work. Darryl is the pilot, and has FML ready to go when I arrive about 0745 hours. Laura won't be going today. She really wasn't invited by sister Carol, and, after all, she's the boss! Carol says that she spent most of her holiday down in Victoria, but didn't get to the sea shore place of her friend. They just didn't make connections.

FML fires up at 0805, and we taxi out to runway "one-two," where the tower monotones, "FML, clear for takeoff, track 207, 8,000, right turn."

Darryl advances the throttles slowly, then to the hilt, and bends them against the firewall as FML leaps ahead and clears the ground at the first intersection. Carol is telling me that poor, little Vivian had od'd. That's why she was in the hospital. Poor, little thing! Carol doesn't tell me what the agent was, but I felt a little sad about that. So, that's why she was crying when I saw her in the hospital. Here I thought it was "boyfriend" or something simple like that. Poor, little thing.

It's amazingly clear today. No clouds, but no haze, either. I have my CME test to correct. The new one arrived with the top off the "latent image" pen, just like last year. I wrote to them then, and had them send me another pen. The top was off that one, too. And when the juice leaks out, there's no way to do the exercise. It's a waste of my time and their money (my money). I'll have to write to them again about that.

Darryl is fidgeting with the panel, checking and rechecking, so busy with his head inside the cockpit that he doesn't notice that the autopilot has slipped off somehow, and we're making a rather steep left bank. Abruptly he discovers it without my saying anything, and apparently he's delighted. It gives him something to do to get us back on track. Actually, from the Finke one can almost see to Ernabella. Mt. Connor and Ayer's and the Olgas all stand out in a straight line chain. All the lakes of the top are full of water. They had ten inches of rain at Ayer's Rock this last week. It looks like the Mississippi delta! It's green, too!

There's a story going about that a group of tourists got lost going to Ayer's Rock. At first that sounded crazy. After all, there's only the one road going to the Rock. But from the air one can see how that could happen. If you come to a bog, you may stay on the high ground, and start around it through the desert, either to the left or the right. Then if there's another bog, you'd go around that, too, and pretty soon, you'd lose the real road with all the other wandering tracks that ramble through the desert stations on their way to nowhere, or a water hole, or whatever.

Darryl cranks off the autopilot and we begin our descent. A quick pass over the settlement, and a smooth landing. The strip is just a little soft from rain, but not bad. There's not a breath of wind. We sit on the metal cases waiting for sister Julie Peters to arrive in the Toyota and take us into town. Small sounds abound as we sit quietly. Little birds chirp, insects whirr, the grass rustles to a small animal making its way towards friend or foe, and then the hum of the Toyota's engine between town and us.

Julie is her usual quiet self. Ann is still at the station. I discover that her whole name is Ann Messinger and she was born 27 March 1958 when I sign her recertification petition for nursing in the Northern Territory. The road is a mess! Julie says that she's never seen it rain so hard and for so long. The little creek has washed out the road on the way to town, and we have to make a diagonal circuit down one bank and up the other. We approach the settlement up the river from the east (actually, it's down the river). It's about three-hundred yards wide, sandy, with lots of junk in it, and the water is still almost fifty yards wide! The town has literally been cut in two by the river. There's kids swimming, and families doing total wash; clothes and bodies. Some of the bodies are in the clothes and some of them with clothes in hand. And some camp dogs. Gee, there's sure lots of things you can do when you have water running through town!

Scattered along the river bed are three concrete pipes, about five meters long and a meter diameter. "There were six of them under the river crossing on the other side of town," announces Julie. "That's three of them there, and the other three have just disappeared."

There are reeds growing along the bank of the river already. No reeds there six weeks ago. Nothing but red sand. It's amazing what water can do.

Heather Hess is the first patient. Heather is 35/52, 82.5kg, 110/70, and good fetal heart tones. She has some nasty varicosities of the left saphenous system. She says she feels good. Wendy Plane is pg, too. Wendy is Rh neg; obviously, she's European. Aboriginals do not have Rh negative blood. Wendy is 25/52, 56 kg, 110/70, too. She has a trace of protein and a mitral murmur that is unchanged.

Makinta is twenty-four, 80 kg, 120/70, 20/52, and I can't hear fetal heart. That's funny. I checked her out last month, and recorded 20/52 at that time, too. I hope there's nothing wrong in there. She says she feels well. Next is Fairy Nelson; thirty-two years old, 24/52, 62 kg, 100/60, + protein in her urine. Her right foot is sore on the extensor surface from prolonged walking. It seems that they ran out of tucker out bush in the rain, and they'd walked about ten miles rabbit-ing. There's no damage to the foot; just sore. I'm not sure I hear a fetal heart here, either. The clinic is kind of noisy. Yilpi is twenty-seven. She has pain in the left chest. I can't find anything wrong with her. Her blood pressure is 110/70. Let's treat her symptomatically for musculo-skeletal pain.

Mitikiki is a young man age fifteen. He speaks good English but won't talk to me. He's been having hematuria. He's been seen by Dr. Martins at ASH before, and nothing was found. His blood pressure 132/70. Palpation of his belly reveals some tenderness on the left umbilical area, but I don't feel any kidney. I really think he should have a workup again. Make sure that this isn't glomerulonephritis.

Helen is twelve. Her Mom says that she doesn't hear. Her notes show that she had a cholesteatoma removed from the left ear some years ago. Examination reveals a strange looking canal. It just ends in a blind tube. It looks like there never was a tympanum there at all. It's just skin all the way. None of the usual landmarks are visible, and there's not even any wax in it. The right ear shows us a big lump of cerumen. That's probably why she doesn't hear. She's built up that wax in the good ear. We'd better send her in to sister Janet Conners for audiology at the Community Health Centre, and then have Dr. Geoff Hauptenhausser, the ENT man, take a look at the ears to see what can be done besides suctioning out the wax.

Chris Wells is thirty-eight. He has pain in his right costal margin. It's up under the rib, but about the anterior axillary line. Not where you'd think of gallbladder. His notes say that I checked him for this last year, too. I didn't find anything then, and the pain went away. Now it's back. We draw an FBC, and an LFT (liver function test). Maybe he has a liver abscess.

Ah, here's Amonia from Fregon with the big abscess in her left heel. Amonia is forty-eight years old and a diabetic. You've met her before. Only here in Ernabella, she spells her name Amanyi. She has another area of swelling almost to the medial malleolus now; about four centimeters in diameter. I'm almost certain she has a piece of mulga in there. Then, Julie says that she's told the tribe that they took out a big piece of mulga in the Alice when she was there before. The docs there told me that they didn't find anything. Somebody's got the story mixed up. Let's give her some Vibramycin and see if the thing comes to a head.

Merridy Levers is twenty. She had a missed ab (abortion miscarriage) last year. Now she has recurrent uti's, but the urine is clear. I think it's musculoskeletal. We'll treat her with brufen.

Alec is fifty-five. He has pain in the second rib, right. His pressure is 118/82. I think that's also musculoskeletal. We'll treat him with Indocin. Then I find that Alec is chief of the settlement council. More about him later, when we have tea at Julie's. Billy Long (Ilpilitja) has the bilateral cataracts. I saw Billy the last time I was here, and we referred him to Dr. Barker, who was due through the settlement, for transfer to Adelaide for surgery on those cataracts. That is, if the council will let him go, since he has a good pension for being blind. Billy accepts my statement that we're still waiting for Dr. Barker to send him on, but I don't think he really understands. I think he thinks that the dumb, white doctor is putting him on. I wonder what he said to the others under the tree out there about the medical system of the white man.

Next is twenty-six month old Chrissie. She's well, except for a huge patch of tinea capitis right on the vertex. Julie doesn't have anything much to work with except some Whitfield's ointment. I order her up some Daktrin (miconazole). Meantime, till they get that sorted out, I'll send her down some Micatin from my own supply. Lizzie is Chrissie's mother. Lizzie is twenty-four, and has a lot of pain in her left side. Examination reveals she's really tender in the lateral abdominal wall muscles. She also has protein in her urine. I can't feel anything in her belly. I don't find a hernia, either. I don't know what it is. Then, when Lizzie gets up off the bed, she reached down, grabs Chrissie by the chest under her left arm, and swings the child up on her left hip. As she does, she winces with pain. So, that's the diagnosis! We'll treat her with Indocin, too. Chrissie is pretty big to lift, and Mom's getting sore muscles from doing it. Lizzie's tribal name is Moodoo. I thought you'd be interested in that piece of information.

The next patient is Lizzie's younger child; Norris, who was born on 20 November 1981. Lizzie just wants a newborn check on him. Exam finds he's a healthy, happy, well fed little kid, and should grow into a fine young man. Jason Caroll was born 1 March 1982. He's checked over. He's going to grow up fine, too.

Then, here's Yakiti. Yakiti has been stuffed with Largactil, and is quite stupified. That's chlorpromazine. It seems that Yakiti's illness is due to a "mamu." There are two types of mamu in the aboriginal culture, and both cause illness. The first is a cat-type being, who can become invisible, but moves about in the same space as people. The second type, and the one that is responsible for Yakiti's illness, is a more sinister type. This is the spirit of a person that has died, and is trying to return to the living. The danger is that, during dreamtime, the living spirit (Yakiti) will be talked into joining the mamu in the spirit of the dead. Yakiti's mamu is his father, who died recently. It seems that Yakiti came into the store the other day with his rifle, brandishing it at people, and generally holding some of his friends responsible for his problem. I have an excellent booklet/paper done by Annette Hamilton, a young student who studied this, and wrote a thesis on "Socio-Cultural Factors in the Health Among the Pitjantjatjara." It should be in the library of every serious student of the aboriginal culture.

I'm getting away from my story. I talked with Yakiti for some time. His affect was schizoid, with expressions from happy to anger moving across his thirty-year-old face like shadows of rain clouds across the desert floor on a blustery spring day. I had been told that he did understand English, but I couldn't get much out of him. Only when I asked if he were Christian did his face come alive—briefly, and then go blank again. How could he believe in "mamu" if he were Christian? They can, and they do! I told Julie to keep him on the Largactil, but slowly decrease the dosage.

"He's not schizophrenic," said Julie. "He's bombed his mind with petrol sniffing. He's been on that since he was eight. He'll never come right."

The next patient was sister Julie Dorn, up from Fregon. I forgot to ask if Mark and Fanou had left. Apparently, Andrew is at Amata. Julie has these bites on her ankles and feet, and they're being excoriated to bloody messes. She's tried about everything on them, she says. Julie was born 1 October 1955. She's also having menstrual cramps, and has a rash on her neck, and she starts to cry. Poor Julie. She's due for her holiday in four weeks, though. She's going down south, and will be away for eight whole weeks. Maybe she'll come back all cured. She feels unlovely, unloved, lonesome and underpaid. I think these sisters are doing a fabulous service for their government out here, and really aren't appreciated a decimal of their worth. That's what I have to offer Julie. She brightens up, and feels useful again.

Sister Julie Peters is my next patient. She wants her Microgyn refilled. Done. I wonder why she would need that out here? The last patient is Ann, for her nurse's registration certificate. The only time the clinic lagged today was when Julie left to have a smoke, and Ann took over. She's not quite useless in the clinic, but almost. Poor thing. Be nice to her, doc, or you'll have another one break into tears.

Then comes Purki, a diabetic, born in 1936; on penicillin for some reason. She's complaining of pain down her legs and in the quadriceps muscles. She doesn't take her insulin regularly; doesn't do anything she's told to do. Probably has her diabetes out of control more than in, and her problem is probably diabetic neuropathy. Then I find that Purki was the original health worker of the settlement, and sister Carol tells me that Purki used to sit in the clinic when Carol was there, and say to her, "I'm chief in this clinic, and you're my servant, and when I want something, I'll have it, and you'll get for me whatever I tell you to."

So, Purki is a racist. So be it. I tell her that she has to keep her diabetes under control, and that she'll have to take her insulin every day or the pain in her legs is going to get so bad she won't be able to walk. I don't think I impressed her.

Tea time at Julie's brings out some interesting politics. It seems that Dr. Trevor Lorenz and John Ballinger were granted $10,000, via Elliot, to do a study for one week on the activity of the four settlements that I cover. They've been around poking here and there, and generally rediscovering the facts of the health care available in the communities, that could easily have been taken from the file of the aeromedical service. It's apparent that the government really doesn't want the system to change. Then there's discussion about the million dollar hospital built four years ago at Papunya, with its beautiful x-ray machine that no one used for a whole year because there was no one who knew how to run it, and that the windows are mostly broken out of the hospital now. Then there's the lovely hospital at Docker River, reduced to rubble now, because the authorities decided to build it down the valley a ways from the settlement, and, of course, when the building was unattended at night, it was demolished. Even the bricks from the knocked-down walls had been broken in two, each and every one "to dust returned!"

This last week the Docker River community had the police, under the direction of Constable Heintz, doing food drops by helicopter to the people out there who had no way to get supplied, except by air, since all the roads were awash. It seems that there was a lady at Yuendumu who went into labor with twins. She'd lost her previous pregnancy a year before, and might well need a Caesar for this one. No way out on the road from Yuendumu. Could they get a helicopter?

"No way," said Constable Heintz. "Those poor people at Docker River need the helicopters to deliver food or they'd starve."

Finally, John went in with the little Baron onto the mushy strip and brought the lady back to the Alice, where she delivered twins about twelve hours apart. All were doing fine. Constable Heintz had actually hung up the phone on the aeromedical service when they were trying to get his assistance.

The conversation ended at Julie's when Mr. John Landsdown strolled in. John is down at Fregon doing a survey for the health department. Isn't that something? It seems that medical service to this part of South Australia is going to get worse before it gets better.

Julie drives out to the strip. The desert is beautiful. There are tiny, little bluebells growing with tiny, white, daisy-like flowers just an inch or so above the ground. Everything looks like the reefs off Santa Barbara; not a square centimeter that something isn't growing on. Darryl opens up FML. We get the metal boxes stored, and take our places. The radio comes alive. Darryl warns local traffic that we're taxiing on the ground, and then the radio says, "FML? There's a request that you divert on the way home to Mt. Ebenezer to pick up a patient there. It will be a sitting patient."

"How's the strip there?" asks Darryl.

"Wait one, and I'll inquire," says the radio.

Soon; "There was a two-oh-six that left there about half an hour ago. They said they had no trouble."

"What's his call sign," requests Darryl. "I'll ask him directly."

"He's already on the ground at Curtin Springs, and won't be on the air. But reliable people at Mt. Ebenezer say the strip is quite good."

"Fine, we'll go there," says Darryl.

He fiddles with the inside of the cockpit until we turn and hurtle down the runway and lift of into moderately bumpy air on a course of 321 degrees. There's so much water down there. One can see where the track runs into big puddles, and where water has come down from the mountains in apparently raging streams, cutting a bank out of the desert floor six feet high where there isn't even a river.

Julie has told us about some folks that got bogged down on the way out of Kenwood Park. Julie was there, and said that the water came up so fast, that the Toyota was soon up to the floor boards. The wheels didn't spin; they just started to sink! She got out and waded to the shore, waist deep in water, and could feel her feet sinking into the sand, like quicksand! She talked with some people on the other side, and they took the jacks out of their car and walked back through the quicksand to the Toyota, which was going deeper and deeper. She didn't go into detail about how they did this, but apparently they placed the jacks and jacked the car up front and back and let sand sweep under it until it was back into shallow water, and then she backed it out of the stream. Sounds like a pipe dream? It could happen in the desert of the outback! Sounds strange that one could actually drown in the desert, but it happens at home, too.

Then, right over the nose of the plane, the few little buildings and windmills that are Mt. Ebenezer appear. Great dead-reckoning piloting by Darryl. Mt. Ebenezer is on the bitumen road from the South Road to Ayer's Rock. We've been in there before. Darryl makes a long downwind looking things over.

"It looks soft," he murmurs almost to himself.

It does look soft. I'll get out my movie camera and make a film of this approach. It's green. The grass is lush on the strip, but it does stand out from the surrounding green. It's a different color on the strip. The plane touches down, and without braking at all, our forward speed drops rapidly. Darryl guns the engines to get us up to the east end of the strip where a 4-wheel drive is unloading three men and three women.

Darryl stops FML, but leaves the engines turning to cool the turbos off a bit. The six people march in front of the turning props. In my horror, I forgot to film this. It's like a doomsday parade. Two Europeans leading the parade, then three ancient aboriginal women, one carrying a blanket, and then the aboriginal man. Darryl shuts down the engines to prevent a disaster. It would be great on film. Darn! We disembark. It seems the lady has a belly ache. Carol is angry.

"Doctor Rutten, you examine her and see if we should take her with us," she demands.

"Gee, Carol, If Dr. Bell has already said to evacuate, I can be nothing but wrong if we don't take her with us."

I do a quick check, though, to make sure she's stable from a cardiovascular standpoint.

"Damn!" exclaims Darryl. "Look at those tires!"

It's true. The wheels of the heavy Navajo have sunk into the octagonal mud squares that lay under foot on the strip. This has all been under water just recently, and the Navajo is sinking! Darryl scrapes the mud with the toe of his boot. An inch below the surface it gets damp, and damper the deeper he digs.

"Let's get moving before we can't move at all."

We hustle the patient (Bonnie Armstrong, about forty-five years old) onto the stretcher. She's not moaning or groaning, and I really don't know what Dr. Bell has diagnosed by radio. The school teacher is substituting for sister here, and is also the expert on runways.

"I don't know anything about them except what I see," he defended, when Darryl criticized his expertise, "and it looks just fine to me."

No use arguing. The parade less the one with the dirty blanket, proceeds across the front of the aircraft again, and over to the parked 4-wheel drive. I missed getting a picture of it that time, too. The engines on FML fire, and Darryl has to advance the throttle quite a bit, like 1,500 (revolutions per minute) just to get us moving in the spongy ground. There's not much wind blowing, and it's from the east; maybe 3–4 miles per hour, but Darryl elects not to taxi the whole 3,500 feet to the west end just for that. We swing FML around, and the throttles go to the firewall, and again and again, Darryl pushes them against their stops. FML moves out rather sluggishly.

"Do you feel it sinking in?" he asks the world.

"Yeah, I sure do," I reply.

And you can! FML will get up a little zip, and then you feel the drag as we hit a soft spot. This would make a good movie sequence. I see the rest of this through the view finder. The ground just isn't moving very rapidly. My eyes come away from the view finder and look at the airspeed. Gosh, just about sixty and not moving up. The Vce is about eighty-four knots. That's still a long way to go. I think she'll come loose from the ground about seventy-two. Back to the view finder.

The engines are roaring, but there just isn't that feeling of acceleration that is so usual with FML. The strip is fast running out of grass, and those wattles at the end of the runway are getting bigger and bigger! Another soft spot; the plane slows perceptibly. No more grass in the view finder.

"We're not going to make it," I vocalize softly. Then there's a jerk, but upward.

Aaaagghhht squawks the stall-warning horn. My head almost hits the burnt orange corduroy guarding the air vent on the ceiling as Darryl drops the nose. We're flying between the wattles, but we're off the ground, and showing almost one-hundred knots on the airspeed. We've made it!

Darryl tucks up the gear with the reassuring *klunk, klunk, kabunk.* He's quiet, and he's angry, I think. Sister Carol is reading. I don't know if that scared her or if she wasn't paying attention. It will make a dandy movie sequence. I wish I'd had the parade on the same film. It would make a great scene for viewing by friends back home! Oh, well—next time!

The rest of the trip is routine. I complete my CME course, and then we're cleared for landing. The touchdown and the roll out on the beautiful runway at Alice Airport. There's an ambulance for Bonnie. Maybe I can still make it to the APO for the mail it's only 1645 hours. At the door of the APO my watch says 5:02. The door is locked. Oh, well. I can get the mail tomorrow. I'm glad to be home. It sure is fun making these trips with the Aeromedical Service. I hope the next doc enjoys it as much as I do.

15 April 1982

It's a crisp, sunny morning in the fall. The sun is just at treetop level coming eastbound on Memorial Avenue around the Alice Springs High School playing fields. The uplifted McDonnells are pink in the sunrise. It's about five miles from the house to the airport, and it's always a beautiful drive. The new gum trees are making themselves seen between the older gums all the way out to the south road turn. Because of all the rain, the grass beside the road has grown tall, and been mowed for about thirty feet on each side of the bitumen, and then disced as a fire break between the mowed area and the fenced range for cattle.

Past the old timers' home, and the original settlement; past the tip road and the drive-in movie. Past the Blatherskite Park area and the Turf Club. Past the 8-AL radio station and the Yarara college, and the Chateau Hornsby turn-off. Then the South Road turn-off, and the road to the airport bears eastbound toward Santa Teresa Mission some forty-seven miles away.

It's John warming up FML this morning. Then sister Carol arrives with Bob Worthing. She's carrying baby Gregory; about ten months old. He's just over H. "flu" meningitis. It's a real morning for the Great Australian Salute this morning. It's something one isn't aware of as you drive out, but once outside the car, the flies are thick and persistent. These are tiny flies, maybe four mm long, and apparently in love with moisture, because they love to invade your nose and your ears and your eyes, and even, if you're talking, they'll fly into your breath, and into your mouth if you don't pay attention. They won't go away with a wave of your hand. They will be right there after a hand pass, and that's why the Great Australian Salute. When you see someone talking with someone else, and their hand is waving in front of their face as though they were keeping cool from a fan, that's flies! It's a good day for it today.

Carol and John are talking. "Yeah, I had to make the flight for him yesterday," John is saying. "He still had three hours to go on his time, but he didn't take his beeper, and no one could find him. I reached him at the Golf Club and his speech was slurred. He said he'd come out."

"He did," said sister Carol, "and I sent him away. He was too drunk to fly. He doesn't listen to me when I tell him that all the heavy things have to go in the nose or wing lockers, and not into the cabin with me. That's why this aircraft has lockers outside the cabin." She's really upset!

John doesn't say much more. The aircraft is loaded, and we're boarding. Sister Carol nestles Gregory against her shoulder. It's Darryl they're talking about! I never thought he'd do a thing like that. He's the senior pilot. Do you suppose there's some chicanery going on here? I wouldn't think that of John and Carol. Poor Darryl. He's been just taken over the coals for sure.

The radio is saying, "Foxtrot Mike Lima, follow the Friendship to runway three-oh; you'll be first to depart."

It's the Ayer's Rock Ansett special; a Fokker Friendship that takes tourists out early in the morning and gives them a chance to tour the Rock and the Olgas, have lunch or opt to climb the Rock, and then brings them back. I didn't see how many people got on it, but there weren't all that many. I don't know how Ansett pays expenses on that run, even at $220 a seat. John wheels FML around as the Friendship reaches the end of the runway and advances the throttles. The engines purr reassuringly and sweep us off the ground smoothly.

There's a puff of black smoke over the Spyce Byce. They must have fired off one of the diesel generators at the power plant. John turns southbound; the 207 radial, and we climb to 5,000 feet east of the highway. There's a Cessna 210 also on the way to Fregon that's talking to us. He says we're on his eleven o'clock and he's at 6,000 feet. I look backward, scan the sky until my own vitreous floaters look like aircraft, but I can't see him. John gazes around too, but we don't see anyone. No matter, If he's not straight ahead, or straight behind, he won't bother. John isn't nearly as nervous about something like that as Darryl is.

It's a beautiful morning. The Palmer Station slips beneath us. There's Mt. Connor in the southwest, blue in the distant haze. I read a little cardiology. The desert is green and brown, and there's still a lot of water around, although the salt lakes on the Ayer's Rock are about half empty now. There's Ernabella strip, and we pass over a lot of "sacred" sites, and begin our descent. There's the Cessna calling again, and sister Carol spots him. He's at our eleven o'clock and high. He tells us that he'll stay up there until we make our landing. John cranks FML around in a short base, and we touch down lightly and roll out. The Cessna lands behind us. It's 0935. There's very little wind blowing. It's a beautiful morning.

Sister Julie Dorn comes for us with the Toyota. We load the things into the car. Julie says that Dr. Lorenz is here on his "survey," and has had a look at Mr. Nigel Fulton and demanded a stat FBC because the man has leukemia. It turns out the count is normal, and the man has tonsillitis. So much for that. I won't have to see that patient

On the radio at the clinic it's Amata. "Aren't the Aeromedical Service coming here today?"

"No," says Carol. "You didn't need us last week. We'll be by in three weeks unless you have something urgent. Cheeahs."

So much for this being a long day. She's just cut off the other clinic that I thought we'd have to attend. The first patient is Maxie. We saw him a couple of weeks ago with the big node in his neck. Now it's down to two small nodes in place of the one, and he's all well, symptomatically. He's delighted that there's no more to the visit than that. Angela is a big youngster for fifteen. She has a history of prophylactic penicillin, but Julie says it's lucky if she's getting three pills a week. That's been going on for the last nine months. She's also just completed the course of Bactrim for trachoma; two tabs bd for three weeks. Well, let's just stop the penicillin all together. It's probably doing more harm than good in the dosage that she's absorbing.

Gee, the flies are terrible in here! Imitjola is 30/52 weeks pregnant. Weight is 82 kg, bp 85/50. Norman is about three. He has a really juicy chest. His Mom is warned that half the treatment is chest physio. She has to get that junk out of his chest. Norman is most unhappy about being upended on her lap, and being pummeled on the back. But that's what it is going to take.

On the blackboard in the clinic is drawn a flag, with the top half of the field black, the bottom half red, and, in the center, a yellow circle that has a diameter of about half the flag. It's the flag of the aboriginal: *Black Man, Red Sand and Sun.*

Purki is down from Ernabella. We met her last about two weeks ago when we were there. She's the original health worker at the clinic and was complaining of pains in her thighs last time we were there. Now she's complaining of right-sided headaches, and the vision in her good eye, the right one, is failing. She's really worried. Her left eye was destroyed in a childhood accident. She's diabetic, and last time we thought her leg distress might be diabetic neuropathy. Wow! What would you think if this is polymyalgia rheumatica! Temporal arteritis, and poor Purki is going blind!

"Let's give her eighty milligrams of prednisone stat, and draw an FBC so we can do a Westergren ESR," I advise.

"We don't have any prednisone," says Julie. So much for that. We'd better bring Purki back with us in the plane. Yes, she's willing to go, and with alacrity! She's scared. Purki is only forty-six, but then you can't depend on their records for true age. She might be ten years or more than that. We'd not want her totally blind.

There's the sounds of the p.a. system floating in through the window. "They're having tribal council meeting today," explains Julie. "They have about a hundred people from the tribe. I don't know what the whole thing is about. They're going to have a big barbecue, too."

Sandra is seventeen. She is pg again. Her last one was born on 9 April 1981 (that's the April last year), and she's now 29/52. Fetal heart is good. She weighs 53 kg, and 114/82. Here's Millie Harding of the pseudocyesis fame, and the congenital dislocation of the left hip. She's complaining of epigastric distress today. I imagine she has a worm burden, and maybe some giardia. Let's give her a dose of Fasigyn; four grams stat. Maggie is anemic. We'd better get a blood on her. She's been on iron. Let's find out how effective it is. She also has trouble with her right ear. Exam reveals a big plug of cerumen in there. We'd better use some cerumenol.

"You don't have any? We'll send you some down on the mail plane."

What's this? The largest lipoma I've ever seen. At least I think it's a lipoma. It's under her hair, over the cervical spine, almost symmetrical in shape with the long axis up and down right over the spinous process. It's fifteen-by-eight centimeters! If I were going to do that, I'd first prep it and then, after a little infiltration anesthesia, I'd put a needle into it to see if it aspirates.

It's so fluctuant you can't be sure it's not cystic. I listen with the stethoscope. No bruits. Man, that's huge! Well, nothing to do for it here. It doesn't seem to bother Maggie all that much. Matter of fact, I think she's proud of it.

Then here's old Louis. He's the congestive failure that we picked up a few months ago that was being treated with penicillin. He was doing great last time we saw him. Dr. Lorenz has increased his digitalis to 0.5 mg/day, and the old guy has gone into an arrhythmia. No wonder. We'd better take him out with us, is Dr. Lorenz's advice. Sure, if he'll write the admission slip to the hospital. After all, he's treating him, and he'll have to be responsible for the admission. I saw Louis about the March 4. His blood pressure today is 160/100. But he's in an irregular bradycardia.

Lastly is Peggy Thompson who is 37/52 weeks. She can come in on the mailplane on Tuesday next week, unless she delivers in the clinic. She's a multip; could handle it all by herself, probably.

That's the end of the clinic. Julie's legs look much better. She says she's increased the B–1 to 100 mg bd, and the bugs are leaving her alone. She's due to leave on her holiday this next week. No tears today.

Outside, the clan has gathered under the big trees in the village circle. Two wooden tables end to end, with the obvious leaders around the table, one with the microphone in hand, and the speaker up in the tree. There's a European at the table, too. I don't ask his capacity. Obviously, a government representative of some sort. Then about ten feet from the head table are a row of chairs, about ten of them, filled with an assortment of male members. Then, scattered around in the dirt are perhaps sixty-five or so aboriginals of both sexes, with their numerous camp dogs. There seems to be grouping of people, though not inter-mingled; kind of like you'd know that each little grouplet was a tribe. I don't know what they're saying. It's all Pitjantjatjara, and sounds to me like "numma-numma-numma" over and over through the tinny speakers in the tree.

To the south of the trees, towards the craft shop, there's an area of grass, about fifty meters by ten meters, with a concrete slab in the middle, and a water faucet that the kids are having great fun with. That's where they've set up the barbecue pit. It's being fueled with dry wattles, and there's huge pan of meat pieces on the table. That is, I think it's meat under the flies. I ask, but no one seems to know if it's beef or kangaroo, or both.

We stow our gear in the Toyota, and carefully pick our way around the perimeter of the audience on the ground. I feel a bit conspicuous with my cameras draped around my neck like some reporter from the *London Times*, or the *Cavalier County Republican*. We're on our way over to Mark and Fanou's place. Fanou has made some lovely little chocolate ball cookies (biscuits) with coconut fuzz around them. They're delicious! I have a cup of coffee and one biscuit. I comment to Mark on his batik, "It's Indian?"

"Why, yes," he replies, rather amazed at my knowledge. But it looks like one we have at home, the decorated elephant walking along, but he has about four elephants all in a row, and we just have one.

"And that's a beautiful tapestry," I admire.

"It's from Africa," volunteers Mark. It's a black field with gold and red designs in the center and at the top end, with a gold a red border.

"Is it Islamic?" I ask.

"I don't know. I don't think so. It's just African," Mark repeats.

"It looks like a Moslem prayer rug," I persist. "It has the place for the head to point towards Mecca, and be touched with the forehead."

"So it does," agrees Mark. "Maybe it is." I don't mention more on his decorations.

He has a beautiful, huge poster of Che Guevara on his wall, like a black silhouette on a red (Marxist?) field. I don't think he knows that I know who it is. Well, time to be getting on. It's only approaching one o'clock. It's really early. We walk back around the council meeting to the Toyota. Purki is there. So is Louis. We take two vehicles to the strip.

"I've never had a ride in this plane," says sister Julie Dorn. "I'd sure like to hitch a ride with you someday."

"Sure," says sister Carol. "We'll work that out. By the way, Dr. Rutten, which settlements has your wife not yet visited?"

"Why, Indulkana," I reply, rather surprised. "She had the invite from Marg Baxter last time, and they arrived in Indulkana at the strip just as we were to leave to look for them, so she hasn't really seen the settlement yet."

"Oh, we'll take care of that,"says Carol.

Into the plane. Purki wants to lie on the stretcher. Louis is sitting up.

"We'll try to keep as low as we can for him," I mention to John. "He's a cardiac. I don't think I want to go over 8,000 if we can help it."

"Okay," says John. "We'll try to find reasonably smooth air, though."

And with everything ready, FML fires up and John taxis back to the south end of the strip, advances the throttles to their stops, and FML hastens along the runway to a smooth take off and climb out. I get a picture of the crowd on the ground waving as we depart. Then take another of the village from the air. I think I can see the council folks all under the trees. I hope so. That will make a dandy picture. John searches for smooth air. Five thousand feet. Much too rough! Eight thousand feet! Louis vomits into his little bag. This won't do.

"Let's go up to nine thousand." At 9,000 feet it's smooth. Louis stops vomiting; sits with his eyes closed, but his chest is rising and falling regularly. No apparent dyspnea. His eyes open.

"Palya?" I ask.

"Palya," he replies, and circles his thumb to his index finger. He's really a dear, old man.

I make it a point to consult the digital elapsed time clock on the panel, and turn to view Louis every ten minutes on the flight. He seems to be doing fine. Most of the time he has his eyes closed.

Each time he opens them, I ask, "Palya?" And he circles his thumb to his index finger in the universal "OK" sign. One time, just as we're about abreast of the Henbury craters, I turn around, and there's old Louis looking out the window. What's that? He just made the sign of the cross with his right hand against the window. I wonder if that was just a happenstance. or if he's a Christian? I don't think I can ask him. He didn't see me watching him. It would be terribly embarrassing to him.

Did you know that there's no concept or perception of the word "if" in Pitjantjatjara? The word doesn't translate at all. In Pitjantjatjara, the phrase, "If we go to Hermannsburgs . . ." would be translated, "Since we're going to Hermannsburgs . . .", by the aboriginal, and then if you didn't go, the aboriginal would again think of the white man as a liar. That's another thing. The white people call themselves European. The aboriginals call them white men. Talk about racist! And then there's their double negatives. "We don't have any bananas" would be answered by "Oh–ah," (Yes). "Yes, we don't have any bananas." It's a fascinating culture.

I'm sorry to see my tour winding down, and the time approaching to leave this country. But then, there are lots of other things to see and do in this world. John's descending. It's bumpy again, but no one vomits now. We touch down. Purki and Louis are loaded into the St. John's ambulance. It's only about 1430 hours. Lots of time to get the mail today.

29 April 1982

We missed our trip last week. It was supposed to be Indulkana, but I heard that Jennie and Patrick are having a lot of trouble out there yet with the Aboriginal Council. They are just too efficient, and are not willing to quietly sit back and be dictated to when they know that the mandates are inaccurate for the good health of the community. They don't have much help from the politicians with this thing. I guess there have been a few bones of contention between the folks at Chandler and the council at Indulkana, too. I heard also that some woman at Mimili died that week from a misadventure with her medication—overdose, or whatever—and the Council is blaming Jennie and Patrick for that, too. I guess the spears were out for a while.

Speaking of that, our little thirteen-year-old at Fregon, Thelma, with the severe bronchiectasis and rheumatic valvulitis, died last week; on Friday the twenty-third, as a matter of fact.

Poor little thing. Everyone knew that she was going, too. Julie Dorn says that the father got out the spears anyway, and everyone fled, leaving him strictly by himself with her mamu. Funny way for Christians to act.

This morning is cool, almost frosty, and the sun is just peaking above the horizon as I drive the little Falcon out to the airport. Sister Carol had rung me last night and said that we were taking two folks to Ernabella with us; Charley and Nancy Chooka. They've been at the Old Timers' Home here for the last two years. Charley is about eighty-five, they say, and used to be a very powerful man in the tribe. He's going back to participate in the initiation rite this fall. He missed last fall because he was too ill to go. Nancy, his wife, is also going. Both are excited as can be about going "home." When I arrive at the airport, there they are, waiting. Charley with his eyes shut tight; he's blind, a rather big man, wearing a green and blue woven head band around his straggly, gray hair, and a leather "stockman" hat over that. Then a plaid shirt, with a jumper of gray wool, and gray trousers that don't fit too well, and a beautiful pair of gray, suede boots with red and green plaid top bands. They're obviously hand made by some one who must love Charley

Nancy is a thin, little woman with gigantic eyes, magnified by the huge glasses that she's wearing to correct for the aphakia of having had her lenses removed for cataracts. She's wearing a red bandana scarf over her thin, fine, gray hair, and she's chewing on a huge wad of mincobah. I'm mesmerized by the way she can talk and still keep that wad of slimy, brown "pitchie" from falling out of her mouth, or worse, sliding down her throat! I've learned that the "pitchie" that they combine with the tobacco is a plant; looks a lot like cannabis. They grind it up and mix it with tobacco and calcium, and apparently that extracts the alkaloid from the pitchie. Also, a requisite of chewing mincobah is the ability to spit great distances. You wouldn't want that brown juice in close proximity, you know.

Nancy is wearing a brown dress, and a gray, wool, knitted jumper. Sticking out beneath the brown skirt are her spindly, little legs, clothed in white stockings with horizontal stripes; red stripes along with blue on the right leg, and green stripes along with blue on the left leg. Then a pair of what look like well-worn running shoes. That's Nancy. They also have a huge, soft-vinyl "Port" (suitcase). One strap is broken, and the edges don't come together too well, and there are some portions of cloth hanging from the flaps. Charley is carrying a dirty, cloth "ditty" bag in his hands, and Nancy has a grease-spotted, yellow, vinyl handbag with a proper zipper; European style. I'm told that they have become quite Europeanized at the Old-Timers' Home, taking up such things as wearing shoes, and all those belongings! Tsk! Tsk! The conversation between Nancy and Charley and sister Carol is quite animated, and it's obvious that the old folks are in seventh heaven, cloud nine!

John is our pilot today. John passed his flight test with Clyde, the inspector from Broken Hill, yesterday. Clyde is out here today, too, and his victim for today is Darryl. Darryl had the option to fly yesterday, but deferred to John because he's a bit nervous about taking the test. Clyde is a nice young man, probably about forty or so, but it's difficult to tell. His face is a mosaic of skin grafts, some brown, some white, and the tight, strained look of the cover over severe burns. John says that Clyde was a helicopter pilot in Viet Nam, and has awards aplenty as a result of the heroism that produced his burns. His chopper went down and he was thrown clear. He went back into the burning machine half a dozen times to pull out people; saved them all, and in return, had these terrible burns.

He and Darryl are flying the Baron FDE. The are going to a place called Bakail, about 055 degrees from the Alice, and almost to the Queensland border. We're flying FML and John has done the preflight. We load the gear, the big, blue port of Charley and Nancy into the nose locker. Charley for blindness and all, manages to climb aboard and station himself on the stretcher on the deck. Nancy takes the backward seat, and sister Carol in the front-facing seat, across from Charley.

A big sign on the autopilot this morning declares, "Yaw axis inoperable."

The engines fire up easily. John goes through his flight check. The port engine dies. John hits the fuel pump, and the engine sputters back to life. My hair is standing on end.

"Something new I was taught yesterday," explains John. "We're supposed to check out the firewall fuel cutoff each time we start up. Just to make sure they're operative."

That's nice to know. I thought the engine was dying! Down to runway one-two, and the clearance, and we roar down the runway. The sun is just enough to the north to let me watch the gear fold up on my side; shadows on the ground. We hear Darryl identify his ship to the Alice Control as "FML." He's sure nervous. He's giving our letters. I wonder if Clyde will dock him for that? We set for 207 radial. We're to be at 8,000 feet. I read my *American Family Practice* journal and begin the quiz for two hours of continuing medical education.

There's a line like smog ahead of us towards Ernabella, but it's really a line of thin clouds at about 6,000. The ground is dappled with sunlight falling through the clouds, and makes landmarks difficult to identify. Then, as I'm looking out the window towards Mt. Connor, the radio comes alive, "Uniform Delta Papa," and it's Barry Bean from Chartair letting us know that he's on course for Ernabella, too.

Why, there he is, right in line with my view of Mt. Connor. Before Barry has finished his message, I've got him pointed out to John. John is impressed with his observer. We'll be there ahead of his two-ten. John makes a clockwise sweep over the village, and drops gear and flaps for landing. The touch down is smooth, and we backtrack just a little to park.

Julie is waiting, and so are the folks that are going to host Charley and Nancy. We unload the clinic material. Julie is telling about the clinic, and the trouble at Indulkana. Barry arrives, and we share a warm reunion all around. Then, off to the clinic. It's not ready, quite, so we have a cup of coffee while we listen to the radio chatter between the settlements. Somewhere, someone is reporting and is being criticized by the radio-of-the-air doctor for giving such a large dose.

"I'm doing the best I can," he retorts. "I'm the school teacher, and don't know anything about medicine."

The doctor comes back with a much more conciliatory tone in reply. Then, it's time for the clinic to start.

Yilpi is still having pain in the left shoulder. She's twenty-eight years old, and this seems to be a classic Tietze's syndrome (costa-chondral joint pain). We'll give her some Indocin. Next is Robert with a huge belly, who is brought in by the schoolmarm.

Robert is happy; no pain, and looks okay, except for the big belly. There's no history of constipation or diarrhea. Exam is just a big belly that percusses with a lot of tympani. Maybe it's a megacolon. Well, let's treat him symptomatically.

The schoolmarm has a terrible uri (upper respiratory tract infection) but she's already on Amoxil. That's okay. Her name is Marie. Makuiniti is twenty-five and pg, 80 kg, 130/80, and about 25/52. I caution Julie to watch the pressure. Andrew is eight and has a huge, resolving left anterior thigh abscess. He's on medication. We'll leave it alone. Trevor is twenty-eight. He's having trouble with dysphagia (difficulty swallowing). It sounds like a "globus" (globus hystericus—a stress phenomenon characterized by difficulty swallowing). He was in just a year ago to see me about the same thing. I think we'll refer him off to Dr. Hauptenhauser at the Alice. I write his referral letter.

Here's little Clara with Mom, Imuna. She was born 19 February 1981, and is getting to be a big girl, but she has a terribly juicy chest, with a lot of laryngeal stridor. She has four teeth on the bottom now. None on the top, yet. She's sure a mess. They say that her chromosome studies were normal, though. I think we'd better take her back with us. Imuna is quick to agree. She's not chewing her mincobah today. She sure has pearly, white teeth!

Amanari is fifteen. She's Purki's daughter, and diabetic like her Mom. Isn't that something? Purki was happy enough with my care of her that she's now decided to let the tjilpi doctor take care of her daughter, too. Amanari is taking twenty-five units of Montard MC in the morning, and five units at night. Her ocular fundi are okay, and her pressure is 120/80. We draw a blood sugar. I congratulate Purki for talking Multalti into having her hip repair done at the hospital in the Alice last week. Didn't I tell you about that? Well, that will be another story. Purki is still having some trouble with her headaches, and also has a cold. She's on Amoxil already. That's good. We'll give her a ten day course. Then, there's Brian. Brian is still trying to get a pension. There's nothing really wrong with him. It's just that all his friends have pensions, and he feels left out. He was told by Dr. C. Parker in Adelaide at the Aboriginal Medical Service that he has Crohn's disease (colitis), and was sent back to Ernabella for a work-up.

We'd better refer him on up. Brian has black hair, and a snow-white beard. Rather striking in a black man. His pressure is 118/90.

Dwayne was born on 20 November 1981. Lizzie Moodoo is his Mom. He's had diarrhea almost since birth. Exam is NAD. The stool specimen that we'll take back with us looks like normal stool of a breast milk fed baby. Then comes Stanley Evans, born 28 November 1981. Mom is aboriginal. Dad is half-caste eastern European. They've come all the way on foot from Kenwood Park, thirty-seven kilometers away, because they've heard that the tjilpi doctor is expert with problems with the penis of babies. Their little guy has a phimosis, and apparently the word has spread from Indulkana that I can do surgery for this without jeopardizing the initiation rite. How about that? Another honor that carries no increase in salary. But it's kind of exciting to think that these people really do talk about the doc. Stanley is a happy baby. We'll bring our tools along next month. They'll probably stay in Ernabella for the month waiting for me instead of walking round-trip again to Kenwood Park. How's that for loyal patients?

Last patient is Kristy Eckert, born 9 October 1980, and she has an aversion to her bath the last couple of days. She screams bloody murder when Mom tries to put her into the bath. Exam of her bottom reveals a small laceration along the right labia. That's what's the matter; the soap is stinging her. Well, that won't last but a day or so. There's no real evidence of infection. I query Mom about the last time I saw her. She was in the throes of a miscarriage.

"Yes," she says. "I lost it all that night. But things went along nicely, and I think we're about ready to try for another one."

Then over to Julie's for tea. There's a lot of politics in the talk today. I mostly sit and listen. They feel comfortable with me, and do give me a few compliments that make it all seem worthwhile. I'm suppose to look up the notes of Colin Tunku, who apparently hurt his neck on a trampoline, of all things, about a year ago. About an hour of gossip, and we're ready to leave. Over to the craft shop. Imuna is waiting with Clara. We talk for a while in the craft shop, and look over some artifacts. There is beautifully done batik yardage there, but it's awfully dear; like $63 for three meters of the stuff. I don't buy anything.

three meters of the stuff. I don't buy anything.

Back out to the strip; load up FML, and we're off. It's kind of hazy going back until we climb out on top at 9,000, and look down on the icing on the cake of the "Red Centre." Not cumulus this time; more like stratus, and where it was awfully bumpy underneath, it's clear and smooth on top. Clara dozes. So does Imuna. I finish my lesson. Then the descent. Again it's awfully bumpy. We land smoothly, as John always seems to do. Darryl and Clyde are there. It seems they never got to Bakail. FDE suffered not only an open door in flight, but also a cracked crankcase on the port engine. Poor Darryl. Today wasn't his day. I don't have to courage to ask if he's passed his test, or if he has to go out again tomorrow with Clyde. Guess I'll just hasten on to the APO and pick up the mail.

6 May 1982

It's another beautiful morning this morning with just a bit of very cold mist on the windscreen of the little Falcon. It isn't going to take much more cold and this is going to be a thin film of ice. It is getting cooler in the mornings. Winter is fast approaching. There's kind of a haze in the air this morning, as though the world is aware that things are cooling off. But, fortified with a reheated lamb chop, a bowl of hot rice, a piece of toast and a cup of coffee, I don't mind the drive out to the airport. The sun isn't quite up yet; just a blush on the northeastern horizon, but it will soon come up and turn the few high cirrus clouds into pink halos.

I heard that Impita Baker, our little old lady in Amata that the family wanted to abandon to the Old Timers' Home a few months ago, died in the family wicki-up. I guess she went down hill very rapidly when she finally started to go. The family was approached by Jennie and said, "No, she can stay here." Of course, that's so her mamu doesn't have to wander around looking for home. Jennie told me about this in a quiet moment between patients. She had to go out to the wicki-up and crawl over the filthy mat between the camp dogs to reach Imita. It's not a pleasant job, and the family didn't really care whether Jennie came by or not.

John and Carol are there this morning at the airport. FML is to be the vehicle; the flying carpet, so to speak. John has done all the preflight check. The little sign is still on the auto pilot, "Yaw axis inoperable." But the plane fires up immediately. This time it doesn't bother me at all when John checks out the fire-wall shutoff of fuel. We taxi out to runway three-oh. But what's this? Here's another plane taxiing down towards us as we make our turn.

John has his earphones on, and 8-AL playing on the middle frequency radio, so I can't hear the conversation. 8-AL is the local Alice Springs ABC (Australian Broadcasting Company) station, and is half of the stations that can be reached from Alice by standard band radio. John makes another turn to the side. We're to let this plane go first. It's a beautiful thing. A Chartair Cessna Conquest propjet. TFG is its call sign, and on the nose in beautiful script is, "First Lady." It's a charter flight of tourists to Ayer's Rock. That, now, is the way to go to Ayer's Rock. TFG departs with a hum. I don't hear the clearance from the tower for us, because John still is on the earphones, but he lines up, forward with the throttles, and the familiar leaping into action of FML takes us off the ground smoothly in about a thousand foot roll.

It's quite hazy this morning. Initially, we're assigned to 2,500 feet. That's fun to watch the ground. Then at 15 DME, we're cleared to 8,000. I sit back and read *Scientific American*. The lakes still have some water in them, but only in the centers, and the edges now are concentrically ringed with deposits of snow white salt. We cross the Henbury craters, then the Ayer's Rock road, and pass just to the east of Mt. Connor. Now the descent for Amata; the sweep over the settlement, and the turn over the small mountain to the west of the strip. I suppose I'm looking at a sacred site. John touches down smoothly with just a bit of cross wind.

We unload the cartons from the plane. Sister Carol isn't that happy about getting out of the warm plane. It is quiet on the strip. A zigzagging haze appears to the south, low over the bush, and between the wattles. It's an erratic motion, like a Brownian movement of dust motes in a shaft of sunshine on house-cleaning day, moving toward us. Then straight up into the air over us, where they shine brilliant green in the morning sun. "Budgies." Parakeets! There must be more than a hundred of them. Little blue shafts of feathers on the wings when you can see them. Otherwise, more brilliant green than emeralds!

Then they're gone, and the Toyota is here with Jennie and Bev. The talk is about Impita, and other problems. There seems to be some controversy with the council here, too. I think it's the politicians who are making such a mess of this; not the aboriginals. I really think they'd gladly do what they were told to do. They're just being told by the wrong leaders, the wrong things for the good of their community. Politicians!

Craig Seneca is a European baby, about two years old. He's had asthma before. I think you remember when we were trying to give him some theophyllin, but only had adult doses to try? Well, he's had a pretty bad time, but is on nuelin now; 50 mg tds, and he swallows the tablets okay. He sounds pretty clear this morning. Reward for this? You bet! A kiss from Craig when I'm all done. He's a sweety! His brother, Garth, is also crook. He's about five, and has been having episodes of epistaxis (nosebleeds). Exam reveals it's from the septum on the right. He was in Alice Springs hospital a year ago for upper respiratory infections and epistaxis. We'll try some quarter percent Neosynephrine and pressure when it bleeds.

Jacob is next. A classic aboriginal face, with a dirty, red head band around his blond-brown hair. He's fifty-four, but not gray at all. He has pneumonia. No breath sounds in the right base at all. He's on Amoxil, and isn't feverish. He has a tight cough. We'll keep him on the Amoxil. He'll do okay. The rest of his exam is NAD.

Then comes Walter. Walter is in charge of the store, and Walter will know about the ten boomerangs that I'm supposed to take back with me. I ordered them about two months ago. They are for a departure party for some of the base people. But we didn't make it to Amata last month, so I didn't have a chance to pick them up. First, though, better get Walter feeling better. He has a piece of the root of the first molar on the lower left that is giving him trouble. The tooth is gone; just a piece of root that's sticking up.

"Gee, Walter, I don't have the tools to take that out," I tell him.

"Oh, I do!" exclaims Jennie, proud to be prepared for any emergency.

"No, you don't understand," I tell her. "I don't want to do it here. There's too much chance of getting into trouble with that, and besides, it's not really an emergency. He's not in pain. It's just sharp. He'd really better come into the Alice some time and have them do that at the dental clinic."

So much for Walter's problem. "If it hurts, you can put a little oil of cloves on it."

Here's old Punch. He's been down to Adelaide and had the cataract extracted from his right eye two weeks ago. He's delighted! His left eye is still opaque, but he can now see through his new glasses, and is proud to point out that he can see my face, and Jennie's, and the light, and the small gas space heater, and just all sorts of things that he hasn't been able to see in years. I look in the eye. There's still an awful lot of debris in there. I don't know how he can see around it. The retina looks fine, though. Maybe a lot of the debris will settle out. Punch is fifty-five. He's a nice, old man. We encourage him.

Sally Harper is ten and has a rather nasty monilial rash in her groin. We do have some Nystatin for that. That should be fine. Apply it twice a day, and continue for a few days even after it seems to be all gone. Kukika was born in 1955. She has pain in the costal margin all the way across, and also in the right shoulder. Exam reveals that the costal margin pain is a red herring. The pain is really a right deltoid bursitis. She's even point tender. But I won't inject it. We'd better go along with one of the non-steroidal anti-inflammatory agents.

This is a different Ivy than the one you've met so many times who had miliary tb. This Ivy is about as old; born in 1908, but she's short of breath. Her brother, Peterkin, is on brondecon. She'd like some, too. Her blood pressure is 126/82, and I don't hear a thing in her chest. We'll just carry her along with TLC (tender loving care). Tjalimuaya was born in 1942. She has a sore throat, hoarse, and has a lump in the throat. Her exam is NAD. We'll treat her symptomatically. Yuminia is fifty. She has hypertension. She's taking 160 mg a day of Inderal, and 250 mg of Diuril a day. Her pressure is still up at 240/120. Let's add 25 mg of Apresoline to this and watch her.

Here's Gladys Raymond. Gladys has returned recently from ASH having given birth to Stella on 2 March 1982. Gladys is nineteen. She's had a nasty breast abscess on the left, and hasn't been breast feeding Stella on that breast for about ten days now. She's taking Amoxil, and the breast is organizing that abscess quite well. They did open it at the hospital and put in a drain. Jennie has taken out the drain just the other day. The incision is clean; no pus now, and is healing from the bottom. It looks like she can start to nurse again when the incision is completely closed.

Meantime, let's look at Stella. This is a cute baby, from the top of her head to her costal margin. From there on, nature has dealt her some sort of cruel blow. She has what is apparently an agenesis of the lumbar spine, and the sacrum is all screwed up, too. The baby is alert, smiling and cooing. Her fontannels are fine; little black eyes that sparkle as they follow my movements. The mouth is clear; ears are even intact, and not draining. There are no cervical nodes. The little arms are well formed. The chest is clear, and the heart sounds normal. There's a good startle to the Morro reflex, but there the good news stops.

The abdomen seems to have turned into mostly a genital crease, and mostly perineum is below the navel. The part that is the belly seems to be all right, and the anus is patent, as is the vagina, but almost too widely so. Bowel sounds are normal. She has a terrible, wet, macerating exfoliation over the entire perineum. Palpation of her back reveals a mushy feel, as though the spine ended at the ribs.

There seems to be no sacrum, and the femurs almost look as though they were not there, and instead, the ilium on both sides has taken its place. The thigh is almost scaphoid in shape, and I don't really recognize the muscle groups. Are they quadriceps and adductors? Or are they gluteal muscles? The little knees are fixed, and remind me of the last joint in a wing of a baked chicken. Then the tiny feet, perfectly formed, but only about three centimeters long, like they'd stopped developing when the fetus was about three months old. How odd! Poor little thing! I don't know what you'd call this anomaly. I wonder if they took x-rays of her? Her Mom's HR# is 4424. I'll have to look it up. What a mess. I coo at the baby, and she coos back. I tell Gladys that she's a beautiful baby. But I can read the pathos in Gladys's eyes. This little beautiful baby is doomed. How sad.

Well, on to other things. Craig was born on 11 November 1980, and is failing to thrive. It's said that he has a lactase deficiency. I think he's just too little to fend for himself at the breast or the table. Maybe we'll take him in to the Children's Health Unit.

"No," says his Mom.

That's that. Maybe next month he'll be ready to go. Sara is four. She has a macerating dermatitis in her axillae. We'll try some Burow's solution soaks to that for a while, and then add a steroid cream. She'll come right. Hildegard is about seven months old. She has a grotty chest. She's cute as a picture, with her little ponytail all done with a proper tiny barette. She sounds clear now. We'll continue with another shot of bicillin (not really like American bicillin. This is a mixture; more like American Wycillin). Larry is next. He has symptoms of a urinary tract infection. He was born in 1930. Examination reveals that isn't his complaint at all. He has a bad cold. His GU (genito-urinary) tract seems okay.

Then comes Leonard who, I'm told, also has a uti (urinary tract infection). Not so, again. This time it's a left sacroiliac strain from playing football. We'll take care of that with a little Indocin. Then we have an antenatal. Sandra is seventeen, and is 56 kg. 94/50, FHH 144, and she's about 30/52. Lillian we saw a couple of months ago for right upper quadrant abdominal pain. She was to have had an x-ray at the Alice on the March 17, but absconded from the hospital in favor of a party down in the Todd river, so we didn't get a picture, and now she's back with the same problem. She can be treated symptomatically until we have a chance to get her back to the Alice. No use sending her there again for another party.

Impintiri is thirty-four and has an elevated BP since December. She's on Clotride and Aldomet. She's 154/104 today. Let's add Apresoline, 25 mg daily to her routine, too. One wonders if they really take the medicine that is given to them, or if they barter it away. Janet is thirty, and has a xiphoid migraine equivalent. I can't find anything wrong with her. We'll treat her symptomatically, too.

Here's little Susan Jack, back from Adelaide. She was born on 3 October 1980, and last time we were here (remember, we skipped Amata last month? They weren't ready for us) we sent her down to Children's Hospital, and she had her surgery for that terrible squint and strabismus! She's a beautiful baby now. Nice, straight eyes, and a big smile, and her mother is absolutely ecstatic! Isn't that rewarding? Both to Mom and the tjilpi doctor!

Last patient of the day is Glenda with a huge carbuncle on her right buttock. She's only twelve. A bit embarrassed as she lies with the lesion exposed on the dirty bed. We take a culture. Jennie hasn't had her on any antibiotic. She's just kept the sinuses open and draining. We'll give her tetracycline for this until we get back the culture. It's smelly; probably not just a staph. It smells like there might be coliforms or even pseudomonas in there. I hope not. Maybe it's bacteroides. Maybe we'll be putting her on something like Flagyl or such. We don't have any Gentamycin anyway, but we do have lots of tetracycline.

That's the end of the clinic. We load up the vehicle and drive up to Jennie's. The coffee is on, and Jennie has some biscuits with a red jam of some sort in the middle, and there are some cheese sandwiches and some made with cucumber and tomato. I have two of the biscuits and my coffee. John tells that he's been watching a lot of kids sniffing petrol while he's been sitting there.

"If they come by the window is it all right if I take a picture of them?" I ask Jennie.

"You can do whatever you want with them if they come by," she replies. She's upset.

Then, there they are! Four of them. Nice, young boys, probably between about eight and thirteen, with their tin cans in hand, and teeth flashing in happy smiles. They don't even look sick! But they will be! They sit for a while on some overturned oil drums, alternately talking and laughing, and taking a big drag on the can; holding it to their face without hands, just with the suction from inhaling against the can. It's scary! Then they come by the window, shade their face with their hands, and peer in. Jennie says something in Pitjantjatjara, and they run away laughing and jumping. How sad. The ultimate in permissiveness.

"Can I take a picture of the graffiti on the community building today?" I ask Jennie.

"Sure." We gather up our things.

"This may be the last trip out," says sister Carol.

It's like a bolt from the blue. She's known this all day and waited until now to tell us. It seems that the Northern Territory has billed South Australia for the RFDS/AMS service for the year; $1.5 million dollars! S.A. is objecting and refusing, at this time, to pay. Therefore, the N.T. is out of funds for the RFDS/AMS, and we won't be flying until they solve the problem! Incredible! What will these people do without the docs?

"They say we're to send them in by plane; emergency evacuations," says Carol.

"How will you know which ones to send in?"

"We'll just send them all in. That'll get their attention."

"Wow! I bet it will!"

We leave. Still, I have to stop by the craft store and have Walter get our boomerangs. The craft store is a demolished house in the center of the square of camps. People and dogs in small groups around smoking fires, nursing babies, sleeping, drinking soft drinks, cooking food and on the wide veranda of the house, playing with old auto tires; rolling them just like we used to when I was a child. We find Walter near the camp fire. He doesn't have a key for the store, and Peter Yates, who is in charge, won't be back until tomorrow. Bad news. Well, maybe we can get in. He tries to pry out a window with a stick.

"This one is open, or at least unlocked," I whisper to Jennie.

"Can you open it?"

"Yeah." I use my lessons taught some years ago in breaking and entering, and gently coax the window open. Walter is delighted; jabbers something to a small child, and lifts him through the window. In a second the door is open. We go in. The house is demolished inside, too. In one room that is a store room, and whose lock is picked by Walter with a sharp stick, are bales of artifacts, ready for market.

"To Ayer's Rock," explains Walter. "I'm not supposed to

open them." We find three boomerangs about the size I want.

"Ten dollars for two and a half of that for one," quotes Walter, in logical aboriginal math. That's not too bad a price, but there are only three, and I need ten.

"I'll get on the radio tomorrow when Peter gets back. We'll have them to you this next week," promises Jennie.

So, we leave the building, and head for the strip, with just a short stop for the pictures of the community center graffiti.

"You couldn't do that in Warrebrei," says John. "They'd take your camera and try to stuff it you know where." No, I guess I wouldn't take a picture of that in Warrebrei.

"But it's not people," I object.

"It's a lifestyle," says John. I'm learning.

We load up FML. John fires up the engines. It's been a good clinic. I'm sorry to leave. I hope we'll get back here again. John advances the throttles. FML refuses to move. Now what?

"I've left the chocks," laughs John. We shut down everything. John gets out, puts the aluminum chocks back in the nose locker, and climbs back in. FML fires up again. We taxi to the end of the runway, and roar back towards the north. Lift off; the climb out. There's Mt. Connor. Up to 9,000 feet for the trip home. I read some more in the *Scientific American*. My mind is busy with what I've seen and heard and lived.

13 May 1982

Crisp and cool, and the sun is making the McDonnels pink as I leave the drive this morning. The windscreen wipers take away the almost-ice dew that has accumulated, and my breath steams up the car which starts with a very cold nose. The heater is on, but about the time I get to the airport, it will come alive and start to warm things up. The hoses in the school yard are powering rainbirds, but one of the hoses has split, and is sending up a cascade of water twenty feet into the chill morning air, and leaving a cloud of steam behind as it condenses on the downwind side. Actually, there's hardly any wind at all, and there's frost on the grass of the school yard where the water isn't settling.

Darryl has run up FML this morning. It seems that poor old FDQ is really out of it. I don't know what's happened to it, but they say it's in the shop. Poor thing. Carol arrives in the car with Bob Worthing, just about the time that I decide to put my cameras into the plane. I fold down the steps and enter, with my back in a C, carefully putting one foot in front of the other in the narrow passageway. A small, electric shock runs from about the 2nd lumbar vertebra into both buttocks. It's enough to make me stop walking and sink to my knee. It's gone. Back up into the C position, to continue forward to place my cameras and my book in the right front seat. It's like being shot. I'm back down on my knee before I know what's happened. Paralyzing pain to both buttocks from the lumbar spine, but not into my legs. This isn't the balloon of a ureteral calculus. This is the old backache disaster of 1979 revisited! I'm not sure I can move. I begin to slide my knee along the passage back to the door. I leave my cameras and my book on the stretcher on the floor of the plane. By the time I've set my left foot on the top step of the ladder, the pain is gone, but that threatening feeling of impending spasm lingers on.

"You right today?" queries Carol, as she busily brings her things to the plane.

"Oh, right!" I assure her. "Have to hit the loo first, though." And with that I proceed into the Aeromedical rooms in the hangar and get to the bathroom. I extract a half grain codeine with Tylenol from my left hip pocket; the one I carry with me all the time now, just in case there's a stone to pass. Palming water in my right hand from the tap I wash the tablet down. It's 0800. Well, we'll see. Back to the plane, so I can help load it up. Carol has a Pavlova that she's made for the morning tea after clinic.

"Everything that could go wrong has gone wrong with this poor thing," she complains. I don't offer any comment. The Pavlova is about two inches thick; it should be five inches thick. The meringue has collapsed into tasty concrete.

"It looks fine to me," I lie.

"It's Fregon, isn't it?" questions Darryl.

"Right-e-o," affirms Carol.

I fake it, making the three steps up into the plane in two, and pick my way forward. My God! One has to be a contortionist to get into the right seat when one has a crook back. I settle in uneasily. The back support of the seat does hit me just about right, though, and it is comfortable. It's a challenge to turn around to pick the shoulder harness off the seat behind me. Darryl comes in the auxiliary door on the pilot's side, and sits down; turns on the power, and the digital clock comes alive. That's good! Now I can watch for twenty minutes, plus seven will put me at the time of my dose.

Small talk. Darryl is listening to the terminal information. We move along the taxi way towards the runway, and wait while a small Cherokee finishes his approach and turns off. Then to runway one-two and clear for departure. It's the 204 radial at 8,000 with right turn amended to 2,500 feet to east of the Stuart Highway. Darryl advances the throttles after checking every switch and button in the cockpit. We leap ahead. This morning the sun is lower enough than last week to almost make the re-traction of the gear invisible by its shadow, because it's too far behind. The right turn. I always think I might see a "roo" down there in the scrub. I haven't, so far, and there's none today, either. It's so clear this morning that the mountains 40 miles away dis-tinctly display their canyons.

Reaching 2,500, we're cleared to 8,000, and report back DME 15.

Carol reaches forward with a sheaf of papers. It's all the reports on patients that we've seen at the clinic over the past month or so. Lilian did have an x-ray of that gall bladder after all, and it didn't show anything, so Dr. Finley had run her through the ultrasound, and there was no stone there, either. So, Lilian may have right upper quadrant abdominal pain, but is isn't from gallstones. I haven't looked up Colin's x-rays yet, either. He had the trampoline accident some time ago, and I'd promised to look up his films. I must get at that one of these days. He was seen on December 10 last year. Dr. Parke says he has nerve entrapment.

Little Clara has been diagnosed as a Crouzon's Syndrome. That's nice to know. Now it has a name. Sue Quayl, the audiol-ogist, says that she has 80 decibels deafness bilaterally. I didn't know that. She did fine in the hospital, says Carol, and is now home again. Poor little thing.

Helen, m/Tyulkiwa #011090 was the little girl that I'd sent in with the funny looking external auditory canal that looked like a tube of skin. History had her having a cholesteatoma removed some time ago. Not so, says Dr. Hauptenhauser. He removed a whole bunch of epithelial debris, and apparently down at the bottom of the mess was a proper tympanum. He did this on the April 20. Helen was born in 1969. Maybe she'll be able to hear after all.

About this time Darryl is fidgeting in his seat. He's had word that there's another plane on the way to Fregon, besides ours. He's like a Tibetan prayer wheel as he spins round and round looking for the bogey. Just like last week, I point with my finger. Darryl is impressed. I'm glad to see him relax for three seconds.

Now we're descending. I've been trying to read *A Town Like Alice* by Mr. Shute, but the time has gone by so quickly, what with reading the reports and such, and it shows 1:05 on the elapsed time clock on the panel. The air is still clear. Darryl makes his sweep around, drops the flaps to decrease airspeed, then down with the gear. He anticipates the flare-out about 10 feet off the ground, and the Navajo balloons just a little. He quickly recovers, and the touchdown is smooth, but he's a little disgusted with the porpoising. I compliment him anyway.

Fanou meets us with the brand new Toyota. This one is brown, but with white vinyl trim on the inside. It won't stay that color very long.

"I don't have any clinic for you today," she apologizes, with her thick French accent. "Zay are to be bringeeng in zee bodee by zee road," she explains.

It's Multalti, who had her fractured hip repaired at the Alice on the counseling of Purki, after I had intervened when she wasn't going to let Dr. Reed do it. She was doing fine; then suddenly died. Probably threw an embolus. But the mamu will be loose until the body is into the burial ground at Fregon. And it was Impeta Baker at Amata last week, and Thelma here at Fregon on the April 23.

"Zay have all gone out boosh until zee vehicle arrive," she apologizes further.

"Oh, well," says sister Carol, lightly, "then we'll just have a cup of coffee while we wait."

So, we unload the Toyota of its cargo of metal cases and organize the clinic room. That's when Rupert appears. Rupert is about 40 years old, and is complaining that he can't see to do close work. Funduscopic exam reveals no problems at all. It's too bad we don't have a big box of near-vision glasses for these people at each settlement. It did work once at Amata over a year ago for one patient. I don't remember now who it was, but now I have to send them all in to the Alice for the proper examination in order to get a low power magnifying glass. So be it. That's what we'll do with Rupert, and I write the referral. Rupert gets up to leave, and Albert Lennon takes his place.

Albert is about 42, and has a fever and hematuria (blood in his urine). His blood pressure is 112/70, but he also has exudate on his tonsils. It's probably a bad throat. Maybe strep? We'll take a culture and start him on penicillin. A Bicillin now, and then tablets four times a day, if he shows up. Meantime, if we find the culture positive, we'll just track him down for another big dose of Bicillin. He leaves, and in comes Murray Minkulyn, about 70, and he had a carcinoma of the thyroid treated in December 1980. He has no cervical node, but I have to lift up his long, gray, beard to see the transverse surgical scar across his throat. He seems fine. He's taking 200 mg of Thyroxin a day, and pretty faithful about it. His pressure is 182/96. We'll leave him alone.

Tyanngawa appears. She was born about 1908? She's taking Clotride and Inderal for her blood pressure, which is recorded at 208/94. She has no dependent edema, but she's using Ventrolin for her asthma. She has a gallop rhythm, and rales in both bases. She's in congestive failure. We'll give her 0.25 mg of Digoxin a day, and see if that doesn't clear up her asthma.

Valerie Farmer was born 4 April 1931. She's European, and gives a good history of giardiasis (intestinal parasite). Examination is essentially negative. We'll treat her with a single dose of Fasigyn, 2 grams stat. Her husband is on Sinemet, she says, but denies strongly that he has Parkinson's disease. He'll be coming in to see me. He runs the store.

Imityala is twenty-nine and showed a positive pregnancy test on the 11th. She had a perforation in her left tympanum, but the right one is intact. She had a tympanoplasty in 1972, but she's deaf as a board. Her belly shows a fundus at about 14 weeks. She's already had five babies. We draw her blood.

Do you remember Sam Munser? A European baby born on 28 December 1981? We saw him here on the March 18 because he hadn't gone "pooh" for two weeks. Well, now Mom says he's vomiting all the time.

Sam looks happy as a clam; not at all dehydrated, and he's laughing and cooing at me. Mom's face is dead serious. I examine Sam all over. Soft belly. Good bowel sounds. Not at all fussy, but he's sure drooling a lot; cutting some lower teeth, I expect, and as if to verify this, his little finger goes into his drooling mouth and massages the front of his lower gum. Even with the doctor poking his fat, little tummy, Sam doesn't as much as regurgitate a spoonful. Happy, healthy babe, but here's a Mom having trouble coping with the outback, I'd suspect. Lots of reassurance for Mom.

Then comes Tommy, and his wife Katy. They both want glasses for near vision. Rupert is spreading the word out there. A quick look at Tommy with the ophthalmoscope. Why, he has a dense cataract in his right eye. I can't see through it at all. The right one looks pretty good.

"Sure, Tommy, we'll send you in to the Alice and get some glasses for you."

We'll also have the doc make a note of the cataract. No use doing anything with it at all, though, until we begin to have some trouble with the other eye. Katy was born in 1933, says her notes. I'd guess Tommy is about five years older than that. Katy's eyes are fine, but she does need glasses for close work. We'll sort that out for her and see that it gets done.

Fanou tells us that Julie Dorn has just received her approval from the Pitjantjatjara council in the Alice to serve at Fregon. She's been here almost eighteen months, and finally got permission to be here. Fanou says that she's been here six months now, and doesn't expect her permit for another six months. Isn't that awful? And they want full hospital facilities at each of these settlements. That's absurd!

Iwana has a "ringworm," I'm told. Examination reveals that she has an allergic dermatitis involving her left cheek. We'll take care of that with a little antihistamine. Then here's Alan Farmer from the store for his script for Sinemet, although he doesn't have Parkinson's. He's on 100/10 Sinemet, one a day. I write him for a hundred from the Alice. He thanks me with a continuing nod of his head, but a deadpan facies, as his shaking hand accepts the script. I'm sure glad that's not Parkinson's.

Ray Bergen is the engineer of the settlement. He's an Eastern European, it looks like. He has a left sciatica, which he describes like he's read it out of a book, even down to the little toe on his left foot. He's had it a month. His pressure is 192/108. Ray is about sixty-two. We'll give him a bit of Indocin, 25 mg three times a day, and see if his sciatica doesn't go away. He's already on Clotride for that pressure. Then it's Ray's aboriginal wife, Nellie. She's diabetic and supposed to be taking Daonil daily. On November 27 her sugar was reported at 5.7 mmol. That's not bad at all.

"Fanou, you're losing your credibility," I remark between patients.

"What do you mean?" she defends.

"I mean, you said there wasn't any clinic today, and the patients are flowing through quite regularly. If you said there was a busy clinic some day, I'd better bring my tooth brush."

"They saw that it was you," she explains. "They know you, the tjilpi doctor, and they will come in to see you because the truck has not yet brought the body. They have trust for you." Isn't that nice? I'm appreciated. That's a real rewarding feeling.

Pompey is next. He was born about 1938, his notes say. Pompey has tinea corporis on his neck. They've tried Whitfield's ointment without success. Let's try him on some griseofulvin for a couple of weeks if he'll take it. Let's say 500 mg daily for about four weeks. He'll probably take it until the itch gets better, then, regardless of how much rash he has, he'll stop.

Then there's Chris Wells. You remember Chris with the pain in his right upper quadrant that I once thought might be a liver abscess? Well, he was sent to ASH on 1 April 1982 and was to have seen Dr. Quinn at 1400 hours on May 7, but we don't have any notes on that yet. His pressure is 158/102. He still has his pain, but I'll have to get his outpatient notes to see what went on. I'll ask the AMS to get them from the hospital and send them over to the CHC (Community Health Centre, where my "town" office is located) for tomorrow afternoon, and see what the docs thought. Until then, there isn't much I can tell him or offer him. Sorry about that.

That finishes the clinic. Not too shabby for no clinic. We pack up the things, and carry them out to the vehicle. Here's Muntaltja with a year-old baby with "fly eye."

"You'll have to come back after the plane leaves," admonishes Fanou. "We've been here all morning, and you just come in now. You'll have to wait."

It's apparent that Muntaltja was probably afraid to come until she saw all those others coming, and by the time she'd screwed up her courage against the mamu, we were leaving. Oh well. A little Chloroptic drops will clear up the eye.

Mark is waiting for us at the house. He has the coffee pot on. Fanou is showing us the baby eagles that she rescued from a group of small boys the other day. They were using them for a game of catch, throwing the birds from one to the other.

"They didn't even have feathers then," says Fanou.

But now the little things (well, not so little really; they look about as big as a frying chicken, but with a heart shaped, white face that's outsized for the body, and looks like someone glued it on crooked) have a down of white fluff.

Carol is putting her Pavlova together. She squirts Reddi-Wip on the top, and then the peach slices from the can. It's tasty! There's a big cartwheel of cheese and bread on the table for sustenance, but it's not eaten. Jennie is there, too, and Rosa. I'd been told that Jennie was bringing the boomerangs across from Amata, but Jennie says she doesn't have them. Mark says he'll look at their craft shop. I really should have ten of them. Jennie says that they promised that they'd be on the mailplane on Tuesday for sure. Sister Carol says that when they arrive, she'll collect them and pay for them, and then I can reimburse her. They're ten for $5 each. The health worker comes in. There's a message from the radio that they want us to divert to Docker River to bring in an accident victim.

"We'll have to refuel at Ayer's Rock," says Darryl, and immediately whips out his calculator and his map and starts to figure.

Jennie passes around Dr. Lorenz's report on the medical care at the communities. It's largely a buck-passer, blaming the sisters for poor quality health care, and demanding that there should be a hospital and a doctor at each community so that they wouldn't have to send so many people away to the Alice. That's pie-in-the-sky at its political best. The people that do the work are disgusted with the report.

Mark and Darryl and I walk over to the craft shop, while the sisters finish up with the lunch things. The door is locked. No one asks me to break in today. I'll just have to depend on Jennie being sure the boomerangs get on the mailplane on Tuesday. The Toyota comes across the dusty plaza and we get in for the ride to the strip. We unload and then re-load the metal cases.

"Those are the biggest paddy melons I've ever seen!" I exclaim.

"They're not all paddy melons," says Fanou. "Those are watermelons." So they are. How they ever managed to grow like that in this poor, sandy soil is more than I can imagine.

"They won't ever get ripe," says Fanou. "The kids will make off with them before they're ready, and just play ball with them."

It's 1440 hours as FML fires up. Darryl fidgets for a while, and then FML lifts off, and Darryl points the nose at exactly 325 degrees, and climbs to 8,500 feet. Sure enough, as the plane clears the first range, Ayer's Rock is visible on the horizon. I read a little of my book. There's more haze now in the air, and things aren't nearly as crystal clear as they were on the way out.

We begin the descent. The call for traffic in the area of the rock reveals there are two tourist planes in the area. One is an Ansett Fokker Friendship; the other is a Chartair Navajo. We make our pattern. There will be no one in attendance at the fuel site, but the radio has informed Darryl to just take the numbers from the counter, and record it on the pad, and that it will be signed out later. It seems that the attendant has taken a group of tourists out for the ride in his 206 Cessna. Darryl comes in on runway one-one. He levels out about 10 feet high, and the Navajo balloons a tad, then touches down easily. Darryl is upset again.

"That's twice," he mutters to himself and me.

"It was a smooth touchdown, Darryl," I try to help.

We roll out to the pump. Darryl gets out and looks at the

machinery. There's a coach full of tourists at the fence watching the spectacle of the Royal Flying Doctors' plane doing its mission of mercy. They're taking pictures of us. I take a picture of them. Darryl is disgusted.

"I don't know how to get this thing going. We'll just have to wait until the attendant gets back."

I walk over. It's a diesel pump, not at all unlike the ones that I used to fire up for compressors for diving chambers.

"I can get it going if you'll crank it, Darryl," I offer. "I've got a bit of a crook back, and don't think I can swing the crank."

"Can you do that?" Darryl is unbelieving.

"Sure."

I check the oil level, then move the cylinders off compression. Darryl gets the flywheel turning, and I cut in the compression, and in a cloud of smoke, the generators fire up. The tourists are delighted. So is Darryl. This is getting to be a long day for him. The thirsty tanks take 328 liters of fuel. We shut down the pump engines.

Darryl gets everything in order, and we fire up and begin to move just as the attendant touches down with his happy tourists in the 206. Darryl takes off a bit downwind, but straight westward towards the Olgas. It's 1555 hours, and we're on 283 degrees. I begin to read a little, and take a picture of the Olgas. With the haze after we pass the Olgas, it's like flying over an ocean. One can look north and south, and see nothing but flat, unbroken desert, clear to the horizon, except for the few spotted rises that look like islands in the sea.

At 1635 hours we're on final for Docker River. I've got a good view of the strip and the settlement. I take some more pictures. Judy Shepard is the aboriginal patient. She's about thirty-five or so, and has been in a fight with another woman, who settled the argument with a metal pipe. It looks like a fractured left zygoma. It happened two days ago. Mary Simpson is the sister, and doesn't tell us too much about it, but is obviously happy to get Judy out of the settlement.

"You can sit anywhere you like," Carol tells Judy, "except in my chair. No one sits in my chair!" Carol is talking about the frontward facing seat.

"I lay down," says Judy, so there's no argument.

Darryl closes things up, and at 1646 hours we're off and away. It's getting towards sundown now, and the mountains are getting all purple and pink. A quick check on Judy also reveals that she's had damage to the maxillary division off the 5th cranial nerve, and a badly swollen right hand. Then the radio comes alive again. Would we return to Ayer's Rock? They have a tourist there with a fracture of the humerus. Darryl grits his teeth and changes course to 110 degrees.

There's the Olgas with long shadows leaning towards the northeast, and Ayer's Rock behind it. I take some more pictures. These are just beautiful to the human eyeball, but I wonder what they'll look like on film? The pattern here is around the south side of the rock, and then a left pattern at the strip. Darryl makes the approach. The sun is at our backs on final. That's good. If we were coming in from the other end of the strip we'd have it right in the face.

Darryl lands about ten feet high. The plane porpoises again before setting down smoothly. It's been a tough day for Darryl. I don't even try to make light conversation. We roll out and Darryl shuts down FML. Annie is the sister here at Ayer's Rock. She comes walking across the dirt with an elderly lady, whose left arm is in a sling.

It's Mrs. Jean Warren from somewhere down near Newcastle. They've been on a sixteen-day coach trip, and the following morning she was going to celebrate her seventy-second birthday. But this morning she tripped over a tent peg, and fell on her shoulder and forehead. Annie has diagnosed it as a fracture of the humerus. So be it. There's not too much bruising of the forehead. Mrs. Warren is of good spirits, but terribly disappointed in leaving the scene of her intended conquest. Actually, even though she says that she's been walking a lot of the last ten days getting into shape for the climb, this accident may well save her life.

"Take any seat you want," says sister Carol.

She can't really mean that. There's only Carol's seat and one other. But Mrs. Warren has already settled into the forward facing seat. I'm a tad incredulous as sister Carol assists with the seat belts, and then sits in the backward facing seat. What an old softie! Lots of talk about "my seat" but when the chips are down, she's a real, soft-hearted, super sister! Darryl mumbles something.

"Do you want to sit up here?" I ask Carol.

"Oh, no," she responds. "I'm perfectly comfortable here."

Darryl faces into the blazing sun on the horizon at the end of the runway two-nine. I sure hope there's no one coming down final. The radio has been quiet. Maybe he's had a better look than I did, since I was turned around talking with Carol and Mrs. Warren. Annie had also been telling me about Mary at Ernabella who is senile, and is going to need care at the Old Timers' Home. It's 1745 hours when we depart the runway at Ayer's.

"Make a circle and fly over the rock," Carol directs Darryl.

"What?"

"Do as I say," she admonishes.

Darryl puts FML in a left turn, and we cruise back around and over the rock so that Mrs. Warren can see the cairn at the top; the object probably of her entire crusade on this trip. She's absolutely delighted! That's nice. We head out on the 058 radial. It's getting darker. There's a pink glow all around the horizon, and blue over the top. I can't help but think of babies; pink for girls, blue for boys. We climb up to 9,000. I read until I can't see anymore. Periodically, I turn and interrupt Carol and Jean in their conversation, just to make sure all is well.

Jupiter comes alive in the sky as the evening star. The ground gradually fades from view. Here and there over that vast outback there are small points of light on the ground. The DME is wild; anywhere from 87 to 37 registering on the display. It's still searching. The panel lights come on. Darryl isn't saying anything, but he's nervous. The sky darkens. The pink and blue fades to an orange glow on the horizon to the north and west. Jupiter glows splendidly. There's Mars, too, and Saturn, and the stars are unfolding.

The exhaust is visible through my window on the starboard engine. It's glowing oranger than the horizon. The EGT (exhaust gas temperature) says it's 1,450 degrees Fahrenheit! It's 35 DME now, and there are the lights of the Spyce Byce. I point it out to Mrs. Warren. She's delighted!

"The rest will never see that!" she exclaims. She's very proud. "I wonder how much it's going to cost me for this," she worries. "I'm a pensioner and was pretty well strained just to make the trip in the first place."

"Don't you worry," says Carol, "AMS will help you make arrangements."

Mrs. Warren is thinking about hotel accommodations after she's released from out patient. The lights of the Alice are brilliant on the other side of the gap. Darryl makes a left hand approach for runway one-two. He follows the markers down, levels out about ten feet too high, and the plane porpoises. That must just about wreck his total day. It's 1847 hours. That is a long day.

St. John's ambulance is waiting. So is Bob Worthing. We unload. I remain in the plane with the patients until everyone is ready outside. It's been a long day. What a wonderful way to help people. I hope they gave Laura the message that I was going to be late.

20 May 1982

It's another beautiful morning as I leave the house for the airport. It's frosty this morning; no ice, but not far from it. I think the radio said It was two degrees. The sun is just making a big blush on the horizon behind the gum trees, but it isn't up yet. This morning it's Mark in charge, and sister Carol, of course, and we're taking FDQ which just returned yesterday from its total refurbishing in Perth. John has had her up already for a checkout flight, and says he's pleased with it, according to Mark.

There's been a big to-do this week. It seems that there's a West German film crew in the Alice that's doing a documentary on the RFDS/AMS, and they wanted to fly along beside us today down to Indulkana, filming the thing that the Royal Flying Doctors do, but the council down at Indulkana said no.

So, they had to find a way around that somehow, and I guess they've got Darryl and Dr. Hugh Wilson and sister Di Staples flying to Papunya to pick up some little kid with pneumonia. They'll be in FML. That sounds about par for the course. They've really picked out the movie stars true to form. I think Mark is a little disappointed. So is sister Carol, I think. She'd pooh-pooh the whole thing, but she likes to be the center of attention when possible. I'd not have minded myself, come to think about it. Oh, well, they can discover my talent later when I've matured a bit.

The Graham Pitt is really bigger than the John Hawkins by about 18 inches. They've taken out the cab insets under the floor stretcher that made it so high. Now it's a proper height for CPR anyway. And they've put in another wash basin, but again, there's no water storage facility for the tap, and the drain doesn't go anywhere. The seats are done with dark blue corduroy with gray lambskin insets. They're beautiful! They didn't put carpet on the floor, though. Just the panels with the recessed lift pins. I don't think that looks so good. She sure fires up nice, though. Mark has already done his preflight runup. The tower gives us runway three-oh, and Mark taxis down there.

"Foxtrot Delta Quebec, clear for take off; track by the 184 radial at 6,000, left turn," says the tower, and Mark advances the throttles and we leap ahead in the usual reassuring manner.

It's a takeoff away from the sun today, so I don't see the gear retract by shadow. It's a nice, clear day. I have a bad cold, and my ears are all plugged up. I have my *Scientific American* along and read most of the way down. About the S.A. border, sister Carol is there with half a cup of black coffee for me, and black with two sugars for Mark. It's good. I can't taste it very well because of my cold, but it feels nice and warm. Then we're letting down for Indulkana. Mark sets me up for a nice picture of the settlement. I'm not sure I've got a good one from this angle. Then we turn on final, and land eastbound. Marks does a smooth job, as usual.

It's Patrick waiting for us with the vehicle. "The council said that the Germans were coming down to bomb the airstrip," he tells us. "That's why they wouldn't allow them. I don't know where they got the idea that Germans bomb airstrips, but that was why they wouldn't let the film crew in."

We load the boxes and drive up the dirty street to the clinic. It's chilly this morning and there's a southeasterly wind that's stirring the dust and papers and tumbleweeds against the wire fences in the settlement. The usual aboriginals are sitting under their wicki-up shelter, but now they have dirty blankets around them to keep out the chill air. The clinic isn't very full. Mrs. Pitts is there, and she's a little peeved that we came in from the west and didn't circle Chandler to let all the folks there know that the doctor was here. No problem, I'm sure; they'll all be here soon enough.

"Don't have much of a clinic for you today," apologizes Patrick.

Jennie is up in the Alice with someone, so she won't be here today. Almost like last week in Fregon, though. As soon as they saw it was the tjilpi doctor, they start coming in. Susan is here first. She's twenty years old and delivered little Ingrid on April 18, and wants a check of the baby. Examination reveals all is well with little Ingrid, except she has a terrible case of fly eye. This is a conjunctivitis caused by the flies that are so terrible at this time of year. We'll give her a little chloromycetin eye drops, and that will clear it up. Otherwise, she's a beautiful baby. We put Susan up on the bed, too, and make sure her uterus is properly involuted. All seems to be well.

Jeannie/Purki is eleven years old, and has a sore right ear, and a pharyngitis. Not too feverish, but not feeling well. We'll put her on a bit of amoxil. Next is Maxine. Maxine is pregnant, and if you recall, about the last visit we weren't sure if there were one or two babies in there. She's had an ultrasound at the Alice, though, and it says there's just one baby. Fetal heart action was observed, and the biparietal diameter is 53 mm. Maxine was born in 1948, and is 23/52 weeks by ultrasonography, and has blood pressure of 100/70, and weighs 67.5 kg.

Then we see Noleen Bridley. Noleen has been sent down to Adelaide about a month ago to see the ophthalmologist. Noleen is from Mimili. She came back with a diagnosis of dendritic ulcers and was placed on Stoxil, chloromyx drops and predrol drops. That sounds strange for treatment of dendritic ulcers. Noleen is only seven. The doctor down there is named Searle. I've not heard of him, and don't have anything in writing, either. The folks at Mimili are just giving me the story. She has a rather fierce photophobia, and when I look in her eyes, I see strange, little, rounded densities that seem to be either within the substance of the cornea or in the anterior chamber. It's really hard to see, because she moves her eyes around and blinks or closes

them because of the photophobia. I'm a little worried, because
I really don't know what it is, but I'm sure it's not good. We'd
better take her in to the Alice with us. I understand that one of
Dr. Markman's registrars is there from Darwin right now, and
can have a look. Better than having something terrible happen
to her vision. Her Mom says, "Yes (Oh-ah)," so there's no problem
with this. They'll be waiting for us about tea time or so at their
wicki-up.

Margo has been having an infertility problem. She's just
twenty-two. But now she's having belly pain and diarrhea. It
sounds like giardiasis. She's already on Amoxil and Fasigyn.
Examination reveals no significant abnormalities. Her belly is
tender, but not that tender, and bowels are normal to active.

Do you remember Susie? We saw thirty-year-old Susie about
November or so with a rock in her right ear. She's been putting
them in there before, apparently for attention getting or something. Last time I was so disgusted that I just left it; figured it
would get really sore sooner or later, or else fall out, but that I
wasn't going to get excited about it and make her happy with her
little game. Well, it got infected behind it, I guess, and she did
end up going to the Alice, and they had to give her a general
anesthetic and make an incision behind the ear to get a leverage
from the tympanum side to push the dumb thing out. She now
complains of a sore ear again. Exam today reveals no silicon
material or precious stones; just wax. We'll use some cerumenol.

Kaylene Miller is thirty-two, 26/52, and 70.2 kg, with BP
100/80. We take her antenatal blood. Then Mabel is here. She's
forty-eight, and you saw her once before with me when she was
taking Tedral that belonged to her sister for her asthma. We decided that since it didn't seem to be hurting Mabel, and the sister
felt better while Mabel was taking the medicine, we'd let her go
ahead. Now she has an abscess on the left lateral knee. She has
a little lymphangitis there, too. Let's put her on Amoxil and take
her off the Tedral, and then after ten days we can wean her off
the Amoxil, and maybe her sister will stay well, and Mabel's
knee should be better. Right-e-o!

Now the Chandler contingent arrives. First is cute little Elizabeth Pitts. She's just back from the Alice, having been evacuated
by sister Di Staples about ten days ago for giardia. In July she'll

be two. She's just cute as can be. Rhonda says she's still complaining about her stomach. I can't find anything wrong with her. I guess we'll just leave her alone for now. She looks fine to me.

Then there's Billy. "He vomits every morning," says Rhonda with no emotion. It's kind of like she's telling me that his shoelace is untied. I look him over. His belly is soft, and he has no hernia. I don't even try to reassure Rhonda. I don't think that's what she wants, anyway.

"Did Bill get the job with the railroad down south?" I ask nonchalantly.

"No, I don't think that's going to come through," she says, haltingly. So, that's the trouble with the kids. They're still going to have to put up with parents that hate Chandler, but have no place else to go to work.

Then we see little Adam Parkinson. He's two this month. "He needs a check-up," says his Mom.

"The notes say that the last one was in January," I remind her.

"See, I knew it had been a long time," says his Mom. Really, I don't think there's too many communities in the world where you'd take your child every four months for a check-up, but then, there's not much else to do in Chandler.

Kym Borke is next. "He had a fever of 39.5 last night," his Mom tells me. He looks fine today. No fever, either. Another reason for a Chandler Mom to see the doc, though.

Cathie Manapol is thirty-one, and has a wog (flu) that has nausea and vertigo as it's major complaints. We'll just treat her symptomatically for now. She has no fever. We also look at her son, Adrian, who is also two this month. He had a dose of Fasigyn yesterday for worms. He seems fine today. The clinic is quiet. I've run the clinic without having my own red stethoscope. Someone has copped it from the equipment case. The ones that Patrick has aren't as good. But, we've made do, and the clinic seems to be over. We close up the cases.

"We'll have some tea at my house," says Patrick.

The workmen have arrived from down south to put the clinic in order with repairs. Every so often it seems that the government decides to update the facilities, and a crew comes up from down south to do the work. They move right in, and apparently there's some sort of union agreement that there're no disputes, so an electrician can put in a light globe instead of waiting for a maintenance union worker to do it, and a plumber can cut a hole for a pipe fitting without waiting for a carpenter, and that sort of thing. They've really been going at it this week, according to Patrick. That's nice to know that the Australian labor unions can get along sometimes.

As we unload the cases into the Toyota, the bus from the south comes up the hill and into the town just ahead of a blowing cloud of dust and dirty debris. It stops at the store, directly across from the clinic. It's fun to watch the tourists on the bus aiming their cameras through the windows at the aboriginals lolling in the protection of whatever there is to keep the wind off them. Probably no more than three minutes and the bus is underway in another swirling cloud of cold, bleak dust.

Patrick does have a proper house. It was originally built for the inspectors who would come up from Adelaide on a regular, like quarterly, inspection of the settlement. Then the inspections got less frequent, and less regular, and finally they stopped all together, and the house has been vacant for about two years. Patrick and Jennie asked for it, because they have Jennie's two grown daughters by a previous marriage living with them. It's a nice house, by Indulkana standards. Patrick has it decorated with his batiks, wall hangings, and his books and cassette tapes. I don't know what the tapes contain. The tea is good, what with my plugged nose and hoarse voice.

Olive, the cat, has gone bush again. Remember Olive? She's disappeared again. Mitzou, the dog, is still here and still affectionate, and now Patrick and Jennie have two German shepard puppies. Huge feet! Frisky enough to make shambles out the ordinary home. The talk is mostly medical political. Patrick really doesn't think a lot of Dr. Trevor Lorenz. It seems that after making his $10,000 report, Dr. Lorenz has named himself to the $50,000 a year post as medical director of the settlement of Indulkana. How about that?

Patrick implies that Trevor had paid the aboriginal council to have his initiation rite performed; and that anyone who would pay to have his genitals mutilated can't have everything altogether upstairs. It's obvious that Patrick doesn't think very much of Dr. Lorenz, or the medical politics of the situation. There's other talk of Tanya from Chandler and PCIS (Parent Child In-compatibility Syndrome), or there's another name for it now; somebody's syndrome, no less, or child abuse—whatever. There's talk about the baby twice being left on the table in the hospital and falling off onto the floor. So far, no damage, but how long can one be that lucky? Then, the burns on the little chest. Patrick is sure they represent cigarette burns. The child is about two. I didn't see him today. They sure don't care for Tanya.

Time to go. Back down the wind-whipped, dusty, filthy street. The same aboriginals are huddled out of the wind in their blankets beside the store. Into the Toyota, and down to the strip. First to stop by and pick up Noleen and her Mom. It's a house that they live in, but it's been destroyed. The house is just a shell that they keep things in to protect them from the elements. The family really lives outside in the V of two wrecked automobiles that are resting on their tops. A battered stereo cassette player lies smashed on the chassis of one of the cars, apparently having seen its best days some time in the past. The bedrolls are lying on the perimeter of a fire pit, maybe seven feet on a side. No wonder some of these kids get those terrible burns. If you roll off the bedroll, you roll right down into the fire pit. Sheesh! There must be a better way.

"You all set?" Carol queries Noleen's Mom.

"Oh-ah."

"You have money?"

"Oh-ah." They pile into the Toyota. Noleen's Mom has a plastic bag for her travel case, and, I suppose, for Noleen, too. It's not a very big bag.

The gallahs are holding the airport when we arrive. Huge clouds of them, squawking and arguing, but they're beautiful. They're a parrot-type bird. I don't know just where you'd classify them, but they are really intelligent birds; or seem to be. They have a human way of community spirit. They're gray-white on top, and with brilliant, reddish breasts. We load the airplane. Mark makes sure the passengers are all settled, then fires up the engines. The circus is leaving the town. I didn't see that when we were there. They must have been there this last week. On the

sides of the trucks that are passing on the road to Chandler are
five or six trucks with letters saying *CARNIVAL*. My gosh! What
would the aboriginals do with a carnival in town, and not a West
German photo crew? Wouldn't that have made a story for the
photo crew?

FDQ roars down the runway, and Mark has a clearance for
3,000 feet. That's MSL (mean sea level), so for us it's just about
a thousand feet above the ground. There's a big cloud of dust on
the track below heading north, and quite a ways ahead. As we
pass, it's the bus; the same bus that was leaving town when we
went for tea. It's terribly bumpy at this altitude. Noleen is screaming with fright and clinging to her Mom with white knuckles.
She's not been in a plane before. It must be frightening for her.
I go back to my reading.

An hour later, we're putting down at the Alice. Noleen is
quiet by now. What's this? It's FML with Sister Di cleaning out
the interior with her bucket and sponge. It seems the child with
pneumonia spewed vomit all over the thing. Not too exciting to
put into a documentary. And what's this? It's Dr. Hugh Wilson
with *my* red stethoscope slung over his neck, like a real pro. I
guess it is more photogenic than a black one, at that. I wonder
if I'll ever see the documentary?

27 May 1982

This morning on the way to the airport, I note that there's
a cloud line to the south. It looks almost like a ridge of mountains
way out there, but there are a few little bumps on them that
suggest that they're cumulus instead of stratus. Well, it's still a
beautiful morning; crisp and cool, but sunny. Mark is there, and
he's taking FML to Papunya. Nervous Darryl is also there, and
we're going to be taking FDQ. A little politics this morning. It
seems the federal minister, Mr. Wilson, is touring the settlements
to get firsthand knowledge of his "portfolio." I'll bet he gets a

surprise or two for his interest. I wonder if, perhaps, the council at Indulkana will refuse him permission to visit the settlement? Sister Carol is her usual effervescent self, as she busily stores things on board.

It's just 0800 when Darryl fires up the engines. The tower gives us permission to line up on runway three-zero, and then relays, "Foxtrot Delta Quebec, clear for take off. Fly the Alice two-oh-seven radial at 8,000. Left turn."

Darryl advances the throttles after running his finger over every instrument and button in the cockpit. Then he pushes them some more. I wonder what would happen if, someday when he's pushing like that, the dumb things broke off in his hand? The Ansett Friendship for Ayer's Rock is sitting on the taxi way waiting for us to go by. We retract the gear just as we come abreast of him. At 6,000 it's ten degrees on the OAT (outside air temperature). At 75 miles DME we're just under the front line of those clouds that I'd seen before. They're perhaps 1,500 feet above us yet, and there are wisps of rain coming from them that ping off the windscreen. I've got my AFP (*American Family Practice*) continuing medical education lesson that I'm doing, so don't see that much of the outside.

Darryl seems content to fiddle with things in the cockpit, and when we get to the Ayer's Rock Road, sister Carol serves us our usual coffee. That tastes good! It's clear under the clouds. Ayer's Rock and the Olgas and Mt. Connor all line up just about the time we start our descent at the S.A. border. Darryl makes a swing over the settlement. There's still quite a bit of water in that creek. The clouds to the north that we've just come under are all pink and orange away up there. That's really beautiful!

Julie meets us. There's the usual banter about things at the settlement. I guess there's a new sister at Amata; a young thing, just six weeks out of England; a real "Pohme!" (An acronym for "prisoner of Her Majesty's Empire," I've been told.) Poor thing! I'll bet she's been surprised by the kind of medicine she's obliged to practice! At the clinic, Purki gives me a warm greeting. She's still appreciative of my efforts for her and her daughter. I guess I don't give her as much attention as I should have. I was preoccupied with other things. I'll have to make that up to her next time I'm out. But now it's time for the first patient.

It's Beverly, and she's 24/52 weeks pregnant, and her birth date is 17 March 1968. That's right. She's just two months past fourteen years old! She's 61 kg, 120/80, and looks happy as a clam. We draw blood from her. The fetal heart tones are normal at 138/minute. Then poor, old Mary. She has gentian violet painted on her lower lip. She's also looking at me with a left eye that has an opaque cornea. She's to have a physical for entrance into the Old Timers' Home in the Alice. I look closer at that left eye. There seems to be a hole in the superior portion off the iris, as though she's had an iridectomy for something. But I can't really see all that well because of terrible corneal scarring. The right eye socket is covered with skin. The lids are stuck together. There's no globe there at all, just an empty socket. Otherwise, Mary is a classic, old aboriginal lady. She's about seventy years old, I'd guess. Blood pressure is 122/82, and I really can't find anything much else the matter. She tells me that she can see some light through that left eye. So be it!

Remember Charley and Nancy Chooka? They rode down with us to Ernabella from the Alice in the April 29. Well, they tell me that they eventually went back on the mailplane. Now, the mailplane is usually just a Cessna 182 with a pod slung under the fuselage. It's difficult to imagine how Charley, with all his bulk, could possible get squeezed into the backseat of that plane. But the funny part of the story is that when he and Nancy got aboard, they had a tin with them that used to hold powdered milk, but empty. When asked what on earth they wanted that for, Charley replied, "for compo." He was going to use it for a urinal. That would have taken a real contortionist in the backseat of a 182, let alone someone with Charley's bulk.

Jason was born on 1 March 1982. Julie is worried about him. "He has white spots on his throat that almost look like pieces of bread," says Julie.

Examination of Jason reveals that he does have a conjunctivitis of the right eye that is giving him a bit of proptosis, but otherwise I can't find anything wrong with him. He's not even febrile. But he sure can yowl when I keep poking that tongue depressor into the back of his throat to make him gag so I can see the posterior pharynx.

"I thought it might be diphtheria," says Julie.

"Gee, Julie, I don't think so. He'd be a lot sicker than this if he had that."

Poor Julie. Maybe she's been out here too long. Wendy Plane is the next patient. Wendy is 34/52, 62 kg, 110/70, FHH 136/minute. She's a reasonable twenty-six-year-old, and she's had mitral valve disease in the past. The murmur is unchanged, and she says she feels fine. Tjinkuma is 34/52 weeks, with a really big tummy, 72 kg, and 118/80. Julie's worried about the big tummy because back in 1970, Tjinkuma miscarried with triplets. No, I only find one fetus in here, and his fetal heart sounds are at 148/minute, and he's ROA (right occiput anterior) presentation.

Makinti is twenty-five, and we were worried about her having more than one in the hopper last time we saw her. But now that she's had ultrasonography at the Alice, we're aware that there's only one fetus and that on May 7, biparietal diameter said gestation was twenty-eight weeks. Well, clinically, she's thirty-six weeks along, and I suggested that about a week from Tuesday they send her in on the mailplane, unless they'd like to deliver her themselves.

Here's poor, little Gregory. He's not able to hold his head up, although he's a year old on the twenty-sixth of this month. He's a post H. flu meningitis, and has seizures and is taking 20 mg of phenobarbital a day or so. He's also has his testes up in his canal, but there's no apparent hernia. He's just going to have a tough time in this life. Next is Dick. Dick says he's a doctor. He well might be, too. He's about seventy years old, I'd guess. He has pain in his chest and into his right arm, or he did have it there when he was walking across from Amata. It's gone now. You've met Dick before, too. He has the big, left inguinal hernia that he's so proud of. Dick's pressure is 130/84, and he has a regular rhythm and no rubs, and the lungs are clear. Maybe he does have angina. Next time he has pain, give him a little sublingual nitroglycerine, and see if the pain goes away. If it doesn't and he gets a headache, it's not angina.

Malpiya is forty-five and has throat pain, just along the course of the left mandible. But I can't find anything either inside or outside that would cause that. I don't know what it is. The rest of her exam is negative. I guess we'll just have to treat her with aspirin or Panadol or whatever when she complains, and keep looking for the cause. Sharen Troy is here for her check-up. She's a European baby, born 22 May 1981, so just a year old. She looks great, and Mom is reassured. Would you believe? That's the end of the clinic.

So, we pack things up and make our way over to Julie's. Sister Carol has a number of items that she wants me to look at, so over a cup of coffee and the pound cake with pink frosting, I look at reports on Colin, who was seen by me on 10 December 1981 for neck pain. He's had this for a long time, apparently from a trampoline injury a long time ago. He's been seen by Dr. Parke, whose writing is illegible. On February 18, it seems, the diagnosis was entrapment neuropathy, or that's what it looks like he's written. His hospital number is 2672 if I want to look at his films. The report says that there's a narrowing of the C—3 and C—4 foraminae bilaterally. His aboriginal name is Pintjuanta, and he's from Fregon, and his mother's name is Mutjiwa, and he's about twenty-five years old now. He's apparently still in pain. He's had some brufen. Would cervical traction help?

Then there's the paperwork yet on poor, old Jackie and his wife who have been trying to get into the Old Timers' for so long. It seems that they were told that they had to have an admission to the hospital and evaluation first, and then they could get into the home, but there haven't been any beds available at the hospital for that kind of examination, so they're still waiting around. Poor, old things. I can't help but wonder if Mr. Wilson, the federal minister, will hear about things like that?

Time to go. Back to the airstrip and load the metal cases aboard. It's not all that late, only abut 1315 hours. It will be nice to get home a bit early. Darryl meticulously checks out everything in the cockpit, and we fire up. The taxi to the end of the strip, and he's opted to take off downwind directly towards the Alice rather than take off against, and have to make a 180° turn. It's a fair wind, too; maybe 6 to 7 knots. FDQ has no problem, and we're airborne with lots of strip left.

The radio comes alive, "FDQ, we have a burn for evacuation at Mt. Ebenezer. Can you divert that way?"

Darryl gets his computer out of its case, and his map, and assures them that we can get there. It hasn't been raining for a couple of weeks. That strip should be well dried out by now. I sure do remember the last time we were in there, though. He sets up 300 degrees on the compass, and I go back to my reading. Then, put it away, as I'm aware that Darryl is scanning the horizon like a radar gone amok. We're just about at the lakes, and nothing really looks familiar out there. There's still cloud cover above us, and periodically, the drumming tattoo of rain on the windscreen. I see some buildings just beyond the lakes.

"There it is," I tell him.

But when we reach there, it's a station, not Mt. Ebenezer. Darryl turns westward, following the Ayer's Rock road. We know we'll find it, 'cause there's no other bitumen road within a hundred miles, and Mt. Ebenezer is on the bitumen road. There's the mountains now that look familiar. We'd drifted almost 40 miles to the east of our intended course.

Darryl descends. There's Ebenezer. A bit of flaps to take off some airspeed, and the gear is down. The landing is smooth, and the strip is just as firm as a board. Good! Darryl taxis up to the Toyota and shuts down.

There's a number of unhappy aboriginals around the Toyota. I get out and look at Cyril. He's about fifteen years old, and is lying on a dirty mattress in the back of the Toyota. He has on a dirty pair of jeans, but the skin on his back is hanging in black strips, with oozing areas of bright pink showing through. The burn extends all the way around on the left side almost to the midline. His left arm is also burned; the extensor side. I'd guess he's got about a ten percent total body burn here. Below the top of the jeans, the burn continues over his buttocks. He's going to be in real trouble. It happened just a couple hours ago, so he's apparently still in shock. He walks to the plane and lies on the stretcher, prone. He says he's not in pain. Sister Carol feels badly that he doesn't want anything for the pain.

She asks me.

"No, let's wait until we get airborne and see if he gets into pain. He's going to have enough pain medicine for a horse before he gets over this episode."

Darryl fires up the engines. This time when we take off from Ebenezer, there's no soft spots to scare me, and FDQ lifts off easily, and we're about 300 feet in the air by the time we pass over the wattles that we flew between on the last trip here.

The remainder of the trip is uneventful. Cyril never does complain of pain. Sister Carol is really soft hearted. She pampers him and takes his pulse and just clucks and coos at him like a mother hen. She's what everyone has in mind when he thinks of the typical sister of the Aeromedical Service of the Royal Flying Doctors.

3 June 1982

A bit of an epilogue on Cyril that I thought you might find interesting. I made rounds on Saturday morning and discovered that Cyril had "nicked off" on Friday, burned back and all. Apparently he went to find friends down in the Todd River. The hospital appealed to the aboriginal council in town, and shortly, they had found Cyril. They had just brought him back to the hospital when I was making rounds. They had him in the ICU (Intensive Care Unit) area, in the whirlpool tubs, but they said that Cyril wouldn't get into the tub.

Sister took me down there, and on opening the door to the tub room, there was Cyril standing naked in the middle of the floor, with his hands tightly clasped over his genitals, and a look of bewilderment on his face. I felt sorry for him at the same time as relieved that he was there. A nurse's aide stood about fifteen feet from him, properly gowned and masked for the debridement that she would carry out on the burns once Cyril got into the tub. He couldn't imagine anything more embarrassing than to have a woman clean his naked body.

"Cyril, the burn has to be washed. Do you remember me?"

Cyril nodded his head affirmatively.

"Cyril, get into the tub and let sister do what has to be done."

Cyril looked at me with big, pleading eyes, but gray hair, a generation removed, as old as your mother's brother, and that's a pretty powerful place to be in the aboriginal culture! Cyril caved in to my authority, and gingerly settled into the tub, and I left. That's what makes this story fun. I'll let you know for sure the next time I run into Cyril.

The third of June is clear and cold again. It's John and sister

Carol again in the Graham Pitt. Dr. Bell is just leaving in the Baron for someplace. Darryl is flying him. John is wearing the earphones, so I don't hear the tower conversation as we fire up and taxi out to runway three-oh. It's two degrees Celsius outside this morning. It's 0815 hours. I had wakened with a small balloon from my kidney stones this morning and taken a Talwin about 0645. I'm not in too much distress right now, but there is a fullness in my right flank, and over the crest of my right ilium. Not enough to really make me distressed, but the threat is there.

John advances the throttles, and FDQ races down the runway. John comes back on the wheel just a little, and slowly the nose wheel rises, and the plane flies itself off the ground. I've forgotten to bring anything to read, so will have to just watch the ground this morning. The Spyce Byce slips by on the starboard wing, the cattle ponds to the southwest of the base are outlined by the shadows of the wattles, all long and pointing in the same southwesterly direction, like strokes from a paint brush. A curious movement catches my eye. Across the mirror face of the cattle pond just below and to the right, a shadow whisks. Then another. But there are no clouds. Then I see them, rising from the eastern edge of the pond. It's like the pond is steaming, but I don't really see the steam. I see the shadow of steam. I look carefully to see if there's a fire on the bank of the pond. No, that's not it. The pond is steaming. Maybe it's that the water coming from the ground into the pond is warmer than two degrees, and is condensing. It looks weird. But then, it was only a fleeting glance, and it's gone below the wing. The other pond is too far away to see the reflection that well. That's strange.

At 0830 sister Carol is offering us our coffee. I slip a Tylenol out of my back pocket, and swallow it after I make sure the coffee won't scald me. It's fun watching the ground. Just like the pond, cattle standing on the ground are identified by their long shadows rather than by actually seeing them first. One can follow the shadow back and then spot the steer, but the shadows subtend a much greater visual arc than the animal alone. No "roos" are seen. We cross the Hugh and the Finke Rivers, and then the road that Laura and I drove to Wallera Ranch and King's Canyon only a week and half ago. It sure doesn't look like much of a road from up here.

John points out the location of Palm Valley far to the northwest of where we are. And there's Mt. Connor, straight ahead, and Ayer's Rock and the Olgas off to the right a bit more. It still seems curious how Mt. Connor is sitting in a rocky saucer, tilted so that the western edge rises and the eastern edge sinks, but a saucer all the same. There's cirrus cover at 80 DME, and the temperature at 8,000 feet is eight degrees; warmer up here than it is on the ground. As we pass Mt. Connor, the cirrus cover changes to scattered alto stratus. John starts the descent. I wonder how many "sacred sites" I'm looking at. John puts down a bit of flaps, and then the gear, and we sweep in for our approach. A fair wind right down the pipe this morning, and John sets FDQ down as softly as a fluff of down on a peach skin.

It's Jennie that meets us with the Toyota. The new sister is here now, Feona Vorne, and she's a bright Pohme only three weeks out of England—page boy hairdo, beautiful black hair, and polished nails, and such a contrast to Jennie, who has been weathered by seven years out here in the bush taking care of aboriginals. Well, we'll see if Feona weathers or caves in the next few weeks.

The working crew has been through, and the hospital is brightly painted with new white paint with brown trim. It almost looks like a brand new building. The little washroom adjacent to the examining room has its stainless steel sink just glistening! But it's cold. Jennie has the little gas floor heater lighted, and the electric heater element on the wall is glowing cheerily. We'll see the first patient.

With that thought, the power goes off, but we still have the little gas heater for warmth. Sandra, born in 1965, 57 kg, 116/40, 36/52, although her notes say that she's twenty-eight weeks along. I think we'd better move her in to the Alice in the next couple of weeks. First I've warmed my hands at the little gas heater, though. I wouldn't want to put my cold hands on Sandra's warm tummy. Heart sounds of the fetus are strong at 140/minute.

Sally Mullen is European, nine years old, and Sally is going to be going to Adelaide to see Dr. Tally. Sally has external ear pinnae like Dumbo; they literally stick straight out from her head, and are of most generous size. She's starting to take some rubbing from her peers about the ears, and she can't wear her hair back in a ponytail because she looks like she's ready to take off if there's a wind blowing. Poor thing. We sign her IPTAS form (Isolated Patient Travel and Accommodation Service). That will reimburse both her and her Mom for the airfare to Adelaide. Also, her pubic rash is back. We'd treated it as a monilia before, but Mom said that it just flared up, and that the cortisone cream seemed to be best for it. Let's try a little micatin. I brought that tube down with me a couple of weeks ago. Let's see if that will make it better.

It's 1000 hours. I'm squirming in my seat with discomfort in my right flank and groin. "Jennie, can I have just a little drinking water? Just enough to wash down a pill with?"

"Are you all right?" scolds sister Carol in a high voice.

"Oh, sure. I just don't want to let it get ahead of me. I'm fine!"

Carol looks at me with a skeptical eye. Jennie brings the water. Down with a Talwin. Back to the patients. Sammy is thirty. A number of years ago his horse got tangled up in some fence wire, and Sammy took a bad spill, apparently fracturing his clavicle, according to the history. Now it's hurting. Examination reveals perfectly symmetrical clavicles, with good muscles and no limitation of motion at the shoulder. I don't know what he's got, but maybe some Indocin will help it.

Then comes fifteen-year-old Jonathan. He's running a temperature of thirty-nine degrees celsius. That's pretty hot! No other complaints. I do a screening physical on him. ENT is clear. His chest is clear. He has no cervical nodes. His belly is soft with normal bowel sounds. What's this? He has a bandage on his right leg. It's filthy dirty, and soaked through with pus. Unwrap it. There's a vesicular, purulent area about three centimeters in diameter over the right shin, about mid leg, with swelling all around, but no tenderness over the groin or along the saphenous vein. That's his problem. No telling if it's really deep, or if there's a foreign body in there. I don't think so. We take a culture. Let's give him a Bicillin now, and again on Saturday, and meantime give him Amoxil, 250 mg three times a day as often as he'll come in for it.

Yuminia is next. You've met her before. She's hypertensive, and I wasn't sure if the inderal and HCTZ that she was taking would hold it. We had discussed giving her some Apresoline if she continued with diastolic over one hundred. Jennie says she's been at 136/80 or so since I left. I take the pressure. It's 210/122! I take it again, and I still get a level over 200 systolic and over 120 diastolic. I put Jennie's cuff on Yuminia. 142/82. Oh-Oh, there's something wrong with Jennie's cuff. She has a new one. It's one of those kind that people can use for taking their own pressure. Let's see what that shows. I take Yuminia's pressure. I can't hear anything at all. Let's take sister Carol's pressure. Yuminia stalks out of the examining room. As far as she's concerned, we're wasting her time. Jennie is upset.

"That's all right, Jennie. Just continue to give her the 140 Inderal bds, and the clotride, 500 mg daily, and if the diastolic stays there above 110, go ahead and add the Apresoline," I tell her.

"And here, you take our sphygmomanometer, and I'll take yours back in with us, and have it fixed," offers Carol.

That's nice. Jennie's eyes brim up with tears. "She has no right to be that way."

I guess Yuminia has given Jennie lots of trouble in the past with demanding.

Next comes fifty-four-year-old Harry. Harry has a toothache. He shows me his left upper central incisor. There's terrible periodontal disease here. The dentine of the tooth is showing at the margin of the receded gum line.

"Loose, too," announces Harry proudly, pointing to his lower teeth.

I put my finger on them. They are all loose as swamp reeds in a high wind!

"Harry, I can't treat you for that. It's going to take a specialist to save those teeth. We'll have to send you first in to Alice Springs to see the general dentist, and then he'll have to send you on to Adelaide to a real specialist to save the teeth. You're too young to have no teeth."

To Harry, I'm sure this is the height of the white man's stupidity. Why doesn't he go directly to the specialist in Adelaide? Harry's right, of course. Indeed, why not, but that isn't the way it's done.

"That's another thing," says Jennie. "There's money allocated for dental clinics every year; lots of money! There hasn't been a dentist through here in the last two years. The money is going into someone's pocket!"

We make plans for Harry to get to the Alice.

"I'll drive my car," he advises us in perfect English. Harry's got it all together!

Iris is supposed to be pregnant. She's fifteen. Her test is positive, but I can't feel a fundus. I guess we'll just watch her. I don't think I'll take blood this trip. Reva was born September 10 last year. Reva has been doing well until a month ago, when suddenly she stopped growing, and lost from 8.6 kg to 7.2! No apparent illness. Not even a fever, but something is sure going on. Malabsorption? Parasites? Then I remember what Dr. John Martins, the pediatrician at the Alice, told me some time ago; when the kid suddenly loses weight and starts off the percent chart for height and weight, it's a urinary tract infection. These kids have a more than average (genetic?) incidence of ureteral reflux with infection. They need gu (genito-urinary) work-ups when this happens, and if reflux is demonstrated, they must have correction of the problem or they'll die.

"We'd better take her in with us. Will you go to the Alice, Malpiya?" asks Jennie.

"Oh-ah," says Malpiya, and that's settled.

"We'll pick you up after noon tea here at the clinic," says Jennie.

Next is Claire. Claire is from Warburton settlement, well out into Western Australia, and said to be a tinder box of racial tension. She's got a headache and swollen glands on her left neck, and a festering, five-centimeter laceration of the left scalp. Someone's taken a "nulla-nulla" to her in the past and done her some damage. Examination reveals the fundi clear with no papilledema, and no blood in her ears. I guess we'll clean up the wound, put a drain down in there, and give her Amoxil, 250 mg three times a day. Claire is twenty-nine years old.

Ngantinja is fifty-two. "She's a real forward thinker," says sister Carol.

Ngantinja is one of that breed of aboriginal that makes the Europeans think that maybe, somewhere down the pike, there's hope for this race to take its place in the modern world. She has empathy for others in distress. She can count to more than two, and she was the first aboriginal woman to come in to the Alice hospital to have her baby. That was back in 1960, and it was quite a landmark. Ngantinja has a lot of pain in her low back, particularly around the left sacro-iliac joint. She's had a work-up for this some time ago, and she has marked degenerative disease of the spine. She also has some sort of belly ache, so we lay her on the bed and feel the belly. It's a strange belly. There's a long, transverse scar, side to side, that's well healed, and according to the notes, was put there to correct an old umbilical hernia. But they've taken away the belly button. There's not a sign of it! She looks like Eve! I don't find anything in her belly. Jennie mentions Claire to Ngantinja. Ngantinja is sympathetic.

"I remember when I was eleven years old, seeing my first white man," says Ngantinja.

I'm amazed! I thought that the takeover by the white man was some sixty or so years ago. Not so! It was only about forty years ago. Then come out some stories about the "pink flour." It seems that the white man would bring in flour for the aboriginals to make their damper from, and it would be laced with poison. There would be whole tribes wiped out by poison.

"I can't believe that. Forty years ago?"

"That's right. And I remember my mother telling me about the fellow who found the big pile of skeletons. Apparently a whole tribe had been rounded up and summarily executed by the white man with guns. And it's still going on. Warburton is a bad place. So is the area to the northeast of the Alice in the Hartz range," insists Ngantinja.

No wonder there's so much tension with the aboriginal people. No wonder they feel "ripped off." It hasn't been that long ago that they were being purged. Surely the black man is as sensitive as the dingo, and look how wary they are of man! Let's give Ngantinja some Indocin and see if we can make her feel better. I feel like I've been exposed to a really filthy experience in what I've just heard. I suppose I should take it with a grain of salt. But then . . .

Karina is eighteen. She's 74.5 kg, 110/54, 24/52, FHH 132/minute. She's fine.

"Now I want you to see Ungakina," says Jennie. "She's down in the hospital. You saw here when you were here, and she had a stroke, and you thought it might be tabes dorsalis, but it was a stroke, and she's come along quite well, but two weeks ago she fell into the fire one night, and her dress caught fire, and she's taken a rather bad burn on her buttocks and legs."

We march down the hall to the hospital. Some health workers stop us on the way. It seems that someone has decided to give Ungakina a bath! Jennie unlocks the bathroom, and sure enough; there are two health workers standing beside the trapezoidal tub, lots of lather, and this classic, sunken-eyed face with the sparse, gray hair that is tumbled with suds. They're washing her with Ajax cleanser; the blue kind that has hypochlorite in it! My God, that must burn! But Ungakina seems happy as a clam, albeit, a bit embarrassed at being naked in front of the tjilpi doctor.

"Let me see your burn," I request.

She laughs, coyly, but with a lot of extra motion, seizes the rails for support on the wall by the tub, and with the assistance of the health workers, gets to her knees. She has the classic hyperlordotic curve to the back, with the steatopygia of the buttocks, but the left one is white with the cleaned burn, an area of about 30 by 25 cm, and her right buttock also has a burn about 15 by 10 centimeters. It looks clean. The bath water would be suitable for planting rice! I can't imagine that all that mud could have come from this lady! It's chocolate brown mud, a layer about a quarter inch deep on the bottom of the tub!

"What are you using on it?" I ask Jennie.

Jennie is terribly upset. She can hardly speak. She's so angry with the health workers for giving Ungakina a bath when she wanted to have the doctor see her in bed!

"SSD cream, but I don't have her on any antibiotic by mouth," says Jennie.

"Gee, she looks good, though," I repeat.

It's amazing how these people seem to respond to medicine. I guess it's because there are so few germs about the settlement that have been exposed to antibiotics.

"You're doing fine, Jennie," I persist. But Jennie is fighting inside herself, and the tears well up and brim over.

"I just can't take it anymore. I've worked so hard with these people, and they have no feeling at all about the effort I've put in," she weeps.

"Come on, Jennie, they really do appreciate it, and remember, a lot of the compensation for what you do here lies right between your own ears. You know what you're doing."

"It's not the compensation that matters," she sobs. Poor Jennie. What does one say? "It's also Dr. Barker. Mr. Carter came up with a terrible statement on the phone, and then a letter, and he blames all the problems out here on the inefficiency of the sisters, and their lack of care for the people."

Jennie has been caught up in the politics again. That's too bad. If the politicians keep this kind of thing up, there soon won't be anyone out here at all except the black man and the red sand, and the sun.

"There's no one else for the clinic," says sister Carol. "Let's pack up and go have some tea."

At Jennie's we have some gingerbread and some home-made bread from Fregon, and a cup of hot tea. Jennie has settled down, but the wound is still there. Feona joins us, eating daintily with her polished nails and soft, white hands, and shimmering black hair in the page boy style. Sister Carol is taking a holiday in July, and intends to drive her little red car to Perth. But not the usual way to Perth! She's going to go through Ayer's Rock and to Docker River, and to Warburton, and then on down to pick up the bitumen north of Kalgoorlie!

"It will cut off two thousand kilometers from the usual way," says Carol. "But I'm going to pick up a friend of mine, one of the health workers, at Docker River to ride with me. I don't want to be in Warburton alone. Better to have an aboriginal friend with me."

I don't know. That sounds dangerous to me. But you can bet if Carol wants to do it, she'll do it!

It's time to go. Malpiya and Reva are waiting at the clinic. Out to the strip. There's a Cherokee Warrior sitting there with a man in it.

"Who's that?" questions sister Carol

"I don't know. I've never seen him before," says Jennie.

The Warrior fires up as we load our cases. John settles things into FDQ and we taxi out. The Warrior has disappeared after takeoff. John advances the throttles, and we're off, too.

John has contact with the Warrior. He's at 7,500 feet. We'll stay at 7,000 feet until we see him. It's funny how your eyes play tricks on you. You just know that there's a great big airplane right in front of you, but you can't see him. John spots him first, and he's really not that far away. Amazing how your eyes can miss something like that. I think of all the hawks that we've flown by at four to six thousand feet. "Surfing," is the word I use, because if they weren't just having fun riding the thermals there wouldn't be any reason for them to be away up there. We pass the Cherokee, and climb to our 9,000 feet, and I watch the ground the rest of the way along. The cirrus has stretched all the way to the Alice now. Reva is quiet. St. John's ambulance people are there waiting for Reva. It's been a lovely day. There sure is going to be a decision day somewhere in the future for Australia. There has to be a melding of these cultures before civilization can carry on. It's probably going to be a violent melding when it comes.

10 June 1982

It's a fine morning with a few scattered alto cumulus off to the north and east, catching the rising sun with orange and pink borders. It's cool, but not cold this morning. A fine day to fly to Fregon. About the time that I'm ready to leave the house, the phone rings. It's our neighbor, who has a four-and-a-half-year-old daughter with chronic chest disease. Actually, I've not seen the child except as a neighbor. She's been under the care of a pediatrician, but this morning her Mom would like me to see her because she has a fever and needs an antibiotic. Laura explains to her that the child should really have a throat culture done prior to starting an antibiotic, particularly since she is complaining of a sore throat and cough. Laura explains further, that this could probably be done at the health clinic even in my absence; that one of the sisters could do this. The child's Mom isn't very happy with the advice, but then, I've got to be at the airport for the 0800 takeoff, too, and adding up the cost of the plane, the pilot's salary, and that of the sister, there's quite a costly venture that is scheduled to get under way, and if I start making morning house calls on the days that I fly, I could really mess up a lot of people, both here and at the settlement where I'm going. No, I think Laura has given good advice. The child can be seen by her own doctor or by the health clinic. And I depart. Funny, though, I don't really feel good about it.

Mark is pre-flighting FML this morning. Margaret, his fiancee, is sitting in her little car, waiting for Mark to finish the preliminary work. They're going to be married this next month, and have signed up for a honeymoon in China. Mark is pretty excited about it. He has it all laid out. I hope Margaret goes along with him. Sister Carol arrives driving her own little Chrysler; a red jobby with a hatchback. It's cute, but hardly the car to drive across the Western Australia desert, I think.

Mark shuts down FML, and we load the metal cases.

"Did you hear the good news this morning?" Carol asks. "The aboriginal minister is saying that the Royal Flying Doctors aren't giving good service to the aboriginal community. I almost choked! Did you know that the Rev. John Flynn was a bit of a racist himself? The Mantle of Safety was never designed for the aboriginal. It's supposed to be a service to the Europeans on the remote stations and their people. And now they've turned the whole thing around as though it had always been for the black people. Politics!" she snorts in disgust.

I just soak up the conversation and will relay it to you like I'm hearing it, and without comment. It's been interesting sorting out what's politics, and what's really in the interest of aboriginal people. More politics, me thinks, than interest. I take the right front seat.

The tower answers Mark with, "Foxtrot Mike Lima, track the Alice 204 radial at 6,000, hold west of the Stuart Highway," and we taxi down to three-oh, and the throttles advance and we lift off at the taxiway intersection.

The same stock ponds are there as last week, but they're not steaming today. There's other traffic in our area, and the tower keeps us separated with changes in altitude and direction until about 15 DME, and then we're cleared to 8,000 for the trip to Fregon. I have the proceedings of the annual meeting of the Undersea Medical Society along today to read, and become engrossed in this. Mark is talking with Carol, who produces the standard half-cup black for me. Mark has everything trimmed out, and leaves his seat to go back into the cabin to talk with Carol. That's a funny feeling. FML keeps right on track, but there's no one in that left front seat. It really doesn't bother me, but I can imagine that a non-flyer might be really upset with that empty seat.

There's kind of a dirty layer of haze on the horizon, but it goes all around us, so it must be dust in the air below us, and not smog. There's nothing out here to make smog with. FML drones on, indicating about 160 knots at 2,300 R.P.M. (revolutions per minute) and thirty inches of mercury (manifold pressure). Outside it's four degrees celsius. There's the Ernabella strip in the valley off the starboard wing, and then Mark is back in his seat, and we start the descent.

Darned balloon in my right flank, and shifting over my right iliac crest suddenly. Heck! I thought I wouldn't have any problem today. Oh, well. Mark drops a little flaps to bleed off speed, then the gear, then more flaps, and FML settles nicely onto the runway. Almost no wind at all, and the little there is comes from the east.

Fanou is waiting with the vehicle. As we unload, I ask her if she can give me a little water when we get to the clinic; rainwater, just enough to swallow a pill.

"What's that?" questions sister Carol, with her ears at the alert. "Are you all right?"

"Oh, sure, Carol. I just don't want it to get ahead of me."

"Well, if you don't feel well, we just call the whole thing off. There's no need for you to be a martyr."

We climb into the Toyota and make room between the jerry cans that are in the back seat.

"I was told that if I carried zem in zee back of zee vehicle, and zey jostle, zat zey would explode," announces Fanou in her thick, French accent.

"No, they won't explode," reassures Mark. "They're capped right and are safe as long as they are full."

It's a short drive and we're at the clinic. The work crew has been by and the clinic is painted a beautiful white with the red cross on the arch of the gable, and some beautiful aboriginal batik designs painted on the side walls in blue and black. It's very attractive. The store is also painted up with scenes of a sad sun and a happy sun, and mountains and a "roo," and all sorts of things. I'll have to take a picture of that.

The first patient is poor, old Louis. You remember we brought Louis back once before with us. He was in congestive failure, and we were told that he had chronic renal disease with marked proteinuria. Well, now poor Louis, born in 1914, is back with a huge liver almost down to the crest of his right hip bone, and just a faint trace of ascitis (fluid in the abdomen) now, and poor old guy is really in pain. His lungs don't have much breath sounds below about the fifth rib, and he has a gallop rhythm. My notes show that I'd said that his digitalis was perhaps his most important medicine, but at the hospital last time, they stopped that. He's been on one Lasix a day. It's like disciplining a tiger with a feather.

"We'll take him back with us," I tell Fanou. "I'm sure he'd want to die here in Fregon, but for your peace of mind, let's have the hospital people have one more whack at him and tell us that he's a hopeless case."

Fanou agrees. "Louis, will you come into the hospital with us when we leave after tea?"

"Oh-ah." Last time when I went to visit Louis in the hospital in the Alice, I discovered that he speaks perfect British English. He's a really neat, old man.

Next is Chris Wells. Chris continues with pain in his right costal margin. No one can find any reason for it. He's thirty-one and is hypertensive. Blood pressure today is reading 158/96. He's on Clotride. Maybe he should be on something more. I don't know what his pain is from. He does have an allergic dermatitis on his arms. We'll give him a little Polaramine. That's the only antihistamine that we have available. I don't know what to do about his pain.

Next patient is Ralph, who is eight years old. Ralph was doing well, but suddenly came "crook" and dropped his weight from 25 to 22 kg. Fanou gave him a course of Fasigyn, and he's doing better now, but still not gaining weight. I check him over.

"He looks okay now. If he starts diarrhea again, go ahead with another course of Fasigyn," I instruct Fanou.

Ralph also has had rheumatic fever, and is receiving regular monthly injections off LPG (long acting penicillin G).

Peter Hillmans is the European mechanic at Ernabella and is about twenty-five. He smacked his index finger, left hand, with a hammer while holding a chisel about a week ago, and now the blood blister has ruptured and he can't move the distal joint, he says. He's also had a terrible fracture of his left forearm sometime in the past.

"Had many operations on it," he relates. "Had pins in it, and all sorts of screws and stuff, and the scar is pretty tender." He does have pretty good pronation and supination there, though. "And I have this lump on my shin," he continues, "from an old accident years ago."

Inspection reveals that he has a callus there, probably from an old periosteal injury from the accident. It's a bit tender, too.

"And I have this pain in here, too. Really bad and makes it hard to walk." He points to his right instep.

My God! Here's poor Peter falling apart at the tender age of twenty-five. I explain the mechanics of the injuries to him, but think we'll put him on some Amoxil for the infection in his finger.

Rita is seven. She was diagnosed and had treatment started by the radio contact this last week. Rita has produced a urine specimen that's grossly bloody. We'll take it in with us. She's been placed on Bactrim, 7.5 ml a day. Her puffy cheeks combined with the bloody urine suggest that Rita is going to recover from a nephrotic syndrome. I can't find anything more on her. Her blood pressure is 96/60.

Then we see Rita's daddy, Treacle. His blood pressure is 132/96, and he has a history of previous albuminurea. We'll check out his "compo" and see if he still has proteinurea. Then we have Tony Thompson who just wants the physical for his driver's license. Done!

Ray Bergen comes in to happily state that his sciatica responded well to the Indocin that we gave him last time. His blood pressure this morning is 232/120. We'd better add a little Inderal to his hypertension medicine, and if that doesn't get that diastolic below 100, we'd better come on with some Apresoline, like 25 mg each morning. Ray is a happy person. We let him talk on about his children. He's mighty proud of them, and he has a lot of them. "Three wives," he announces proudly.

"My God," says sister Carol, "no wonder your pressure is so high!"

"Oh, no," laughs Ray. "They've been one at a time. The others have died," he says without emotion.

Anslem was born on the 23 October 1981, and has a juicy chest, and a fever. He's given half a bicillin now and then another one in two days. Colin Brown is twenty-eight, and has pain in his left lower abdominal quadrant; "inside," he tells me. Exam is NAD, though. Let's check his urine for blood. He could be passing a kidney stone. It's 0940, and Fanou has brought my water. I swallow a Talwin. Langaliki is a buxom child of thirteen, and has tinea corporis marking up her black skin. It's too big an area to treat topically. We'd better start her on griseofulvin, 500 mg a day, and continue until the rash is gone if it seems to improve in a week.

Mawitza is thirty-two, and has a pain in her right hip. Her blood pressure is 122/84. Let's give her some Indocin for that. Then comes Carol. She's born 11 January 1976, and has a three-centimeter abscess over her left clavicle right at the neck. It really should be opened. Carol is screaming and wriggling so that it's almost impossible to feel how fluctuant the abscess is.

"Give her fifteen milligrams of Phenergan," I instruct Fanou, "and we'll get at that thing in about forty minutes." My own pain is starting to subside.

Tinimai is forty-nine, and diabetic. She need glasses for near vision. Examination reveals no disease in the fundi. Her pressure is 208/92. She's on Clotride. We write the note for the Alice for her to have reading glasses fitted. Next is Iwana. You've met her before, and she was thought to have a fungus infection of her face that wasn't clearing on griseofulvin. So, we had her try some Chlortrimeton, but that didn't help, either. It's really itching and spreading to the other side of her face. Let's get her back on the griseofulvin, and we just happen to have some betamethasone cream here, so we'll put that on topically, and see if it helps. What a mess! Iwana is thirty-five, and she, too, needs reading glasses. Exam shows normal fundi. So be it. I write the note.

Millie Harding is next. Millie has had polio in the past and walks with a terrible, swinging motion to get that bad left around to support her. She always looks like she's pregnant, but that's just the way the muscles have developed around that gait. She's twenty-three. She has pain in the left hip. No wonder! Let's give her some Indocin, too. It's a good thing we have lots of Indocin. Here's Robyn with myalgia. Exam fails to reveal any other significant abnormality. Indocin!

David Mott is a European with a birthdate of 21 August 1959. He's really an outgoing chap, but likeable. He's got a crook knee. He strained it getting into the auto pit. We give him a support, and some aspalgin for the pain. Now we get Carol back. The Phenergan hasn't made her a bit sleepy. As a matter of fact, she's even more active than she'd been before. No matter. Father can hold her well. We drape her from a disposable pack, prep with betadine, prick in a little xylocaine, and make the stab with the #11 blade. There's an upwelling of yellow, thick pus, and some blood. I take a look at the cord-like, external jugular vein right beside the abscess, and decide not to make another stab at this squirming mass of shrieking humanity. The job is done, anyway. We take a culture and dress the wound. Whew!

"I'd like you to see Daryl," says Fanou. "He has this terrible infection in his hand, but he's segregated for initiation, and can't see the women. I'll go get him if you don't mind."

I don't mind. Isn't that strange? Daryl can be seen by white women but not by black.

"He was in the hospital for this last week, but nicked off. I don't know how he got back here. It's a mess."

"Sure, get him and we'll look."

Shortly, Fanou returns with Daryl Stanley. He was born 1 November 1963, and has his left hand wrapped in a dirty bandage soaked with pus. As the bandage comes off the putrid odor of gram negative bacilli assails the nostrils. What a mess, indeed! The index finger is swollen to about four times normal size, and along the flexor surface is a great, gaping opening that's draining pus. The skin of the palm of his hand has separated from the infection, but there's no evidence of lymphangitis. He tells me that there's no feeling in the finger, but I note that the nail blanches and pinks with pressure. There's circulation there. They've brought back almost $100 worth of flucloxacillin for Daryl, but he's been on that before at the hospital and stopped it about ten days ago. Maybe we'd better go for something that's a bit more specific for gram negative infection.

"Do you have any Keflex?"

"No."

"How about tetracycline?"

"Yes."

"Good. Let's give him 500 mg tetracycline four times a day. Daryl, do you understand that you must take this medicine or you may lose the use of that finger?"

"Oh-ah." Maybe he'll take it and maybe he won't.

We pack up the metal cases. "I have a sore ear," says Fanou.

We take a look. She has a eustachian salpingitis secondary to her uri (upper respiratory infection), and a really retracted tympanic membrane on that side. Let's give her some decongestant, and she'll come right.

On the way over to her place for tea, I stop and take a picture of the painting done by the women of the community on the freshly painted white store. It's quite a mural. Then into Fanou's for tea, and she has a 15-kilogram wheel of cheese there, made in Norway. It's delicious. It tastes almost like a mild cheddar.

"We don't eat meat," Fanou explains. "Not that we have anything against it. We just found it was expensive, and we didn't care for it all that much. So we don't eat it. Oh, maybe once in a while some ham. We don't seem to suffer, and we're alway quite well."

It's a comfortable rest after the busy clinic. As we leave her home, Mark points out the box under the "extra" roof above Fanou's place. There, in a cardboard box sitting on edge, are two owls. They are the same ones that we saw last time we were here that were just covered with down then. I climb the little ladder, and from three feet, take a picture of the two of them. Their territory has been infringed, and they let me know by blowing up their necks, and making clicking sounds with the facemask like rim around the head. How interesting!

Back to the vehicle. There's old Louis with a clean shirt on, and his "going away" checked brown and gray slacks. He's really a proper looking elder. He has a thick envelope in his hand.

"What's that?" asks sister Carol.

"Money," answers Louis. "I'm going to buy a car." Sister

Carol holds out her hand, and Louis puts the packet into her hand. She counts it.

"Six hundred and forty dollars! That's an awful lot of money, Louis. I'd better keep it and take it to the bank, and have them make out a check to you for this money. Otherwise, you'd lose it at the hospital. Ninti cheque?"

"Oh-ah," sighs Louis, and we're off for the strip.

The cases are loaded on board, and Mark fires up FML. The plane rises easily into the clear sky. There's no diversion today. Louis watches the landscape folding out from under the plane.

He smiles when I turn and ask, "Palya?"

"Oh-ah," with a big grin and a circled thumb and index finger. This time I don't see him make the sign of the cross. I wonder about this old man. I'll have to keep track of him at the hospital.

We're on final for the Alice. Mark touches down lightly, and we taxi to the ramp. St. John's is there with the training vehicle ambulance. Louis gets in.

"Now, I have your money, Louis," reminds sister Carol, "and I'll bring it back to you in a check that only you can use. So, it's no good to anyone who steals it. Palya?"

"Oh-ah," agrees Louis, and then the ambulance won't start. Everyone has a shot at it. We even pour petrol into the carburetor. It won't fire. Good thing it's not the aircraft! They radio for another ambulance. Louis is having a fine time, and enjoying all the attention. I wait until the other ambulance arrives, and see Louis safely on board; then depart. I have to get the mail. I wonder if our son, Raul, will be coming in this weekend from Miri?

17 June 1982

By golly! It's really cold this morning! Even though the Tropic of Capricorn is only about seventeen miles north of here, the winter mornings can be downright cold when the sun is just peeking over the horizon. There are a few high cirrus that reflect the dawn off the desert, but not much haze. The car has a cold nose, and is reluctant to get started, but with a little coaxing, we do get under way about 0725. At the airport, John is running up FDQ. Carol isn't there yet.

There's a rather beat-up, old Holden sitting on the edge of the ramp, with a tall, curly haired, young man and a young lady in a shapeless, gray, warm-up flannel outfit. He has a backpack, another orange canvas carrying bag that looks a bit like a bag for diving gear, but has a label on it, "National Geographic Society." He also has a metal case about twenty-four by eighteen by eight inches with the same label on it, and various other paraphernalia that would make even the uninitiated believe that he's a journalist with the National Geographic Society.

John shuts down FDQ, and the young man gets out of his car and moves toward the plane with both hands loaded down with gear. I wonder who he is? Bob Worthing, with car #009, rolls up with Carol scrunched down in the left front seat keeping warm in the chill morning. I help her carry over the cases for the clinic at Indulkana, chatting small talk of people and things that we both have interest in. The tall, young man with the curly hair (looks like he's had a permanent?) stands with us.

"I'm Jack Rutten. I'm the doctor with the aeromedical service. Gee, you look familiar, like someone I should know."

"Yeah," he answers laconically, "I guess I look like a lot of people."

John loads the cases into the nose locker. The young man swings his heavy, orange canvas bag into the cabin.

"Not there!" orders sister Carol. "I won't have that heavy stuff in the cabin with me. If I'm going to crash, I don't want to die from someone's heavy gear hitting me on the head. It has to go in the wing locker!"

John and the tall, young man pick up the gear and take it to the starboard wing locker. I turn over one of the tags that says, "National Geographic." Maybe his name is on it. Nope.

"What's his name?" I ask Carol.

"I don't know," she replies. "And I don't know what he's doing on board this flight, either." John and the young man return to the port side to board.

"All right, Dr. Rutten, in you go first," orders Carol.

I move forward to the right front seat. Carol takes her seat, John enters on the port wing and through the access door at the pilot's left front seat. The tall young man takes the very rear seat behind Carol, instead of taking the backward facing seat in front of her.

"This is Dr. Rutten," Carol announces to the tall, young man. "What's your name?"

"I know Dr. Rutten," replies the tall young man.

"That's not what I asked you," presses sister Carol. "What's your name?"

"Denny Gordon," replies the tall young man. Okay, now we have a name for this "different" person.

"You're going to Amata?" queries Carol. "What are you going to do in Amata?"

"I'll be there for about three or four days," replies Denny.

"That's not what I asked you," Carol repeats. "What are you going to be doing there?"

"I'm going to be doing a story on cattle," answers Denny.

John is firing up FDQ. He has on the earphones so that I don't hear the conversation between him and the tower, but we roll out and westbound to runway one-two. Apparently John has received clearance, and he whips the plane around, advancing the throttles as he does so, and FDQ roars down the runway and lifts off easily into the morning sun. Periodically, John presses the "talk" button on the control wheel and says something into the mike projecting in front of his mouth. It looks like we're to be at 4,000. It reads 179 degrees on the compass, and 175 on the autopilot. We're following the iron compass, though (the railroad). It's smooth with only occasional bumps.

I've got my "AFP" journal along, and read on injuries to the hand and fingers. I steal a glance over my shoulder. Denny is busy in the back seat with pencil on pad industriously putting something down on the paper. John pulls the same thing this week that Mark did last week. He leaves the front seat and goes back to sit on the stretcher opposite Carol and talk with her. I don't know if that impresses Denny or not. He seems to continue to write.

There's Chamber's Pillar to the east, and Palmer Valley station to the west, and FDQ drones on across the sky. By-and-by

John returns to his seat. "We've got a 30 knot head wind," John tells me.

It's going to be a bit longer this morning than it has been. John advises that he's going to drop Carol and me at Indulkana, and then he's to take Denny to Amata, but he's going to have to stop at Ayer's Rock for fuel. Then he has to come all the way back to Indulkana for us. It's about an hour's flight across to Amata. "He's paid for the flight," says John.

But that's impossible. The AMS/RFDS is certainly not a charter air service, and there's no way one could pay for a trip like this. That's what Chartair (now Chartill) air service is for. As a matter of fact, just carrying Denny is illegal. Somewhere, someone is going to get trouble for this trip. It's going to take about two and a half hours of plane and pilot time, and something like 350 liters of fuel to deliver this young man to Amata. Hmmm!

Without asking, Carol produces half a cup of black coffee for me and a cup of milk and two sugar for John. She turns to Denny. "Coffee?" she offers.

"I'll take tea," says Denny. Carol looks nonplussed.

"You don't have tea?" suggests Denny.

"No."

"I never drink coffee." And that's the end of the conversation. There's the surf of the Mintibi tailings, and the range of mountains, and off to the left is Granite Downs. We don't go there now, since Marg and Murray Baxter have left for the big sheep station in Western Australia. I wonder who the folks are at the station now? Maybe we'll get to meet them one day.

John is descending. The wind at the strip is just about straight cross wind, and from the looks of the sock, is blowing with some moderate intensity. John comes in from the west; starboard wing down against the wind, and touches on the right wheel first, smoothly as can be. Jennie is waiting for us with the Toyota. We unload the cases for the clinic. Denny gets into the right front seat that I've vacated.

There are two new sisters at the settlement. They just arrived two weeks ago. Lynn is chubby and young. Andrea is well-proportioned and young. Lynn has come out with Jennie. John invites her to ride to Amata with them. Lynn is delighted. I don't think she's been in the plane before. As we sit in the Toyota waiting for the plane to depart, Carol announces the existence of Denny to Jennie.

But Jennie has a story, too. She had a night call over to one of the settlements down the track from Chandler this morning, or last night, actually. In the black of night she had a flat tire. She didn't have a torch along, so had to change it in the starlight, mostly by feel. Then on the way back, the fan belt broke. She managed to rig the thing to keep the fan turning while she came slowly home. Good thing! About 15 kilometers south of Chandler, she hit a bullock. No damage to the vehicle. The bull bar did its job. The bullock staggered off into the dark. She didn't go look for it. It was probably awfully angry, if it were alive! Such is the life of the "outback" sister!

During the coffee break on the plane, I'd managed to swallow a half grain of codeine for the developing balloon that was making my right flank and iliac crest ache. Now I could feel the pain moving into my groin and down the inside of my leg.

"Could I have a little drinking water when we get to the clinic?"

"Sure," says Jennie.

"Are you going to be all right?" worries Carol.

"Oh, yeah. I just don't want to get behind it, Carol."

Up the dirty road with all the papers and soft drink cans, past the store and the bus station, to the front of the clinic. Gee, they didn't paint the outside of the clinic like they did at Fregon. But there are some heavy plastic slabs of clear material that make the self-closing door at the clinic now. I carry in the material. Patrick is already holding clinic. His greeting is warm and sincere. I remember when I first met Patrick and he found out that I worked at the Spyce Byce. He wouldn't talk to me almost the first two months that I was coming around. Things are certainly different now.

"It's going to be a long clinic," he warns me.

"Has Olive come back from out bush yet?" I ask.

"No, and we really don't care if she ever does," says Patrick. "We've put too much worry and care into that cat already. Fine if she comes back. Fine if she doesn't."

It's really a cop-out, I know. They really do care, but they have to have some defensive mechanism to still the ache in their hearts.

Kym Borke from Chandler is the first patient. He was born in November of 1981. He's had worms, but Mom is looking for a trip to the Alice to have him looked at for his pigeon-toes. Kym is cooperative; walks back and forth well. He has a right meta-tarsus varus. No evidence of tibial torsion at all. He'll do better without any treatment at all, except keeping him in proper straight last shoes. Tanya isn't happy with that. She really wanted the "IPTAS" to the Alice. Tanya's birthday is 23 June 1962. She does have some plantar warts. They should be taken off. I don't have anything here to do it with. She'll have to have that done sometime when she's up in the Alice, but it sure doesn't need an emergency med-evac.

Maxine is next, and is a Grav VII, Para VI. She was up to the Alice on June 3 for ultrasonography, which said she was twenty-five weeks gestation. She's 65 kg, BP 100/60, getting monthly serology to follow her response to treatment for syphilis, and her fundus is at thirty-three weeks, despite what ultrasound has said. Cynthia Brown is also pregnant, 100/60, 70.3 kg and is twenty-seven weeks. She's twenty-eight, and is having some nausea. We do have Debendox for her nausea.

Heather Marson is the thirty-one-year-old wife of the com-munity advisor. She's very tall, and very haughty. She's also pregnant. She's also a nurse, I'm told. She has her own specialist in Port Augusta, and is having nothing to do with the Alice doctors, or even the AMS, for that matter. She's willing to let me feel her tummy, but I can't feel a fundus. She's apparently less than twelve weeks. 126/86. I really do wonder if she's even pg. Her son, Conroy, born 12 August 1980, has a nasty "fly eye."

"It's the sixth time in six months," announces Heather. "He should see a specialist."

Let's keep up the cholormycetin drops anyway, until we get him to a specialist. Heather departs, regally, her head almost touching the top of the doorway. Norma is a more realistic preg-nancy. She's 59 kg, 35/52, fetal heart at 136, and BP 132/68. Hughie was born in 1932. A long time ago he was kicked in the right knee by a "brumby" (wild horse). I'd seen him before in February with costo-chondral pain. This right knee has a lot of strange callus medially around the tibial plateau, and a lot of chondromalacia patella. Maybe some brufen will help him; about 200 mg tds.

Then I'm asked to write scripts for OCP (oral contraceptive pills) for both Ronda Parkinson and Tanya Borke. They're using Microgynon 30 ED. That's the kind with twenty-eight pills, seven of which are white placebos. It's easier to keep track if you don't want to count days. Done!

Here's Bill Pitts. It wouldn't be a complete day without seeing some of the Pitts family. But Rhonda and the kids aren't here. Bill really looks pretty good. He tells a sad tale of his grocery money being taken from his check again. It leaves him with nothing much for spending after taxes and such, he laments. But he's had a promotion, and they're finally moving. He has a painful, infected perianal hair follicle. I do a rectal on him. NAD. Let's put him on some Amoxil. Later I find that he's bought a Betamax, and the payments are being taken from his check. That's why he has no money left after he receives his paycheck. My own thing is coming on. At 1120 hours I swallow a Talwin.

Here's poor, old Tommy. Tommy has finally had that big abscess node on the left mandible opened and drained in the Alice. I remember when I first saw him, though, I discovered that he also had a marked cardiac arrhythmia, cardiomegaly and congestive failure. He has a past history of mitral valvular disease. He's never been put on Digoxin, though. He's forty-seven. He's having a lot of distress with dyspnea. His lungs show rales in both bases, and he has a gallop. Let's put him on 0.25 mg Digoxin daily for ten days, and then drop him to 0.125 mg a day. He did have stomach ache this last week, but that's gone now. I'll also look up his x-ray that he had done when he was in the hospital on May 7. His number is 53090. Tommy's wife, Lily, same age, also wants to be seen for pain in her right leg. She's been smacked there, and has a hematoma over the area of the tibial tubercle. We'd better cover her with an antibiotic, like Amoxil, to make sure she doesn't come up with an osteo (osteomyelitis) here.

Then Cathy Manapol with low backache and headaches. She has a port-wine nevus on the right side of her face, just lateral to her mouth. Her exam is otherwise NAD. I think her problem is stress. She's thirty-two. Here's her problem: Adrian, age two. He has a uri. Let's give him some Benadryl elixir. It will slow him down, if nothing else. Then we have Amanda Flint, born 1 December 1981, and her Mom, Irene, who has a stiff neck from being the victim of a rear-ending collision on the road. We'll keep her moving. She has a collar from a friend, but I think we'll do better with Soma or something like it and a little heat.

Molly was born in 1942. She had GC (gonorrhea) septicemia in December which was treated at Alice Springs Hospital. Now she has pain in her left hip and arm. Let's draw a serology. Then Leslie, who has been having urinary retention, and a lot of belly pain. Sister says that his urine has been essentially NAD. Leslie agrees to let me do a rectal exam for prostate when the sisters leave the room. His prostate is moderately enlarged, and quite boggy. No other masses there. We'll treat him with tetracycline. That's about all we have to use except Amoxil. Maybe he'll get better. No one is going to give him rectal prostate massages, that's for sure!

Here's Rosamond Tine, age twenty-two, wanting a refill of her Nordial 28. Then little Martin, whom I had done the dorsal slit on before. Martin isn't very happy when he's placed on the examining table. He remembers, I think. There's sure no phimosis there now.

"No, it's really coming loose now," says Rosamond. She's quite pleased. Martin was born on 30 April 1981. He's been having a little diarrhea. He's a little dry. Let's keep up the fluids.

Nyuniwa was born in 1942. She has a chronic proteinuria, and some pain in her left groin. Her BP is 122/70. About the only thing we have for pain, other than aspirin, is Doloxine. We'll try that. Linda was seen before in October 1981 for asthma. She's fifty-six. She has decreased breath sounds on the left. Her BP is 142/84. Let's give her Amoxil and Neulin. She opens her dirty, white purse. She has all her medicine in here. She's pretty good about taking it. All the labels are done with the sunrise, midday, sunset and nocte. I think I've described those labels to you before.

Why, here's the new folks from Granite Downs! Rhoda Larkin is greeted warmly. A younger-than-Marg, but almost as red-haired woman. She's really a nice person. She had been bitten, some time ago, by a red-back spider, and when given the antivenin, had a reaction. She was watched overnight in the hospital, but never did develop any laryngeal edema. She's worried, and says that the medicine kit at the station has no adrenalin. We'll get things up to date for her. She's a delightful person.

Here's Fanou! She's driven all the way across from Fregon! That's almost two hours by terrible road. She didn't know that she could call on the radio and have us diverted. She has two men with her. One, she says, has a sore on his scrotum, and the other was kicked in the testes playing football. And, yes, she's ordered 15 boomerangs for me! Leslie is the man with the sore. He's nineteen. He has a chancre (primary lesion of syphilis). We'll give him LPG now and weekly times three.

David is the other man. He's thirty-two. When I look, though, there's no swelling and no ecchymosis (black and blue) of the scrotum. His penis has been sliced during his initiation ceremony, longitudinally, and in such a way as to separate the meatus and urethra from the cavernosa, leaving just the spongiosum half of the glans to a point about two centimeters distal to the base of the penis. That's where the urethra now opens. Thus, the meaty side of the penis rests on the scrotum, keeping the whole thing moist there. But the chancre is there, and looks a bit wetter than the usual. How about that? In twenty-three years of private practice, I don't think I ever saw a chancre. I think the only one I've seen was at San Diego Naval Hospital when I was an intern. And today, I've seen two of them, back to back, so to speak. Amazing! We'll give him LPG, too.

Sadie Singer is the first patient of the day, I think. Sadie has an awfully sore right hamate (one of the small bones of the hand) bone. Her husband kicked her there. Not intentionally, though. Sadie had been holding the bloke her husband was fighting with, and when the husband kicked the guy, he accidentally got Sadie on the wrist. It's swollen, but there's nothing broken. She'll come right. I show Jennie how to place a plaster slab, and wrap it with an elastic bandage to keep a little support under this wrist for a day or two, but still give Sadie the option of taking it off when she wants to.

We pack up the things. That's when Biddy arrives with her kids. Biddy is the "number 2" wife of Captain 2. The "number one" wife has three kids, and is pretty, and good to the kids.

Biddy has three kids, too, but couldn't care less. She's the one that Carol has been upset with a long time ago, when I first got here, and had announced that if Biddy got on the plane, she, Carol, wouldn't.

Tea time at Patrick and Jennie's. Patrick's Mom is here on holiday! Heather. She's going to be going up to the Alice, and taking a proper, nine-day tour with CATA to Ayer's Rock and such. There's lime cordial, so that I can swallow another half grain codeine for the pain that's still in my right groin. Then, half a cup of coffee and a biscuit. The talk is smallish.

"What happened to the Martins?" I question. "That's the only family from Chandler that I didn't see today." Everyone laughs.

"They're on holiday," chuckles Jennie. "Otherwise, I'm sure they'd have been here."

Patrick is telling Jennie that he started out for Chandler with the new vehicle, the same one that Jennie had all the trouble with earlier this morning, and the steering snapped. Now it's totally incapacitated. What is this with Indulkana vehicles? John is sitting there. He had returned from his trip to Amata with Denny.

"Cheeky fellow," says John. "He wanted to open the side window in flight so that he could stick his camera out. I told him absolutely not! And then he had the nerve to say that the plane wasn't very good for taking pictures from, and I told him that this wasn't built for a tourist transport. I hope he finds some wild bulls for his story. Maybe they'll introduce him to petrol sniffing. Maybe they'll get him for the $500 a day for being there without a permit."

John isn't being very solicitous. I don't think he cares for Denny. The *National Geographic* is going to have some PR debris to clean up after Denny leaves the area.

Then it's back to the plane. The loading up, the take off. The auxiliary tanks register just a bit more than a quarter, but the mains are a bit more than half full. The radio comes alive. They want us to divert to Mt. Ebenezer. "Okay," says John, and sets the course of 340 degrees.

It's 1520 hours. At 1605 we're on final. Baron UUP is on the ground there from Chartair. He's brought in Mr. Donders and party; the minister of Works and Transport. The raggedy procession of aboriginals comes to FDQ across the strip. It's a baby, about two, really looks sick with green pus from his left ear, yellow/white snot on his upper lip from his nose (but so do all the other little waifs in the family party), respirations of 48/minute, and a pulse rate of 192/minute. He has no breath sounds on the left side. We'd better take him in. Stephen Cook (with a "ph") is his name.

Peter is the aboriginal health worker with his left upper incisor missing from initiation. Peter advises us Stephen stopped breathing last night. Sister Carol puts on a white, cotton examining gown, all nice and clean, and takes dirty little Stephen into her arms. He has a pair of tan, flannel jeans on and a red (I think it's red under all the dirt), cotton T-shirt, probably the only clothes he's been into (and not out of) for the last six months. He clings to her, chest to chest, like a little koala bear. Not a peep out of him. Mom explains that she'll be coming into the Alice by road in a day or so. It's been a while since payday, and she probably doesn't have any money.

At 1625 hours we're airborne again. There are alto-cumulus to the west, and the sun is lowering into them, painting shafts of light between them to the desert floor. John tells me that there's been an aircraft crash at the Alice airport. Four people killed. It seems they hit a flock of birds on takeoff. Gee! FDQ drones on at 7,000 feet. Stephen sleeps; Carol holds him with one hand and her book with the other. John is flying the auxiliary tanks dry. There's the Henbury craters to the right. They're not so big from the air as they are from the ground. There are some green rectangles of lucern (alfalfa) at Palmer station. And there's the Alice. We touch down at 1715 hours. There's no wreckage to be seen around the airport.

"It was a disaster drill," the tower tells John. "It was a disaster. No one seemed to know anything about anything, and I guess they'll have to do it over."

So much for the Alice Springs disaster committee. Back to the drawing board. I wonder who's in charge? It used to be Dave Winding. Oh, and John Hampton seems to be the person who accepted Denny's money for the flight with the RFDS. At least we have the name of the guy who's going to go to jail for that!

I'm home by 1800 hours. The same neighbor is there waiting. Last week she wanted me to see her four-and-a-half-year-old daughter when I was leaving for the airport. This time she has been waiting for me to come home because she thinks she has the flu. She's sixteen weeks pregnant, and doesn't want to take aspirin. I check her over, and suggest that she call her obstetrician in the morning and see if she wants Brenda to have some medicine.

8 July 1982

Cold! There's ice on the windscreen of the little Falcon this morning. But it's fun to be going back out to the airport to fly with the Aeromedical Service of the Royal Flying Doctors. I haven't been out for the past two weeks. Dr. Cahill was making her regular six-months trip to Ernabella two weeks ago. She drives out about every six months; won't fly. She says she's scared. With her there, there wasn't much reason for me to go. Then, last week there was a closed runway at Amata. I don't know if it was the council arguing again with the Transport Department, but the strip was closed. So, this week we're off for Fregon, and I'll be able to pick up the boomerangs that I ordered a month ago.

John is running up FDQ when I get there. There's old Louis sitting on the bench in front of the AMS operations office. There's a sweet little girl, about three, sitting beside him; flimsy, little cotton skirt, a jumper made of moderately heavy synthetic material, no shoes, and a nose that looks like it's been wiped so often that it's taken the skin off the upper lip. Ahh! Civilization! It can even wipe out runny noses! Her name is Eva. Eva has come in to the Alice from Fregon with Mommie, but Mommie went to the hospital and had a new baby, and so we're actually smuggling Eva back to Fregon. She's a cute little thing; and smart! I'm sure she speaks good English, but nary a word comes out of her. She does talk to Louis in little whispers, and that's in Pitjantjatjara.

Louis looks radiant. He's lost a lot of his fluid. There's no evidence of ascites now. The big, flowing, white beard is impressive. He's wearing his felt hat with the proper crease, and a gray shirt. It might have been white once, but it's gray now. A dark suitcoat covers the shirt and keeps him warm. It's pretty ragged and awfully dirty. And then, the brown and gray checked pants; also pretty dirty. No shoes, just those black, leathery, bare feet. But he's happy! I talk with him for a while. He has no notes. I guess he's on one Clotride and two Slow-K a day. I think the practice of sending these people sans notes on treatment back to the poor sister in the aboriginal camp is tantamount to malpractice by the specialist at the hospital. But that's the way they do things out here.

Carol arrives with Robyn Pelt. Robyn was the switchboard operator at the base until a week ago, when she and her husband bought out Bob Worthing's limousine service. Carol is her usual bubbly self. She announces that next week she's indeed going to be driving her car, via Ayer's Rock and Docker River, to Perth. That's going to be some drive! John shuts down FDQ, and we load up. John is pretty quiet this morning. He's not feeling well. In the plane he keeps his headphones on so I can't hear the tower. It's runway three-oh, and FDQ performs beautifully, except the red light on the panel tells us that the booster fuel pump on the left engine is inoperative. Hmm.

We're at 8,000 feet, so I take out my diary. I'm counting up the times that I've had balloons (kidney stones) over the past year. It's a lot! There's considerable haze today, so from 8,000 feet there's not all that much to see. I look up once, and we're at the lakes, and then again, and we're abeam of Ernabella and ready for descent. John does everything right, and the plane touches down easily. Here's Julie Dorn back. Julie is beaming and happy, and has had a marvelous holiday, she tells us.

The clinic building is sporting some beautiful batik designs painted on its white walls. It's not finished yet, so I don't take a picture. I probably should have. By the time I get back again, they may be all gone. We set up the clinic, and the first patient that we have is Henry Barkley. He's the community advisor, European, and perhaps a tad smarter than the average aboriginal. Henry has recurring furuncles. He's on Bactrim for them, and they're clearing up. Maybe we'd better check his urine to make sure he isn't a diabetic.

Fanou has gone for a ten-day holiday, says Julie. Mark is still here, and to prove it Mark comes in and we do a driver's license exam on him. I guess that's their way for handling holidays. They take them separately. The next patient is our little friend, Rita. Rita had what I thought was a nephrotic syndrome last time we were here, and was clearing up nicely. But the last two days, she's suddenly developed hematuria. We'd better take a specimen back with us. After she passes the specimen, and I see it's gross blood, I decide that we'd better take Rita back with us. Treacle, her father, is willing. Treacle is a Christian. He's a big man, but a very nice man. Rita is seven.

Here's active, fat, little Jason. He's had diarrhea. He was born on 1 March 1982. He has really active bowel sounds, but he doesn't look too bad. His belly is soft. We'll give him a little kaolin and see if he comes right. Malyunka was born in 1957. She has a really tender node on her left groin. She's a little shy on examination, but the node is sure there. I thing she might have a venereal infection here. Let's give her 500 mg of probenecid, and then in about an hour we'll give her three grams of Amoxil stat. That should make things subside.

Little Julie is brought in next. She's just five years old, and for the last ten days has had bilateral lumps under her nipples. Exam shows these to be breast buds. A tad precocious, but we'd be wise to leave them alone. Lena is five. She had chills and fever last night, and fever today. Examination reveals runny ears and the usual runny nose, but I can't find anything until I run across an abscess over the right achilles tendon, and by golly, there's a node in the right groin. She's got cellulitis and lymphangitis. Two mils of Bicillin IM (intramuscular injection) should take care of that. Lena you met last January when she had a fracture of her right arm. We put it into a sugar-tong splint, and she had four plasters after that. But it was hot, and she'd play in the water, and those plasters would just come apart. Amazing! The arm is perfect, and she has full function.

Trevor Smith is twenty-one, and has blown his brains apart with petrol sniffing. He's in today with pain in his left lower chest. Exam suggests that he has a pneumonitis here. It's probably secondary to sniffing petrol. He's already had Bicillin and crys-topen. We'll give him some more. Then we have a little, blond European girl, Amelie Farmer, who has recurrent tonsillitis, says her Mom. Amelie's tonsils really aren't that large. She's allergic to everything except erythromycin. She doesn't need that now. I'll talk with Dr. H. about her when I see him, though. No medicine this time.

Payula is angry with me for calling her that. I'm supposed to call her Manyuritjanu. Okay. So be it. Better not abbreviate that name, either. She's antenatal, I'm told. She's 78 kg, 136/80, and Dr. Cahill says she's twenty weeks pg. You met her last March when she had the sore hip from lifting up the other baby. Remember? I can't feel a fundus down in there at all, but if Cahill says she's pregnant, I guess I'll say so, too. I don't hear any fetal heart.

Imitjara is stone deaf, twenty-six years old, 47 kg, 90/60, and is 24/52 with FHH 148/minute. Christine Irish is twenty-four years old, European, and has pain in her left scapula with no trauma. I can't find a thing here; no limited motion or anything. Let's try one of the non-steroidal anti-inflammatory agents, like brufen. Then here's Narella. She's Tali-tali's baby, born 8 August 1981. She hasn't put on any weight at all since March. She's been afebrile, but Julie was worried about her.

When Tali-tali brings Narella in, Julie is even more worried. The baby is listless and apethetic. She rolls her eyes back into her head, and really looks terrible. She's dropped 300 grams since yesterday. Examination reveals the usual runny ears, and she cries weakly when I palpate suprapubically. Dr. John Martins had said that failure to thrive in these little people often means urinary tract infection. Narella also has a peculiar hump over the lower cervical vertebral spines and carries her head funny. We'd better take her with us. Tali-tali hates Alice Springs Hospital. She also has five other children. Tali-tali is a classic aboriginal woman, with the protruding mandible, and the mincobah stuck in the side of her mouth, and her eyes sunken back into her head. But she's adamant. She won't come. She'll send the baby with sister Carol, though. That's okay. The child really has to be evaluated at the hospital. That's two patients and one adult escort for evac today, already. It's a busy day! Julie says that Narella's sister, Feona, also has hematuria, but she's walkabout with some other family and isn't here.

That's the clinic. We'll go and have a cup of tea. Here's Leah, who used to be a sister out this way, and her husband, Chris, and four-year-old son, Nicki. They're on holiday and just coming through. It's a nice family, and Leah has brought a big, round damper, fresh out of the oven at the bakery, and with a golden brown crust. Yummy! I head over for the craft shop and pick out the fifteen boomerangs that I'd ordered.

"They just don't seem to be into making boomerangs," apologizes the aboriginal craft superintendent. She has a basket full of about twenty or so, and then there are some more that are done really tourist style, with all the fancy markings.

"They're not really Pitjantjatjara art, you know," she reminds me.

"Yes, I know. But back in America, they think all Australia uses boomerangs, and if I brought anything else back, they'd think it was not *Australian*," I tell her.

She gives me fifteen for $75, and throws in a packet of printed tags that say, "An Original Pitjantjatjara Work of Art, from the Aparawatatja Crafts Centre, Fregon, South Aust."

Back to Julie's, and the tea is on. John still doesn't feel well, I'd given him one of my half-grain codeine with Tylenol when we first landed, and he's had a nap. Maybe he does have a touch of virus. There's cheese and the fresh damper, and carrot sticks. Four-year-old Nicki climbs on his mother's lap, and she nurses him while he comments on the flashing reflection of the sun on my watch band tracing circles on the ceiling. Strange to watch a big child like that nursing. Then he's down and over to the table for damper and cheese and a carrot stick. It's only two o'clock, but we're ready to depart.

Back to vehicle. Treacle is there, with his red Pitjantjatjara bible in hand, and Rita. We drive a back road to the wicki-up of Tali-tali, past the discarded auto parts and the paper and bottles that have rolled to the fence line. Past the camp dogs and the children playing in the cold breeze, naked, but apparently having a wonderful time.

On a mound of dirt, littered with empty cans and bottles, sits the family group; filthy blankets wrapped around them, a stocking cap on one, a head band on another. The fire is a glow of embers down in a pit about a foot deep and three feet in diameter. A smoke-stained pot holds a piece of boiled chicken. A man lifts it up with his fingers and holds it above his mouth, juice running into his mouth and down his clothing. Tali-tali rises and brings the baby. There are now nine people in the Toyota. At the strip, Tali-tali sits in the dirt and nurses the baby one last time. We load the metal cases into the plane. Treacle climbs in with Rita.

Carol says, "Okay, Tali-tali, bring the chi-chi."

Tali-tali comes forward with the baby, like an offering, held out to sister Carol on extended arms. Tali-tali's eyes well up and spill over with tears. The mincobah trembles at the corner of her mouth. The baby is listless and unaware of the transfer to the white sister. Carol bubbles on and on. It's good. It's a touching scene. John takes his place and fires up FDQ. On the way home I think a lot about what I've seen, and finish my task of sorting out the eleven trips that I've made to the hospital this last year for treatment of kidney stones.

15 July 1982

Yesterday, sister Carol rang, and told me that she hadn't been able to get the notes on Louis, nor Tommy from Indulkana, nor Simon or Carol, but that she'd reviewed them, and was sending along the information from these for my review while flying out Indulkana today. Louis you remember. He's the old man from Fregon with the Santa Claus beard, whom we brought back about five weeks ago in massive congestive heart failure, and with the big belly from ascites. We took him back to Fregon last week. Tommy also is a congestive failure from Indulkana, probably mitral valvular disease, too. They sent Tommy back to Indulkana, apparently improved, but sister Carol couldn't get any information on what medicine he might be on.

Simon is from Ernabella and had a penetrating eye injury

that had been treated by Dr. Richey down at Flinders in Adelaide. Simon is about 12. They may want me to drop by Ernabella on the way home and have a look at it. Carol is the little girl that we'd seen down in Fregon a month or so ago with the big abscess on her neck. She's six years old, and apparently has been up in ASH for evaluation for retarded. All those problems are out there with no notes available to the doctor for follow-up. I think Dr. John Stein, administrator (superintendent) of the hospital is carrying his privacy thing to the ultimate ridiculous end. Anyway, we'll do the best we can within the system.

At the airport, I park the car and watch as a pilot whom I don't recognize tries to start the port engine of FDQ. The starboard engine is running smoothly, but the left one is just cranking away and not even firing. My own feeling is that he should give it a shot of primer from the booster, but I just sit in the warm car on this chilly morning and watch the effort.

The limousine car is a brand new Volvo, and is sitting up near the fence, also watching the starting trials. But it's not Carol in the limousine, it looks like Virginia Gretchen. I pick up my cameras and my brand new *National Geographic* and walk over to the limo after locking my car.

"Good morning," says Ginny. "Come sit inside. It's too cold out there." Bob Pelt is the driver. I sit in the back seat.

"Who's the pilot?" I question.

"It's Neil from Chartair," Ginny replies. "He's chartered today because Darryl has something important with some film people today."

Well, Neil is sure having a time. The plane won't fire. He shuts down the starboard engine and departs the plane. He talks with some people who are loading up the police Navajo on the tarmac, and one of the pilots comes over, climbs into FDQ, and manages to get the engine started, but it's running terribly rough. That will never do. The engine is shut down again.

"Last week the left fuel booster wasn't working," I remind them.

"Yesterday, coming back from Ayer's Rock, we lost the alternator on the starboard engine when it threw a belt," says Ginny. It sounds like FDQ had better stay in the shop. Neil comes up to the limousine.

"I rang Darryl, and he says we should take the Baron. Do you mind?" continues Ginny.

"No, that's fine with me," I reply. "It'll probably mean that we'll get diverted and have to evac a lot of people because we have the smaller plane," I predict.

We push the Baron out of the hangar and load up the cases. The Baron is smaller, but actually a bit faster than the Navajo. FDE fires up easily, even in the cold morning air.

"I'll sit up front going, and you can sit there coming back," I offer Ginny.

"Fine!"

The panel on the Baron looks almost like the panel on the Bonanza, and the visibility is much better than from the Navajo. Ground control directs us to runway one-two, and we're cleared to fly the 184 radial at 6,000 feet. The Baron rockets off the runway, and Neil banks us over sharply to pick up the radial. It's a little hazy this morning.

Neil is young, maybe twenty-three. He looks a lot like the old pictures of Howard Hughes in his flying days, with a narrow, little mustache on the upper lip. He's handsome, really. He's a bit chagrined at his problems with FDQ. We chat a while. The configuration of the interior is right and left brown leather seats, then on the port side behind the pilot is a brown leather seat with lamb's wool pad, and behind that on the port side, another seat just like it. On the starboard side is a stretcher, and the Baron has a double door on the starboard side to receive the stretcher. It's compact. There's not a lot of leg room in the back. Behind the last seat is a bit of room for storing linens and equipment. I pick up my *Geographic.*

How about this? Here's a story on Papua, New Guinea! A tribal warrior in mask and head dress glares at me. What's this? Photography by Denny Gordon! Well, I'll be darned! I wonder if Denny ever got his cattle story from Amata? There's a short editorial story about Denny on the editor's pages. That's sure interesting. I wonder if they know back there what a reputation he has out here. It says he's been here in the Australia for eight years! I'll bet he's done a lot of damage in that time.

There's Chamber's Pillar. The sun is warm, and the engines drone, and I nod off into that peculiar shadow land where one isn't really sleeping, yet one's dreaming and not really awake. It's most comfortable. A dip wakes me up. Neil has switched off the auto pilot; we're descending. I doze off again. ZZZZRRR!! The plane bucks as the gear descends. Now I'm fully awake, and there's Indulkana straight ahead. Neil banks us from southbound to westbound just past the settlement, and we make a standard right-hand pattern for the strip. He touches down easily. There's Patrick on the dirt strip with a warm greeting. His Jenny is up in the Alice having the vehicle repaired.

"Where's sister Carol?" he asks Ginny.

"She's taken her little red car and is on the way to Perth via Warburton and Docker River," answers Ginny.

So, she really did get off and away. I was wondering about that!

"We've sent a vehicle over to Mimili to get some patients from there," continues Patrick. "I've got about fifteen down here, but none have fronted up yet. It's going to be a bit disorganized today. Would you like tea first?"

"I think not," I answer. "I think we'll get on with the clinic, and have the tea when we finish."

I'm thinking of the possible diversion that we still have to make for a look at Simon in Ernabella. As we enter the clinic, the Amazonian dimensions of Heather Marson, the community advisor's wife, fill the entryway. She's well proportioned, and pregnant. She's just terribly big! She must be six foot five and weigh 185 pounds (that's 195.6 cm and 14.25 stone). Actually, I find later that she weighs 191 pounds. There's no one visible from Chandler. I wonder if there's something in the wind.

First patient turns out to the school marm Carol Wagner. Carol is thirty, and gives a history of having severe sudden onset of cramping abdominal pain about a month ago. It was intermittent and intense, and seemed to be related to the lower belly and to urination. She was treated with a course of Bactrim in spite of her urine being okay. That didn't seem to help much. Then she was given a course of Amoxil, and she's still having some trouble with it. Her periods were a little mixed up for a while. In March she had an IUD removed, and there was a lot of tugging and the string broke. But things have been okay now, with the last period about three weeks ago. She's afebrile. Exam shows fullness in the right lower quadrant, and, as a matter of fact, one can see the subtle outline of a mass showing in the horizontal light. She's got something in there. It's easier to see than to feel. It's soft. A cyst?

"We really should do an internal exam," I tell her.

"That's fine, doctor, I don't mind. I'd like to find out what that is." Patrick sets us up.

"I won't need a speculum. I just want to feel."

The glove, a bit of lubricant. There's the cervix, and it feels like a normal uterus, and here's a cystic mass that's moderately tender on the right. It does measure about eight centimeters.

"It's a cyst," I explain. "You'll have to go to the Alice. Can you come with us?"

"Yes," she laughs. "My husband is there in the hospital with an ulcer. Do you suppose they'll allow a man and woman in the same room?"

"Sure, but I don't know about the same bed," I laugh, as I think of John Stein, and how he'd receive something like that with dour lack of humor.

"Will I go with you?"

"I don't know, Carol. We may have a diversion. We'll let you know as the morning progresses. If we can't take you, you could come up on the bus at noon time."

Next patient is Heather, and she is pregnant. Her attitude is much improved over the last time I was here.

"Did you get to the specialist in Adelaide?" I ask.

"No, I couldn't get away."

"How's your little boy?"

"Oh, he's just fine, thank you."

Her face brightens up to think that I'd remember the problem of a month ago. I've just won a friend, I think. She submits to the antenatal exam. Now I can feel just the tip of a fundus above the symphysis. It's probably fourteen to sixteen weeks. That good. I don't hear any heart sounds.

"Sure seems like all is well," I tell her. She's 87 kg, 120/90 (watch that diastolic!), and thirty-one years old.

Here's Janet Moodoo. Poor little Janet. She's four months old with gastroenteritis. She's gone from 5,150 grams to 4,600 in two days. That's a lot to lose. Her ears are draining and so is her nose,

and the snot and pus have dried all over her head and face, and
her little tongue is dry. She's crying, but not too strongly.

"She's got to go in," I advise. Mom stands mute in her filthy,
black dress and cardigan.

"Can you be ready when the plane leaves?" Patrick asks
Mom.

"Oh-ah," she whispers.

"We'll pick you up back here about 1300 hours," Patrick
soothes.

"Oh-ah." Poor, little thing. I hadn't felt anything in the belly
except an irritated bowel churning away, and a smelly diarrhea.

Maxine Steward is a gravida VII, and has a little pretibial
edema. She's thirty-three, 64 kg, 104/60, and the fetal heart is
clicking way at 140/minute. She's maybe thirty-six to thirty-seven
weeks. We draw her antenatal blood.

"She'd better come in next week or so," I tell Patrick.

Pansy Woods is thirty-eight and had a headache. It's all better
now. Her blood pressure is recorded at 110/60. The exam is NAD.
I don't know why she came to see me. There isn't any treatment.
Linda Kadashi you've met before. She's the asthmatic that we
put on Amoxil last month. We've got to keep her on her Neulin.
She has a lot of rales in her chest. Her blood pressure is 144/88.
Do you remember Suzie Lambina? She had rocks in her ears. She
has pain in her chest now. Exam reveals nothing much. Her chest
is clear. The heart sounds are normal. Her blood pressure is
102/80, and then I find the tender xiphoid.

"You've been hit with a stick?"

"Oh-ah." So that's it! Exam doesn't show much of a bruise.
I guess she'll come right without treatment. Give her a little
aspalgin for the pain.

Nginta is twenty-seven and is still having abdominal pain.
We saw her a number of times since last January, and always the
same complaint. She has a Cu–7 in place since January. That's
probably what's causing her pain. She still hasn't had it out. No
wonder she's tender in there.

"You've got to give Dr. Cahill a chance to take that out,
Nginta."

"Oh-ah."

"You go up to the Alice on the bus. Sister will make an

appointment for you with Dr. Cahill.''

"Oh-ah.''

"Now, you do this! It will probably stop the pain.''

"Oh-ah.'' She probably won't.

David is the next patient. He's a big man, red head band, handsome, classic with the heavy brows. He's dressed warmly and rather clean. Pressure is recorded at 162/112, but the heart sounds are normal and the chest is clear. He's forty-two.

"Let's draw an FBC on David, and start him on one Clotride a day. If the pressure hangs up there over 100 diastolic after a week, let's add on 40 mg of propranalol A.M. and P.M.,'' I tell Patrick. Patrick is a good sister. David will get the medicine.

"We'll check him out next time.''

Biddy King is next. She's one of the tribe from Mimili that's come in on the vehicle. She's twenty, thirty-two weeks pregnant, 100/60, and 60.5 kg. The fetal heart is good at 148/minute. We draw the antenatal bloods.

Kangi is Tommy's wife (Lily). She's back again with the same tibial tubercle prominence that she had last time. This time the infection is gone, but the bump is there. I explain to her that the bump isn't going to go away. That is part of her, and she really needs the bump to make her leg move. No mind that she doesn't have a bump like it on the other side. This one is just fine, and people can't really expect to have two. One is usually enough.

"Oh-ah.''

Sadie also has a bump on the right tibia, but hers is about mid shaft anteriorly, and is from a stick, although she denies trauma. She's thirty-two. She could have an injury here with a potential osteomyelitis. We'd better give her a bit of Amoxil. The area is about five centimeters and swollen and quite tender.

Tanya is only five. She has a ganglion on her right wrist. We admire it. Tanya is happy that we won't do anything with it, and her Mom is pleased with our advice. Anita is a new born on the seventh. Neonate exam reveals a beautiful baby and a happy Mom. We check Mom out, too. Teresa is nineteen, and Anita is her first, and she's involuting very nicely. Then there's Puna, who won't front up for the exam, but Patrick says that it sounds like she has hemorrhoids, and he has no cream for that. I order up a script for Proctosedyl ointment, a thirty-gram tube. Andy

Barr, the chief chemist from the Alice Hospital Pharmacy, was supposed to be with us today, but didn't make it for some reason. Andy is going to be responsible for supplying all these settlements.

Then we have Rita with a fever, and not feeling well. She's European, but not from Chandler. She's twenty. After a general exam we find a huge abscess on the right posterior thigh.

"But I didn't think that could make me feel this badly," she says. We'll put her on seven days of Amoxil.

That's the end of the clinic for today.

Back to Patrick's for a cup of tea and a biscuit. Discussion turns to opals.

"There's lots of opals right here," advises Patrick. "You can walk down the street here kicking the dirt, and turn over opal. Over at Mintibi, the big operators go in with the big machines, and just take out the big stuff, and then the black people come noodling along after them and pick up some as big as your thumb."

"But they don't have much fire, do they?" I ask.

"Oh, yes! Some of them may be worth several hundred dollars!" exclaims Patrick.

Then I tell him about Wally, and how I'd still like to have a bag of opals before I go.

"I'll pass the word," says Patrick.

Then the talk goes to politics. I mention the trouble with getting information from the hospital notes.

"Don't tell me about that!" Patrick is inflamed! "I sent a baby up to the hospital about six weeks ago. Dr. Martins saw it. The Mom couldn't go because she has five other ones here. I assumed all was going well. Mom would come in every day and ask me how the babe was doing, and, because I hadn't heard, I'd say, 'Oh, the babe is fine.' Later I heard that the babe wasn't fine. They'd transferred it down to Adelaide, and it died. Dr. Rutten, it died! And it was nine days until they told me, and then I had to tell the Mom."

"Gosh, Patrick, that's awful!" And it really is!

We finish tea, and walk back to the clinic. The bus is in. There's Carol Wagner getting on board. She's heard that we have the baby and the Mom to go.

"Do you think they'd mind if I took a picture of the bus, Patrick?"

"Take it if you want it," he replies.

So now I have a picture of the bus at Indulkana, with all the dirt and filth piled up along the road, and the tourists taking pictures of us taking pictures of them.

Little Janet Moodoo is there with her Mom. But now Lizzy is dressed in a quite clean, blue skirt and cardigan, and even a golden chain around her head. Janet has been cleaned up with her hair all combed and shiny, and her face cleaned of the dry exudate, and she's been tucked into a brand new, fluffy, pink bunny bag, complete with zipper up the front. What a contrast with the filthy baby we just saw a couple hours ago in the clinic.

"We have to go to Fregon to pick up Louis," says Neil.

"Louis? Why, we just brought Louis back from the hospital last week! What's wrong now?"

"I don't know. They just said that he's in a lot of pain."

"Do we have to go to Ernabella?"

"No, they've called that one off."

At 1330 hours, we're off the ground in the Baron. I've traded seats with Ginny, and she and Neil are in animated conversation up on the flight deck. I continue to read my "Geographic." Lizzy and the baby sit quietly behind. Periodically, Lizzy brings out the breast for the baby when she cries, but she doesn't take it too avidly. Poor little thing, she's too weak to do a good job of sucking.

It's only about twenty-three minutes to Fregon. Neil hits it right on the head, and we drop down onto the strip. It's Fanou, back from holiday.

"It's Louis," she tells me again. "He has somezing wrong wiz zee scrotum and zee penis." She's really excited. I pick up the equipment case.

"You folks can stay here with the plane," I tell them.

Fanou and I leave for the settlement, but not to the clinic. We make our way between the bush and wattles, and past junked cars, and abandoned drums and camp dogs and kids, and finally on the outskirts of the settlement is the camp of Louis, and about four of his friends. I don't know how to describe the abject filth and chaos that represents the living environment of these people.

There's a "house" of sorts on the fringe of the camp, but as far as I can tell, this is used only for storing things out of the weather; things like auto parts and perhaps some old clothing. Perhaps the women and children live in the shelter of that roof, for I don't see anyone walking about except these three old men that seem to have their swag within the same confines of the camp as Louis. There are three wooden posts and two metal stakes, worn and bent, that support three sides of what would be an octagonal enclosure made of old tarpaulins and canvas, perhaps three feet high.

The wind is blowing from the open side of the enclosure, though, so there isn't much protection from the occasional sprays of grit and blowing tumbleweeds that come through the camp. The fire pit is so close to the four-inch-foam pad that constitutes Louis's home, that I have to warn him as he tries to stand, not to put his feet in the fire. The fire at this time is a single mulga log, about two feet long, that is covered with gray ash, and occasionally glints red as the wind blows the smoke directly onto Louis's three-by-seven foot, four-inch thick bed.

He's lying on the bed with two filthy blankets over him. I move the blankets off. Louis has a dirty shirt on, and a second one with the tails tied around his waist, and the collar draped in front like a loincloth. Beneath this is a scrotum about the size of a football! Poor Louis! I can't tell if this is full of fluid or if there might be a hernia here and that this is bowel. There's some suprapubic swelling and tenderness. But the belly is generally soft. His eyes are watering and his face grimaced with pain.

"Louis, are you in a lot of pain?"

"Oh-ah." What a stoic. I feel his scrotum. I can't feel anything in there, it's so distended. It does transilluminate, though.

"Louis, can you stand?"

"Oh-ah."

Fanou is flitting back and forth, and somehow, the men tolerate her in spite of her womanhood. I think she's afraid that I'm not going to take Louis with me. I extract the stethoscope from the kit. His heart sounds reveal a regular rhythm. He has some rales, but that's sure not his problem.

"He's been taking one Clotride and two Slo-K a day," helps Fanou.

"Louis, I'm going to take you into the Alice in the airplane."

"Oh-ah."

"Can you put on your pants?"

"We-ah." So, we'll leave the shirt as it is, and wrap a blanket around him.

Fanou is obviously relieved. Louis sits back down on his bed. He reaches for a box that is stuffed between the bed and the dirty tarpaulin. He extracts a filthy pillow case. That's his "port." He stuffs in the (once upon a time) clean white and brown trousers that he wore home from the hospital last week. A small envelope of bills is stuffed into his top shirt pocket, and then removed, and carefully placed in the pillow case. I glimpse a set of aluminum cookware with orange exteriors and fitting lids inside the box. The inside of each pot is caked with perhaps a quarter inch of dried food and grease. I don't think they ever clean them out after cooking. My eyes drift around the camp. Two scrawny camp dogs lie quietly between the fire pit and the other man's "bed." One little dog is lying so quietly that I fear he's dead. Later he moves a leg, so I guess he's not.

The periphery of the camp area is slightly mounded with dirt and debris that has been scooped back from the fire pit over the years. Old bottles, rusted tins, pieces of wood and broken glass and cardboard; paper and an occasional piece of torn, filthy clothing; a streamer of loose cassette tape, ashes, and here, right beneath, a shiny twenty-cent piece. I didn't pick it up. I looked at it and let it lie there for future archaeologists to muse over.

Back to Louis. Another look at that scrotum. The posterior portion is excoriated, and almost bloody from resting on the sponge rubber pad. A fluid wave is easily discernible rippling the thin skin. There's a white, crusted sore, about 1.5 centimeters in diameter over the head of the penis, and the end of the penis that has been mutilated in the initiation rite looks like Louis has been trying to empty the scrotum through the urethral meatus by widening it with a stick, perhaps.

Fanou has gone back to bring the vehicle closer. I help one of Louis's friends lift the old man with the Father Christmas white beard to his feet. We finally get him into the vehicle.

"Where's my bag?" he asks.

"Right here, Louis. Right here."

"Oh-ah."

Poor Fanou was afraid, I think, that I wasn't going to take Louis out with me. We circle the plane, and park as close as prudent to the starboard door. Ginny gets the stretcher ready. Louis struggles, in his pain, to raise his bottom high enough to get it onto the stretcher backwards, as he tries to avoid the glances from Lizzy Moodoo. He's finally horizontal, and we cover him with a clean sheet and the yellow comforter. His head is forward. We close the door, and I board from the front, and then walk between the front seats to sit beside him. He has his eyes closed and is moaning. Lizzy says something and reaches forward to him with an opened can of soft drink.

"We-ah," says Louis softly.

The baby cries and Lizzy pops her breast out of the dress and into the baby's mouth. Neil fires up FDE and we taxi to the south end of the strip and roar for takeoff. As we climb out, I write the admission note on Louis. We're going to 9,000 feet. It's not so bumpy up there, but I recall that Louis is only one week out of the hospital with congestive heart failure. He seems to be doing all right. We level out at 9,000. A tap on my shoulder from the rear seat.

"May I borrow your *National Geographic?*" asks Lizzy Moodoo in perfect English.

"Why, yes," I answer in great surprise. "It's got a good story on Papua, New Guinea."

"Yes, I know." she says.

Past Ernabella, Louis queries, "Are we at the Alice?"

"No, Louis. We're just past Ernabella." Then, to Ginny, "Can I give him one of my Talwin that I use for kidney stone pain? Maybe it will take away his pain."

"Sure," says Ginny, and produces a cup of milk from the tea service. Louis swallows and lies quietly. Then I notice Ginny fishing behind her in the pocket of the seat she's sitting on; a burp bag. I help her get it.

"It's Neil. He's sick. He says he has to vomit, and he has pain in his chest and numbness in his left arm," she tells me.

"Oh!" Neil puts the bag close to his right hand, but keeps flying.

"Do you know how to fly it?" I ask Ginny.

"I think so, if I had to."

"Well, I've flown Bonanzas, and would have no problem with it, if worst comes to worst. You'd have to get him enough out of the seat to let me get my feet into it, though. Let me know if things go bad."

I relax into my seat. What a circus! Neil carries on, though. At DME 15, we start our descent. It's bumpy! No one is talking. I find that my little green Bible is in the pocket of my windbreaker, left there from last Sunday. I read a few Proverbs. Nothing dramatic. The final is a tad steep, but Neil greases it on the runway, and we taxi up and shut down. The ambulance isn't here yet. Neil departs to lie on the lounge at the AMS operations office. He's feeling better. There's Darryl with a bunch of well dressed people boarding FML. And there's the television camera crew. Good old Darryl! Right in the front line with the celebrities, and with his handsome epaulets flashing the three shining gold bars of the senior flight captain. I wonder who the celebrities are?

22 July 1982

Louis is dead. Louis Wirultukur, the thoughtful, black man from Fregon with the full, white Father Christmas beard; the man who signed the cross while flying over a sacred site on the way to the hospital, left his mamu in the Alice and took to the permanent dreamtime this last week. I'd seen him after we brought him to the hospital. He was sitting naked in the center of the white sheeted bed, slowly rocking back and forth with his eyes closed, concentrating all the pain in his body in the wrinkles beside his eyes and on his brow. His scrotum, grotesquely distorted with ascitic fluid, was lying on the white sheet, gently supported on both sides by Louis' hands. A fluid wave could be seen to move across the thin, black skin on the top of the scrotum as he rocked, and the bottom side, the side against the sheet, had been rubbed raw and bloody by the friction with the starched material.

The doctors said that he died of an overwhelming sepsis. Somehow he'd gotten an infection into that scrotum, or maybe it was the chronic renal failure, or maybe it was just that his old heart gave up. But Louis is dead. We forgot to bring his old felt hat with him when we left Fregon last week.

This week is different again. It's FDQ, and it's John Everett pilot, and sister Virginia Gretchen for Ernabella. John is disgusted this morning. Neil, he says, left the plane in a "grotty" condition. It's also leaking oil from the port engine; probably a rocker pan that's loose, suggests John.

"Ginny, you can sit in the right seat if you want," I offer.

"Oh, fine!" she exclaims.

But then she doesn't go up front. Maybe she's afraid of John in his blue funk this morning. She sits in the backward facing seat. That's okay with me. I walk past her and settle into the right front seat. John has the earphones on, so I can't hear the tower conversation. John sets up the panel. It's going to be the 208 radial at 5,000 feet. There are some little puffy strings of cumulus sitting at about 9,000 this morning. We'll be just below them. John wheels down to runway three-oh, and we turn and roar back towards the northwest. The Ansett Ayer's Rock special F-28 is sitting at the taxiway waiting for us to go by. The familiar "Klunk, klunk, kabunk" as the gear settles into its well, and we're climbing out east of the Stuart Highway.

The sky is about eighty percent overcast with the cumulus, and it makes a dappled pattern on the desert with here and there shafts of light between the clouds illuminating the floor of the desert with spot-lights of brilliance. Somewhere ahead of us is a new Chartair Cessna 402, but I can't spot it. John can't either. Not until we're on our descent pattern over the low hills to the north of the Ernabella strip do I spot the Cessna making its base leg over the settlement. John flies the pattern, and touches down facing into the brilliant morning sun.

Julie Peters arrives with the Toyota, and we pile in. They've had some rain during the night, and the desert has that washed, dusty smell, almost like something good is cooking in the kitchen. The mountains are splashed with light from the ground, too. Someone set the desert grass on fire two days ago, and there's a burned area of about twenty acres to the west of the airport.

That will make the little spring flowers come on strong, I'll bet!

The first patient we see on arrival is Cyril (Gerald) who is about twelve years old and has a terrible burn to the right leg. I guess he was sniffing petrol and smoking at the same time, and dropped the can when it caught fire. It got his pants leg, and he has a raw burn, circumferential, from about five centimeters above the ankle to about ten centimeters below his knee. It's a clean, but deep second degree. He's going to need a graft. I hear that he was in the Alice all this last week, but didn't go near the hospital. He went walkabout in the Todd river basin instead. I explain to his Mom that this is going to be like pork rind barbecue if we don't graft it, and that it will shrink up and stop his foot from moving in flexion and extension. Mom understands, and agrees that Cyril will go back with us on the plane when we leave after tea. Mom and younger brother will go along, too.

Mark Carlson is here from Fregon, and doing some carpentry repairs to the clinic. Mark puts his left wrist through a glass window. Just like that, right in front of us! He has a nasty laceration of the volar left wrist at the palm. It's cleaned with salvon and we find enough material to suture it with 4-0 silk after we give him a little Xylocaine anesthesia. Poor Mark. He sits there like a good fellow until we're all done, and then, when I look up, his face is the color of unbaked pie crust, and his eyes are rolled back into his head. He's fainted without making a sound. No matter. I gently lay him down on the bed that he's sitting on, and by and by he opens his eyes and gets up slowly and goes back to his carpentry.

Mulayenga is there with the knot at the junction of the middle and outer thirds of his left clavicle. He broke it in a football game on June 15th. He's twenty-five years old, and can swing that arm around pretty good. No limited motion. I reassure him that the callus on that fracture will mold and resorb, and that in another eight months or so, one won't be able to see where it was at all. Roger Webb is there for a driver's physical. Done!

Ruby has a sore back. She's also hypertensive and fifty-four-years old. She's also fat; 85 kilograms, and she has an old laminectomy scar. That's why her back is sore. She winces when I touch the scar. At least she's not having disc disease with pain like that. We'll give her a little Indocin. Meantime, her pressure is 192/116, and she's on 120 milligrams Inderal twice a day and one HCTZ. Maybe we'd better add on 50 milligram Apresoline to bring that diastolic down a tad.

Winifred Hillmans is the European lady who is in charge of the craft shop, and whom we see almost every Sunday at the Flynn Uniting Church in the Alice. Winifred is about sixty-one, and is having trouble with her hammertoes rubbing on her shoe when she walks. She's talked with Dr. Charley, the surgeon, about it in church, and he needs a referral. I write the letter. She'll have them fixed when Stephen gets around to it.

Dutchy is a fourth of July baby, cute as a bug's ear, but has a nasal obstruction on the left. Choanal atresia? Adenoid? He sure is a snuffly baby. I reassure Mom that he may grow out of it yet, and I think we'll use some oxymetazoline drops when he's nursing. If he's not better by the time I get back this next time, we'll send him on in to Geoff Hauptenhauser. What's this? They already have the drops. They got them when he was discharged from the Alice hospital. Good!

"You'll have to come outside to see this next one," advises Julie. "Bring your stethoscope."

I follow her to the concrete pad that forms a patio between the garage of the clinic and the back door. There's Harry, sitting Buddha fashion on the cold concrete, naked except for what looks like an earth color, felt greatcoat covered with camp dog hair. His face is black and thin, and the eyes are sunken into their sockets, and rheumy with chronic infection. His belly looks like the thirty-eighth week of pregnancy, and laced with huge superficial veins that are carrying the portal circulation around a scarred and useless liver. I wonder what his esophageal varicies look like? He also has a large umbilical hernia, but the abdomen is so tight with fluid that it feels like a pumped-up football. About every third breath, Harry coughs a weak, gurgling, juicy cough, but nothing comes up.

Beside him sits a woman. Her eyes are sunken in almost as far as Harry's, but hers aren't rheumy. Hers are steamy with cataracts. She wears a filthy knitted stocking cap, pulled down over her sparse hair, and her dress seems little protection from the cold air, except for the synthetic cardigan she has pulled about her narrow, skinny shoulders. Neither of them is wearing shoes; just the thick, leather skin of years of exposure. She has her gnarled left hand resting gently on Harry's shoulder, and in her right hand is a hunting stick, about an inch in diameter, and about a meter long, polished smooth and shiny from years of being rubbed by that hand. She looks expectantly at the tjilpi doctor as he bends over her man. Harry is having a tough time breathing.

"Gosh, Julie, he's in bad shape. I don't think that's congestive heart failure, or backward failure, I think it's primary liver problem. Cirrhosis, most likely, and I think he's not going to make it. I think we should take him in."

"Harry, would you come with the doctor to the hospital in the Alice?" asks Julie.

"Oh-ah," whispers Harry. We leave them there and return to the clinic.

Yanyi Baker is thirty-three and 20/51 weeks pregnant. She's 76 kilograms, BP 100/60. The clinic is awfully noisy and I can't hear fetal heart sounds. She's going to be okay. Joy Ann is European and also pregnant. She's thirty years old, 52 kilograms, and 138/70. We'll have to watch that pressure. She's maybe ten to twelve weeks pregnant. I can't really tell where the top of her uterus is. Her pregnancy test is positive, though. She has some nasty veins that gave her trouble with her last pregnancy. She has the support stockings from the last time. I encourage her to wear them, starting now.

Here's Imuna and little Clara. Clara is wearing a green and white parka that looks pretty new . . . and clean! Clara sits on the floor while I check Imuna. She's pregnant again, and not very happy about it. She's thirty-four, and of course, she's worried that she'll have another one like Clara. Imuna weighs 45 kilograms and has a pressure of 100/70. She's about nineteen weeks pregnant. Next is Marge McEgan, with tonsillitis. She's European, too. We take a throat culture. Julie will put her on some penicillin. She's twenty-seven.

Yuminia is Imuna's sixteen-year-old daughter, and she's in with abdominal pain. It's down on the left lower quadrant. This has been intermittent for the last year or so. She had a uti a month ago that was treated with Amoxil, but this other has been going on for a long time. I think it might be a chronic p.i.d., but she'll need an internal exam before we'll know for sure. Maybe she can come on in to the Alice and see Dr. Cahill in the next week or so. I'll bet it's a smoldering tubo-ovarian abscess.

Here's Mary Pirmangha, sitting on the bench out in the clinic. She was born about 1906, and she's babbling away like a child. Her right knee is swollen and ulcerated. The ulcers look clean, though. Let's take a second look. It's a burn! She's kneeled in the fire, it looks like. We'll give her Bicillin and dress the burns with furacin. Trkula is twenty-seven and has a sore throat. Exam shows this to be a resolved peritonsillar abscess. She's already almost better. Continue with her Bactrim.

We'll have to refer Ruth down to Adelaide for an evaluation. Ruth is post-polio, and you've met her before when she had the hip pain from trying to move about fast. She now gives me a history of sitting in school and watching the world tilt sideways from her, and then she gets a headache in the middle of her forehead. She's disabled with this for a period of minutes to hours when it happens, and it's happening more and more frequently. Examination reveals normal ocular fundi, and her pressure is fine. I don't know what it is except possible a migraine equivalent. But I think we deserve to work her up for this. We'll get her an appointment down south for evaluation. She can also have someone look at that right knee then, too.

Barney has a blood pressure of 134/102, and is taking Vibramycin for his chest pain. I guess that's as good as anything. His pain is over the right pectoralis, and identified with the tips of his fingers. Barney has had a previous heart attack, I'm told. We'd better get him on a little HCTZ for that pressure of his, or he'll be having another one. Langoliki has had diarrhea and cramps for a year. Yes, I think it's time we brought her into the Alice for an evaluation. She's thirty-two years old. No, she doesn't have to come with us this time on the plane. The clinic is dragging along, and I find that I'm not paying as much attention to some of the problems as I should. After about three hours of this, one gets a "burn-out." And there are other things on my mind like Cyril and Harry.

Alec Munchukoa is thirty-eight and wants a driver's license, and then Julie Dorn is here from Fregon. Julie says that when she was down to Adelaide, she saw a dermatologist who biopsied those lesions that I thought were scabies. It seems that Julie has hypertrophic lichen planus! How about that? She's improving on diprosone OV ointment, b.i.d., and she needs another 30 gram tube. Also she needs her Trocholor, ten orange, ten brown and eight white tablets, to keep her from getting pregnant in the spring and winter air. We write the script! That's the end of the clinic!

Who? It's Patrick on the radio for me. "It's George," he tells me. "George says that he has access to some really nice opals. What kind do you want? Over."

"Gee, Patrick, that's wonderful. What I'd like is about five or six in a sack for $500 to $600; solids with lots of flash, and cut and polished. Over."

"Do you want any roughs? Over."

"No, I think not, Patrick. I'd like to have them cut and polished. I'm not going to be here in Australia long enough to get them polished here. Just solids with lots of flash, and five or six for $500 or so. Over."

"Roger, Jack. They'll be here for you next time when you come down. Anything else? Over."

"No, Patrick, that's all. Roger Papa Sierra clear." How about that? That's for the next time to Indulkana, and we'll have some opals to take home.

Tea time. Slabs of cheese on rye krisp-like crackers. Then coffee, and some delicious banana bread that Julie has made. The talk is small talk, mostly between Julie and Julie from Fregon, with Virginia adding a little. It's shopping talk, and yes, sister Carol drove straight through from Warburton to Perth in one lump. A terrible, long trip, but she got there in only three days. She lost the chrome strip off the bottom of her little car on the right side somewhere, but otherwise, it came through just fine.

Then it's time to leave. John gathers up his "Brideshead Revisited" and we head back to the clinic to pick up the metal boxes. There's Cyril and his Mom and brother. Julie Peters will take them in her vehicle. And here's Harry and his wife.

"There's not room for you in the vehicle, Maminyi," says Julie Dorn. Maminyi stands there with her polished, dirty stick in hand, her cataracts beseeching the world to let her come along with her man.

"There's room Julie," I venture. "Ginny can sit on my lap

or John's. Let's make room for her.''

Harry has struggled to get his huge belly into the back seat of the vehicle. Ginny moves up front and sits on John's lap. Maminyi wriggles her skinny frame in beside her husband, and I close up the empty spot on the outside of the back seat.

"See whose lap she prefers?" I tease Ginny.

"But he's younger," defends Ginny.

"Yeah, but I'm safer," I laugh.

The vehicle is under way. Maminyi seeks out her husband's hand in a clandestine closeness. It's quite a job to get Harry into the plane, but finally we're all in, along with Cyril and brother and Mom. It's a full plane. Virginia sits in the very back seat. Harry is on the stretcher, but almost upright to keep his big belly from compromising his lungs. Maminyi is standing in front of and to the left of the plane as I settle into my right hand seat. I take out my camera; a picture, quickly taken. I hope it comes out.

John settles in. FDQ starts easily. We taxi to the end of the strip. The wind is straight across the strip. John pours the throttles open, and FDQ leaps into action. We race past the little figures standing beside the vehicles on the ground, waving at us. The stocking cap turns to follow the plane as we rise from the runway. We climb out to 9,000 feet where the air is less bumpy, and we're above the remnants of the cumulus string. I read my *National Geographic* that I didn't get to read last week. The trip is smooth.

I look back at Harry. "Palya?"

"Oh-ah."

Cyril is having a good time with his brother, looking at the sights and talking animatedly. He'll get that graft, and then, I suppose, back out bush to more petrol sniffing. But he'll be able to walk like the other kids. Maybe it's a waste. Oh, well.

The St. John's ambulance is waiting. There's Shane Pine, Vivian's husband. He's a nice looking man. He greets me warmly. I tell him about Cyril and Harry. It's quite a struggle getting poor Harry onto the stretcher, but he's finally on his way. He sure looks a lot like Louis. Oops! We're not supposed to use that name anymore. Never! The mamu will hear and accompany you from there on. I heard that Chartair charges the family of the deceased $400 for the one way trip back to the traditional grounds. That's kind of a rip-off, it seems. They have to carry the mail out anyway, but that's the way it is out here in the bush.

29 July 1982

I did see poor old Harry this last week at the hospital, and he didn't look very well. He still had his big belly with the dilated veins trying to drain the portal circulation around his umbilicus. I heard later that they'd tapped the tummy, and that they'd taken a lot of fluid off. I'm not sure that's all for the good unless they also replace some of the albumin loss. What's the poor bloke to do for osmotic stability if they remove all his osmotic force? No matter; Harry is still going.

This last Saturday, the twenty-fourth, son Raul arrived from Singapore via Perth. It was so good to see him. We've really enjoyed the week visiting the sights in the Alice and environs. But today is going to be the big day. The trip was to be to Amata, but there seems to be some difficulty again with the Dept. of Transport and the Council of Amata, and the strip has been closed. Sister Kay says that we're going to have to go to Ayer's Rock anyway to bring out Captain I. Would I mind?

"Heavens, no!" I do feel a little bit guilty, as if they are making this whole thing up just so that Raul can have a flight to Ayer's Rock via the Aeromedical Service.

They insist that we have to make the flight. Sister Di Staples is going to be going along, and then the scenario changes. There's a bus driver down at Victory Downs with severe chest pain, and they say they'll motor him over to Mt. Cavenaugh strip and would we take a look at him first before we proceed to Ayer's Rock.

"Why, sure!"

It's good old Neil warming up FDQ when we get to the airport. Sister Di is already there. She really enjoys this, I think. I introduce Raul all around, and it seems like a happy group. We're arranging for an 0900 hours takeoff, but Neil is fidgeting around and seems to be having some trouble getting his thing together. Finally we fire up, and there's no trouble with recalcitrant engines. Everything is moving along just fine. Neil is even wearing his bright blue shirt with the two-and-a-half gold bars on the epaulets! It's runway one-two, and at the end of the strip is Navajo "KTU," but we taxi right up in front of her. I guess it's a student taking lessons.

Neil gets the clearance, but I'm chatting with Di and Raul is in the right front seat. I do look up at the gauges and see that it's to be at 8,000. The power roars to life and FDQ leaps down the runway and into the air. It's a bit hazy this morning, but there are no clouds in the sky. I read my CME in the *American Family Practice* journal as we head out. Neil isn't much of a tourist guide. I look up, release my belt and move forward to inform Raul about the Finke River and Chamber's Pillar, both of which are coming up at about 35 DME.

The "iron compass" is below us, so I know that Neil is on track. Finally we begin the letdown. They've changed the venue of the landing from Mt. Cavenaugh to Kulgera. Goodie! I've never been there before. The low sweep over the settlement, about eight buildings with metal roofs and a "proper" looking station, and Neil is making his approach. He really makes them steep, but seems to touch it on easily. Let's have a look at this first patient.

His name is Danny Liefsen, and he's a big bloke. He has a terrible cough that makes him grab his chest with the flat of his hand mid sternum each time he coughs. He's raising green and yellow sputum, and after he takes his jacket off in the shelter of the plane from the cold wind, he's sweaty underneath. Poor guy. His temp reads 37.6 Celcius and he has a lot of amphoric sounds in his chest, but no decreased breath sounds. His heart sounds are normal and his BP is recorded at 122/78. It's a severe bronchitis. Sister from Victory has him on Vibramycin, 100 milligrams daily. That's good. He says that he's feeling better.

"O.K., Danny, you should stay on the Vibramycin for the next seven days, and don't go back to work until your temp has been normal for twenty-four hours."

"How will I get back to the Alice?" asks Danny.

"There's a bus will be coming through here about 1430 hours this afternoon. It will take you to the Alice in about six hours," I tell the bus driver.

Look at the big expert in interstate bus schedules. But I know Danny thought he could ride with us.

"We've got to go on to Ayer's Rock for a med-evac, Danny," I tell him. "And from there we may be diverted again, so we can't take you with us."

"Oh, that's fine. I'll make it on the bus this afternoon. How much do I pay and to whom?"

"No, Danny, there's no charge for this service. It's the service of the Royal Flying Doctors, and the 'blanket of safety' of John Flynn." Isn't that neat?

Neil taxis us to the western end of the strip and checks to make sure the temps are in the green. The radio comes alive. It's Julie Peters from Ernabella. She has Mary Tinpulya there with a sudden illness, and she's afraid that the thing is terminal. She wants us to stop by if we can. Remember Mary? Last week I saw Mary with the abscess on her knee. She was babbly then. I wonder what's gone wrong.

"Sure, Julie, we'll come on by. Should be there about 11 a.m."

Now it's Jennie from Amata. "What's your ETA (estimated time of arrival) for Amata?"

"We're not coming by Amata, Jennie. Your strip is closed."

"But I have a lot of people here that are waiting to see the doctor, and he hasn't been by for almost two months," complains Jennie.

"Sorry, Jennie. The Dept. of Transport says that you only have 500 meters of runway available, and the Navajo minimum is 800. We can't come. Can you drive your people to Ernabella?"

"No, we'll think of something else." Poor Jennie.

I can just see her with the responsibility for some really sick people, and the politicians have mucked it up so badly that they're going to make someone squirm. But it's going to be poor Jennie instead of some other politician. Like I said before, these sisters sure earn their money!

Neil advances the throttles, and we move down the runway. A big circle to the right, and we head back for Ernabella to the west. I can't see the surf at Mintibi. Sister Di is babbling on about something, and I'm only half listening and nodding my head in agreement. Poor Mary. What a coincidence. Mary Tinpulya is the wife of Captain I whom we're going to Ayer's Rock to evacuate. Ironic. Neil gets us to Ernabella about eleven o'clock. It looks like a convention with two planes already on the ground. Neil is talking to them on the radio. We make the pass over town and line up for the northbound runway. Again the steep angle of approach. I remember one of my instructors, when I was learning the Bonanza, who told me to always come in high enough so that you know you can make the strip when you shut down your power.

Julie is already there with the Toyota to take me into town. Raul rides along. Small talk on the way in, and the desert flowers, the red wild hops, and all the others, are blooming. There's not much wind blowing, but it's chilly. At the clinic, Julie leads me down the hall to a room with a bed. The patient isn't on the bed, though. In true aboriginal style, she's lying on a pallet on the floor. Mary's vacant orbit on the right is closed by her eye lid. The left eye is looking at me and blinking, but I don't think it's seeing. She's in Cheyne-Stokes respirations (a slowly increasing respiratory rate until suddenly interrupted by a long pause in breathing). It looks pretty bad. She has her knees and elbows flexed in mild decerebrate, fetal position. I quickly check her over. The blood pressure is 122/78, and she has a sinus rhythm. She's stroked out. It's probably an occlusion of the vertebral artery. I wonder if it's a thrombosis or a bleed.

"I think she'll be dead in a few hours," predicts Julie.

"I think you're right, Julie. If she goes on past five this after-noon, maybe you should raise a bottle of saline. It's hard to know if they may have periods of consciousness with a stroke like this, and if she gets thirsty, she'd have no way of letting you know. That would be a tough way to have to die." Julie doesn't say anything. I have the feeling that she isn't going to raise a bottle unless Mary asks her to.

"Would you talk to her daughter, Tjimpuna?" Julie asks.

"Sure."

Tjimpuna is sitting outside the clinic on the sunny side and out of the cold breeze. Her black face is shiny on her cheek bones from the tears that are welling over the lower lids.

"Tjimpuna, Mary is very sick. I don't have any medicine that will make her well. I don't think there'd be anything in the hospital at the Alice that would make her well, either. We can take her with us or leave her here. I think she'd want to stay here. Do you think so too?"

"Oh-ah."

"She's not in any pain. I don't think she's going to wake up again, Tjimpuna."

Tjimpuna says something in Pitjantjatjara to Julie, who reassures her with some words in the same language. I touch Tjimpuna's shoulder as I rise. We move to the Toyota and are on the way back to the strip. It's rather a solemn drive, past Ronald's grave on the west side of the church, through the river that is still running a little water. Strange how much salt has leached out of this land what with the river running almost all winter. Back to FDQ. Di and Neil are sitting in the plane out of the breeze. Now for Ayer's Rock.

Neil cranks things up and we move to the south end of the strip, and roar into life. There's a small balloon in my right flank. Sister Di breaks out a bit of coffee, and also some pancakes that look like they were left over from breakfast. Everyone cheers up with the warmth of the coffee. I slip down a half grain codeine with my java. Maybe that will hold that pain off.

"There's Mt. Connor," I inform Raul.

But it really is so hazy that one can't see it all that well. I take up a little of my reading again. Di is chattering on like a magpie. Occasionally I nod my head and say, "Oh, really?" That keeps the monolog going. Then a glance out the front windscreen, and there's the rock. Raul is enjoying it!

Neil descends, and then flattens out just a bit below the level of the summit of the rock, and we proceed from the airstrip counterclockwise around the monolith. About opposite the climb area, Neil begins to raise the nose, and banks a bit more to the left, and suddenly, we're on a level with the summit, and there's the summit cairn just out the port window. I get a picture of a few tourists standing by it waving at us. We must be only about a hundred feet or so above it.

A glance at Di. She's got her eyes squeezed shut, tightly, and is muttering to no one, "I just hate this!"

So, that's her weakness! Poor Di. Neil swings us around, and we make a downwind for the eastbound runway, one-one. Again the steep approach. I have my movie camera out and record this approach. It will be fun to show Raul again someday.

Wendy See, the sister at the Rock, is nowhere to be seen as we shut down FDQ.

"We'll go over to the hospital while Neil fuels, and Raul can then ride on with Terry to the climb area," instructs sister Di.

It's rather a dirty "ute" (utility—Aussie for pickup truck), but Raul and I pile into the back, and Di and Terry take the front. It's not too far to drive to the clinic. Raul and Terry lumber off after a quick visit to the outdoor "loo."

Di and I check out the clinic. It's closed. A small signs says, "Sister is at the camp or at Uluru or the Red Sands." That's neat. We don't have any wheels. Guess we'll just have to sit here and wait until someone shows up. A huge four-engined RAAF turboprop lumbers into view. It has a stinger magnetometer on the tail, and it's about the same altitude as we had been making the counterclockwise circle of the rock. It's probably giving some government VIP the same view of the summit as we'd had. It's not unpleasant sitting under the tree in the sun and out of that cold breeze.

Then chubby Wendy arrives, gazing through her Coke-bottle-bottom glasses, and telling us that the "patients" are already at the airstrip. Swell! Maybe it would be nice if the doctor had a chance to evaluate the necessity of the med-evac prior to departure, and what's this about the plural of patient? I thought there was just Captain I.

"Oh, no," Wendy informs us. "There's a tourist lady with a severe asthma that has to go out. I gave her nine milligrams of IV aminophyllin this morning, and there's another man with chest pain that has to go."

"Oh, is that so?"

"Yes, they're all waiting for you at the strip."

Back into the utility, and we're off for the strip. I wonder where Raul is now on his trip up the rock? There's a big, white St. John's ambulance on the strip, backed up to FDQ. Let's meet Veronica Conraad first. She's already sitting in the airplane.

She's a thin, little lady with a peaked nose and sucking at each breath like it was semi-solid air coming in. She has an inhaler of Ventolin, but she's still in trouble. A quick check and a bit of history. Wendy already has the evacuation papers filled out. Yes, I guess she really should go, although it's going to be a bit tough deciding whether we want to stay out of the bumps or keep her below 6,000 feet for her dyspnea. A quick check of the oxygen bottles reveals that they've already been turned on, but there seems to be plenty there. Let's see who else we have. Yes, there's Captain I lying on a stretcher in the ambulance. He seems fine and oriented, but he can't move his lower legs, Wendy tells me. He's been having a lot of trouble anyway, and just the last few days, he can't stand at all. He has his set of well worn and polished crutches beside his stretcher.

I bend down. "How are your feeling, Captain?"

"I'm a little cold. May I have another blanket?"

"Sure. Captain, I saw Mary at Ernabella just a little while ago. She's very sick."

"Oh-ah," he says, and his eyes seem to fade into looking through me instead of at me, but he shows no other emotion.

"I left her there with Tjimpuna. Is that all right?"

"Oh-ah," and the eyes look back at my face.

Captain has a long, scraggly, white beard, and is a very high man in his tribe. If you'd like to see a picture of him, you should look into the book *The Red Centre* and you'll see Captain almost naked, standing on a sand dune with his spear properly resting in his woomera preparing to bring down the big game. He's there on those pages in full color.

A quick check revealed no significant abnormalities in blood pressure or heart sounds. I don't know what Captain's trouble is. Maybe it's a peripheral diabetic neuropathy. He really needs to come in. Let's look at the other patient.

Jim Greene is a local worker in one of the hotels here at the Rock, and he's had a bad bronchitis for a couple of weeks. It seems that last night he gave out with a cough, and had sudden onset of sharp pain in his left chest laterally and anteriorly. He's really in quite a bit of pain. A quick check reveals that he has no decreased breath sounds, and he seems fit from a cardiovascular point of view, but I think he's fractured the eighth rib and maybe also separated the costo-chondral junction on that side.

"I don't know why he has to come in, Wendy."

"Well, I've already done the work on him and I think he needs an X-ray."

"What good will that do? What he need is support of this

fracture and some medication for pain. It's going to take five weeks for the fracture to heal even without an X-ray."

But Wendy is adamant. Jim has to be evacuated for some reason know only to the "sister-play-doctor."

"I can't take the weight," announces Neil. "There's room for Jim on the stretcher, and Captain I on the other stretcher, and Mrs. Conraad in the forward facing seat, and the doc on the backward facing seat, and me and Raul on the flight deck. But I won't have minimums on this short a strip to get us off," insists Neil. Fair enough! Let's not test it!

"I'll stay with Jim and we can take the Fokker back on the commercial flight," announces Di.

Good on her! She has an invitation to a free lunch at the hotel, and can travel back in the comfort of the commercial flight, and leave the doc to handle the sick ones. So be it. That's the way it's going to be. Di and company leave for the hotel to make the arrangements (and also to pick up Raul at the climb area). It's getting on to 1400 hours. Jim is really in a lot of pain. Wendy produces two elastic six-inch bandages, and we wrap him securely and I give him one of my small supply of Talwin. That should help. About twenty minutes later he is feeling better. Here comes the red Toyota on the other side of the strip. A figure leaps out and races across the strip. It's Raul.

"Where are they going?" I ask him as he comes up, not even short of breath after the sprint.

"They're just driving around the end of the strip, but I thought you might like to leave early," explains Raul.

With that, the Toyota arrives. Captain I is loaded in. Veronica is checked again. She has a blood pressure of 152/72 and was born on 31 July 1912. Her birthday will be this Saturday! Happy birthday!

The tourist Cessna 208 is warming up. They're getting into position for takeoff to show a load of tourists the Olgas and the Rock. But there are eight passengers and the pilot in that single engine plane.

"They're called 'widow makers' back in America," Neil tells me.

I can see why. The plane is coming down the strip with the engine screaming all the power it can get from its 300 horses.

With only about three hundred feet to go it gently lifts off the strip and proceeds out over the scrub at about fifteen feet altitude. That's scary!

Now we're ready. Down to the end of the strip for one-one. Neil advances the throttle. I wonder if Di is going to be happy. I've sure got my hands full. Captain I reclines easily on the stretcher. I don't know what's going through his mind.

"Are you palya, Captain?"

"Oh-ah."

Mrs. Conraad has informed me that she really doesn't care for small airplanes. She sits tense and stiff opposite me.

"We'll get you some oxygen once we're in the air," I reassure her.

We're off the ground. It's bumpy. Mrs. Conraad is a good scout. She doesn't seem to mind the bucking aircraft. At 6,000 feet the bumps stop, but she's really cyanotic. I turn on the oxygen. What's this? It's a pediatric mask. Oh, well. I give her the mask at about nine liters/minute flow, and work my way back to the kit in the after locker.

"What's that, Captain?" He's tugging at me as I go by.

"Is my bag in?" He has a dirty pillow case, much like Harry did, that was with him in the ambulance. I'd been told by the ambulance driver that he had a big wad of bills in there.

"Yes, Captain, it's right here." I raise the dirty bag to show him. He brightens up. I think he just now thought of it, and was worried.

I search the kit, but I can't find an adult mask. We'll just have to make do with the peds mask. Poor Mrs. Conraad. When she takes the mask off, you can see her start to turn blue, and when she puts it back on she pinks up like litmus paper in vinegar.

"It makes my mouth so dry," she tells me.

"I'll get you some water, but it's going to be hot."

I go aft again and get some leftover coffee water. It's welcome to her. The flight seems to be a long one, but then we're starting our descent, and there's the Space Base, and we're cleared in on runway one-two. Neil makes another of his steep approaches, but again, pulls off a "nine" landing. St. John's is waiting for our patients. It's been an interesting day. We've really earned our wage today with all this evacuation. Raul and I help Neil clean up the aircraft.

"Thanks, Neil, for everything." I explain to the St. John's officer about our patients. Everything is going smoothly.

"Is my bag there?" queries Captain.

"Oh-ah, Captain." I set his bag on the foot of his stretcher in the ambulance.

Neil tells me that he's had word from Kay at the Aeromedical Service that Mary died at 1400 hours. Ah, well. God bless her. But I don't think I'll tell Captain I just now. We wave "g-bye" to the ambulance that's departing.

5 August 1982

I checked up on poor old Harry this last week. He has diarrhea now, and is a constant mess. They did do a paracentesis this last week removing about 1,200 milliliters of fluid from his belly, but it really didn't help him much. His poor little wife managed to find her way up to the Alice from Ernabella, and sits in the chair beside his bed, looking away from the tjilpi doctor when he's visiting, but looking at her man when she thinks no one else is looking. She still is wearing that funny little stocking cap, but it looks so much cleaner, that someone must have run it through a bucket of water some place. Captain I is sitting on his bed like Buddha yet. He can't move his legs very much, they tell me, and he's scheduled for the Old Timers' Home. I couldn't find Cyril to find out how the burns were coming. I guess he's been grafted and is probably over at the Children's Health Unit. It's hard to keep track of all these people when, for most purposes, the hospital feels that I'm supposed to have nothing more to do with them, except fill out the IPTAS forms (Isolated Patient Travel and Accommodations Service).

Today it's to be Fregon and we have Mrs. Sue Miller going with us to meet Neil, the schoolmaster and be introduced to aboriginal settlement schooling. Sue has a Bachelor of Science degree in Elementary Education from Cortland State University in Cortland, New York, and also has twenty-three graduate credits from the American University, Washington, D.C.; the University of California, Berkeley; and the University of Virginia in remedial reading. She has taught American Schools for six years (grades three to five); has three years experience in remedial reading in elementary schools; has tutored remedial reading for five years, and is presently volunteer teacher, Ross Park, Alice Springs working with a ten-year-old aboriginal child, and is a most interesting person to talk with. She's quite excited about our trip this morning, and has been waiting patiently for the doc to arrange this opportunity. Only yesterday afternoon did the council finally announce to Aeromedical Service that it was all right to bring her along today.

Sister Carol is back from her holiday to Perth. She really did drive all the way across the western desert by herself in her little Chrysler. She did the Warburton thing all by herself, but had written a letter to the petrol station there with a check for $30, asking them to reserve petrol for her when she came through.

When she arrived and inquired, the manager said, "Oh, my wife wants to see you. She knows you."

Sure enough, Carol and the manager's wife were old schoolmates. So they had a good reunion, and, though they tried to persuade Carol to stay, she headed on out over the desert. She had some interesting experiences with gangs of "roos" and emus. She even managed to clip an emu on the foot when it challenged her on a narrow, winding mountain road. Total problems with the car, though, were a lost wheel disc and a trim strip from the bottom of the car. She's her usual bubbly self today.

Darryl is the pilot. Mark and Margaret are at the airport too, but Mark is going out in FML to Utopia. Margaret is just there. They had an excellent honeymoon in China, Margaret says. Darryl is loading the boxes. He looks sharp! It's time to board. I direct Sue to the backward facing seat, which makes Carol happy. I slip into the right front seat next to Darryl. The Ansett Friendship, Foxtrot Oscar November is lined up on runway one-two, and the tower is telling them that there's a bunch of birds at the 6,000 foot length of runway. "FON" advises that they'll be well off and above at that distance, and they're cleared for takeoff. The F–27 does leave the runway well before the halfway distance, but the little truck then proceeds down to the end and shoos the birds away.

We're next, and Darryl opens the throttles after checking all the switches on the dash, and inadvertently cutting both mags to the starboard engine, making a rather startling sound as the engine dies. He quickly switches both on again, and the engine roars back to life. Now, with the throttles all the way forward he strains against them like he was pushing them through the firewall. FDQ lifts off considerably shorter than Foxtrot Oscar November. It's to be the 204 radial at 6,000.

"Stay east of Stuart Highway until 5,000," advises the tower, and Darryl does as he's told.

I have two bulletins from the Santa Barbara County Medical Society to read. The one has the Editorial by Society President, Tom Ross, on "The Jealous Mistress." Most interesting. I'll have to tell you about it some time. Meantime, I also try to point out the sights of interest to Sue, but she's reading the *Centralian Advocate* and doing her own thing. Sister Carol is polite, but conversation is limited. Carol provides us all with coffee about the SA border. We've been trying to spot the Chartair 210 that's supposed to be going in to Ernabella, but neither Darryl nor myself can find it. At one point I see something moving against the floor of the desert. "Contact!" I cry out.

"It's a truck on the highway going northbound," says Darryl without enthusiasm.

So it is! Good grief! It's only a spot; must be 6,000 feet below us and five miles away. I thought I'd really pulled off an "eagle eye." Oh, well.

We're letting down for Fregon. Sue hands her Instamatic to me for a picture of the settlement. Done! Darryl sweeps around to approach from the south and touches down smoothly. He's upset that there are two vehicles in what he thinks is the plane parking area. But it isn't the parking area. It's the vehicle area just west of the cattle grid.

"I think it's too soft, Darryl. The other guys always park over by the strip markers there; the half-barrels painted white."

"That's illegal," scoffs Darryl. "That's on the strip. We have to park off the strip."

With that he taxis FDQ down to the north end and beyond the markers for the end of the runway. He shuts down. The vehicles have a time deciding what's going on, but finally come down the 400 or 500 meters where we're now parked. It's Fanou in Mark's vehicle, with only a front seat. The other vehicle is an old Dodge truck, with a mechanic driving. We all pile in and head for the clinic. The building is now completed. The batiks painted on the wall are vivid in color and quite pretty. I'll have to get a picture of that. What's this? We've forgotten the medical kit again.

"Do you have a stethoscope and sphygmomanometer?"

"Yes," says Fanou. "I have all the equipment you'll need."

Good old Fanou! The clinic can start. First comes Mark. His wrist looks just fine where we sutured him a couple of weeks ago at Ernabella. Fanou herself is having some trouble with pain in her right arm and wrist and hand. It sounds almost like carpal tunnel syndrome, but on testing she has some suggestion that this might be C–5,6 cervical disc trouble.

"We should have an X-ray of the cervical spine," I tell her.

She's agreeable and is going to be in the Alice this week. Fine! We'll get an X-ray request for her. She's going to be going soon to McClellan Medical Unit Neurological, Alfred Hospital, Commercial Road, Prahran, Victoria anyway, and can have things looked after there.

Next is Brian Smart. Poor Brian has terrible psoriasis, and says that he came to Fregon just because he feels too ostracized by humanity because he looks so terrible. He says that he should take his shirt off and get sunlight on it, but he's so ugly of skin that he can't do that. He's been on methotrexate before for it, and always had good results. Can I give him some more? Sure, I can. We'll draw a blood count and watch for side effects, though. He also uses betamethasone cream, .05% for it, too. We fix him up with a script. He's shown me his legs. Not just a few patches. Brian is covered with the stuff. It really is ugly, too. Poor guy!

Then sister Julie Dorn would like to have a letter of referral for a new class that she's going to attend at Lincoln Institute in Community Health and Maternal and Child Welfare. Sure, I'll write a glowing letter for her. She's dedicated and has the combination of a sense of humor and compassion that's rare in young people of Julie's age.

Next is Rich Norton, born 30 September 1961 and he's had mono, he says. He has a crop of boils that are giving him trouble. We'll draw an FBC on him too, and put him on some Amoxil. That should take care of the boils. Howard Stuart is from Warebrei. He says that he's come to Fregon "forever." Apparently there has been a disaster of some sort in his family life. Carol asks him in Pitjantjatjara if he has a father or mother.

Howard answers, "No."

"Brothers or sisters?"

"No."

Either they are dead, or Howard has committed some tribal crime and been expelled from his tribe. He's just eighteen years old or so. He says that he saw a witch doctor, but still isn't better. He did get a few capsules of Amoxil from a sister at another settlement, but still has pain in his right chest. He's running a fever of about 38.6 and on examination has decreased breath sounds in the right base. He has pneumonia. Poor Howard. The world is treating him rather shabbily. We'll put him on some Keflex, 250 milligrams, two caps twice a day for about ten days—if he'll take it. He seems grateful.

Ylipi is huge! 97 kilograms, and she says she's pregnant. BP 114/62, and maybe there is a uterus in there. Let's guess that she's about fourteen weeks. Margaret Carroll needs LPG for a positive serology. She also has a toothache. That's fine. We can fix both things at the same time. Her blood pressure is 94/68, and she's about 30/52 weeks pregnant. She has fetal heart tones at 148/minute. Let's give her LPG now and again in a week and again a week after that, and save this baby from a terrible fate.

Next comes Peggy and baby Patrick. Patrick was born April 20. He has his first neonate exam. He's just fine, except he has a curious adduction of his little fingers at the proximal IP (interphalangeal—the joints between the finger bones) joint. Peggy wants a Lippe's Loop (intrauterine device), but I can't put one in out here. She'll have to have Dr. Cahill do it in the Alice. Douglas Miles is a great big man, wearing a stocking cap; wants benefit money.

"Sit down money," he says.

"What's the trouble, Douglas? Why can't you work?"

"Broke arm ten years ago, and in March (Easter time) was hit by a car and hurt it again."

I put the arm through a range of passive motion. There's nothing wrong with this arm. He's just big and lazy. The notes say that he was born about 1937 or so. We produce an amazing array of papers of different colors. Each is going to have to be filled out by some social worker before we get to the green one, which is the one that I would certify that he needs a pension. It will take him a year to get back to me.

"Here's what you have to do, Douglas."

With that we present Douglas with his first lesson in bureaucracy. He takes the papers and doesn't seem discouraged. He seemed to expect that this would be necessary. Maybe he'll follow through and come up with a pension some day.

Imityala is twenty-nine years old and weighs 48.5 kilograms, and has a BP of 110/70, and is thirty-seven weeks pregnant. "Jingaroo next week you come in on the mailplane to the Alice, Imityala. Then you can have the baby there." She nods her head and smiles. She's deaf as a stone.

Manyuritjanui is twenty-seven weeks pregnant and 80 kilograms, and 120/80 and is still hoarse. I don't know why, but when she comes in for her delivery, I think Geoff Hauptenhauser should take a look down there. She sounds like a recurrent laryngeal nerve is gone. She's thirty-seven. There's no thyroid abnormality visible. Collin has a terrible periodontal infection. He's on erythromycin. We'll refer him to the dental clinic. Then here's little Julia with her breast buds again. She's just five, but last time we checked them out we told Mom to let me have a look at them next time I came, and here she is. Yes, they're still just little breast buds. We'll leave them alone. Last patient is Chris Wells with the pain in his right upper abdomen and costal margin. I still don't find anything wrong with him. We draw a serology anyway, since his wife is Ylipi, and we've already given her LPG to protect her and the "ity" (baby).

That's the end of the clinic. Gee, it was a nice clinic today, and people seemed really friendly, and the time has gone by fast. It is almost 1215 hours. Time for a cup of tea. We proceed to Fanou's place. No Sue around. I wonder where she is? Here she comes.

"Can we go to the craft shop? I've been all morning with Neil at the school and have to go to the bathroom, but I don't want to miss a chance at the gift shop."

"Sure, let's go over there right now when you finish in the bathroom."

She disappears and shortly reappears ready to go. I leave my half-finished cup of coffee and we walk across the compound. She's had a wonderful time with Neil. She's had a chance to sit and watch the teachers. Sue thinks that they seem too indecisive in their program.

"But that's because the kids don't have to be there if they don't want to," I try to explain.

She still thinks that they should keep the class moving more rapidly, because the kids have such short attention spans anyway that they lose interest while the other kids are reciting. She's probably got a point. It sounds like she was right in her element during the morning. To tell the truth, I'd kind of forgotten all about her. But then, I knew that she'd find her way to what she wanted to discover. She's resourceful and not shy. Apparently, she did win over Neil, who can be a terrible road block to the community acceptance of a visitor if he isn't pleased.

Lorraine is in attendance with some of the ladies at the craft shop. They've done some painting today, and are just leaving their tables for lunch. Lorraine is most patient. Sue begins her shopping for Christmas. Why, they have some beautiful shields available. I'd wanted one for a long time. They run about $45 in the Alice. Here there is a beautiful one that attracts my eye. The faults in the wood have been patched with spinifex gum. It's beautiful!

"How much?"

"That one is $23."

"Sold!"

Then there's another one, wider and with beautiful white and mahogany colored grain.

"How much?"

"That one is $25."

"Can you put it away for me for next time?"

"Oh-ah." Sue rounds up her purchases including some beautiful paintings of the tribal designs.

"Oh, those ideas for the designs come from the design of the dry lakes that you fly over on the way to the Alice," says Lorraine.

But these designs have been part of the culture of the aboriginal for more than a hundred years. How did they ever get to see the lakes from the air? It's a mystery like the huge paintings in the deserts of South America. All in all, Sue spends the major portion of a hundred dollars, but does come away with some beautiful artifacts that would cost at least twice as much in the Alice, and be totally unavailable in America. She's pleased.

Carl and Fanou and Darryl arrive with the vehicle. It's one o'clock, and they're anxious to leave. We pile in and head for the airstrip. This time we have Sue in the right front seat. I'll sit in the backward facing seat. The engines of FDQ roar to life. Darryl fidgets while the needles come into the green. Then full throttle to the firewall, and FDQ leaps down the strip and into the air. A circle over the settlement, and we head for smoother air at 9,000 feet. The radio: "We have a stretcher patient at Ayer's Rock. Can you divert?" It's only 1330 or so.

"Sure." Darryl turns to about 300 degrees and we climb on to 6,000. It's bumpy all the way. It's also a bit hazy.

Sue is enjoying the ride. Carol and I talk about the probability that the land below is all underlain with beautiful layers of opal. Here and there the white dirt of opal country sand is showing through the scrub. Then we're descending. There's quite a bit of activity on the strip. The Cessna 208, the "widowmaker," is just departing downwind on runway twenty-nine heading for the Olgas. Behind it is a Cessna 206 also leaving downwind. Darryl flies a wide left downwind pattern, giving them time to get underway. The new Uluru village that is to be the international "jet set" headquarters is still only patterns in the desert sand, although the new airport with its 10,000 foot runway is now sealed with black bitumen.

Darryl swings a broad base leg, slowing FDQ down. Then onto final. I turn in my seat to look at the view that I'd had through the view finder of the movie camera last week when Raul was along. It's not as steep an approach as Neil makes. Darryl fidgets with everything, but comes in much flatter and with a bit more power on. There has been no buzzer or honking, but I notice that there's also no green light for the landing gear.

"You are going to put the gear down, aren't you?" I question as we come about 200 meters from the threshold at about 200 feet altitude.

Darryl takes his eyes off the strip to the handle of the gear, and casually flips it down. "Klunk, klunk," and Darryl's eyes are back on the strip for a smooth landing and roll out. There are the ambulance people and the ambulance that we saw last week, and there are two bus loads of tourists taking pictures of the Royal Flying Doctors making their mercy call. Darryl taxis to the parking area and shuts down.

There's Wendy. This time she's really worried. Mr. Kenneth Barkmint, a worker at one of the hotels at the "Rock," is writhing in agony on the stretcher in the ambulance. His IV is plugged in but isn't running. Between gasps of pain, Ken tells me that the pain started at about 1030 hours this morning and has been burning in character, and now is almost unbearable. Wendy has given him 75 milligrams of pethidine (Demerol) at about 1215, but he's sure hurting. We don't have any tools, but Wendy has brought along their kit. Our kit isn't even in the plane—the emergency kit. So we have no IV material or any medications at all. The ambulance departs for the clinic to bring us back some new IV material and some more pethidine. I give poor Ken another 100 milligrams of pethidine at 1430 hours.

"Have you had any trouble with ulcers, Ken?"

"Yes, I had a bad thing with them about six months ago."

So that's probably the problem. He's perforated a peptic ulcer. Gee, we'd better get this show on the road. First an IV line. Carol works efficiently providing the material. The IM demerol is now taking hold, and Ken is sitting much more quietly. The lines goes in and the flow of .45% saline, four percent glucose runs well. Ken settles back on the stretcher. There has been a continuous whir of cameras and clicking of shutters as we work, but one is aware of it only peripherally. There's just so much to be done quickly, but the tourists are having a field day putting this all on film for posterity or whatever. Too bad we can't scatter a little ox blood around just to make it more interesting. Now we're ready to depart.

As the plane is being cleaned up of various debris from the administration of medications, Darryl moves beside me and explains, "I couldn't get that gear down until I'd slowed her down. I was going too fast to drop the gear, but I hadn't forgotten."

"Sure, Darryl. I know. I didn't mean to talk up. That's just the way I've always done things when I was flying with my good buddy, Vernon back in the old days. It's just a habit I have. I didn't mean to be critical of you." I wonder if he believes me?

The trip back is bumpy. We're at 9,000 feet to get smooth air, and then Ken is in distress as he tries to find a comfortable position. We put on the oxygen flow. The IV is running well.

"Can I have another needle?"

"No, Ken. It's only forty-five minutes since the last one. You'll do okay. Sit up for a while if you like."

Finally, he relaxes again, and lies back down. Darryl isn't talking to anyone. I'm in the backward facing seat, so I can't see his face. Sue nods and finally settles her head on the head rest and the starboard window. Carol monitors the vital signs on Ken and records dutifully.

"What's the diagnosis?"

"Perforated hollow viscus, query peptic ulcer."

With the business of attending the patient, the trip goes quickly, and now we're descending. It's really bumpy. The landing. There's the St. John's crew. Shane is in attendance again today. Ken is able to walk from the plane to the stretcher on the tarmac. It's been a rewarding day. We make our good-byes and head for our vehicle.

I find out that they took Ken straight to "theater" (surgery) and that he indeed had a perforated peptic ulcer. I saw him today. He has an "NG" (naso-gastric) tube still through his nose decompressing his stomach, but he looks great and feels much better. He's grateful. So am I. He'd not have survived a road trip in to town, I'm sure.

Oh, yes. I also saw Mrs. Conraad. She's still in ICU but is much better, and not requiring oxygen now. She'll come right soon. I also had a talk with sister Di Staples today. She agrees that there was no reason for the evacuation of Mr. Greene with the broken rib. But as I recall, she wasn't resisting very much when she had to take him on the commercial flight back from the Rock two weeks ago. They looked at him at the hospital, she tells me, and taped him up and sent him back. They never admitted him to the hospital or even gave him pain medication. Let's blame that one on Wendy. I wonder if we'll get there again next week—the "Rock" that is.

12 August 1982

On the way to the airport this morning, there's an interesting mirage to the south. There are chalk cliffs standing up straight; looks like about fifteen miles south, and the cliffs must be about a hundred feet high by the looks of the mirage. The specter is so clear, that one can see the brush growing on the outcroppings from the cliff. This wall stretches for about fifteen miles. It's really interesting.

It's like old-home week at the airport. There's Mark and Darryl and sister Ray, and Dr. "Dede" Stapleton, and then Carol drives up. Darryl is flying Ray and Dr. "Dede" to Yuendamu in FML, and Mark is taking Carol and me to Indulkana in FDQ. Everyone seems to start up at the same time. "Mike-Tango-Juliett" is a Cessna 210 that is taking a station manager's wife back to her station. They are waiting at the helipad line for tower permission to cross to the main strip, but the Ansett Fokker F-27 is already down there at the end of runway three-oh, and about to start his takeoff run. FML is directly behind us and "Uniform Uniform Papa" is behind them. Quite a parade. Here comes Foxtrot November Oscar, and by the time he's opposite us on the taxi strip, he's retracting his gear. No birds this morning. All four of us that are waiting, taxi on down to the threshold of three-oh, and make a counterclockwise circle, with each departing as the tower releases.

"Foxtrot Delta Quebec, clear to track the Alice 184 radial at 6,000. It will be a while until I can give you left turn clearance. Would you make a right turn clearance?"

"Affirmative, Alice."

"Foxtrot Delta Quebec, clear for takeoff; right turn approved. Stay east of the Stuart highway below 6,000."

Away we go, making a right turn out over Hornsby's vineyard and the Racecourse housing area. I've never taken off that way before, so just have to take a couple of slides of that direction. Then we settle down on the radial and follow the railroad south towards Kulgera. Mark is telling me about his and Margaret's honeymoon trip to China. Actually, they flew Air Cathay to Hong Kong, and then took a hydrofoil to Canton, and were there a few days and took the train back to Hong Kong. One meal was a twenty-four course dinner, Mark says. He really did have a good time, I guess.

Sister Carol serves coffee and biscuits, and Mark leaves me reading my cardiology text and goes back to talk with Carol. I watch Kulgera go by; we really should be starting our descent. Mark comes back.

"Why didn't you take us down?" he asks half seriously.

Actually, I'd have been delighted to do so if he'd told me to, but as right seat occupant, one doesn't touch anything on that panel unless told to do so, or in the event the pilot is incapacitated. The strip at Indulkana is terrible. There are weeds and grass growing on it, and there are patches where the sand has gone soft. This will be the next strip to get shut down, I suppose. Mark touches FDQ down easily, and we taxi back.

There's Patrick sitting in the Toyota. "Big clinic this morning," he announces.

Indulkana is still just as dirty and trashed with discarded paper and bottles and tins as it ever was. No one ever bothers to pick anything up, and the camp dogs here are the scrawniest and mangiest of any of the settlements. Irene Flint from Chandler has been hired as the janitress. I suppose it was a job below the dignity of any of the aboriginal folks. She's doing a good job. The clinic looks clean.

Jennie is my first patient. Sister Jennie has a sore left thumb that is getting weak. Jennie's full name is Jennifer Mary Markham, and she was born on 16 November 1945. From the history and examination, it would seem that Jennie has some sort of nerve root problem at the C6-7 level.

"Gee, Jennie, I think you should really be seen down in Adelaide and have an EMG (electromyogram) and a CAT (computerized axial tomography—a form of X-ray examination) scan to find out what's really going on."

"Oh, I don't want to get that involved with it. Do you think something like Indocin will help?"

"I don't think so. I think the best thing to do is find time to go down and have it worked up. It will only get worse. You don't have any atrophy of the thenar prominence yet, but that's going to come along if it gets worse."

"Well, I'll have to think about that."

So much for sister Jennie's problem. Next is Cynthia Brown who is thirty-six weeks pregnant and is to have another Coombs test. Cynthia was born in 1954, 74 kilograms and BP 100/70. She should be thinking about heading for the Alice soon. Biddy King is thirty-four weeks and 60 kilograms. She was born in 1962. Her BP is 105/65, says Jennie, and the fetal heart is clicking along at 160/m. Then comes Kantji, a very "ninti" (knowledgeable) tribal leader, who is seventy years old and wants an exam for his driver's license. He's an opal expert, I'm told. I can't find anything really wrong with the old man. He has some cataracts, but they're not very dense. I approve his license.

Gilpin Ward is sixty-five years old and limping. He's hypertensive and his pressure has been up to 214/110, says Jennie. I get 172/92. He's taking colchicine for his gout, and was taking allopurinal as well, but they ran out of that. He's also taking Aldomet and hydralazine for his pressure; no diuretics because it made his serum uric acid go up. He's having headaches, but has no gout pain. I tell Jennie to give him another hydralazine if his pressure goes up.

Pirimulga was born in 1949. She's very shy, but Jennie says that she has condylomata (venereal warts) which are very painful. We'll have a look. Sure enough! She has a lot of them.

"Pirimulga, you'll have to take the bus up to the Alice and have Dr. Cahill fix these for you."

She looks away, and softly whispers, "Oh-ah."

But one can tell from the way it's said that she isn't going to go until they get much worse. That's up to her. She can stay here until they really get to be a mess if she wants to.

Jennie is gone, I notice, and Patrick has taken over. The nicotine fit that these "environmentalists" get is surprising. I never can deduce the logic that compels these people with the activist ideology of environmental protection to smoke cigarettes, or pot or whatever. Somehow they can twist this into being all right. Patrick brings in Puna. Puna fell four days ago and hurt her right arm. It's in a neat back slab, and Patrick cuts the binding off. There's a mild table fork deformity of a Colles fracture. It looks still to be slightly swollen. No use trying to send her up to the Alice. In the back slab she's comfortable. Puna is about twenty-seven.

"Patrick, let's leave the back slab on for about another four days, and then put her into a circular plaster. I want her in the position of function with her thumb point at her nose and a little wrist extension, and the plaster should come down to the distal palmer crease, but leave the fingers and the thumb mobile at their joints. Proximally, you can leave the elbow open to extend and flex. The pain, if there is any, will restrict her enough so that she won't move it that much, and if we immobilize her elbow, she's going to tear the whole thing off. Better half a loaf than none. She'll have good function when it's all over."

Here's the Pitts family from Chandler. Scrawny Rhonda; hubby is home with a sore back. They don't have a job. I guess Bill blew that, too. Rhonda is twenty-six years old. She's having inguinal pain. Exam reveals that there's no hernia. She has a well healed scar in the RLQ (right lower quadrant) of the abdomen (previous appendectomy) and also suprapubic. I can't find anything wrong. Billy has tinea capitis (ringworm of the scalp). We'll try some micatin on this six-year-old, and if that doesn't work, let's give him a bit of griseofulvin. Little Elizabeth looks fine today. So much for the Pitts family.

Nyuniwa brings in daughter Inmantjulai. Nyuniwa has a mincobah sticking out the side of her mouth that looks awful. But apparently it fulfills the same thing for her that the nicotine in Jennie's cigarette does for her. I don't think the mincobah is as carcinogenic as Jennie's cigarette, though. Inmanjulai is six and has a left lower lobe pneumonia. A look in her mouth tells you why. Every tooth in her head is a carious mess! Every time she bites down she must inject pus into her little blood stream. She just has to get up to the dental clinic in the Alice and get those teeth attended to. In the meantime, let's give her some erythromycin. She's had enough penicillin in the past to make these bugs probably resistant.

Meantime, Mom, (Nyuniwa) has a recurrent uti (urinary tract infection) and left flank pain. She's already been scheduled to see Dr. Tompson in Adelaide, but she does need something for pain. Patrick doesn't have any codeine, but he does have Fortral. Let's give her that and see if it holds down the pain. I have lots of empathy for Nyuniwa. She's forty years old now.

The clinic seems to be losing momentum. Now Patrick has gone away, and Jennie isn't bringing in the patients as snappily as she did at first. It seems as the hours go along, Jennie and Patrick really don't have a feeling for the work. That's different than it used to be when they were over at Fregon.

The next group of people is rather difficult to sort out. It's a family arrangement that isn't condoned by the tribes, and wouldn't exist here, either, unless David, age about forty-four, weren't high in the hierarchy of the tribe. David is a big man, and rather handsome. He's hypertensive, and is wearing a red head band. His blood pressure is 142/92, and he's taking a Clotride, one daily. He seems fit otherwise. Lilly is his wife and is the mother of Michael. Lilly is forty. She has a reflux esophagitis that is hard to define, because the words that she is using in Pitjantjatjara are unfamiliar to any of us. But it comes out that the burning of the reflux is the main problem. We'll try some Mylanta see if that gives her relief. The etiology of this is probably set into some rather strange family arrangement that comes along with the next patient.

Debra is Audrey's daughter, and is just past three. Debra has an eight-centimeter abscess in the left femoral canal. It's really swollen and tender, and for a while I almost thought she might have an inguinal hernia here. She holds the leg adducted and flexed at the hip to take the pressure off. The abscess is not pointing, and I can still feel a good femoral pulse.

"Audrey, we should really take her in to the hospital to have this taken care of. Is that all right?"

"Oh-ah."

"We'll come by for you after noon tea time; maybe about 1400 hours. Is that all right?"

"Oh-ah."

I guess Audrey is worried about this, too. Audrey is about twenty-three or so, and is, at the same time, the daughter of David and also his second wife. David is the father of Debra. Michael is the son of Lilly and David and is six. Jennie is worried that he has undescended testes.

We check it out. David wisely puts the handle where it belongs. "It's cold."

That's exactly true. Michael has retracted his testes up into the canal because it's cold. Both of them are there, and there isn't any hernia above them. The relationship between Michael and

Debra is best sorted out by genetics rather than family.

Here's Amanda Flint. She's nine months old and Mom is worried about a "dent" in her head where a traumatic hematoma has subsided. No problem. Mom is reassured. Mom is Irene, and is twenty-nine. She has some stasis dermatitis on the left medial leg just above the ankle secondary to a broken leg after a road accident some years ago. She's reassured. The clinic drags some more. I finally walk out of the room and into the main reception area.

"If you aren't going to supply the patients, we'll call the clinic to an end."

Jennie hustles in the next patient. Barbara Tunkin is twenty and has a uti, and is taking Bactrim and is also pregnant; about twenty-four weeks. Everything else is okay with her. Her sister, Pollyanna, wants a loop out.

"Jennie, I don't do that out bush. She'll have to go into town and have Dr. Cahill do that."

"We were told that all you had to do was gently take hold of the string and pull, and if it didn't come out, then send them in to town."

"Okay, Jennie, I can do that, and I have done it lots of times at the Community Health Centre, but if I pull that out and we get into the airplane, and two hours after we leave, Pollyanna starts to bleed, what are you going to do? I think it's just a lot more sensible to send her in on the bus to have that done under sterile and controlled conditions. If you want it done out bush, then you can sit down here now and do it, and I'll watch." That settles the argument.

Roberta is pregnant, too. She's twenty-two and about nineteen weeks pregnant. She weighs 58 kilograms and BP is 100/70. Sister Carol misses the vein for the pre-natal bloods. I lay her down, and I miss it too. We'll leave her alone and catch it next time. Roberta leaves pretty well disgusted with European medicine. But we're all getting tired of this interminable clinic. Here's old Jackie Walsh, born about 1912. He has gout and hypertension and cataracts. But aside from all that he's in good enough shape to go walkabout. We just talk with him for a while.

Do you remember Tommy? He looks a lot better than he did when he was in congestive failure. Tommy is about forty-seven and has a terrible mitral stenosis. He's had two episodes of hemoptysis (spitting up blood) and now has a bradycardia (slow heart rhythm), probably a junctional rhythm, but it sure sounds better than the supraventricular tachycaria that he had a couple of months ago. He feels much better. He still has fluid in his lungs, but he looks a lot better. We reassure Tommy.

Phillip was born in 1966. He has a burn on the outer lower limbus of his right eye. It looks like maybe fire or battery acid or something. It's about a millimeter in diameter, but there's a massively inflamed conjuctiva. Let's put some chloromycetin eye ointment in there and patch it for a couple of days. I don't see anything wrong with the central cornea or the uvea. Here's another Biddy; pregnant and weighing in at 106 kilograms. She's about twenty-four weeks? Who can tell with that much belly. She looks happy. Her BP is only 122/70.

Lastly is poor Linda; 1926 is her suggested birth date. The hair on her chin is long and poor Linda looks more animal than human. Her lungs sound just awful. She still has her purse with the medicine in it, and she's taking it faithfully. That's probably why she's still alive. Poor old thing. Her BP is 142/82. Rales filling both bases of her chest. Now she says her back hurts. I shouldn't wonder. We'll give her a little aspalgin or something. I really don't know what we can do for the poor thing.

That's all! Thank God! The clinic today has really dragged on, but I think it's a lot to do with the lack of enthusiasm of Patrick and Jennie. On the way out I run into George. George was going to have a sack of opals for me today, remember? Well, he doesn't. He says he didn't understand what I wanted. After all that time on the radio from Ernabella. Nuts! He says he has some nice rough stuff at his house, but he's off for Mintibi straight away, and won't have time to show me any.

"Okay, George. How about next time?"

A cup of coffee at Jennie and Patrick's. Mizzou, the cocker dachshund is there. No, Olive never did come back. Finis Olive! We listen to Jennie and Patrick detail their struggles with the establishment and overtime pay. I guess they have a point. There's isn't much pay and there is a lot of overtime.

Finally we head down to the airstrip. We pick up Audrey and Debra and Lilly and David at the clinic, and Mark fires up

FDQ. It's a hazy day, but after leaving the ground, Mark climbs to 9,000 feet where it's smooth, and I doze in the sun. There's the thirty-five-mile DME, and the Finke River. There's the Alice, and we're cleared to a right base for one-two runway. Mark settles us in neatly. St. John's is there to pick up Audrey and Debra, and so ends another day with the AMS/RFDS.

19 August 1982

Different morning this morning, with a hint of springtime in the air. There are puffy little alto cumulus up there, maybe about 9,000 feet, that look pretty dark in patches. Do you think there might be rain? It's still. No wind is blowing at all. At the airport it's Richard running up FDQ. I haven't seen Richard for a long time. He has a beard that looks a bit scraggly, but he offers a warm greeting when he shuts FDQ down. Carol arrives with Robyn in the limo. She also has Damien with her and Cyril. Damien is about eighteen months old and walks like a duck. He is cute and fat, and has blond hair and a pink hospital ID on his left ankle. Cyril has had the graft on his leg, but is active and running. There's sure no restriction of motion in that achilles tendon now. There's a bandage around his lower leg, and also one around the thigh where the graft came from.

We load the boxes. Carol gives Richard the devil for putting one of the metal card cases into the cabin instead of the wing locker. Carol wins. Richard takes it from behind the last seat and places it in the port wing locker. Not too much traffic this morning. I can't hear the clearance because Richard is wearing the earphones. It's runway three-oh though, and we climb to 7,000 feet.

Not too much conversation. I have my new *National Geographic* along, and read about the Bahamas. It brings back some great memories of one of the first international trips that Laura and I ever made. We'd been to a General Motors meeting in

Miami Beach, and took a holiday up to West End, Grand Bahama Island. I think it was two nights and three days for two, all inclusive, for $99. Not each. Ninety-nine dollars for both of us, and that included the airfare, which was by DC–6 that was loaded with people and ducks and geese and chickens. Ah! Those were the days!

Richard brings us in a long descent towards Ernabella. It's a crosswind blowing here, and pretty freshly, too. We're almost under the southern edge of the clouds here, though.

Julie meets us with the Toyota. Damien is delighted with seeing his family. What's that? Cyril's folks are up in the Alice. We can't leave him here. We'll have to take him back with us.

"How come you never let us know that they were up there?" Carol asks Julie.

Here comes the Chartair Cessna 402. Old senior pilot Murray is at the controls when it lands. These planes look so ungainly. The 402 has a terribly long nose, and the access door almost touches the ground. Another vehicle drives onto the strip. It's old Charlie and Nancy. They've been out here again for a visit. Nancy still has on the green striped stocking on her left leg and the blue striped one on her right leg. They've both fallen down around her ankles. I wonder if she's ever had them off since I saw them both about four months ago? We watch in wonder as huge Charlie wiggles his bulk into the narrow door of the 402. It's like stuffing a big marshmallow into a little bottle. He sits in the narrow chair in the cabin of the plane with his broad bottom overflowing the tiny seat. That entry would have made a great movie sequence. I had my camera, too, but from good manners I didn't unleash it to record the event.

The clinic is clean, and doesn't look too full. Julie always has her clinic pretty well organized. First patient is little Dutchy with the snuffly nose. We saw him before. They've been using the nose drops on him, and it does help, but he's still snuffly. I guess we should send him up and have Geoff Hauptenhauser have a look at that. They've been using .125% neosynephrine. That's a bit strong. Bradley was born 18 July 1982 and has rales in his right lung base. We'd better give him a blast of Bicillin. Bradley's mom is fourteen years old!

Joyann McElwell is European. She's the school marm, and

is pregnant again, and has some terrible varicosites recurring in her left leg. She's thirty years old, and about fourteen weeks pregnant and weighs 54 kilograms. Her pressure is sure up yet. It was last time, too. But now it's at 142/80. We'd better watch that. Milyika is twenty-four, 25/52, 120/65 and 50 kilograms. I wonder about hydramnios here. Her belly is so soft it's hard to pick up the edge of the fundus, and I can't hear a fetal heart. Oh, well. Next time we'll double check.

Here's Imuna with little Clara. Imuna's pregnancy is coming along. She's now thirty-four, 49 kilograms, 100/70 and 23/52 with a mincobah sticking out the side of her mouth. We also check out Clara. Crouzon's syndrome, and she's chesty. But we won't give her an antibiotic unless she starts to run a fever. Ampiyi is 51 kg, born 22 October 1952, 110/70 and about thirty-three weeks. FHH 136/minute. She's holding little Gregory, who is a post-meningitis with marked mental retardation. Poor little kid. He's just as cute as a bug's ear, but periodically goes into opisthotonus and fits for a few seconds. That's sad. He's got a bit of a chest, too. Yanyi is thirty-two, 79 kilograms, 130/76, and 22/52 weeks. There's a loud placental bruit that makes the fetal heart sounds uncertain.

Jackie Baker is Yanyi's father. He was born about 1908 and he's heading for Hettie Perkins' Old Timers' Home. He looks pretty good; a little hypertensive at 162/82, but dressed really nicely with a gray-knitted cardigan and matching stocking cap that looks remarkably clean. I wonder if someone just made it for him? He's diabetic and you met him once before when I described his lipomatosis. He still has the great big one in his left inguinal area.

Nelson is seven weeks old and has a left lower lobe pneumonia. We'd better give him a half Bicillin now and another half in two days. Rowena was born on 27 April 1982, and has a draining abscess in the right groin. She had bicillin on the tenth, but none since. Let's give her some erythromycin by mouth now, and for the next five days, at least, if she can be found.

The radio is saying that there's been a stabbing at Fregon? No, the message is that Nungalka/Dicky, about sixty-three, has been bashed as of yesterday by her daughter-in-law, Ilyipi. There are three lacerations of the scalp that bled a lot yesterday, and

look like they might be infected. No, she never lost consciousness, and she seems to be okay except for the wounds. Carol tells
Fanou that we won't come down just to check it out.

"But if anything happens to Nungalka, they'll kill Ilyipi,"
wails Fanou.

"That's not our problem. We just sort out the medical problems, not the social ones," Carol reminds Fanou. "Besides, Ilyipi
has already fled from Fregon. As a matter of fact she's here in
Ernabella sitting right in the clinic."

Oh? My hair feels ruffled at the back of my neck. I'm glad
Nungalka is okay. I'd really prefer not to have to treat a spearing.
The radio tells us that Jennie in Indulkana has a belly patient
that she'd like to get an opinion on when we're on the way home.
That's our first diversion. I agree that one does need to be seen.
Fanou's was really a social rather than a medical problem.

Cliffie is here for a newborn check-up at the tender age of
one month. He's a fine looking, traditional facies aboriginal baby
boy. Then Julie Dorn arrives with a Toyota full of patients from
Fregon. Amanyi is hypertensive. Born 1933, and she's running
a pressure of 260/120 today. She's taking Clotride and propranalol, but she's also been previously diagnosed as renal failure.
Let's add a little Apresoline; maybe 25 milligrams in the morning
for a week, and if it doesn't come down below 200/100 we'll add
another 25 milligrams at night.

Tjangawa was born about 1908 and is also a little hypertensive at 160/100, but her problem is that she was bashed on the
right elbow and has a really firm mass sticking out about the
lateral epicondyle. Exam shows that it's a hematoma. There's no
limitation of motion here. We'll just put her in a sling, and give
her some aspalgin for the pain, and she'll come right.

Here's baby girl Amyala, 13 August 1982. She's fine! Probably make a good friend for Cliffie as they grow up together.
Imitjana is her Mom, and Julie is a bit worried about the laceration
that she has of the birth canal. Amyala was born in the bush.
They place Imitjana on the table on her side, and draw her right
leg up a bit. It's an unfamiliar view of the perineum, and at first
the size of the introitus scares me. Then as I look some more, I
can sort out the anatomical landmarks and separate what's edema
from what's damage. She's not too badly damaged. She's come

along fine. But that's a new experience. I've seen that view with animals after birth of offspring, but not with humans. That's kind of a shocker!

Audrey has pain in her fifth rib on the right lateral side. She's had it for about six months off and on. Julie wonders if it could be gallstones. I take a look. Audrey denies trauma. I don't know what it is, but that rib is sure tender. The lungs sound fine. I guess it might be a residual from herpes zoster, maybe. I really don't know. We'll just treat it symptomatically. It sure isn't gallstones, though.

That's all? Yup, the clinic is over. That was interesting and it didn't take too long, and it was well organized. It sure was a change from the clinic that Jennie and Patrick put on for us at Indulkana last week. Let's go over to Julie's for some tea.

We load the cases into the Toyota. Here comes a little donkey, just wandering along the road. Gray with a black neck band that almost looks like he's wearing a collar. He stands only about shoulder high. Remember, don't let him get to where he can put those hind feet to you. He approaches and stops. He's close enough to touch. I reach out slowly, and put my hand between his ears and scratch gently. I become involved again in small talk and suddenly find the head has searched out my hand so that my fingers are again between the ears. We start walking slowly towards Julie's. The conversation is about Fanou and Nungalka and Ilyipi, and it looks like I've found a new friend in the donkey. When we enter Julie's house, the donkey expresses his displeasure at being left out with some loud braying.

Richard is looking at his sectional for the trip to Indulkana. There's something that smells delicious! Julie Peters and Julie Dorn, bless their hearts, have produced a real, true pizza. Out of the oven it comes! All melted cheese and pepperoni and tomato sauce, and steaming hot!

"It's your last visit, and we thought we'd like to do something special for you," the sisters explain.

"Oh, Julies, that's so nice of you. But I will be back one more time before we leave for home."

"You will?"

"Yes, it's still five weeks until we leave."

"Well, we have something else for you, too."

With that they fold out a lovely green sweatshirt with "Pukatja Community" in white letters on the top, and then a perched Magpie, and then "Ernabella" below. It's hard to express thanks for something like that when it comes as a "thank you" straight from the heart. I'm really overwhelmed. I put it on. It fits, too. Isn't that nice?

"Gee, that's so nice. Thanks to all of you. How thoughtful." No use getting emotional about it, but I really am impressed.

Carol and the sisters talk a bit of politics. We've still got to round up Cyril and go by Indulkana to see Jennie's belly patient. So, we move on from the house to the Toyota, bidding good by to my friend the donkey on the way. Cyril is playing with friends at the school.

Out to the aircraft; load things up, and Richard lifts FDQ from the strip, and heads about 110 degrees for Indulkana. It's rough! There are more of those little cumulus clouds around now, and each has a solid bump under it. They're at about 9,000 feet yet, and we're below them. It's hard to read with that kind of motion, and then we're on final for Indulkana. The strip looks just as bad as last week; loose sand and lots of grass and weeds growing on it.

Jennie is there with her vehicle, and quite apologetic about bringing us all the way across. "That's okay, Jennie. Let's have a look at the patient."

Tjanala is heavy, and lying in the hospital bed. It's a different hospital bed than you'd think of, though. This one is a metal bed with a gray blanket, and the whole appearance of the room is more like a storeroom than a hospital. There's no window in this room. The window is missing because there's a fire exit on that wall instead. It's rather dark and dreary. Tjanala says that she's been having this kind of pain about every period time now for several months. Exam shows that she has a tender belly, but the bowel sounds are normal. I think it's endometriosis, and tell Jennie so. We'll have to get Tjanala up to the Alice for Dr. Cahill to see one of these days. Meantime, we can start her on some oral contraceptive pills and see if that will make the pain go away.

David is standing on the porch of the hospital as we leave. I recognize him by his red head band. He's going to be going up to the Alice with some money for Audrey, he says. I tell him that I saw Debra yesterday, and that they got a lot of pus out of that abscess on her right thigh. Poor little Debra. I did indeed see her. She was sitting on the floor of the TV room in the peds ward at the hospital, just crying like her little heart was going to break. Just lonesome, I guess. But when I'd reached down to pet her hair out of her eyes, I discovered that she was burning up with fever. From somewhere she'd gotten quite an infection. I had called it to the sister's attention. I didn't tell David all this, though. He was telling me about how he was bringing money to Audrey, and in his best authoritarian manner, standing straight and tall. I didn't see his wife, or his son.

Back to the strip. Cyril is making quite a trip of it today. Back into the air, and again it's almost too bumpy to read. The miles slip by. It's hazy enough so that even the sightseeing from 7,000 feet isn't all that good. I doze, then watch again as the familiar landmarks creep up. There's Chamber's Pillar, and the Finke, and then the Hugh River, and then the mountains, and we start our descent. Richard greases FDQ onto the runway.

"Let's give him an eight for that," I tell Carol.

"Gee, you're sure generous!" teases Richard. FML is just firing up to depart for somewhere as we taxi in. Never a dull moment with the AMS/RFDS.

2 September 1982

Yesterday sister Carol rang me at the CHC (Community Health Centre) and announced that the council has given permission for Laura to come with us to Fregon today. Neil is doing his thing out there, and I guess last month he was pleased with Sue Miller, so this month he's mellowed to allowing white people to come to see the settlement. Also, it didn't hurt that Mrs. Miller has spent the better part of $100 there, and also the tjilpi doctor spent a bundle and has a $25 shield still to pick up and pay for.

Laura is excited, and she isn't wearing her little white hat this week. I hope that doesn't portend doom and gloom.

It's overcast this morning. It's to be FML because FDQ is back in the shop with something or other drastically wrong with its innards. FML is sitting a little nose low, though, and Mark announces that we have a flat nose wheel. It might be an hour or so before we have it fixed. He's phoned to tell Carol, but apparently she's already on her way. We could take FDE, the Baron, but then Laura probably wouldn't be able to come along because there wouldn't be room to evac a patient if necessary.

Here comes Carol. It isn't in the limo, either. Carol now has her own Datsun Bluebird station wagon, all done in blue with its walnut dash and a console CB and just all sorts of nice things. The Health Department decided that the sisters should have their own vehicle. If they come in with a patient that is ambulatory they can take the patient straight to the hospital without St. John's ambulance. I guess the charge from the airport to the hospital by St. John's is $186. That's pretty steep! In the course of two years the little cars will pay for themselves just from St. John's savings, not to mention the savings of the limo. I feel a little sorry for Robyn and her husband who just bought the limo service from Bob Worthing. I imagine the AMS was a sizeable chunk of their business. Oh, well, that's economics. Meantime, back to the flat tyre.

The shop men have arrived and begin piling sandbags on the port horizontal stabilizer. The nose comes up higher and higher, and finally, two of the men lean on the stabilizer and the nose wheel is off the ground. The flat tyre comes off and the wheel from the nose of FDQ replaces it. Now, in addition to its other problems, FDQ will have a flat nose tyre. But it's only ten minutes, and we're ready to go. I hope they didn't bend the bolts in that horizontal stabilizer.

Laura takes the right front seat beside Mark, and I take the backward facing seat. FML is clean and trim. It's a nice plane. Carol tells us that Captain One has gone back to Ayer's Rock. He didn't go to the Old Timers' Home after all. He can get around with Canadian crutches. How about that? It's runway three-oh, and left turn to radial 204 at 5,000 feet. Its amazing when one is in the backward facing seat how you feel your back being pushed away from the seat with the acceleration of the plane.

Laura and Mark are chattering away. I read the *Centralian* that Carol has brought aboard. The Americans *won* the Henley-on-Todd regatta again this year, but lost it because the crew had been fed on imported food instead of local food. (The accusation was that there had been McDonald "rooburgers" imported for them!) Also, none of the American crew were in possession of their passports, and were therefore declared illegal immigrants. So the Aussies won again, continuing their unbroken record of success against the Yanks. The Aussies compare it to the Americas Cup in reverse.

The lakes that I've been mentioning in my logs all this time do have a name, I discovered when I looked at Mark's section of the area. They are call the Ephemeral Lakes. That's apt! They're salty dry now, and there's Mt. Connor and Ernabella and Mark starts us down. The wind is about across the runway, so Mark makes a whole circle and we land from north to south and taxi back. Mark has no feeling about parking on the strip by the markers, unlike Darryl.

There's Jennie from Indulkana to meet us. Julie Dorn is on holiday and Fanou is here, too, but Jennie has come down to help out. I wonder if the clinic will stay on course this time, or if we're going to be held up by nicotine fits? They've done some more work on the drawings on the side of the clinic. They really are beautiful. We carry in the cases and I note on the blackboard that there are going to be two dentists coming through the settlement on September 9, who will stay for three or four days. That's neat!

Our first patient is Alan Farmer, the store manager. Alan has a non-Parkinson's for which he's taking Sinemet 100/10. But it isn't holding down his non-tremor, so he's increased to one-and-a-half tabs a day with some improvement. We check him out and everything else seems okay. Let's get him on up to two tabs a day to further reduce his non-tremor. Alan is tall and gray-haired, and really a nice man.

We have a nice talk, and then we see Amelie. She's also European, but she's the caboose of a family of five siblings all of whom are married with their own families. Amelie is nine and has a problem with eneuresis (bed wetting). She has pharyngitis with nodes in her neck. We'll put her on erythromycin since she's allergic to penicillin and sulfa. Her urine is NAD anyway. I discuss the eneuresis with Mom. Mom isn't worried about it, and it isn't every night. Malpiya is in again and is now 45.5 kilograms, BP 95/60 and about 24/52. FHH at 136/minute.

Margaret is 65 kilograms, 105/65. She's getting her LPG yet for syphillis. She was born in 1956. We'll have to keep an eye on her. Then come Payula with her chronic cough. I really do want Geoff Hauptenhausser to have a look at her when she comes in for her delivery. She's thirty-seven and has had three previous C-sections. She'll have to think about going to the Alice on the mailplane soon. She's thirty-two weeks now, and 81 kg! BP is 105/60. Mowita is thirty-three years old and has pain in her low back. She's a classic pelvis of the aboriginal, though, with a marked lumbar lordosis and steatopygia, and paraspinal muscles as thick as my arm. Maybe a little Indocin will help.

Fanou is still having trouble with her right hand and arm. They took the films at the Alice, and I looked at them and they looked all right, but they didn't take a film on the oblique (obl-eek, not obl-ike) so I don't know if there's narrowing of the foraminae or not. She'll have to go back for more films. She isn't too happy about that, but I try to explain that it isn't my fault that they didn't take the total series.

Then comes little Samuel Munser, born 28 December 1981. Peter, his daddy, is teacher, and Mum is plump and cheerful. Sam is a juicy baby, just getting into his teething and he has a cough. I don't find anything wrong with Sam except that his BCG is draining. I still have mixed emotions about BCG. I reassure Mom, and we get to Mantua who is thirty-eight and having musculo-skeletal chest pain. She has huge breasts, and I think that's the problem. No such thing as a "good" supporting bra for these people. We'll have to try to give her relief with aspirin or Indocin or something.

The last patient is Brian Smart. His psoriasis has almost cleared. The methotrexate has been amazing. Did I tell you that I received a very formal note from the chemist through Dr. Wilson's office, stating that the medicine was dangerous and that the patient should have blood counts and such? I wrote back that I'd be responsible for my patient's care. Brian has another FBC drawn, but also had a strange experience this last week. He was out in the bush and had been working on some project or other when Robert, an aboriginal, had accosted him and told him that he was angry with David and was going to fight him.

Brian had said,"Oh, Robert, David is a nice bloke. What do you want to fight him for?"

Robert had replied, "Oh, you want to fight me instead of David?"

Brian had explained that he didn't want to fight anyone, and thought that was the end of the matter as Robert walked away. Brian was talking with another man, when he sensed disaster and turned just in time to throw his left arm up to catch the impact of the brick that Robert was about to crush his skull with. As it was, the blow caused a huge hematoma on the lateral side of Brian's left arm. Exam reveals that there's no fracture, but it's sure a good thing that he didn't catch the force on the side of his head. Brian says that in another week, he's going to take his shirt off and start to let the ultraviolet get to his skin. Fortunately, his face is totally clear of this awful disease.

That's all! The clinic is ended! Jennie hasn't taken a single break for a cigarette to my knowledge. We carry out the cases. Laura has been sitting in the vehicle watching all the activity around the village centre. Maggie has the bakery open. Let's buy a loaf of that delicious bread for a dollar! It's still hot. Mmm! It smells so good.

"Let's look at the craft store," says Laura. I discover that she's already been there.

Lorraine had shown a picture of the staff of Aesculapius to one of the aboriginal craftsmen, who has done a beautiful staff about three feet tall out of red gum. Laura has spotted this and tried to bargain Lorraine down for it, but Lorraine is adamant. Sixty dollars! I pick up my shield. That's another $25, and then Laura selects four mats with the "ephemeral lake" design on them for framing, and the bill is $105. There are two small "pitis" thrown in for a dollar each, and we make our way back to Fanou's house.

Despedida! There's Peter and Mrs. Munser and Sam and Fanou and Jennie and Carol and Mark, and they've put on a party with all kinds of cheese and sausage and even an omelette quiche done in a microwave oven! And there's Spumante! What a feast! There's also fresh bread from the bakery and fruitcake and Mrs. Munser has made a cake with the flag of the aboriginals as decoration, with "Palya?" written on it. How wonderful! It's quite a boost to the ego to have someone do this. How thoughtful!

Time to head for the strip. Mark fires up FML. It's going to be a bumpy ride home, I'll bet. We're to be at 7,000 feet. But by the time we reach Ernabella, I'm dozing in the warm sun. And then we're letting down. I've slept almost all the way. It's a bit windy in the Alice. Laura has permission to come along next week, too. We'll be going down to Indulkana. Laura will have a chance to see the really dirty settlement. I heard from Jennie that the Pitts are really finally moving, now that Bill's back is right. Little Kym's mother took him down to Adelaide, and found another man. That's okay. She wasn't married to Kym's father anyway. Poor little Kym. Maybe the next Daddy will be kinder.

9 September 1982

Strange day for the trip this morning. Sister Carol had rung yesterday, and after the recent rains, the strip at Indulkana has been said to be closed. So, we're going to have to wait for Mr. Marson, the community advisor, to let us know when everything is okay to come on down. Meantime, Carol has also contacted Granite Downs about their strip, but the reception with the new folks down there is a lot different than it used to be with Marg Baxter. Carol was told that the Granite Downs strip is closed. That's that. It's just closed. No one has gone to check or anything. It's just closed. That strip is on quite high ground. I wonder what it's closed for? Certainly not for water. Maybe it's overgrown with grass and weeds, or maybe they have cattle on it. We have to wait, and so takeoff is delayed until 0900.

This morning Laura is wearing her little blue hat. It's a lot like the white one, but doesn't sit as far down on her head as the white one. It looks nice, though, and does keep her hair in place. I imagine it will bring stares of wonder from the natives at Indulkana. John Everett is to be the pilot, and this week it will be FDQ, fresh out of the shop, and without the flat nose tire. John has been running it up, and it sounds good.

Carol arrives in her little "Bluebird," and we unload the cases. I mentally check to make sure that we have all of them. Yes, they're all here. It's bright and sunny this morning, but there is a cool breeze whipping around the corners of the buildings, and there are little puddles of water standing around from the rain. No clouds in the sky, though.

Laura takes the right front seat. I take the backward facing seat, and Carol faces me on the port side of the plane. It's runway one-two, and John has the earphones on, so I don't hear the tower conversation. Laura tells me that John says he can't hear well in FDQ, and Laura insists that FDQ is much noisier than FML. It's to be 8,000 on the 184 radial, right turn, and we're away. I almost slide off the seat as the acceleration of the plane pulls me out of the seat.

It's a bit bumpy to about 5,000 feet and then it smooths out and it's easy to read. I show sister Carol last week's travelog. Then I read some material that Randy sent us with a tape last week. Laura and John are in busy conversation. Laura has been this route before, so I don't have to show her the landmarks or scenery. A line of broken stratus appears ahead of us and lower. There's Kulgera, and John is following the "iron compass;" the railroad.

We start the descent, down through the clouds which are about 3,500 feet altitude, but only about 200 feet thick. Then we're over the railroad with the sun shining in dappled spots through the clouds above. A pass over Indulkana. They've dragged the strip free of weeds, but there are puddles of water at the west end of the strip and again on the northeast side. The middle looks fine, but it might be a little soft. John is a bit upset. We were told only about fifteen minutes before takeoff that Marson had sent the telegram up saying the strip was open. John isn't too happy with him. The landing is perfect, though, and we taxi back to the parking area.

There's Patrick with the vehicle, and the aboriginal health

worker with him. Why he needs company to drive out to the strip is beyond any of us, and it just means that we all have to scrunch into the vehicle. Patrick tells us that Jennie was hurt in a road accident. Patrick was driving the other night and they ran into a bullock. It smashed the bull bar on the front, and the vehicle tipped onto its left side. Patrick fell against Jennie on the low side, and she suffered an injury to her right arm. She had Dr. Parke see it at the hospital in the Alice, but he says it's a torn triceps muscle.

There's a lot of swelling over the elbow area, and she can't flex or pronate/supinate. I guess I can have a look at the films. I'll get the notes when I get back to the Alice and report to Jennie on the radio later. We drive into the clinic. The place is just as filthy as ever. I introduce Laura to the clinic staff, and then she goes on about her own business of seeing this settlement, and I stand by while sister Carol begins to discuss the landing strip with Mr. Marson. The discussion gets a bit heated, as Mr. Marson tells sister Carol what an important man he is in the community, and sister Carol tells Mr. Marson that she's not going to have his "guess" on the condition of the strip jeopardize the plane, the pilot, the doctor, and mostly herself! From now on she wants him to get his lazy body out of bed and go look at the strip and send a telegram of the condition, or they won't have a doctor visit from AMS anymore.

I don't know how it finally ended, because I had left the room when it started to get warmed up, and went to meet Sandy and Sally. Both of the girls are temporary sisters, and have come to help out Patrick while Jennie is incapacitated. Finally, the clinic can start.

Judy is the first patient; born June 30, 1963, and she's said to have Sydenham's chorea. She is athetotic, particularly on her facial expressions, and she's shy to boot. It's hard to get a story out of her. Examination reveals no cardiac murmur and her blood pressure is 122/82 with a sinus rhythm. She has no joint symptoms or signs, and is afebrile. I wonder if this is really Sydenham's? I guess we'll give her a covering course of penicillin and also some phenobarb to temper the choreiform motions. It's interesting that when she has "intention" she doesn't have the problem. She takes my torch and turns it on; then off, transfers it to the other hand. Not a tremor in a carload, and the facial grimacing also stops. I wonder?

Myra is the next patient. Myra is a well-Europeanized aboriginal lady of about fifty. She's on eight committees for the council and is clean. She's hypertensive, but taking one Clotride in the morning and one Aldomet bds. She's also very heavy. I talk with her for quite a while and then opt to leave the medicine alone. She could give up some of her responsibility and lose a bit of weight, and maybe we won't have to increase the Aldomet. I'd just as soon not. She's agreeable.

Next is Riley with a clean red and white logger's shirt. He was born in 1934 or so, and has some sores on his left foot. These are right at the mp (metatarsophalangeal—footbone, toebone joint) area of his 2nd and 3rd toes, and also another small lesion on the dorsum of the foot. But the foot is so caked with mud that I can't really see the lesions. It doesn't look like cellulitis, though. Riley says that he has some mulga in there. But mulga usually festers up with a lot of pus. Maybe it's just because of the mud there that I can't see the pus. Well, let's clean up the foot with some soap and water, and then put Riley on a course of erythromycin.

The next patient is six foot four inch Heather Marson, wife of the community advisor, who has just been lectured by sister Carol. Heather is first of all concerned about two-year-old son Conroy. She wants to know about circumcision. Red lights flash and bells ring in my mind with this apparently innocent request for information. I'm sure she already has a pre-formed opinion or information from other sources.

"Let's look first, Heather." Conroy has a rather small opening, but the foreskin is not really redundant.

"Is the urinary stream pretty full?"

"Oh, yes. He has no trouble with that." I look again. The opening is about four millimeters, but the skin is really thin. We discuss dorsal slit vs. circumsion.

"But if he has no trouble with the stream, I think we'd be wisest to leave things alone. I think in the next six months or so the opening will get bigger, and he'll have no problem. Probably by the time he's four or so, the foreskin will be retractable over the glans and then all will be right. If not, then he can always have something done. The main thing is that there's no obstruction to the flow of urine."

Then Heather wants her pregnancy checked. She's 92 kilograms, 132/75, which is unchanged from last time. Palpation of the belly suggests 22/52.

"I'm twenty-seven weeks. I had an ultrasound in Adelaide five weeks ago and I was twenty-two weeks then."

Not to argue. I don't hear any fetal heart sounds, either. The fundus is about 2 centimeters above the umbilicus. I'll go for whatever she says. The AMS has had enough discussions with the Marson family for this day.

Puna you met before, when we saw her for the Colles fracture of her right wrist. You recall, she wouldn't go into the Alice for x-ray or treatment? Well, she wouldn't leave the plaster on, either. She has on a back slab of plaster, and there's a huge callus formation about four centimeters above the wrist on the dorsum of the arm. But she has good flexion and extension of the wrist and can pronate and supinate. She's now four weeks since injury, and she's twenty-eight years old. I guess we'll keep her in a back slab for another week or so; whatever she'll leave it there for, and then in about six months, I'd expect that the callus will mold away, and the arm will look fine. At least she has good function, and that's the main criterion for a good result. Cosmetic wouldn't mean that much out here anyway, unless there's points for ugly.

Mona has just been recently found to have sugar in her urine. She's thirty-nine years old. Funduscopic reveals no disease. Her blood pressure is 132/82. Let's draw a blood on her, and if it's over 8 mmol we'll start her on diabinese 250 milligrams in the morning.

Little Jamie is whining with mouth ulcers and a draining left ear. His birthday is 28 September 1980, and he has a node over the middle margin of the right mandible. He's already on erythromycin, and Mom is making sure he gets it. I guess that's about the best we can do. Let's give routine toilet to that ear, though. Jamie's Mom is Betty (Biddy) who is thirty-two. She has some sort of arrhythmia, paroxysmal, apparently, that is very disturbing to her. She's doing just fine right now. BP 128/78 and a sinus rhythm. I don't know if she's complaining about P.A.T. (paroxysmal atrial tachycardia) or extra systoles. No matter, if she's normal now, and nothing diagnosable, I don't know what to suggest except to reassure her. We do that; or try to.

Jane Walham was born in October of 1954. She's been having meno-metrorrhagia (irregular, heavy vaginal bleeding) the last two periods. She's not on any contraceptives. She has no other symptoms or signs. Dr. Cahill is going to be down in six weeks or so. We'll have her seen by her. Meantime, if flooding really gets bad, we can give her some Provera.

Here's Andy back with the chronic festering problem of his buttocks. Actually, on exam, Andy looks better than the last time I saw him, according to the notes on the card that sister Carol puts in front of me. It was Andy's wife that had the festering condylomata that seem to be resolving with the LPG. I guess we'll give Andy some aspalgin for his painful butt. Some day he's going to have to have that all undecked and cleaned out. I don't think any antibiotic therapy is going to make it better. Interesting about his wife's condylomata, though.

Iljiya is twenty-eight, 98 kilograms, 110/70, and 19/52 pregnant and has a uti. We'll give her Bactrim. Joan is eighteen, 61 kilograms, 110/70, and 22/52. Her FHH is 152/minute. Rosie has lumps on her left neck that recur, drain, and then recur. Currently they feel like a series of rather large lymph nodes in the posterior left cervical triangle. Examination inside the mouth reveals nothing. I'd suppose that a chest film might reveal some chronic lung disease, like tuberculosis. She'll have to have a workup at the Alice for these. Why don't we send her up next time the lumps fester? Maybe they can sort it out.

During this time I looked out the window of the clinic on one occasion and saw Laura sitting in the vehicle outside. She's been talking with Myra for a while, too. Guess I should tell her that the craft store is just around the corner. I slip out of the clinic for a minute, and discover that she already knows where the craft shop is; she just doesn't have any money. That's fixed! I give her the whole $12 that I have; and after a little small talk, I head back into the clinic.

Now that the clinic is over, we'll go to Jennie and Patrick's and have a cup of tea. As usual, sister Carol has brought a bunch of goodies with her, and there's quite a spread of sausage and cheese and breads and pickles and other goodies on the table.

Laura and I stick to our glass of orange cordial, but do succumb to the offer of the chocolate cake with the pink and white goodies for frosting. We discuss Jennie's sore arm and I make a note that sister Carol will get Jennie's note from the hospital and I'll try to let her know what really is wrong. Dr. Parke did see her, but he's not too communicative, and she'd like to know what the injury is. Yes, we'll do that.

John announces that we have to go by Ernabella yet. It's Cyril with the bad burns that we brought out of Mt. Ebenezer last May or so. Remember? The petrol sniffer who had a friend who threw a can of burning petrol on his back? He has an infection in his arm, and has to go back to the Alice for further treatment. Okay. Jennie over at Amata also wants us to come over and look at a pregnant girl who is having belly pain. It's going to be a long day.

Laura has purchased a painting and a wooden carved snake at the gift shop, but still owes the lady there $15. We'll have to send up a check. Laura also has a picture of Myra, she says, and had the offer of a tempting morsel of malu (kangaroo) that was being cooked on an open fire by an aboriginal family. She declined the morsel. She did ask them if she could take a picture of the meal time; was told "oh-ah" by the men, and "we-ah" by the women, and is now kicking dust because she asked at all instead of just taking it. She says the meat was charred on the outside, and bloody on the inside. No, there weren't any side dishes of salad or veggies or even bread. Just the meat, and there weren't flowers on the table, either. Matter of fact, there wasn't any table. They were just squatted around the open fire in the dirt, tearing off pieces of meat, and throwing bits of the fat to the scroungy, skinny, mangy camp dogs that sat on the periphery of the human circle.

Laura did comment on the healthy looking horse that was at the edge of the settlement, and how upset it was at the kids that were throwing stones at it. She opted not to interfere for fear the kids would turn the stones on her. But, all in all, she's had quite a day in Indulkana.

Down to the strip. Sandy has been invited to fly back to the Alice with us. She's on her way down to Adelaide, where her home is. She's been in Western Australia at a post for a while. She was supposed to just take the bus from Indulkana on down, but now has the chance to see the Alice. She's delighted! There should be room and weight, says John, if we don't have to take on too much fuel at Ayer's Rock, even if we do have to bring in Cyril and the pregnant lady at Amata.

FDQ performs perfectly, and we make a 180 degree and set course for Ernabella. John has been reading *The Onion Field*. I pick it up, since he's busy with Laura and the controls. It's a good book. Suddenly we're descending for Ernabella. The pass over the settlement, and the approach. It's a strange feeling riding in the backward facing seat. One sees the end of the runway first, and then the touchdown, but no idea how far ahead the end of the strip might be. We taxi back and shut down, and all get out to stretch. By and by Julie comes along; and Cyril. What's this? Cyril's Mom, Dora, all 80 kilograms of her! Cyril won't go into the Alice without his Mom. John kicks dust with his shoe.

"It's the weight, Carol. If I have to fuel at Ayer's Rock, I'll be overweight. And I don't have enough seats."

"Oh, if you say the weight is all right, I'll squeeze the bodies in," Carol affirms. John kicks some more dust.

Then comes the port out of the vehicle. Usually aboriginal people have a small sack or even nothing with them for possessions. Dora has a suitcase big enough for international travel! With disgust John lifts it into the port wing locker. Dora and Cyril sit on the starboard stretcher. The rest of the people sit where they were before. John fires up FDQ, and we leap down the strip and into the air; course set for Amata. I go back to my reading, although it really is pretty bumpy. Cyril and Dora point with excitement to Mt. Connor. John isn't heading for Ayer's Rock. He's going straight to Amata. It's only twenty-three minutes from Ernabella to Amata today. It was thirty-two minutes from Indulkana to Ernabella. FDQ is making pretty good time. Jennie is waiting for us at the strip at Amata.

"Jennie, I'm sorry that I was on holiday in February when we were scheduled for our trip here. I really haven't meant to miss you. I'm sorry about that letter you wrote to Mr. Carter."

Jennie had written to the South Australia Aboriginal Commission complaining that the AMS doctor had made only three visits in the first six months of the year. Actually I'd made four. One missed because I was on holiday, and the others missed because the strip was closed. But Jennie in her "activism" had felt that she was being dumped upon. Strange girl. Jane is the patient, and she's about 19/52 weeks, about twenty-two years old, and the story goes that about 0900 this morning she had a belly pain. She came to Jennie, who examined her, checked her out for bleeding (there wasn't any). Checked her for uti (there wasn't any), and, although there had been no more pain nor nausea nor vomiting, Jennie felt that the doctor should see her.

Examination revealed a normal belly that was 19/52 pregnant. A stolid young lady in no distress, wondering what all the fuss was about. I examined her in the plane, on the stretcher, with my wife in the right front seat watching the show. The patient's blood pressure was fine; bowel sounds were normal.

"Well, Jennie, I guess that it has passed. I think she's going to be fine. Let us know if there's any more problem."

With that the patient departs back to the vehicle. Jennie has made her point by getting the doctor down to Amata for whatever political reason. Maybe to show the community advisor that it really is important to keep their strip open or whatever.

John is delighted. Cyril and Dora pile back in, and Sandy and sister Carol, and John fires up FDQ. I really thought he'd be heading for the Rock for fuel, but it's obvious that we're on the way to 9,000 feet. The course is 43 degrees. We're going straight back to the Alice. Small talk. It's hard to stay awake. I read a bit more of John's book.

Laura is all eyes. It's been a fun day. I get a bit more of the story from Sandy of her career, and then she questions my career as the doctor at "Pine Gap." It's funny how, when an Australian younger person says that, there's a mixture of awe and contempt at the same time. It's strange what publicity does for a name. In any other situation, Pine Gap would generate thoughts of clean, tall, shady trees in an environment of perhaps lakes and fish and things. But not here. Pine Gap has the dimension of disaster or the great "unknown." I explain my public health ministry at the facility. It mollifies Sandy. John sneaks FDQ onto the runway, and taxis to the ramp. Another day. It's too late to make the APO. Laura has had fun. We're all excited that we've seen quite a bit of outback that most tourists will never see. I'll have to remember to look up Jennie's notes on her accident.

"Let's stop by Coles and buy one of the barbecued chooks (chickens) for dinner," suggests Laura.

"Good idea. We'll try one of the 'seasoned' ones this time."

We discover that "seasoned" at Coles means that they have stuffing in them. Ah, well. It's good with a salad of fresh lettuce from the garden, a baked potato, some baked squash that's been in the freezer, some garlic toast and a glass of wine. I guess Laura didn't need that feast at the kangaroo table to keep flesh on bones. But it was a thoughtful invitation from folks from the most primitive culture in the world.

16 September 1982

Sister Carol rang me at the Community Health Centre yesterday with the news that we would be going to Ernabella. It really wasn't news, because I knew that we were due to go there anyway, but what was news was when she said, "Is Laura going to be ready to come along with us?"

"Oh, is she invited?"

"Oh, yes. I think it's near enough to the end of your tour that no one should object."

"Gee, sister Carol. That's really nice. She just loves to fly, and if there's room, she'd be delighted."

"Well, the Council has no objection, so you just bring her along."

This morning it's a big, beautiful sky, with cumulus beginning with bases about 10,000 feet, and some of them soaring way up to catch the first of the pink and orange as the sun begins to rise towards the eastern horizon. The bases catch some of the light from between the mounds of fluff, and that leaves some white clouds at the base, and then streaks of black, where double layers of cloud obscure the morning light. It's not been raining, but the smell is there. It should be a beautiful day!

It's like Grand Central Station! Mark is going to be our pilot and he's running up Foxtrot Mike Lima. John is also out here, and he's already checked out Foxtrot Delta Quebec. I guess there's a clinic going to Yuendumu and points to the northwest. Laura is a little confused as she watches the preparations. There's an aboriginal lady sitting on the little bench in front of the Aeromedical operations office, and she has a little girl with her. "Is she going with us?"

"Gee, I don't know. Let's wait and see how it sorts itself out." The wind is blowing from the northwest at a pretty good clip.

"It's going to be 50 knots right on the nose," ventures John.

"It'll be a quick trip to Ernabella," offers Mark. That wind is at only 5,000 feet. I'll bet it's going to be bumpy, too.

There's small talk as we seem to be waiting for something to happen. I don't like to ask. I'll just stand around and wait for whatever it is to happen, and I'll know. Carol is saying that we're going to be seeing another of those patients with the chorea-like symptoms that we saw last week. Also, Milyika, who is having fits, and then Carol tells me that old Dolly, the lady from Amata with the bad burn on her fanny that we described so long ago in the bath tub getting debrided at Fregon, has been in the hospital from June 27 to August 12, and has had that big burn grafted. It's turned out fine, and Dolly is back on the circuit rabbit hunting again in the Amata area. How about that?

There's a dot on the eastern horizon below the cumulus. It's getting larger and it's on approach. It touches down just as we finish loading FML and climbing aboard. Laura is in the right front seat. I'm in the backward facing seat, and after Carol had arrived in her new "Bluebird," the picture had sorted out. Dr. Lark and John and the aboriginal lady, and the little girl and "another sister" are going to be going in FDQ to Yuendumu for their clinic. It's the other sister that is the unknown. Then the story comes out.

About 0230 this morning, Carol had received a call that there's a boy out at one of the eastern mines who'd been bitten by a snake. They wanted a first light flight, and sister Carol had felt that rather than announce to everyone at 0230 that they'd have to get up at 0400, she decided to just have the hospital switchboard ring everyone at 0400 hours and tell them to get up.

It would be less disturbing to the folks involved. The trouble was, sister Ray had already been scheduled as the sister for the Yuendumu flight at 0800, and had rung Carol when the switchboard awakened her at 0400 hours. Carol says that Ray has a wonderful Maori vocabulary, and after documenting the ancestry of all flight personnel, had become the martyred one, and would somehow make the first light and the Yuendumu flight as well. Sister Di Staples could have taken one or the other, but sister Ray was making the supreme sacrifice and would have none of sister Di stealing any of her blood and glory.

Sure enough, this was Foxtrot Delta Echo, the little Baron, that had just landed. Darryl is the pilot, and Ray is getting out and heading for FDQ with a slow, weary, measured step. I didn't see any boy get out of FDE. I wonder if it was a snake bite after all, or if the whole thing was a wild goose chase. Poor Ray. It's going to be a long day for her. Darryl will go home and toss a couple of tumblers of scotch and go to bed. Ray is in for the whole day at the wonderful clinic at Yuendumu on the edge of the Great Sandy Desert.

No matter, we're already taxiing out and Mark has the overhead speaker on so that I can hear the tower saying it's to be the 218 radial from Alice to 8,000 and that we'll have a quartering wind at thirty-five knots. Runway three-oh. The turn is made, and FML rockets down the runway and into the air while Carol and I are still discussing sister Ray and her longsuffering.

I have my *American Academy of Family Practice Journal* along and finish about half the Continuing Medical Education lesson while we're cruising towards Ernabella. The wind has raised a lot of sand into the air, and the horizon seems to fade from view about fifteen miles ahead of us. The bases of the cumulus are still about 2,000 feet above us and every one has a bump. Wait until it heats up this afternoon. It's going to be rough! There's an excellent article on hepatitis B, and another good one on postpartum depression and psychosis.

Then we're starting to let down. Mark makes the turn over the settlement. There are two planes on the strip. It's rained quite a bit down here. There's free flowing water in the creek through the village yet, and puddles sitting around. Gosh! The desert is a sea of yellow acacia and pinked wild hops, and smoke colored black acacia, and blue zinnias, and ghost gums along the river, and where that fire had burned about two months ago, the green grass is making the whole look like a huge putting green on some gigantic golf course. How beautiful!

Mark sets FML down gently and taxis back to the tie down area. There's a Cessna 182 staked out right in the middle of the tie down/park area. It has an aboriginal flag on the vertical stabilizer, and words, "Pitjantjatjara Council" stenciled on the side. Boy, talk about "land rights." These folks have usurped the most of the parking area. That figures! Laura and I both take a picture of that. The other plane on the ground is just a small Cessna 182, and there's a man sitting in there with the door open working the radio. No one seems to know who he is, and he doesn't offer any greeting.

Julie Peters drives up in the Toyota. It seems like it's going to be a big clinic. Jennie has come over with some patients from Amata. That's a two-and-a-half hour drive each way! Fanou has come up from Fregon with a vehicle full of people. Julie says that Indulkana has been on the radio frequency asking us to divert there when we finish the clinic to pick up Ilyipi who is going to deliver something from that huge 105 kilogram bulk of hers in the next week or so. That's the first time ever to be seeing patients from all four primary settlements in one day. So be it!

Small talk as we ride into town. Carol is bubbling over with her usual enthusiasm. Mark sits quietly looking at the beautiful desert scenery, and Laura is listening to the "Strayne" dialog between Carol and Julie with great care, trying to see if there's more to this language than "Waltzing Matilda." The clinic is clean. Not too many people round. A ten year old aboriginal boy is riding my old friend the donkey. Laura is trying to get a picture of him on the donkey, but the boy slides off, and the donkey collapses in a heap in the courtyard of the clinic, and Laura had better watch to her camera, because that young man has his heart set on relieving her of her ownership of that! Laura's savvy. No tricks from the young man that fool her for long. She wanders off towards the creek and the church and the bakery (and the craft store).

First patient is Miljika/Pepai, who is twenty-four, 51 kilograms, 105/60, 30/52, FHH 148/minute, and has had a left lower lobe lobectomy for some disease or other once upon a time. She's fine. Pepai, her husband, is thirty-two and had a road accident on the twenty-ninth. He's been seen at the ASH (Alice Springs Hospital) after the accident and declared to be okay, but since coming home, he's developed this huge lump on his low back. Exam shows it to be a lumbosacral hematoma, about 15 centimeters in diameter. It's painful, but it will be okay. He has no limited motion and no evidence of neurological deficit.

Yanyi is thirty-two, 82 kilograms, 138/72, 156 FHH. She's fine. Watch that pressure, though. The systolic is a tad elevated. Maybe she's in a hurry this morning.

Ah, here's Imuna. "It's doctor's last visit, Imuna," Carol tells her.

There's real sadness in Imuna's eyes. She says something under her breath and around the mincobah in her mouth that has a complementary infection, and Carol says that she's very sad to see me go, and that she hopes that Jesus watches over me and my family. Isn't that nice? Hard not to let oneself get maudlin at times like this. Imuna is now twenty-three weeks along with this unwanted pregnancy, and that's not too good news. This pregnancy isn't developing as fast as I'd like to see. In the last two visits (eight weeks), I've recorded only about four weeks progression. Well, she's due to go up to the Alice soon and maybe they can do an ultrasound on her. FHH 146/minute.

Little Clara is also having more difficulty. She simply refuses to stand up at all. She's getting old enough to be walking around, but she's so far behind. Poor little thing. She has a fullness over the lumbosacral back area that almost looks like her back has been broken. I wonder what that is? Let's send Imuna in for her ultrasound and Clara for another evaluation at the Children's Health Centre. I sure hope I hear the end of the story of Imuna and family.

Joy Ann McElwell is coming along with her pregnancy all right. She has those terrible varicosities wrapped, but says they don't give her too much trouble. She's 56 kilograms today, and the pregnancy is progressing just fine. She also says that she wishes me and my family a safe and happy journey back to our homeland. Isn't that nice? Rahan is twelve. He has chronic bronchitis and is short for his age, and his family is worried about this. He really is only 138 centimeters tall. He has decreased breath tones in both bases, but on the left, it's soundless to the fifth rib. Maybe we'd better send him in and have Dr. Martins take a look at him.

Then Harry Taylor, who is forty-two, amputated the distal tip of his left index finger a week ago. He was sutured at ASH, but they just seem to have ronguered back the bone to the joint, and then put three stitches through the meat of the end of the stump. These are single filament of 3–0 nylon, the blue stuff, and the ends have been cut short enough so that they make stiff little spines at the end of the finger that send shocks of pain through Harry when he touches anything. I can't see the suture, except for the stiff little ends. It has to be soaked in peroxide for a while to get some of the scab off. Let's do that and have Harry back in about twenty minutes.

Jennifer was born on 29 April 1981. She has pneumonia. She's on Amoxil. She's now afebrile. She'll be okay. Her Mom, Esther, was born on 4 September 1963. She's hypothyroid but won't take her medicine. She had a crushed pelvis in a road accident in 1981. I guess she should go in to the Alice for evaluation. Esther may be pregnant again. Jean is twenty-two and has a urinary tract infection. She was on Amoxil and didn't take the whole course, and now has symptoms again. Let's try her on Bactrim this time.

Oh, my gosh! Here's Chris Wells again from Fregon, with his right upper quadrant pain. Chris with the shocking mountain of teased hair that's gold and brown and covers his head with a halo thirty centimeters in diameter! Poor, disorganized Fanou behind him, who reminds me of a mother hen trying to get all her chicks under her wing to lead them to the tjilpi doctor, clucking loudly in all directions to the confusion of all. Chris is thirty. I don't find anything but a fat belly. I really do wonder what the pain is from. I think it's in the chest wall as opposed to the lungs or liver. I just don't know what to do. Otherwise he's asymptomatic. Let's give him some aspalgin.

Fanou is determined to be heard, too. Her X-rays showed nothing to suspect that the weakness in her right arm is neurological. I guess I'll have to send her down to Flinders and have the folks under Dr. Rick Smith work her up. It's tough trying to understand Fanou when she's excited. "Strayne with a French accent." Margaret, Chris's wife, who is to go with us today to the Alice to deliver the new baby. She's had her second LPG so the baby should be born without congenital syphilis. That's nice. But she isn't going to be able to come with us on the plane if we have to go to Indulkana to get Ilyipi. Margaret weighs about 95 kilograms, and with Ilyipi's bulk, poor old FML would have to taxi all the way home. She can come on the mail plane on Tuesday.

Here's poor old Harry back. Now I can see that the reason I couldn't view the sutures before wasn't just because they were imbedded in an edematous stump covered with dried blood. There was an awful lot of dirt there. It's nice and meaty now. I remove just the middle suture. Harry winces, but says nothing. Now Julie can see the other two. They can come out in about another three days or so, but I'd just take one at a time, just in case that stump decides to come apart.

Muwitza is fifty-one years old and has a back ache. No wonder! She's a classic aboriginal lady with a marked lumbar lordosis and steatopygea. Her paraspinal muscles are big as my arm. Let's give her some Robaxin for the backache. Ngintja is thirty-seven and having chest pain. She's got a really skinny chest; the bones sticking out like spareribs. Poor thing! I think it's all just that the bones are right out there where they get traumatized. No bruise, but she's tender only on pressure over the lower sternum. Let's give her some aspalgin.

Next is interesting in that Clifton (a lady) has a patch of vesicles about 1.5 centimeters in diameter right below her right eye. A week ago it was terribly painful and the eye was swollen like a bee sting. Then the swelling subsided, and this patch appeared. It's still sore, but not as bad as it was. The patch is right over the infraorbital nerve. I'll bet it's herpes. I've never seen one like that before. There's no linear distribution, but then if it's the infraorbital nerve, there wouldn't be. The nerve would go straight into the maxilla, and so would the swelling and vesicles. She's had this since September 6th. Let's treat her symptomatically. I wouldn't put any steroid cream on it or anything. Maybe some aspalgin or whatever. The eye looks okay. Here's another Margaret; not Margaret Wells. This Margaret has tendonitis of the right extensor digitorum of the foot; swelling and pain. Indocin will probably help that, too. Nura Ward is forty-one and only wants a driver's license p.e. Done! Aumpi is thirty and is going to have a baby soon. She's from Fregon, about 38/52, and 134/78. She'd better get onto the mailplane on Tuesday, too. The mailplane comes on Friday now? All the better. Get her on it tomorrow. Aumpi has had one breech presentation already, and the other child, Hillary, has had meningitis. We don't need a breech delivery out here!

Poor Fanou. I think she thinks a lot of these problems will go away with prayer. Fanou has also brought up our good friend, Joe Peters. Joe had a near coma the other day, and Fanou diagnosed it properly and raised his insulin from twenty units of Isophane to thirty. Joe feels pretty good right now, but his urine continues with four plus protein and acetone. We draw blood for sugar. Isophane has an action time of onset of three to four hours; peak at six to ten hours and duration of twenty-eight hours. He's such a nice man. He speaks good English, too. And he's humble. He's a Christian. He has a horrible prognosis, though. Two years that I've known Joe I've never seen his urine without four plus protein. It's a wonder he has any kidneys left at all. I wonder what his creatinine is? No matter. There's nothing could be done for him anyway.

Here's Kay Finn from Oodnadatta. I don't know how Fanou got all these people into her vehicle. Kay showed up at Fregon the other day with a history, says Fanou, of "fitting." When shown medications, Kay picked out the Dilantin and she said she took three a day of those. Fanou started her dose and brought her along today. Kay is a classic aboriginal lady in a small mold. She's 34 kilograms only, and about 144 centimeters tall, the sunken eyes with the left one watering over the inner canthus, wetting the side of her nose, the protruding lips, the lumbar lordosis without the usual steatopygia, and a look of pain on her face. When one can get close enough to hear her whispering, she's speaking quite good English, but she's so shy! She's having belly pain. Let's check. She lies on the table. The bowel sounds are normal, but she has a fundus just below the belly button. She's pregnant. About nineteen weeks or so! And it hurts! Let's see if she has a uti. What's this? It's four plus for blood!

"Are you bleeding?"

"Oh-ah," in a very soft whisper. So that's it! She's a threatened abortion! It reminds me of the story about "the dog died"! We'll have to take her back with us.

"Kay, would you go with us in the airplane to the Alice?"

"Oh-ah."

"Are you 'ninti' airplane?"

"Oh-ah." Good! She's flown before.

"Kay, you wait for us and when we finish the clinic and have some tea, we'll take you with us, but we have to go back to Indulkana first to pick up another patient. Do you understand?"

"Oh-ah."

Fanou is dumbfounded. She hadn't any idea that this patient was pregnant. Little Errol slips in while Fanou is talking with Kay. I don't even know if I'm supposed to see him, but it turns out that Errol, 9 December 1979, has had two Bicillin already for his pneumonia. He sounds and looks pretty good right now. Let's give him one more Bicillin in forty-eight hours and he'll come right.

Here's Jennie from Amata and Nini, who was born on 16 February 1974. Nini is another of those strange, athetoid, choreiform kids. I wonder if this is some kind of a strange epidemic? Jennie had originally brought her over for evacuation to the Alice for this, but, gee, if Kay is coming and Ilyipi, I just can't take Margaret or Nini with me. I check Nini over. She has the same facial grimacing as Judy of last week. The same waggling of the arms, too, almost like a Balinese dancer. The child is aware of it, and frightened by it. The intention effort removing the chorea is different than last week, though.

Nini has something wrong with the right arm too. She can turn the torch on and off fine with the left hand, but not with the right. She can hardly hold the flashlight with the right hand, and the grimacing seems to be worse as she tries. I wonder what this is? Dr. Carpenter has said rheumatic fever with Sydenham's chorea for this one, too. I don't think so. Her ESR (erythrocyte sedimentation rate—the rate of settling of the red blood cells in the serum) was reported at 28 mm/hr. She's been this way since the 24th of August.

We'll give her Bicillin now and again in forty-eight hours. Let's give her 30 milligrams of phenobarbital t.i.d. We can alway send her in on the mail-plane if she doesn't improve. I think she really should go south to Flinders, though. I wonder if we're looking at some kind of basal ganglion thing like hemiballismus or something? No end to funny things out here.

Jennie from Amata comes in and Nini is placed over her Mom's lap. The shot is given. Nini screams like a banshee; more than I would have suspected. I wonder if that's part of the disease? Nini weaves her way to the door of the clinic and down the steps and falls on the concrete patio writhing with pain and drawing up that right leg. I wonder if Jennie got that shot on the sciatic nerve? Oh, God! I hope not!

That's all, Julie tells us. I can't believe it! It's been a monster clinic today. I'd sneaked a drink of water from Julie at one point and taken a Talwin for a small balloon that was trying to explode in my right flank. There's another one there now. I guess I'll sneak a codeine with my coffee. We pack up the metal cases. Laura is back from her adventures in the settlement. I'll have to ask her later what she's seen and done.

Julie's is rather a messy place, but sister Carol has brought along some goodies and there are the usual sandwiches and pickles and such. Laura and I have our beverage and make use of the "loo." I slip down half a grain of codeine with my coffee. Carol wants to visit with some friends who will be leaving this week, so she takes the vehicle and heads for the other house. The small talk continues. Fanou seems more excited than usual. I guess she's thinking about her trip to Adelaide for workup. She wants to be a midwife some day. Julie and Jennie from Amata talk away. Time is slipping by. We should really by underway for Indulkana. It's coming along to 1400 hours.

Laura and I walk outside with Mark. Julie has a garden in the rough soil on the north side of the house. There's broccoli and tomatoes and lettuce, and some parsley and other goodies. She'll have a nice garden. Two of the other health workers are sitting on a block of broken concrete by the dirt road. They're reading part of Dr. Lorenz's report on aboriginal health care delivery.

There's little Kay hanging on the fence, watching the house, and being sure that she isn't left behind. The weeping of her left eye from disease gives her even a more pathetic look than she'd have otherwise, but the expression on her face really is one of pain, too. Julie comes out of the house and jogs down the road towards the clinic, cutting across the sandy bed of the river. We keep watching the naked children playing in the pools of water along the rocky outcrop at one corner of the river bed. Here comes the vehicle. Oh, oh! Julie has gone for Carol to tell her that the tjilpi doctor is anxious to go, and I wonder if Carol will be upset. She does remonstrate a little, but not much. The vehicle is packed, and we're off for the strip.

The Cessna 182 is still staked out in the center of the parking area, but here's another plane. It's a smashing twin engine, four bladed turbo prop Mitsubishi! That's a lot of money there! Who? It belongs to the Pitjantjatjara Council? Wow! There really is money in poverty! That plane costs about $1.3 million! We unload the Toyota of the cases and load them into the Navajo. Oops! That left tyre looks a bit sad. Indeed! We have an almost flat tyre on the left. Mark surveys it glumly. Well, if we get underway we can probably make it all right.

We finish the load. Carol sits on the starboard side of the stretcher. I'm facing backward again. Kay is in Carol's seat. The extra seat behind the door hasn't been put in today. Mark and Laura are on the flight deck. FML starts easily, and the gauges come into the green. Down the runway and into the air. The last little bit I wonder about that half-flat tyre at eighty-five miles an hour! Oh, well, we're flying, and it's terribly rough. I'm trying to write up Kay's admission report. Forget it! There's another aircraft coming from Indulkana our way, but he's a thousand feet above us.

Now it looks like there are two layers of clouds. There's the lower layer of cumulus and there's an upper stratus layer about 20,000 feet, and then the dust. The ride is about 40 minutes. Kay is in pain. I give her one of my codeine.

She says, "Thank you," in a tiny voice, but excellent English.

Here we are at Indulkana. The strip looks fine and isn't as soft looking as it was last week. I guess Carol did finally have her way with the community advisor. He must have had a lot of work done here. Jennie waits for us. Her arm is out of the back slab. She says that another doctor has said that she may have a fracture of the head of the radius. So be it. It looks a lot better. (I don't really think so, but I'm not going to argue.) I have a sharp, stabbing, insistent pain in my right flank. I listen as Jennie unwinds about three or four other histories of patients that she's worried about. Let's get out of here.

The tyre by my feet on the left side of FML looks almost totally flat! Finally, we conclude and re-board the plane. Big Ilyipi takes the backward seat. Kay and Carol sit on the starboard stretcher. I can hardly stand the pain! I swallow another codeine. We're off, all the way up to 9,300 feet. It's still bumpy! Ilyipi and Kay doze. Carol is solicitous.

"Do you want a shot?"

"No, Carol. I'll be all right."

"Can Laura drive the car?"

"Yes, Carol. She'll take me home." I try to keep my eyes closed. It makes time go faster.

The tyre bothers me. It really was flat. I hope it didn't tear up when we took off. The trip seems unending! I try to doze. There's the Finke. We'll be letting down soon. Mark approaches runway three-oh. He brings us in left wing high, and touches on the right wheel, holding FML up there on just one wheel as long as he can. Finally it settles on the port wheel, and then the nose wheel. FML runs straight and true. That's neat! It's been a good day after all! Mark slowly rolls us into the ramp, and shuts down. The pain is subsiding a little. We don't help this time unloading the cases.

I head for the car, and we start into town. Not much mail at the APO. Then, we head home. I go for the sofa, take another Talwin, and lie there a minute. Laura sits quietly in the chair watching her mate handle pain. Finally it subsides a bit.

"What did you see and do?"

Laura lets out all the fun things that happened to her while she was at Ernabella. She's taken a lot of pictures and seen a lot of things. Not as exciting as the kangaroo-offered meal last week, but lots of fun. Then she rolls out a spectacular, silk batik that she bought at the craft shop! It's about three meters long and a meter wide, and absolutely spectacular in orange and black and white and gray. She has three scarfs of silk batik, and a wall hanging, and about twenty little wooden carved animals with designs branded on them with hot wire. She's done really well. She's excited, and my pain is going away.

What a wonderful way to spend a Thursday. Even with all the fun and mental satisfaction, I just might have done some good for someone out there in the great Australian outback.

23 September 1982

There are mixed emotions as I start for the airport this morning. It's the last trip of this tour. The last trip to the aboriginal settlements, and the last time I'll see my little patients out there and minister to them. Maybe there'll be a sequel to this. Maybe there'll be a time of TDY (temporary duty) when I'll have a chance to come back to all this and see it as it is several years hence. Better chance that the next time I see this is when I'm a ghostly presence in the outback joining with so many of the other ghostly beings of yesteryear like Burke and Giles and Lassiter and so many of the others. Won't that be a story to write about?

The sky is clear, and the mirage down the south road is standing high in the sky like the chalk cliffs of Dover. It looks like a mountain cliff fifteen miles away and so clear that one can see individual trees sticking out of the palisades. It's not even shimmering. It's just standing there, and if one were an explorer of long ago, one would be looking for signs of a pass or gap through that solid wall.

My thoughts are interrupted by seeing sister Carol unloading the metal boxes at the gate next to FDQ. Her little Bluebird holds them all. I park the Falcon and wander over. An isolette is standing near the fence, and John is running up FML. Seems that they have an emergency at Papunya. Sister Di is to fly with John. Sister Carol announces that there's been a lot of politics this last week at Amata. It seems that sister Jennie Markam and Feona have been critical of the South Australian Aboriginal Council and have complained that the money to be allocated for medical costs in Amata has not been properly spent. Also, something about them being "workers of the people" or something like that, and for their vocal efforts, they've both been fired and are now in the Alice without employment. Poor Jennie. "Soweto Lives!" Sister Carol also waxes nostalgic. She's hitting the big "four-oh" on Saturday. Darryl is his usual nervous self. All the tyres on the plane seem to be inflated. It's climb aboard time.

FDQ fires up easily. Ahead of us, John is approaching FML, and here comes sister Di in her little yellow car. She looks like she usually does. She has an ill fitting blue smock on; her hair is blowing in all directions, and she has some sort of clogs on her feet. Can't take the country out of the girl. Then we're taxiing to the helicopter pad, and Darryl stops while he gets clearance from ground control to proceed. He has the earphones on, so I can't hear the tower. We taxi rather slowly to the end of three-oh runway, and he swings FDQ wide.

"We've got to let FML go first," says Darryl, and sure enough, FML swings around and John has poured the power to her. A diminishing object to an almost invisible dot going straight away to the northwest, and then it's our turn. Two; three; four; five white lines racing beneath the nose, and then the rotation and the quick lift. I look at the horizon and see the mirage. At about fifty feet, the whole cliff in the distance flattens out. It's been the desert floor all the time just reflected into the sky by the inversion layer at fifty feet or so. Isn't that unusual? Like God had put a giant mirror over the desert floor and you're actually seeing the horizontal in a vertical plane. The course is set for Mt. Connor and we're to be at 6,000 feet. It comes up fast.

Darryl levels off. The engines are still guzzling petrol at thirty-eight liters a minute. Darryl fusses with the throttle first, and draws us down from almost forty inches of mercury manifold pressure to thirty. Then the pitch brings the RPM away from the 2,500 red line to about 2,300. Then the mixture brings fuel consumption down from thirty-eight liters/minute to about fifteen. All of this is done meticulously and infinitely slowly, of course, with both the left and right engine needles staying almost exactly superimposed. It's absolutely calm here at 6,000, though. Good thing! Darryl would never get these things lined up to his satisfaction if the plane were bucking around at all.

I've purposely brought no book to read today. I wanted to just look at the ground and the canyons and the stock ponds with the dots of cattle around and in them. The wild hops is growing like great sheets of blood on the desert floor. The trees are casting shadows twice their height in the morning sun. It's just a really nice day for flying. FDQ whistles on.

I notice as Darryl begins to level us out and bring the needles all into the cruise that the outside noise in FDQ is quite an instrument in itself. As the plane comes into cruise and the air speed builds from climb to cruise, the noise of the wind on the plane increases in pitch to where it sings almost a pure note. One can tell instantly if there is any change in power setting or engine performance just by the sound of the wind outside. And there's Mt. Connor in the distance. Gee, it really is clear today.

The Ephemeral Lakes come into view; the Wallera ranch road north and south, Curtin Springs to the west. We cross the Ayer's Rock road. I imagine what it would be like to be walking on the bed of one of those dry, salt lakes. The bowl around Mt. Connor and the low hills between us and Amata. Darryl begins the descent. There's another plane inbound to Amata from Ernabella, Darryl announces. I let my eyes scan the distance about an inch below the horizon.

"There he is," I point with my finger.

Darryl sees the other plane as he sights my finger line. It's way out there, and moving along pretty fast; just a tiny dot. It's the motion not the angle of the arc that the object represents that brings it into view. Darryl picks up his mike and says something. He's telling the "bogey" that we have him in sight. The other plane make a right base, and Darryl drops flaps on FDQ. He swings us on a wide left downwind to let the other fellow in first.

Then it's our turn. There are two big white "X"s on the runway. One is at the far south edge of the strip and the other is about half way up the strip where the low, soft-looking slade lies over the southern third of the strip. The Xs are made out of half forty-two-gallon drums painted white. One wouldn't want to hit those on the way in. Darryl sets FDQ down just past the middle one and quickly applies the brakes. We've only got about 2,500 feet of runway. That's not good. That's part of what Jennie and Feona were crabbing about. When the summer really heats up this desert at 1,800 feet, and the plane is loaded, there's no way with the density altitude that will exist to get it off the ground in 2,500 feet. And the money has already been spent. That's not good.

Two beat-up "utilities" with aboriginal drivers meet us. The other plane is a Seneca, and I don't know who the Europeans beside it are. There's another Toyota over there with them, and a conversation going on. Meantime, we load the cases into our vehicles, and we climb into the back. It's Maureen going to be our health worker today. Darryl and I climb into the back of the "ute" and sit on the metal boxes. We're joined by two aboriginal men. The drive back is through the dead grass and the red dust. Beneath the dead grass is the sprout of the new year's crop of green grass.

The acacias are balls of yellow fuzz, the wild hops make red patches between, and there are jillions of tiny desert flowers in patches throughout the spaces between trees. Past the wrecked cars, the flotsam and jetsam of society abandoned in the outback. A flock of brilliant green budgies zig-zags by like emerald lightning. There's the community centre building. What a mess!

The clinic is really pretty clean. We unload the boxes. The radio is playing up some sort of request for us to divert to Docker River. No sister's house for Darryl to lounge in this time. He's assigned to a rickety metal chair in the clinic with his charts and calculator to figure out fuel and altitude and winds aloft and headings, and things that pilots are supposed to do. Maureen has the antenatal clinic set out first.

Nora; age twenty-five, 83 kilograms, 100/60, 22/52 and fetal heart not heard. Elaine; 1961, 51 kilograms, 128/62, 20/52 and a trace of protein in her urine. No fetal heart heard. Iris; 2 March 1961, 74 kilograms, 19/52 says the card, but she's really 23/52, and BP is 118/64. Jane; 12 June 1960, and on 9 September 1982 she had a lot of pain suprapubically and I saw her on diversion to Amata in the plane. She was okay then, and she's okay now. I still don't know why Jennie had us come all the way over here, but it's okay. Jane is 23/52 and FHH at 144/minute and BP 120/80. Jane is epileptic, but she's taking her medicine.

Itjinaly was born 1950, 27/52, 91 kilograms, 120/82 and FHH

148/minute. Sandra was born in 1965 and is postnatal exam. Her uterus is well involuted. Blood pressure is 116/70. Maureen has it really well organized, and I'm writing my findings both on the AMS card and on my own card, but no one is transposing it to the clinic card. Maureen can't write, of course. Well, they can always get the information by radio, except that since Jennie left, the radio has been having temperamental fits of deciding not to copy continuously, and cuts in and out on transmission and receiving.

Daniel is a twelve-year-old epileptic. He dropped his petrol can on his right foot when his sniffing gave him a fit, and the can caught fire. He's lost most of the skin on the dorsum of the foot and toes three, four, and five. I remove the bandage. It stinks, but it looks clean.

"We'll smear it good with SSD (silver sulfadine) cream and put on another Melolin and then a good cover. Must be kept dry and clean. No, we don't have to evacuate him to the Alice. There's no burn on the flexor surface; just the dorsum of the toes to the MP joint, and if he keeps it dry and we dress it daily, he'll come good in about a fortnight."

Sally Mullen is here. Remember "Dumbo" with the protruding ears? Well, she's had her surgery in Adelaide, and they've done a wonderful job. She's European.

"They've buried permanent stitches," says Mom.

"Do they hurt at all, Sally?"

"Only if I pull them back really hard like this," she demonstrates. There's almost no scar at all, and her ears lie flat long the mastoid. That's really pretty neat, and the child is delighted. I compliment her on her blond hair and pretty face.

Yuminia is back with her hypertension. Remember when she got so angry that time when Jennie's blood pressure cuff wasn't working right? Today she's 152/84 and is taking her Clotride, one a day, an Apresoline, one a day, and Inderal, 140 milligrams twice a day. She's doing fine. She smiles. Good on you, Yuminia!

Nini is next. She's not limping from the shot in her buttock last week that I feared might be on the sciatic nerve. But she's not improved, either. As a matter of fact, she's almost paralyzed on the right. She can't hold the torch in that hand at all. Left hand does well with turning it on and off, but the right hand can't function, and the right leg doesn't know where it is. Cerebellar? Gosh, maybe she's got something growing inside the head. Funduscopic reveals no papilledema, but then she doesn't move the right eye at all when I'm looking in. I wonder if she sees at all with that eye? The other eye will follow the light. Something is really wrong here.

Her Mom, Tinami, refused med-evac last week. Now I talk to her like a Dutch Uncle. Tinami is an older woman, too. She has quite a bit of power in the community. This time she agrees to come with Nini to the Alice.

"Good," says sister Carol.

"Tinami, you and Nini be ready about one o'clock. We'll be leaving when we finish the clinic and have a cup of tea. Palya?"

"Oh-ah."

Tiger is an older man and has a red "T" shirt and a red head band. That's also "power" in the tribe. One doesn't wear a head band in the village without some significance. I wonder what his power is? Tiger has been on Indocin for arthritis, and also had a draining ear on the right. His card says born in 1922. His ear is dry now. There's part of the malleus there, but I don't see any drum at all. No cholesteatoma, either. Lots of dry powder in there, though. That's fine. Let's keep it dry. And keep up the Indocin for the arthritis.

Karina was born in 1964 and is postpartum. She's involuted well but BP is 148/92. Better check that again next week. Her baby is a nice little sausage of a male. With all the proper appurtenances for a male, and good feet, and a lusty cry, he should be the leader of men when he grows up. His birth date is 11 August 1982. Carol chides Karina a bit for not yet having a name for the babe.

Susan Simm was born 3 October 1980 and is now one year since surgery for a really bad squint. Her eyes track beautifully this morning. Great job! She's really supposed to go back down to Adelaide for evaluation by the surgeon. We'll arrange the IPTAS for her.

"It does wander just a little when she gets tired," volunteers Mom.

Craig Seneca is next. He's also European. He has a cough

and has had a number of bad bouts with asthma in the past. He's still taking his neulin. A listen to his chest. No wheezes, it's just a bronchial cough. No real treatment except keep on the neulin. Boyd Simm is twenty-seven. He has a sensitive skin and his joints ache. Coming down with some kind of "wog." Temp is 36.7 and I really can't find much else. BP is 120/74. Chest is clear with no murmur. I guess we'll just treat him symptomatically with aspirin or Panadol and see what comes next.

Manygatja was born in 1942. She describes a left frontal sinusitis, but looking back in her notes, it shows that she complained of the same thing in 1979. Her BP is 162/90. I was going to put her on Amoxil, but instead let's give her Inderal, 40 milligrams b.i.d. and see what happens. Kukika was born in 1958, and is complaining of charley horses in her legs at night. We'll write a script for some quinine bisulphate, 300 milligrams, and give her one tab at bedtime and see if that helps.

Mayana was born in 1939, and today she hurts all over. She had minor cataracts, but not enough to alter her visual acuity. We'll give her some Indocin for her arthralgia. Wally is next, and he's been on tolbutamide for his diabetes. He's also been in ASH recently for SBE, but that's better now. What he really has is scabies. Wally is originally from Maryvale. We'll give him some gamma benzene hexachloride to wash with.

Now it's Maureen's turn. She's been a good "sister" today, and really run a well organized clinic. She's in the middle of an infertility work up by Dr. Cahill, who want a postprandial blood sugar. Done! Ah, but there's one more to the clinic. The girls have made me a cup of coffee with cream but no sugar. As I start to drink it, they hand me a paper for Nini's admission, and then Roger Chapman wants to be seen with a "wog." He's born 25 September 1950. Happy birthday this Saturday, Roger. You're eight years younger than sister Carol. Blood pressure is 120/80. Treat him symptomatically. Ah, but now there's one more. This could go on all day with one and then another straggling in, and we've got to go to Docker River yet, and it's coming up to 1400 hours!

Leonard, born in 1952. Injured his right thigh playing football in August. Now he's got a calcifying hematoma over the right quadriceps. I guess we'll give it another six weeks or so with symptomatic treatment, and if it doesn't get better, we'll have him in to the ASH for an X-ray of that. Leonard is one of the chaps who rode back in the ute with us from the airstrip when we first arrived. He'd jumped in that ute with alacrity then, but hobbles away on his damaged leg now. Ah, the histrionics of it all! Now the clinic is done.

We move all the equipment back into the ute and take our places. This time we have a whole box full of people back there, including Tinami and Nini and Maureen and all the rest. Carol asks one of the ladies to take our picture. She blushes (?) and coyly drops her head onto her right shoulder. One of the other Pitjantjatjara ladies quickly steps up and takes Carol's camera and sights carefully through the view finder like she's done it a thousand times before, and clicks off a shot. I set up my Pentax and hand it to her. Same thing. I now have a picture that includes me! Neat! The ute rumbles down the dusty street; the kids and natives wave at us as we pass.

They know it's the last visit of the tjilpi doctor. They're really wonderful people. The strip is deserted. There's another ute full of people that have come to say ''g'bye.'' Isn't that nice? We load into the plane. Everyone is waving. Everything but the brass band. Darryl runs up FDQ, and we go to the north end of the runway. Down there, about half way down the strip, is the first ''X'' of barrel halves.

Darryl lines up on the east side of the strip so that if we're not off the ground by the time we get there, we'll be going by beside it. That's good thinking. Darryl advances the throttles, and we roar away. He pushes them against the stops until I think they'll break. Just at the point opposite the first ''X'' he rotates FDQ and she leaps into the air. The climb out; the left turn; the 180 and we head back for Ayer's Rock at 6,000. It's bumpy. It's only about twenty minutes.

Darryl makes a left pattern, remembers to put down the gear, and drops onto the strip. They'll be plowing this one up soon and moving everything to the new Uluru International ten miles away. I don't think it's a good idea, but that's the way it's going to be. We fill the tanks. Darryl signs the slip and we fire up again. While waiting, Nini and Carol and Tinami go to the ''loo.'' It's heart rending to watch Nini walking. That right foot doesn't know where it's going at all. Tinami has told us that Nini is naturally left handed, though.

Darryl taxis to the west end of the strip and takes off towards the camp. FDQ uses just about the whole strip to get off. It's getting hotter. The climb out westward past the Olgas. Morpheus overcomes me, and I doze, until it gets really bumpy and I open my eyes. I wonder which of those mountains out there contains Lassiter's Reef of Gold? Darryl drops a little flaps, and then the gear.

It's a nice, long, wide strip. We taxi back. The pole and branch shelter by the Liquor Act sign has had its roof cave in. That didn't last long. We shut down. By and by a Toyota comes along. I can't see who's in it, but Manami comes from the vehicle, with a stocking cap pulled down almost across his eyes. He looks like Beetle Bailey, except black, and must be about thirty years old. We're told he has an "infected eczema," whatever that is. I don't even look at him. The sister at the clinic has already filled out his admission form. Nothing for me to do. We sit Manami in the back seat by the door. Darryl energizes the engines and we roar away again.

This time our course is about forty miles north of the Rock and the Olgas. There they are in the increasing haze. It's starting to get on to the afternoon now; almost 1545. The course is right over Lake Amadeus. I take a picture. I've not been this way before. Amadeus is about forty-five miles long and about five miles wide in places, and forms the western end of the Ephemeral Lakes. Geologically, it's supposed to be floating on huge pools of oil of good quality. My, this country is rich!

Across Amadeus and there's a ridge of hills ahead. It looks like, yes, it is King's Canyon. From the air it's not nearly as spectacular as it is from the ground. From 9,000 feet it's just a huge mesa with a knife-like, right angled cut into the western edge of the mesa. But there's the road that Laura and I drove on, and the water hole that we almost got bogged down in on the way out there. Then we're flying across some of the roughest country in Australia. There's a trail down there somewhere, but it's for four-wheel drive, and one can see why.

The terrain looks like a piece of sun-baked rubber under a microscope. There are so many sharp valleys and ridges that it's a wonder water can find a way through, let alone a vehicle. I'd hate to drive that, but if one did, I'll bet it would be some kind of spectacular scenery. Then we can see the Spyce Byce gleaming in the sun some sixty miles ahead, and yet, behind and to the right is Mt. Conner, and yes, you can still see Ayer's Rock from here. It's that clear!

It's thirty miles DME. Darryl starts to descend. That's when I look behind. Poor Manami has been filling burp bags. I didn't notice that it was rough at all. I guess back where he is, he gets the full see-saw effect of being removed from the center of gravity that I'm sitting almost directly over. Poor guy! Nini and Tinami have done well.

Darryl brings us in on a straight in from over the stock yards. It's a smooth landing. I don't really quite know what to say. Darryl pumps my hand.

"It's been good flying with you, myte," he says. "I hope you get a chance to come back and fly with us again." That's really sincere.

"Gee, I do too, Darryl. I've really enjoyed this tour of duty, and it's you and Mark and John and the other pilots that make it that way. Give them my regards."

"Sure."

"Carol, I'll be seeing you tomorrow. Have a nice birthday. We'll be dropping off that little thing for you tomorrow."

"Not necessary, but we'll be seeing you before you leave."

"Yes, I'm sure."

What more is there to say? I'm going to miss this a lot. Maybe there will be another chance to do this. Live or ghost. There are going to be lots of memories about my Australian black brothers, and the red sand.

Glossary

A

Abattoir—Aussie word for slaughterhouse (French).
Abbocillin—An antibiotic.
Aldomet—Blood pressure medication.
Aminophyllin—Asthma medication.
Amoxil—An antibiotic.
Ampicillin—An antibiotic.
Anorexia Nervosa—A disease characterized by loss of appetite.
Antecubital—Front of the arm at elbow.
Antenatal—Before birth (Aussie); pre-natal (USA).
Aparwatatja—Aboriginal name for Fregon settlement.
Apresoline—Blood pressure medicine.
Artilla—Aboriginal name for Mt. Connor.
ASAP—Acronym for: as soon as possible.
Ascites—Fluid accumulation in the abdomen.
ASH—Alice Springs Hospital.
Aspalgin—Aspirin containing medication.
Atherosclerosis—Hardening of the arteries.
Atrial fibrillation—Heart rhythm abnormality.
Atrophic—Withered.
Axilla—Pit of the arm.

B

Bacitracin—An antibiotic.
Bactrim—An antibiotic.
Ballottable—Sensation of fluid rebound.
BCG—Bacillus calmette-guerin, a vaccination against tuberculosis.
Bds—Abbreviation for twice a day; same as bd, bid.
Benadryl—An antihistamine.
Betadine—An antiseptic.
Bicillin—An antibiotic.
Billibong—A fresh water stream (Aussie).
Biscuits—Cookies (Aussie).
Blepharitis—Inflammation of the eyelids.
Bore—A well (Aussie).
BP—Blood pressure abbreviation.
Bradycardia—Slow pulse rate.
Bramby—A wild horse (Aussie).

Brufen—Non-steroidal anti-inflammatory.
Bullbar—Welded steel pipe frame fastened to the front of a vehicle for protection from animal (bullock/kangaroo) collisions.
Bum (bumm)—Buttocks (Aussie).
Buscopan—Aussie equivalent of vistaril—a tranquilizer.

C

Calomine—A lotion to inhibit itching.
Cardigan—Any type of sweater (Aussie).
CATA—Acronym for Central Australia Tours Association.
'Cause—Contraction of the word because (Aussie).
CDC—Child development clinic.
Cellulitis—Soft tissue infection.
Cerumen—Ear wax.
Cerumenol—Medication to dissolve ear wax.
Chamber's Pillar—A tall geological tower in the desert.
Chelokabob—Barbecued neck muscles of lamb (Iranian).
Chesty—Congested lungs (Aussie).
Chloromycetin—An antibiotic.
Chloromyx drops—Antibiotic solution.
Cholesteatoma—Hard bony nodule in the middle ear.
Chondromalacia—degeneration of cartilage (knee).
CHU—Acronym for Childrens' Health Unit.
Clonic seizure—Alternating contraction and relaxation of muscles.
Clotride—A diuretic.
Cloxacillin—An antibiotic.
COF—Acronym for Chief of Facility, JDSRF.
Compazine—Prochlorperazine—a tranquilizer.
Compo—Aboriginal word for urine.
Condylomata—Venereal warts.
Congestive failure—Heart failure secondary to decreased ability of heart to pump blood.
COPD—Chronic obstructive pulmonary disease.
Corroboree—An aboriginal convention or show.
Costochondral—Pertaining to rib cartilage.
CPR—Cardiopulmonary resuscitation.
Crook—Sick (Aussie).
Crouzon's syndrome—Baby Clara's diagnosis.
Crystopen—An antibiotic.
C-Section—Caeserean section (surgical birth).
C-6 lesion—Spinal cord damage—sixth cervicle vertebra.
Cystic hygroma—Cavernous growth of lymphatics.

D

Daktrin—An anti-fungus cream.

Damper—A skillet fried bread made with soda, flour, and water.

Daonil—Oral anti-diabetic medication.

Deciliter—One tenth of a liter.

Demerol—Pethidine (Aussie); a narcotic analgesic.

Dendritic ulcer—Ulcer of the cornea of the eye.

Dependent edema—Swelling of lower extremities due to obstruction of lymph channels.

Despedida—Aussies use this Spanish word for "farewell party."

Desquamating—Shedding of skin.

Diabinese—Oral medication for diabetes.

Dichlortride—A diuretic.

Digoxin—Medicine for congestive heart failure.

Dilantin—An anticonvulsive medication.

Diuril—A diuretic.

Doloxine—A non-narcotic analgesic.

Dreamtime—Aboriginal heaven before birth or after death.

Dr. H.—Abbreviation for Dr. Geoff Hauptenhauser, the ENT specialist at Alice Springs Hospital.

Dummy—Aussie word for child's pacifier.

E

Ecchymosis—Black and blue bruise.

ENT—Abbreviation for ear, nose and throat.

Enteritis—Bowel infection.

Ernabella—Aboriginal settlement known as Pukatja.

Erythromycin—An antibiotic.

Esky—Portable ice chest (Aussie).

ESR—Abbreviation for erythrocyte sedimentation test—a blood test.

Etiology—Cause of problem.

ETOH—chemical abbreviation for ethyl alcohol.

European—Aboriginal word for white skinned person.

F

Fasigyn—Anti-parasitic medication.

FBC—Abbreviation for full blood count.

FH—Abbreviation for fetal heart.

FHH—Abbreviation for fetal heart heard.

Fistula—Drainage canal in the body for blood, pus, or fluids.

Flagyl—Anti-parasitic medication.

FLK—Acronym for "funny looking kid."

Fluoxacillin—An antibiotic.
Fly eye—Eye infection transmitted by flies.
Fortnight—Two weeks period of time.
Fossicker—Prospector (Aussie).
Frank heart failure—Advanced heart failure.
Fregon—Aboriginal settlement known as Apparawatatja.
Fundus—The body of the uterus.
Furunculosis—Huge skin boils (abscesses).

G

Gallahs—Gray-backed, red-breasted cockatoos.
Ganglion—A cyst in a tendon sheath.
Gastro—Gastroenteritis, diarrhea (Aussie).
GC—Abbreviation for gonorrhea.
Gentamycin—An antibiotic.
Giardia lamblia—An intestinal parasite.
Gingival hyperplasia—Overgrown tissue of the gums.
Glaucoma—increased pressure in the eye.
Goana—An aboriginal lizard deity.
Gorked—Slang expression for diminished cognitive function.
Grotty—Aussie word for dirty, congested.
Gums—Aussie word for eucalyptus trees.

H

Haloperidol—Aussie tranquilizer called Serenese.
HB—Abbreviation for hemoglobin.
Hematoma—A blood clot under the skin.
Hematuria—Blood in the urine.
HF channels—High frequency radio channels.
Homeplace—Residence of station family.
Hydramnios—Excessive amniotic fluid in pregnancy.
Hypospadias—Opening of urinary tract beneath the penis.

I

I and D—Incision and drainage.
Incontinence—Involuntary loss of urine or feces.
Inderal—Beta receptor blocker heart medicine for high blood pressure.
Indocin—Anti-inflammatory medication.
Induration—Hardening of tissues to the touch.
Inf. vena cava synd.—Obstruction of lower extremity return circulation
    secondary to enlarged uterus.
INH—Isonicotinic acid hydrazide—a medication for tuberculosis.

Interphalangeal—Point between finger bones.

Ippi—Aboriginal word for breast milk.

IV/VI—Expresses heart murmur loudness with VI being loudest. This
    murmur is four of six.

J

JDSRF—Acronym for Joint Defense Space Research Facility.

Joey—A baby kangaroo.

K

Kalkya—Aboriginal word for an emu.

Kaolin—An anti-diarrheal medication.

Katajuta—Aboriginal name for the Olgas mountains.

Kaulatus—Aboriginal word for spears.

Kenalog—Hydrocortisone cream for the skin.

Kidochi boots—Moccasins worn by aboriginal witch doctors to conceal
    their identity as assassins. They are made of human hair.

Koplic spots—Characteristic oral mucous membrane lesions of measles.

Kukia—Aboriginal word for gallstones.

Kwashiorkor—A protein deficiency syndrome characterized by marked
    abdominal swelling.

L

Labrynthitis—Inner ear infection.

Laryngeal stridor—Croup.

Lasix—A diuretic.

Lidocaine—Injectable local anesthetic.

Lipoma—Fatty skin tumor.

Lobectomy—Surgical removal of lobe of lung.

Lollies—Aussie word for candy.

Loo—Aussie word for bathroom.

LPG—Antibiotic—long acting penicillin G.

Lucern—Aussie word for alfalfa.

Lymphangitis—Inflammation of lymph vessels.

Lymphogranuloma—Chronic lymph gland infection.

M

MAC—Military Air Command.

Malleolus—Ankle bone (medial in inner).

Malleus—Small bone in the middle ear.

Malu—Aboriginal word for kangaroo.

Mamu—Aboriginal word for spirit.

Mantoux—Skin test for tuberculosis.

Marker beacon—Radio navigation device signaling one half mile to runway.

Maxilon—Aussie brand of atropine.

Med-evac—Medical evacuation of a patient.

Mellaril—Anti-depressant.

M.I.—Abbreviation for myocardial infarction—a heart attack.

Microgynon—Oral birth control pill.

Milkali—Aboriginal word for blood specimen.

Mintibi surf—White earth tailings from opal mines at town of Mintibi as seen from a distance.

Miru—Aboriginal word for a woomera—Aussie word for a throwing stick used to propel a spear.

Mmol/liter—Millimol liter—1/1000 of the molecular weight of a compound per liter of solvent.

Molluscum contag.—Chronic skin disease characterized by pulpy nodules.

Mono—Infectious mononucleosis—a benign blood disease.

Montard MC—Anti-diabetic medication (Aussie).

Motrin—Anti-inflammatory, non-steriodal.

MP joint—The big, proximal joint where fingers meet the hand or toes meet the foot (metacarpophalangeal joint).

Mulga—Aboriginal word for acacia wood (wattles—Aussie).

Mycostatin—Anti-fungal medication.

N

NAD—No abnormal data (nothing wrong).

Neosynephrine—Nasal decongestant.

Neulin—Asthma medication.

Ninti—Aboriginal word for: to have knowledge of.

Nocte—Latin word for nighttime.

Noridal—Oral contraceptive.

Notes—Aussie reference to patient hospital summary.

Nulla-nulla—A club like a small baseball bat (aboriginal).

Nungkari—Aboriginal word for a witch doctor.

Nystatin—Anti-fungal medication for thrush or vaginitis.

O

OCP—Oral contraceptive pill acronym.

Occipito-parietal—The back corner of the skull.

Occiput—The back of the skull.

OCP—Oral contraceptive pill acronym.

Oh-ah—Aboriginal word for yes.

Old Timers' Home—The name for an aboriginal convalescent hospital run by Mrs. Hettie Perkins.
Olecranon—Refers to the elbow.
Opisthotonus—Spastic arching of the back.
Ossicles—The small bones of the middle ear.
Osteomyelitis—Infection of the bone.
Otitis externa—Infection of the external ear.
Otitis media—Infection of the middle ear.

P

Palya—Aboriginal word for okay.
Panadol—Aussie equivalent of U.S. Tylenol.
Papilledema—Swelling of the optic nerve at the retina.
Paracentesis—Procedure to drain fluid from the abdomen.
Paraplegia—Paralysis of lower extremities.
P.E.—Physical exam abbreviation.
Pen-V—An antibiotic.
Peroneal—Pertaining to the outside of the lower leg.
Pethidine—Aussie word for demerol—a narcotic analgesic (generic —merperidine).
Petrol—Aussie word for gasoline.
Pg—Pregnant.
Phenergan—An antihistamine.
Phenobarbital—A sedative and anti-convulsant.
Phimosis—Tight penile foreskin.
Photophobia—Sensitivity to light.
PID—Acronym for pelvic inflammatory disease.
Pine Gap—JDSRF.
Piti—Aboriginal for wooden bowl-like object.
Pitjantjatjara—Tribe of aboriginals indigenous to area shown on map.
Pitting edema—Swelling of legs which retains a depression in the tissue when pressed.
Pohme—Acronym (Aussie) "prisoner of her majesty's empire."
Ponderax—An anti-depressant.
Popliteal—Space behind the knee.
Port—Suitcase (Aussie).
Prepatellar—In front of the knee cap.
Prepuce—Penile foreskin.
Probenecid—Medication which slows elimination of penicillin from the system.
Prochlorperazine—Generic tranquilizer (Compazine).
Proctosedyl oint.—Hemorrhoidal analgesic ointment (Aussie).

Pronate—Turning the hand palm down.
Propranalol—Generic blood pressure medication (Inderal).
Proptosis—Bulging of the eyeballs.
Pseudocyesis—False pregnancy.
Psoriasis—A chronic skin disease.
Purnu—Aboriginal magic wooden rod used by nungkari.
Pyelitis—Infection of the kidney.

Q

Q.I.D.—Four times a day.
Quadriceps—Muscles in the front of the thigh.

R

Rales—Moist breath sounds commonly heard with pneumonia.
Reef of Gold—Legendary outcropping of solid gold found by fossicker, Lasiter.
Registrar—Aussie equivalent of the U.S. "resident" physician.
Right—Aussie word used to designate improving health, as in, "he'll come right."
Road train—Multiple "semi" trailers pulled by a single tractor.
R.P.M.—Revolutions per minute (as in aircraft propellors).
RPR—A flocculation test for syphilis.

S

Sanguinous—Bloody.
Script—Aussie for a written prescription for medicine.
Senecot—Medication for softening stool.
Septra—An antibiotic.
Shifting—Aussie verb for relocating—as in moving.
Sinemet—Parkinson's Disease medication.
Sister—Aussie for registered nurse.
Soma—Muscle relaxing medication.
Spell—To take the place of or to relieve a person (Aussie).
Spinifex—Genus of spiny grasses (Aussie).
Spud—Instrument for removing foreign bodies from the eye.
Stat—Latin abbreviation for "at once".
Station—Aussie word for a ranch.
Stemetil—Anti-diarrheal medication (Aussie).
Stoxil—Medication for treating corneal ulcers (Aussie).
Stryne—Facetious American for "Aussie accent."
Stubbies—Aussie word for bermuda-like shorts worn by men.
Sugar-tongs—A plaster splint for forearm fractures at the wrist.
Sultrin—Antibiotic vaginal cream.

Supinate—Turning the hand palm up.

Swag—Aussie word for personal belongings, usually all contained in a duffle bag.

Sydenham's chorea—A nervous disorder following rheumatic fever, characterized by writhing muscular contractions.

T

Tabes dorsalis—Damage to the spinal cord secondary to syphilis.

Talipes—Deformed (club) foot.

TB—Abbreviation for tuberculosis.

TDS—Three times a day.

Tedral—Medication for asthma.

Tetracycline—An antibiotic.

Theater—Aussie word for a surgical suite in a hospital.

Theophylline—Medication for asthma.

Thiazide—Generic name for diuretic.

Thyroglossal cyst—Congenital thyroid abnormality.

Thyroxin—Thyroid hormone.

TIA—Transient ischemic attack (small stroke).

Tibia—Shin bone.

Tinea circinata—Ringworm of the skin.

Tinea corporis—Ringworm of the body.

Tinea versicolor—Ringworm of the skin characterized by white, de-pigmented spots.

Tip—Aussie word for garbage dump.

Tjilpi—Aboriginal word for a gray haired, wise old man.

Tjuri—Aboriginal word for diarrhea.

Tolbutamide—Generic word for oral anti-diabetic medication.

Torch—Aussie word for flashlight.

Trachoma—A parasitic eye disease.

Transilluminate—Procedure by which a flashlight is held against a cystic structure so that the viewer may see solid contents inside.

Transponder—An electronic device that identifies the specific aircraft to the air traffic controller.

Trapezius—Muscles of the back and shoulders.

T-3 level—Pertaining to the third thoracic vertebra.

Tucker—Aussie word for food.

Tyre—Aussie word for tire (vehicle/plane).

U

Uluru—Aboriginal name for Ayer's Rock.

Undecylenic acid—An antifungal medication.

Uru—Aboriginal word for watery (as in diarrhea).

Uti—Abbreviation for urinary tract infection.
Utility—Aussie name for pickup truck.

V

Vaginitis—Infection of the vagina.
Valium—A tranquilizer.
Vallergen—A tranquilizer (Aussie).
Varicosities—Swollen veins (usually the legs).
Ventolin—Medication for treating asthma.
Vermox—Medication for treating intestinal parasites.
Vertigo—Dizziness.
Vesicular—Blistered.
VHF—Very high frequency (radio channels).
Vibramycin—An antibiotic.

W

Walkabout—Aboriginal word for traveling about tribal territory.
Wattles—Aussie for acacia-like trees (aboriginal word for wattles is
   mulga).
We-ah—Aboriginal word for no.
White man—Any person who is not aboriginal.
Wicki-up (wicki)—Aboriginal word for habitation.
Willy-willy—Aussie word for whirlwind.
Wiltja—Another aboriginal word for habitation.
Windscreen—Aussie word for windshield.
Wira—Aboriginal word for wooden vessel.
Wog—Aussie word for: flu, illness.

X

Xiphoid—Breast bone.
Xylocaine—Injectable local anesthetic.

Z

Zygoma—Cheekbone.